tory

Douglas Haig, 1861–1928

Gerard J. De Groot

UNWIN HYMAN

London   Sydney   Wellington

First published in Great Britain by Unwin Hyman Limited, 1988.

UNWIN HYMAN LIMITED
15–17 Broadwick Street, London W1V 1FP

Allen & Unwin Australia Pty Ltd
8 Napier Street, North Sydney, NSW 2969, Australia

Allen & Unwin New Zealand Pty Ltd with the Port Nicholson Press
60 Cambridge Terrace, Wellington, New Zealand

British Library Cataloguing in Publication Data

De Groot, Gerard J.
   Douglas Haig, 1861–1928.
1. Great Britain. Army. Haig, Douglas,
Earl Haig, 1861–1928. Biographies
I. Title
355.3′32′0924
ISBN 0–04–440192–2

Typeset in ITC Garamond
Printed in Great Britain by Biddles Ltd, Guildford, Surrey.

To Susan

Contents

v

Illustrations

MAPS

Preface

This book began almost ten years ago when, while working as an insurance adjuster in Portland, Oregon, I decided that I would rather be doing postgraduate research in Great Britain. 'Decided' is in fact an exaggeration; this was pure whimsy. I had recently read Leon Wolff's *In Flanders Fields* and Paul Fussell's *The Great War and Modern Memory*, two books which, despite their considerable flaws, left me with an indelible impression of the shattered illusions of 1914–1918. From Wolff, I hit upon the idea of studying British Intelligence in the Great War, particularly the relationship between Douglas Haig and his Intelligence Officer, John Charteris. Applications were sent to many wonderfully mysterious universities and rejections arrived by return post. Edinburgh, however, was willing to gamble.

I am still shocked by my ignorance of my topic at that time. During our first meeting, my supervisor, Dr Paul Addison, assured me that Edinburgh was the perfect place to do my research because 'as of course you know, Haig's papers are in the National Library of Scotland, just down the road'. Reluctant to expose my lack of preparation, I replied, 'Of course.' The next day I began my acquaintance with Haig. Before long I discovered that Intelligence has very little to do with cloaks and daggers, being mostly about boring reports and endless statistics. The really fascinating stuff had to do with Haig himself, a man historians have either exalted or pilloried but seldom tried to understand.

As for understanding, the best one can do is try. The complexity of human nature renders complete comprehension impossible. Historical accuracy is limited by the availability of resources and the subjectivity of the historian. A fellow biographer claims that he has never used the word 'perhaps' in any of his many works. I would not want to presume any such certainty about Haig. I have pored through the 360 boxes of Haig's letters, diaries and official papers at the

National Library of Scotland. I have studied the manuscript collections of his contemporaries. I have read the relevant secondary sources. Yet despite all this spadework, I cannot claim to have uncovered the 'true' Haig because history provides no final truth. What I have uncovered, and the interpretations I have drawn, is inevitably a reflection of my own background. I would not have it any other way. That is what makes the study of history so fascinating. God forbid that it should ever be thought a science.

There are nevertheless professional standards. The historian is supposed to base his conclusions on hard evidence. This rule has prevented me from delving deeply into the private side of Haig. I have been told that Haig was a devoted husband, a caring father and a loyal friend. Whilst I have no doubt that this was indeed true, the evidence to support it is technically hearsay. I apologise for the disappointment I might cause in neglecting this important but unfortunately elusive side of Haig's character.

My work would have been impossible without the painstaking efforts of Dorothy, the late Countess Haig. By her selfless devotion to the preservation of her husband's papers she established what is probably the best memorial to him. I regret that, for the same reasons outlined above, I have not been able to do her justice. I understand and accept that, in her private life, she was much more warm-hearted and charitable than her correspondence suggests.

I am also deeply indebted to Dawyck, the present Earl Haig. Despite being fully aware of the sort of book I was likely to produce, he has never hesitated in providing assistance. Our inevitable disagreements did not give rise to bitterness; it was, he assured me, more important to preserve my integrity as a historian than his peace of mind. His warm-hearted support and encouragement was one of the nicest fringe benefits of pursuing this research.

It was my very good fortune to have Dr Paul Addison as my postgraduate supervisor. His formidable insight illuminated recesses which would otherwise have remained in darkness. My convoluted, verbose style of eight years ago was honed by him into something approaching clarity and brevity. Professor Geoffrey Best, Dr John Brown, and Terry Cole also helped me at the thesis stage. Dr Ian Beckett very kindly read the entire manuscript and saved me from some embarrassing mistakes. Those that remain are undoubtedly my own. My colleagues at St Andrews, especially Alan Sykes, Bruce Lenman,

Hamish Scott and Jane Dawson gave advice and encouragement – quite often without realising it themselves. My new-found friends at Unwin Hyman, Bill Neill-Hall, Elizabeth Nicholson, and especially Janet Clayton, provided the sort of guidance essential to an author wandering blindly towards the publication of his first book.

I fear I imposed terribly on my friend Peter Aeberli who drew the maps. He probably now wishes his talent for cartography had remained undiscovered. My thanks and kindest regards go out to Dr Douglas Duncan and Lt Col J. A. Charteris, for providing photographs of their father and grandfather, respectively. Dawn Waddell and Peter Adamson were extremely patient about the jacket portrait. The rest of the photographs were kindly provided by Lord Haig.

I am grateful to the following for providing permission to quote from material under copyright and for generally assisting me with my research: the Curators of the Bodleian Library; Miss Denise M. Boyes; the British Library Board; Lt Col J. A. Charteris; the Dowager Lady Cholmondeley; the Master, Fellows and Scholars of Churchill College, Cambridge; Elizabeth Cuthbert, Registrar of the Royal Archives; the Earl of Derby; Duke University; Lord Elibank; the Viscount Esher; the Earl Haig; the Baron Hankey; Mr Peter Hippisley-Cox; the House of Lords Record Office; Hunter of Hunterston; the Imperial War Museum; Lady Patricia Kingsbury; the Earl Kitchener; the Trustees of the Liddell Hart Centre for Military Archives; the Earl Lloyd George; the National Army Museum; the Trustees of the National Library of Scotland; Mr M. A. F. Rawlinson; the Baron Robertson of Oakridge; the Public Record Office; and Mr Charles Strachey. Attempts have been made to contact the owners of all copyright material. If I have inadvertently infringed anyone's copyright, I hope that my sincere apologies will be accepted.

Finally, I must thank dear Susan who read the manuscript and soothed my occasional panics but most importantly kept me in touch with what was really important. It is to her that this book is dedicated.

Gerard J. De Groot

St Andrews, June 1988

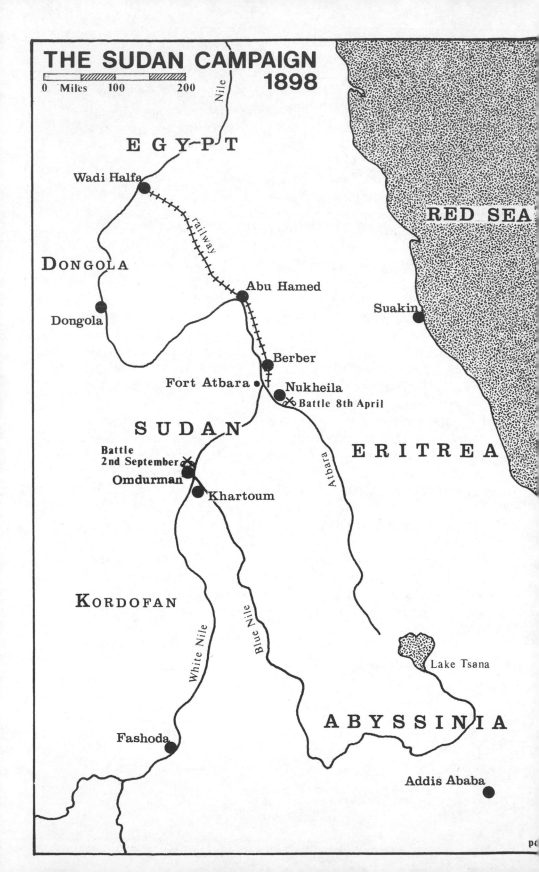

THE SUDAN CAMPAIGN 1898

0 Miles 100 200

EGYPT

Wadi Halfa

RED SEA

railway

DONGOLA

Dongola

Abu Hamed

Suakin

Berber

Fort Atbara

Nukheila

Battle 8th April

SUDAN

ERITREA

Battle
2nd September

Omdurman

Khartoum

Atbara

KORDOFAN

White Nile

Blue Nile

Lake Tsana

ABYSSINIA

Fashoda

Addis Ababa

Nile

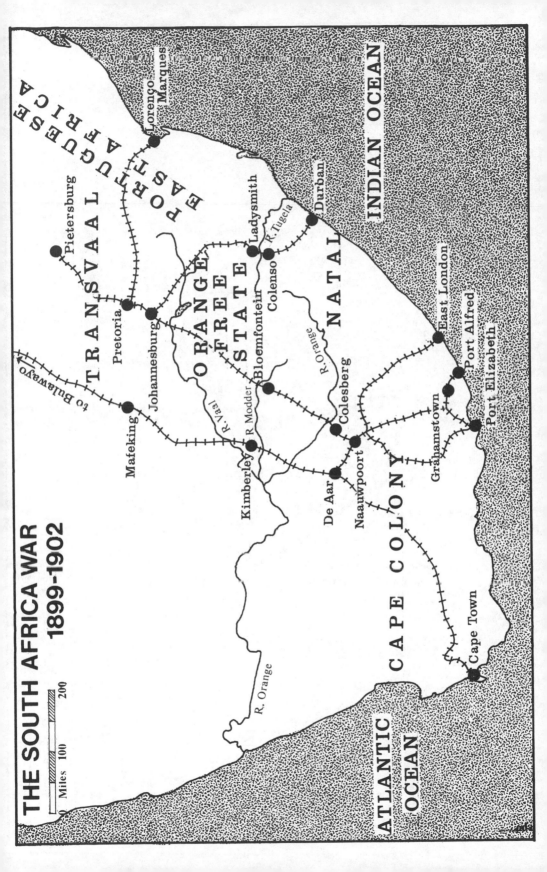

THE SOUTH AFRICA WAR
1899-1902

0 Miles 100   200

ATLANTIC
OCEAN

INDIAN OCEAN

PORTUGUESE EAST AFRICA

Lorenço Marques

Pietersburg

TRANSVAAL

Pretoria

Johannesburg

to Bulawayo

Mafeking

Kimberley

R. Vaal

R Modder

Bloemfontein

ORANGE FREE STATE

Ladysmith

R. Tugela

Colenso

Durban

NATAL

R. Orange

Colesberg

De Aar

Naauwpoort

Grahamstown

East London

Port Alfred

Port Elizabeth

CAPE COLONY

R. Orange

Cape Town

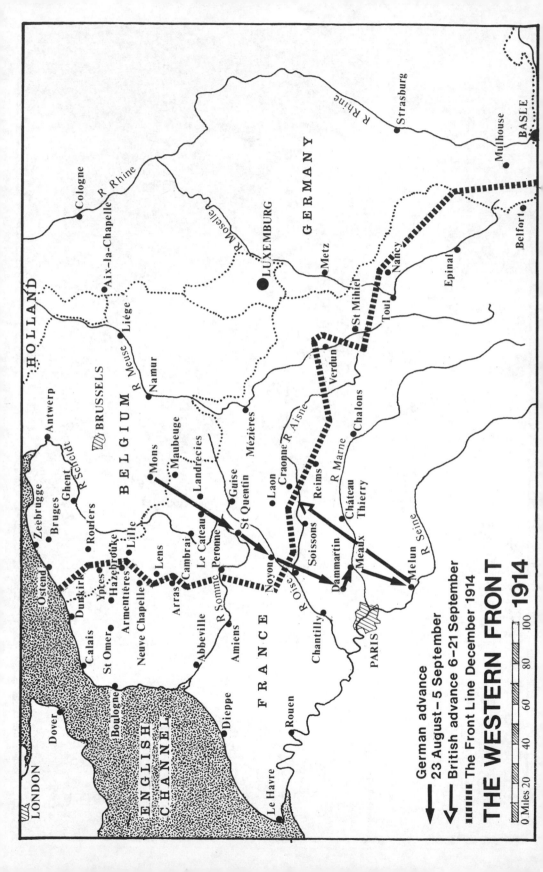

THE WESTERN FRONT
1914

→ German advance
23 August – 5 September

→ British advance 6–21 September

▮▮▮ The Front Line December 1914

0 Miles 20   40   60   80   100

HOLLAND

LONDON

ENGLISH CHANNEL

Dover

Calais
St Omer
Boulogne
Ostend
Zeebrugge
Bruges
Ghent
Roulers
Dunkirk
Ypres
Hazebrouke
Armentières
Neuve Chapelle
Lille
Arras
Lens
Cambrai
Le Cateau
Péronne
Abbeville
Dieppe
Amiens

Le Havre
Rouen
Chantilly

PARIS

Melun
Meaux
Dammartin
Soissons
Noyon
St Quentin
Guise
Landrecies
Maubeuge
Mons
Mézières

BELGIUM
BRUSSELS
Antwerp
Liége
Namur

Château Thierry
Reims
Craonne
Laon
Chalons
Verdun
St Mihiel

Toul
Nancy
Epinal
Belfort

LUXEMBURG
Metz

GERMANY

Cologne
Aix-la-Chapelle

Strasburg
Mulhouse
BASLE

R Rhine
R Rhine
R Moselle
R Meuse
R Scheldt
R Somme
R Oise
R Aisne
R Marne
R Seine

FRANCE

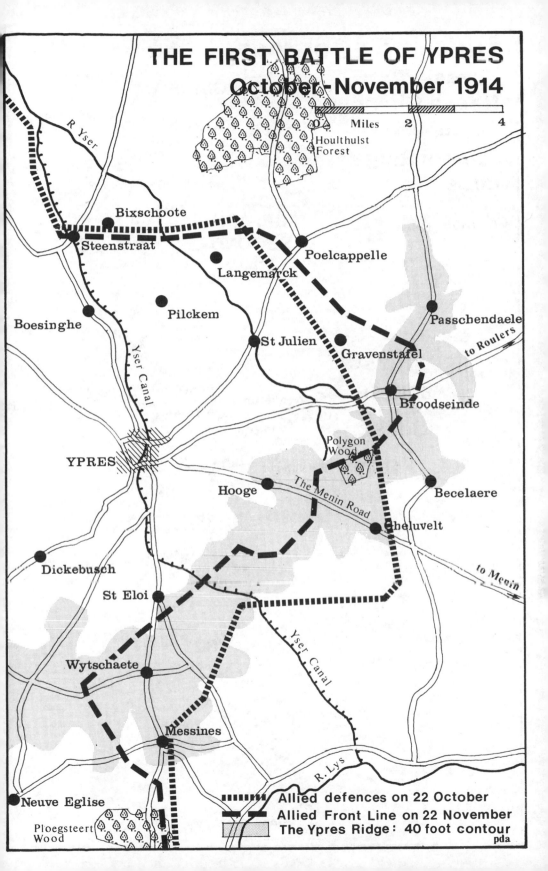

THE FIRST BATTLE OF YPRES
October–November 1914

0   Miles   2   4

Houlthulst Forest

R Yser

Bixschoote

Steenstraat

Poelcappelle

Langemarck

Boesinghe

Pilckem

Yser Canal

St Julien

Gravenstafel

Passchendaele

to Roulers

Broodseinde

YPRES

Polygon Wood

Becelaere

Hooge

The Menin Road

Gheluvelt

Dickebusch

St Eloi

to Menin

Wytschaete

Yser Canal

Messines

R. Lys

Neuve Eglise

Ploegsteert Wood

··········· Allied defences on 22 October
━ ━ ━ Allied Front Line on 22 November
  The Ypres Ridge : 40 foot contour

pda

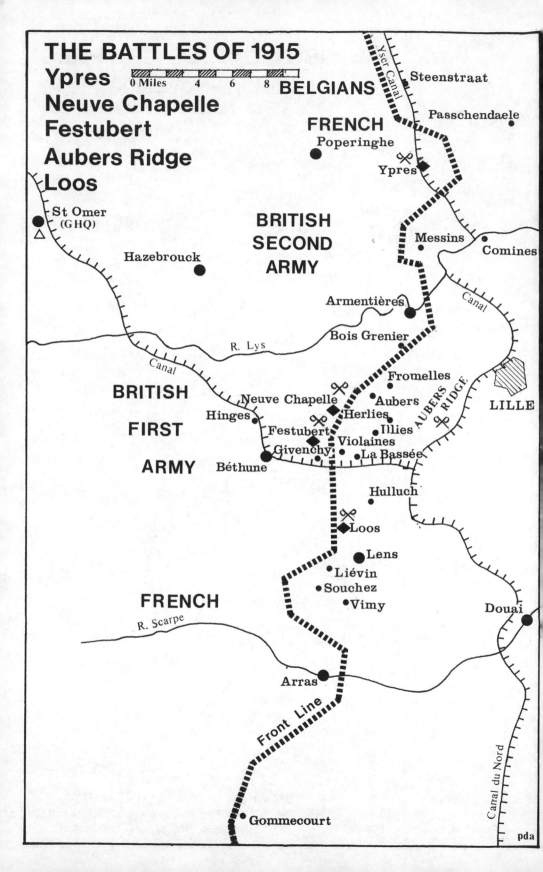

THE SOMME
July-November 1916

0 Miles 2 4 6

Gommecourt

Hébuterne

Bapaume

Miraumont

Warlencourt

Beaumont Hamel

Le Sars

Le Transloy

BRITISH FRONT

Thiepval

Courcelette

Martinpuich

Gueudecourt

High Wood

Delville Wood

Sailly

Pozières

Morval

Ovillers

Longueval

Mametz Wood

Ginchy

Guillemont

Contalmaison

Montauban

Trones Wood

Combles

Albert

Tricourt

Mametz

Maricourt

Maurepas

Bouchavesnes

R. Somme

PÉRONNE

R. Somme

FRENCH FRONT

Dompierre

Barleux

Estrées

Allied Front 1 July
Allied advance 31 July
Allied advance 1 September
Allied advance 1 October
Allied advance 20 November

pda

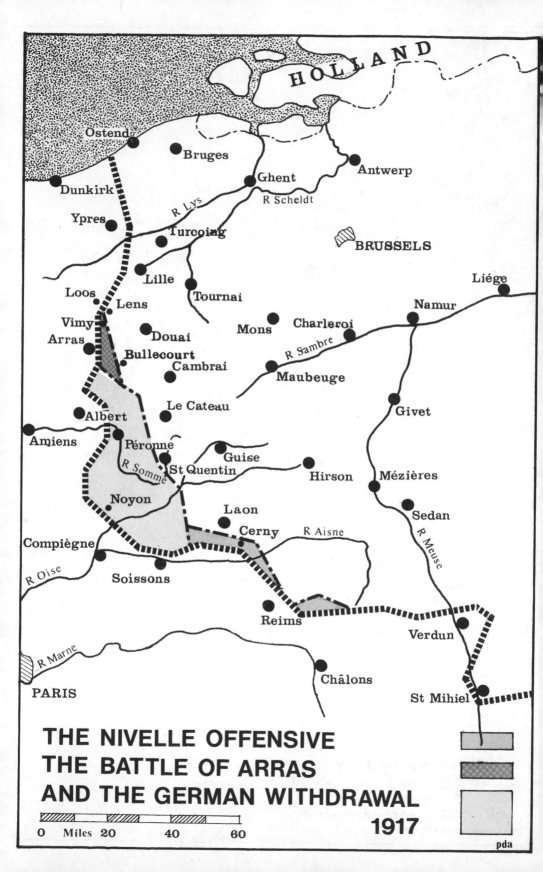

THE NIVELLE OFFENSIVE
THE BATTLE OF ARRAS
AND THE GERMAN WITHDRAWAL
1917

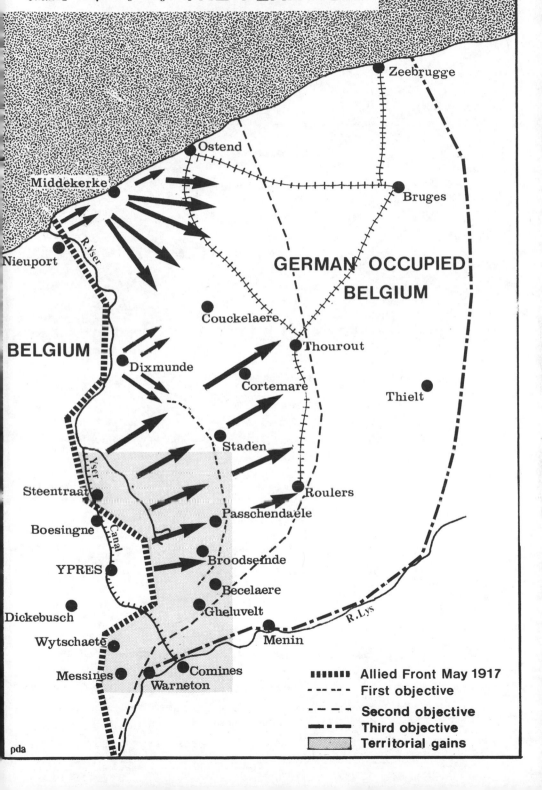

THE FLANDERS OFFENSIVE
THE PLAN 1917

0 Miles 2   4   6   8

Zeebrugge

Ostend

Middekerke

Bruges

Nieuport

R. Yser

GERMAN OCCUPIED

BELGIUM

Couckelaere

BELGIUM

Thourout

Dixmunde

Cortemare

Thielt

Staden

Yser

Steentraat

Roulers

Boesingne

Passchendaele

Canal

YPRES

Broodseinde

Becelaere

Dickebusch

Gheluvelt

R. Lys

Wytschaete

Menin

Messines

Comines

Warneton

pda

■■■■■■ Allied Front May 1917

- - - - First objective

– – – Second objective

–·–·– Third objective

▨ Territorial gains

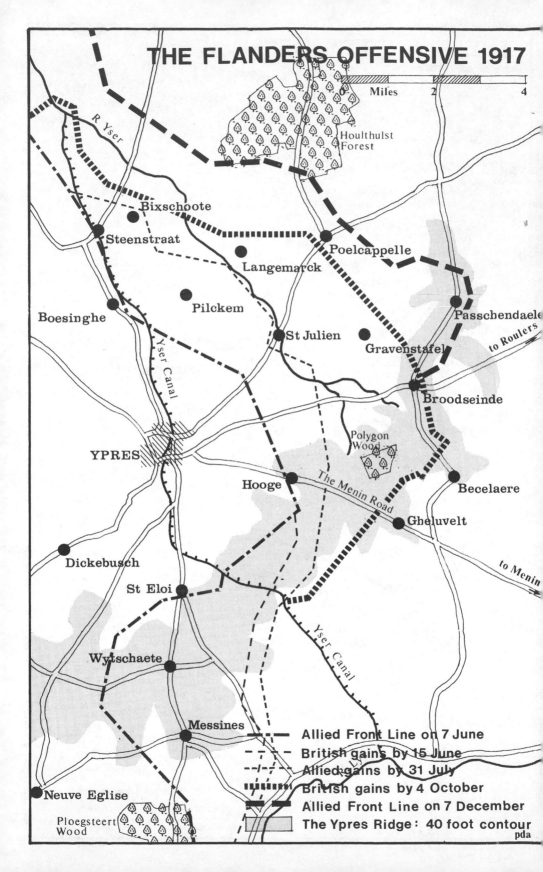

THE FLANDERS OFFENSIVE 1917

Miles   2   4

R Yser

Houlthulst Forest

Bixschoote

Steenstraat

Langemarck

Poelcappelle

Pilckem

Boesinghe

St Julien

Gravenstafel

Passchendaele

to Roulers

Yser Canal

Broodseinde

YPRES

Polygon Wood

Hooge

The Menin Road

Becelaere

Gheluvelt

Dickebusch

to Menin

St Eloi

Yser Canal

Wytschaete

Messines

Allied Front Line on 7 June

British gains by 15 June

Allied gains by 31 July

British gains by 4 October

Allied Front Line on 7 December

The Ypres Ridge : 40 foot contour

Neuve Eglise

Ploegsteert Wood

pda

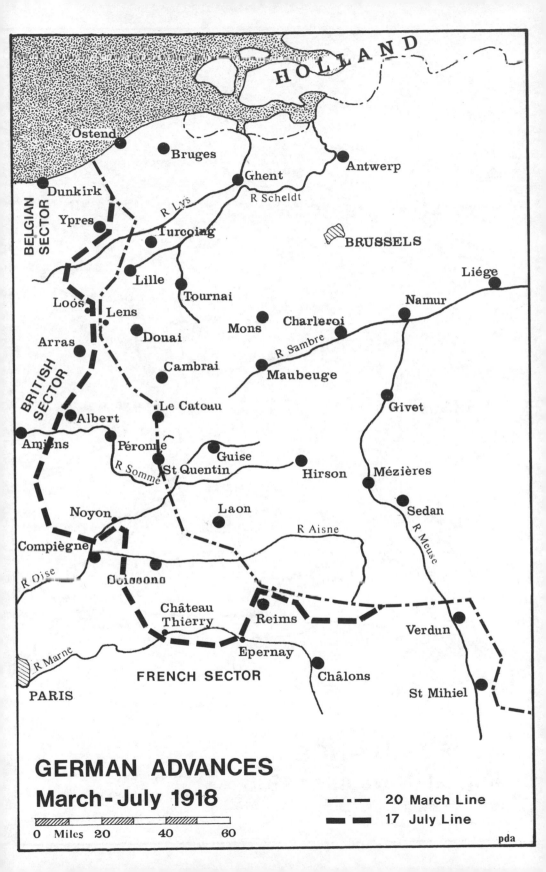

GERMAN ADVANCES
March - July 1918

	20 March Line
	17 July Line

0   Miles   20   40   60

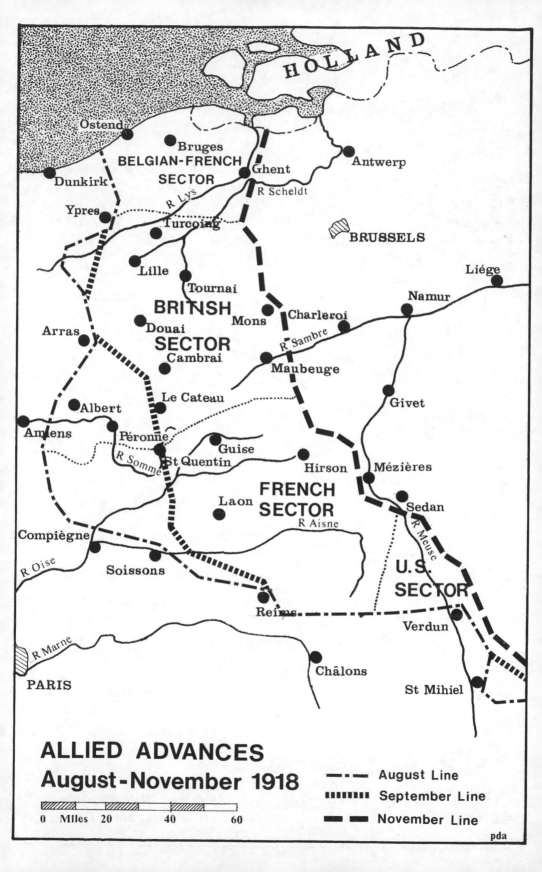

HOLLAND

Ostend

Bruges

BELGIAN-FRENCH
SECTOR

Ghent

Antwerp

Dunkirk

R Lys

R Scheldt

BRUSSELS

Ypres

Turcoing

Liége

Lille

Tournai

Namur

BRITISH

Mons

Charleroi

Arras

Douai

SECTOR

R Sambre

Cambrai

Maubeuge

Givet

Albert

Le Cateau

Amiens

Péronne

Guise

St Quentin

Méziéres

R Somme

Hirson

Sedan

Compiègne

Laon

FRENCH
SECTOR

U.S.
SECTOR

R Oise

Soissons

R Aisne

Verdun

R Marne

Reims

PARIS

Châlons

St Mihiel

ALLIED ADVANCES
August-November 1918

—·—·— August Line

▪▪▪▪▪▪ September Line

▬ ▬ ▬ November Line

0   Miles   20   40   60

pda

Introduction

Visions of the Great War have traditionally been peopled with victims and malefactors. For seventy years, books, films, plays, poetry and television documentaries have presented two contrasting images: the noble Tommy in his wretched trench and the inept senior commander living in luxury miles from the front. The insane orders of the latter, so the story goes, brought about the mass slaughter of the former. Objecting to this iconography, an angry band of revisionists has put forth a different picture. But, hopelessly outnumbered, they have been driven to the opposite extreme, transforming the senior commanders from butchers into saints. The passage of time has not cooled tempers. The argument remains as polarised as it ever has been. The middle ground in the Great War debate remains as sparsely populated as No Man's Land.

The popular view sees the British Army in the war as lions led by donkeys. The line of reasoning is easy to chart. The Great War, it is argued, was the worst disaster in British military history. Since the heroism and skill of the men in the muddy trenches – the lions – is beyond doubt, blame for the disaster must belong to the senior commanders – the donkeys. More specifically, ultimate blame belongs to the supreme commander, Douglas Haig, the most asinine of them all. This school believes wholeheartedly in man's ability to affect the course of events. Unfortunately, in this case, a disaster occurred because a 'Great Man' was not available, or not noticed. It is assumed that there were strategies and tactics in the Great War which would have resulted in fewer casualties. Haig, by failing to act upon these alternatives, therefore proves himself to have been unimaginative, indifferent, obstinate and incompetent – in other words, an ass. A disaster is neatly explained and blame reassuringly apportioned.

Haig's critics argue from the war to the man; his champions take the opposite approach. Their study of Haig reveals a man whose

1

values were the same as those which made Britain great. They glide smoothly towards the conclusion that if a man of such stature could not limit the casualties, no one could have. In other words, no attempt is made to deny that this was a horrible war. The enormous losses are consequently blamed upon its intractable nature. Haig is revealed as all the more heroic for his ability to endure its ghastliness. Lesser men would have crumbled.

Over the years, champions and critics have shouted their arguments across the vast expanse which divides them. In the process, the scholarly landscape has become as barren and blasted as the battlefields of the war. The raids of revisionists and counter-revisionists have not altered the stalemate. The argument is unresolvable because the standards – of human conduct and of war – of each side are not honoured by the other. In this stagnated contest, rhetoric has become more important than subject matter. The pattern of Haig's life and his development as a soldier have been ignored or distorted in the stubborn effort to damn or ennoble him.

The case for the defence has been argued mainly by Haig's biographers. None of the dozen books that has been written about him could with justice be called a critical biography. In the two earliest works, written immediately after his death by George Arthur and by Ernest Protheroe, facts were not allowed to impede the glorification of a fallen hero. In 1935, Duff Cooper's two-volume official biography, still the most complete treatment of Haig, was published. The usual restraints imposed upon official biographers were in this case exacerbated by the vigilance of the distraught Lady Haig. What resulted was, unsurprisingly, a book which made little attempt to separate the myth from the man.[1]

Four biographies fall into the category of personal memoirs. Three of these, by his chauffeur, his personal padre at GHQ and his Chief of Operations, provide snippets of valuable information and interesting anecdotes, but little else. They are in no sense balanced treatments. Similar criticisms apply to Lady Haig's *The Man I Knew*, written in order to repair the 'vandalism' of the official biography which had, according to her, 'slandered my husband's name'. A comparison of it and the evidence in the Haig papers reveals how little she knew of him, or else how blind she was to his faults.

Finally, there are five conventional biographies. Two of these were written by Haig's Intelligence Officer, Brigadier-General John

Charteris, one of the few people who can be said to have known Haig well. This knowledge enabled him to expose sides of Haig which would never otherwise have been revealed. But, though an occasional eyebrow is raised, Charteris stopped well short of serious criticism. His books also suffer from the fact that he had access to few primary sources. Most of the official documents were still sealed. In addition, Lady Haig, who despised Charteris – considering him a vulgar and dirty man – was unsupportive of his work, denying him access to her husband's papers. She then, incidentally, criticised the finished products for their inaccuracies.

It became fashionable from the 1930s onwards to censure Haig. In response to this perceived injustice, three revisionist biographies were written by E. K. G. Sixsmith, Sir James Marshall-Cornwall and John Terraine. The latter, the most outspoken, articulate, determined and devoted admirer of Haig, has set the standard of Haig historiography; all biographies are (and will be) compared with his. Terraine and his soul-fellows take a similar approach, arguing that Haig achieved the most that was humanly possible in an extremely difficult situation. Alternatives to Haig's conduct of the war are judged impracticable and protestations over the huge loss of life are scorned as hopelessly naive. A hero emerges through the back door: Haig is praised as much for his ability to recognise the limitations the war imposed as for any impressive accomplishments. He was, according to Terraine, a modern commander because he accepted the intractable nature of modern war.

The revisionist biographers are also alike in their eagerness to get to the war. Haig's early life is an insignificant road upon which they must unfortunately travel in order to arrive at the real point of interest. But, whilst they race through this period at high speed, the authors do not resist drawing sweeping conclusions about it. Unfortunately, the conclusions are drawn before the subject is investigated. In other words, having decided that Haig was a great leader in a difficult war, the authors assume that his early life must have been full of militarily enriching experiences. It is no wonder that evidence of such experiences is then easily found. This evidence then reinforces the original conclusion regarding Haig's skill as a commander. This ladder of logical conclusions begins with some doubtful and dangerous bottom rungs.

A penchant for twisted reasoning is also exhibited by the other side in the Haig debate. The post-war view of a costly but otherwise justified and well-managed war began to be questioned in earnest with the publication after 1928 of the memoirs of Sassoon, Blunden, Graves, and others. The lion and the donkey were born. This new school of thought was soon reinforced by the highly successful but hopelessly inaccurate *War Memoirs of David Lloyd George*, which were written with the expressed purpose of exposing the 'incompetence of the trained inexperts' at GHQ. Accustomed as he was to exercising power, Lloyd George could not admit the existence of situations in which men were manacled by forces larger than they. Therefore, if the war was horrible, it was natural to conclude that the Commander-in-Chief was incompetent and dim-witted. But, not stopping there, Lloyd George also accused Haig of intentionally misleading the War Cabinet in order to continue fighting the war in his own incompetent way. What is presented is a rather incongruous image of a conspiracy of idiots; the stupid Haig and his fellow donkeys had somehow outwitted astute politicians. That matter aside, Lloyd George provided the lion and donkey school with energy, respectability and authority. His interpretation of the war remains the most popular because it is simple and reassuring. The easiest judgement when confronted with disaster is to conclude stupidity, because in doing so one can avoid looking deeply into the painful question of societal responsibility. Haig is safely judged an aberration, and one is left with the comfortable fantasy that if only a genius had been available things would have been so different.[2]

Among the criticisms of Haig, there has been the occasional attempt at honest scholarship. J. F. C. Fuller and Basil Liddell Hart – the foremost military minds of their day – used their considerable knowledge of war and their direct experience of this war to point out specific faults in Haig's method of command. Though some of their ideas (particularly Liddell Hart's indirect strategies) have not stood the test of time, others remain relevant. Their criticism of Haig's lack of imagination, his blinding optimism and his preference for a sycophantic staff – all of which shielded him from the 'real war' – is justified. But while both were able to expose these weaknesses, both stopped short of understanding them or explaining their origin.

A second generation of critics produced studies which restated the arguments of Fuller and Liddell Hart, albeit with credibility sacrificed in favour of flair. Foremost among these are Alan Clark's *The Donkeys*, Leon Wolff's *In Flanders Fields*, and Norman Dixon's *On the Psychology of Military Incompetence*. The three authors, while pursuing different theses, share a blinding desire to denounce Haig. Rules of historical reasoning are carelessly trampled in the pursuit of this goal. With a crooked judge and warped witnesses, Haig is naturally found guilty of the most heinous crimes.

Dixon's work is the most dangerous because of the way in which an apparently scientific approach is used to prove that Haig was incompetent. Blinded by 'psychology', the reader is apparently not supposed to notice backward and twisted reasoning. Dixon's argument proceeds as follows: (1) the war was a disaster; (2) incompetent commanders are usually authoritarians; therefore (3) Haig, being responsible for the disaster, must have been an authoritarian. Having drawn this conclusion, Dixon then looks for and quite easily finds supportive evidence from Haig's early life. Haig, we are told, had a domineering and oppressive mother who turned him into an anal sadist. (It just so happens that anal sadists make the worst sort of commanders.) The book tells us a great deal more about the psychology and indeed the incompetence of psychohistorians than that of military commanders.

The retrograde reasoning of Dixon, Terraine, Wolff and others is the ultimate consequence of the unresolvable debate over Great War casualties. Behind every study of Haig there lurks the preconceived aim of absolving or condemning him for the massive loss of life. Haig has become the Piltdown man of military history; his diaries and letters have been raided for evidence of characteristics which accord with the authors' preconceptions. After seventy years we know very little about the man.

But the scholarly landscape is not as bleak as I have described it. Whilst the two sides in the casualty debate have proceeded with their stubborn raids on each other's trenches, away from the front a less visible but more sober attempt to explain the way in which the war was fought has been in progress. Geoffrey Best, Brian Bond, Gwyn Harries-Jenkins, Shelford Bidwell, Tim Travers, Ed Spiers and others have stressed a less personalised view of the Army, aiming instead to integrate the institution into Edwardian and Victorian society. By studying the public schools, the Staff College, the social composition of the Army, the societal image of war and related subjects, they have revealed the way in which strategy and tactics were extensions of social trends. In doing so, they have demonstrated that the study of society and the study of war are mutually reinforcing.

Perhaps because of their disdain for the personalised approach, these historians have not, generally speaking, produced in-depth studies of the senior commanders. But the examination of a personality need not be personalised history; the individual can be examined as another expression of social trends. This is, however, only possible if, as in the case of Haig, the study begins at his birth rather than at the outbreak of war. Haig's character developed before he became a soldier. He developed as a soldier before he became a commander. Because historians have so far failed to respect this process, distorted pictures of the man have prevailed.

There is, therefore, room for a new study of Haig. His progress at each stage of his life should be examined in relation to the previous stages not in relation to the Great War or any preconceptions regarding his character. Above all, he must be seen as a creature of his society. This is the approach taken in this book. The reader will notice a reluctance to enter the casualty debate. That debate has done nothing for the memory of the poor men who died, and little more for our understanding of the war. The avoidance of it and indeed of any sweeping judgements upon Haig's command, allows a picture of the man to emerge which is open to widely varying subjective interpretations. If the reader believes that Victorian and Edwardian values and the principles which Haig upheld are worthy of respect or even imitation, then that reader will probably see this as a biography favourable to Haig. If, however, the opposite is the case, this will seem a very damning book indeed.

It is impossible to deny that in the end Haig won the war. But his victory should not be interpreted as a vindication of his methods or an exoneration of his character. Though he was the architect of victory, there were flaws in his design. Whilst he was undoubtedly the best commander available, this reveals as much about the Army as a whole as about Haig. It also reveals a great deal about the society which nurtured, educated, trained and shaped him. Its faults, like its virtues, were mirrored in him.

PART I

A Question of Upbringing

1

'And the Training Makes a Gentleman'

It was whisky, not blood, which initially determined Douglas Haig's course in life. His connection with the main family line and the ancestral home of Bemersyde in the Borders was distant.[1] John Haig, Douglas's father, was a man of secure means but relatively modest pedigree. Though master of the Fife hounds (an appointment which in those days of social snobbery would not have gone to a member of the middle class), his reputation and influence (not to mention his income) was derived mainly from his whisky empire. Thus Douglas's background defies precise classification – a fact of profound importance in his upbringing.

John Haig married Rachel Veitch in August 1839. He was 37; she a beautiful 18 year old. It was a poor match for her, an excellent one for him. The Veitches of Eliot and Dawyck were a proud family upon whom financial misfortune had of late descended. Marriage to a member of the trading community, ordinarily inconceivable, had become pragmatic. John Haig's income of £10,000 per year outweighed the disdain of the dowerless Miss Veitch. The marriage brought him greater respectability and provided her with the resources to raise her children in the style of her class.

John and Rachel settled at Cameron House, near Markinch. Douglas, the youngest of eleven children, was born on 19 June 1861 at an Edinburgh residence used by the Haig children who attended school in the city. By the time Douglas was born, his father had aged well past his 59 years. Troubled by gout, asthma, and the ill-effects of heavy drinking, he spent every winter at continental spas, where the main aim was to dry out. The cures were occasionally, if temporarily,

9

successful. 'Your father is looking so well,' Rachel wrote with delight from Vichy. He had, she told Douglas, for 'the first time . . . done without Brandy, Whisky or Kirsche before breakfast'. Vichy had 'acted like magic on your father'. Nevertheless, the heavy drinking continued until he died in 1878 of 'abscess of the liver'.[2]

John Haig's energies were concentrated upon his business. Though highly ambitious, he was at the same time widely respected as a fair and honest employer. But, as might be expected, he had little time or patience for family matters. He was not a good father. The drinking problem and his ill-health made him prone to fits of rage. His children, frightened of their father, did their best to avoid him. Douglas, like his brothers and sisters, was noticeably silent about his feelings for his father and recorded no grief when he died. A former groom at Cameron House, Thomas Houston, provided a revealing glimpse of the relationship between the two:

> My brother was . . . riding a rather restive young horse . . . Master Douglas was behind a hedge and when my brother came near he jumped out and startled the horse and my brother had a fall, the horse's hoof catching a cheek and leaving a mark quite visible now . . . Master Douglas was sent off to Edinburgh by his mother till his father cooled down.

John Haig, who took little interest in his son's welfare, had a minimal effect upon his development. This situation was probably rued by no one. The eldest brother Willie – the 'moving spirit in the family' – played the surrogate father, providing the administration behind Rachel's motherly inspiration.[3]

Rachel Haig believed that her genteel birth rendered her better able to supervise the children's upbringing. She taught them the manners of her class, not their father's. Her often overbearing attention was in complete contrast to his neglect. A kind-hearted, highly moral and deeply religious woman, she willingly sacrificed herself for her children. 'Her devotion to us shortened her life by many years,' one of them wrote.[4] She was especially close to her three youngest sons – John, George and Douglas – nicknamed the 'three bees' for the way they constantly buzzed around her. Though her health was already failing by the time they were born, she nevertheless made certain that they did not suffer from a lack of attention. Aware perhaps that she would not live long, she was eager to do as much as possible for them while she could.

Douglas was by all accounts Rachel's favourite. Though as an adult Janet Haig could excuse her mother's attitude by claiming that she 'knew herself to be especially blessed in her . . . little son Douglas', when the children were young it caused friction. Douglas was often cruelly tormented by jealous siblings. His long blond curls, which Rachel adored, were on one occasion shorn by his brothers and sisters who had ambushed him while he was playing. Douglas arrived at his mother's knee in tears, the curls tucked in his pinafore. When Rachel died, they were found among her most precious possessions.[5]

Virtually blind to his faults, Rachel turned Douglas into the classic spoiled child. He often got his way by throwing severe temper tantrums and knew how to trade good behaviour for sweets or small gifts. When a nurse found him impossible to handle, she, not he, was more often than not blamed for his misconduct. Like many spoiled children, Douglas stubbornly opposed his mother while at the same time recognising her as his most important ally   his security in a lonely and somewhat threatening world. She supported him unquestioningly in spite of his inability to justify her faith during her lifetime. His status as Rachel's 'blue-eyed boy' gave him an overinflated sense of his own importance, an attribute which, though in time moderated, was never completely discarded.

Douglas spent his first eight years almost constantly in his mother's company. Since he did not start school until May 1869, there was little outside influence upon his early development. He had few playmates (his mother did not encourage contacts with the humble country folk) and no close companions. Rachel was, therefore, Douglas's most important role model. He 'revered and loved his mother', Emily Haig wrote. 'It was her memory that inspired him to do his utmost to live up to her exalted standard of truth and uprightness.' Though some standards were perverted through imitation, there were significant similarities between mother and son. Both were highly ambitious – though it must be said that, society being what it was, Rachel's ambition had inevitably to be channelled through her sons. Both were also determined, confident, wilful and self-righteous – a combination which made compromise difficult. Yet Rachel and Douglas shared an ability to cloak their darker sides in a 'quiet dignity', an image of moral purity and serenity.[6]

This serenity arose in part from Rachel's devout religious beliefs, mirrored by her son later in life. She derived immense comfort and security from her faith, in part because her belief in predestination absolved her from responsibility for the course which her life took. Though certain of every person's ability to shape his or her own destiny, she was equally certain that everything was ultimately the expression of God's will. For her, no contradiction existed between these certainties. Thus, occasional misfortune – such as Douglas's lack of achievement as a child – was never allowed to erode her steadfast optimism.

Rachel kept a watchful eye upon her children's religious training, requiring them to recite their lessons and pray daily in her presence. Whilst away at school, Douglas was instructed to send his weekly biblical texts, accompanied by his comments, to his mother. In her replies, she repeatedly reminded him of 'the All-seeing, loving Eye ever upon you my dear boy'. The other children did not emulate her deep conviction; John, in fact, found her 'perhaps too religious'.[7] Likewise, Douglas, for most of his life, gave only half-hearted attention to matters spiritual. In the Great War, however, an intensity similar to Rachel's suddenly materialised, and with it came the same belief in predestination.

The image of moral purity was also strengthened by the habit of order and cleanliness which Rachel cultivated in her son. This habit was later reinforced at every institution through which Douglas passed, but its source was definitely Rachel. Though lax in her discipline of him, she stressed regimentation in his daily life. Nurses were given strict instructions regarding the care of the children, departures from which were not tolerated. The following is an example:

NURSERY DUTIES

The nurse must devote her time and thoughts to the comfort and well-being of the three little children under her charge – *cheerily – and happily, always being beside them.*

Perfect regularity necessary.

Children's porridge at 8 o'clock. Dinner at 1/2 past one. Tea at 6. Lights out and nursery quiet at 10. Children bathed every night –

their hair washed once a week – their socks changed twice a day. Clothes kept in good repair – and everything connected with the nursery *tidy, and neat*. Day nursery scrubbed out every second night – bathroom twice a week, dirty things counted over and mended before washing on Monday.

Clothes brushed at night and boots and shoes *before they* rise in the morning. Nurse has to rise to wash and do up her own clothes. Nurse gets to church every other Sunday.

Janet commented that 'the "Nursery Duties" remind me of [Douglas's] own orderly ways'.[8]

In the Victorian ethos, order and cleanliness symbolised moral purity, which was in turn an essential attribute of the gentleman. Rachel, above all, wanted her sons to be gentlemen. Part of their training was a classical education at a first-rate public school, which, according to Rachel, enabled the gentleman to rise above the vulgar masses. Her thoughts on education and her objectives for her sons are evident in an 1859 letter to one of Willie's tutors:

Our object is not to make Willie a distiller or anything in particular. We desire to develop in him to the utmost such gifts as he has received from God – to improve those intellectual qualities in which he may be deficient and to cultivate his moral powers: – to see him grow up a humble and earnest Christian – an accomplished, well-informed and liberal-minded *gentleman* – with these qualifications be his lot in life what may, he will command respect and be in a position to derive happiness in whatever position of life God may place him . . . As for myself I attach so much importance to scholarship – especially as an antidote to the vulgarity and narrowness of mind which active commercial pursuits are apt to engender in the best . . .[9]

The ideals of Muscular Christianity could not have been better expressed. Rachel's hopes for Douglas were no less bold, as she indicated in a letter to John:

You must write to Douglas about your prospects – and it will be an immense *spur to him* in his Greek which he dislikes so much –

When my brothers were at school, it was considered that a boy who did not learn Greek was uneducated – and to my idea an Oxford or Cambridge University man *is of a higher stamp*, than those who are not – of course you . . . mix with men *in college* who, in the course of a few years will be the great men of the day, Statesmen, lawyers, etc. and the training makes a gentleman![10]

With Rachel's guidance, a Victorian gentleman was what Douglas became.

In view of Rachel's firm belief in the value of a classical education, it seems curious that Douglas's schooling was at first approached rather haphazardly. The fact that he was given no formal training before he was 8 might be explained by his ill-health, his difficult behaviour, or Rachel's reluctance to part with her youngest, and dearest, child. His first school (in St Andrews, to which he went in May 1869) seems only to have been a convenient place to stow him while mother and father took cures in Vichy. Douglas stayed there only a few weeks. In October 1869, he joined his brother John at Edinburgh Collegiate, a small day school located in Charlotte Square. A master later remembered him as a 'clean, well turned out boy' who was slow and backward.[11]

John felt that his brother's educational difficulties, particularly his problems with the Classics, originated at the Collegiate. The nature of his problems is not known, but it is certain that he was not of low intelligence. Rather, his early problems probably resulted from his late start, and teaching methods ill-suited to his individualistic and somewhat difficult temperament. While his experiences may have caused him some anxiety, there is no evidence that they resulted in permanent psychological impairment.[12]

In September 1871, Douglas again followed John to Orwell House, a preparatory school whose master, a Mr Hanbury, specialised in grooming students for Rugby. Rachel was determined that her sons should go to that temple of Muscular Christianity, but Hanbury refused to recommend any boy who did not meet Rugby's high standards. Douglas, burdened by his slow start, was torn in opposite directions by his mother's unrealistic ambition and Hanbury's depressing realism. His time at Orwell House was therefore his most distressing educational experience.

Douglas stayed at Orwell House until October 1875. Reports from tutors reveal a difficult child with a consistently dismal academic record: 'Douglas . . . is very backward in Latin . . . spelling very poor and writing careless . . . Rather tiresome at times . . . as he is backward he ought to be more attentive.' Despite the problems, Rachel's support remained steadfast. She did not scold her son, but instead encouraged him to improve as gently as she knew how. When Hanbury advised that 'It would not do Douglas any harm if he worked a little harder', Rachel responded by writing 'my own darling boy take the hint and try and work a little harder'. She elevated every rare small success to the sublime, while reminding Douglas not to be burdened by the more frequent failures. 'Do tell me how your work gets on,' she would urge him. 'Tell me all about it, as there is no one, as you know, whose thoughts centre so much on you my darling Douglas.'[13]

Douglas was not allowed to forget that 'your advancement into Big School is my great desire, as you know so well'. Rachel's ambition may have caused him strain, but this was outweighed by her resolute faith in him. This faith, at times blind, caused her to question Hanbury's more objective opinion of her son's abilities. When she learned that he had advised Douglas that 'it is hardly worthwhile his going up to Rugby as he would be chucked out in a year or so', she instead insisted that Rugby was 'not so particular as Mr. H. would lead one to suppose'. Eventually, however, she accepted the inevitable:

> I had a letter last Saturday from Mr. Hanbury writing to know where we thought of placing you, as he could not advise you to go up for Rugby as your knowledge of Greek was so deficient you would never pass . . . Of course, as you know, I was very sorry to get Mr. H's letter, but then I felt satisfied it was for your good as I had so completely cast it upon God to do for you exactly what He knew was to be for your good, and now I have no more regrets about it if it be for your good.[14]

Rachel took Hanbury's advice and enrolled Douglas at Clifton in late October 1875.

Rachel assumed that Douglas would immediately take his place in the School House at Clifton, but the headmaster, Dr Percival, was of a different mind. After meeting Douglas, he found that he was not sufficiently advanced to enter the Fourth Form, and not, therefore, allowed to reside in the School House. He was instead boarded (for approximately fifteen months) with a master of the school, a Mr Marks, from whom he received private coaching. In January 1877, he was finally admitted to the Fourth Form and moved into the School House. His subsequent progress was later described by Mr N. Whatley, the headmaster in 1929:

> He was placed in the Lower Fourth on the Classical Side. At the end of his first term he was promoted to the Upper Fourth. After two terms he was promoted to the Lower Fifth. Up to that time he had made quite rapid progress. In the Lower Fifth he seems to have slowed down, and remained there for four terms, during which he slowly made his way up the form. He was seventh in the form when he left in April 1879.

Whilst this is not the description of an outstanding student, it is clear that Douglas was slowly overcoming the difficulties experienced at Edinburgh Collegiate and Orwell House. His academic record, neither brilliant nor dismal, was perhaps an accurate appraisal of his actual abilities.

John admitted that his brother was 'never very good at games', a critical failing in an educational system which placed at least as high a value on athletic achievement as on scholastic aptitude. This failing caused Rachel some dismay. Concerned that he might become a 'weakly Cad', she told him that 'You must try, darling, try and come out well at your games.' Cricket (as opposed to football!) would, she assured him, 'make you strong and manly'. Her entreaties had little effect. Games bored Douglas; school spirit and inter-house rivalries left him cold. A schoolmate remembered him as someone with 'wider interests' who was 'more grown up than the average boy'. Charteris echoed this appraisal in his biography of Haig:

> His time at Clifton was short, and he does not appear to have made his mark in any way . . . Already at Clifton he was developing that quality of 'aloneness' which was so prominent a characteristic of his later life. He was his own judge, his own taskmaster; he set the standard for himself, and he did not allow himself to be deflected a hair's breadth from his intentions or to be swayed by the opinions of others.[15]

16

Haig was no typical public school product. He spent only two years at his school, hated the Classics, did not excel at games, and was not popular with his fellow pupils. It is therefore safe to conclude that the values the public schools encouraged – teamwork, loyalty, self-sacrifice, anti-individualism, and harmony – were only partially absorbed by him. As will be seen, whilst he expected others to conform to the public school type, Haig himself followed a different set of rules.

Despite his usual difficulties with the Classics, Douglas passed first in Latin in his final term at Clifton. His mother was ecstatic:

> Oh! Such pleasure it has given me! Your report! So satisfactory and delightful and to me *so true*! So true too! . . . This 'decided improvement' is to me the more satisfactory since your time at Clifton *is so short*. I should like you to leave the best of characters behind you – and so would you, yourself, my darling.

As the final two sentences indicate, Rachel now felt that the time had come for Douglas to go on to university. Though neither he, nor his form master, nor Percival agreed that he was ready to leave Clifton, Rachel remained determined:

> by going *early* you will be finished *early* and ready to begin your Profession or Trade at once when you pass – Willie seems to think you are '*quite fit* to pass and go into residence in October' – and 'you have heaps of time' he says to get up for your '*Matric*.' and no time is to be lost – '*You are not too young*' and the time would be lost don't you think, were you to delay . . . going to College.

In a manner typical of the relationship between mother and son, Rachel gently but persistently imposed her will upon Douglas. She was certain that she alone knew what was best for him. He was given very little say in the matter, being instructed to

> do as I have always done in such cases *seek to be directed* – and you may rest assured *God will shew you* – and my dear boy isn't it delightful to feel that you will be *wisely* directed and that you may rest passive in the matter . . . I trust that you will *ask for guidance as the matter concerns much* of your future

17

happiness in life and we know nothing can prosper without God.[16]

Douglas, having only recently settled in at Clifton, quite suddenly found himself on his way to Brasenose College, Oxford.

Haig's university education was, however, delayed by Rachel's sudden death on 21 April 1879. He was deeply grieved at the loss, especially since he was unable to return home in time to see her before she died. The resultant gap in his life could never properly be filled. His immediate reaction to his loss was to shelve the Oxford plans in favour of a trip to the United States with his brother Hugo. This gave him the opportunity to play the wealthy young gentleman abroad and also offered him the time and circumstances to overcome his grief.

Returning from America refreshed and matured, Haig entered Brasenose in October 1880. Though only 19, his chiselled jaw, piercing blue eyes and profound self-assurance suggested character and experience beyond his years. His was a type ideally suited to Oxford of the 1880s. Financially independent, he could enjoy the pleasures and pastimes favoured by the privileged student, unfettered by strait-laced parents. Though self-possessed, he was not at this stage reclusive, nor was he bookish. His lack of athletic prowess did not matter to the extent it had at Clifton. All of this meant that he was fully equipped to flourish in the Oxford environment. And flourish he did. He became an accepted member of an aristocratic circle, a well-mannered, agreeable and impressive young man. The negative characteristics of his youth – sullenness, ill-temper, and aggression – were put behind him as he developed into a gentleman. His mother would have been immensely proud.

Oxford, for a man of Haig's background, was more finishing school than university. Here, young men refined the gentlemanly habits they had acquired at school. In other words, they learned how to enjoy themselves in the accepted Victorian fashion. Thus, social pursuits were infinitely more important than intellectual ones. Though Lord Askwith, a fellow student, claimed that 'No dinner and no club . . . deterred Haig if he was not prepared for a particular lecture or essay', in truth, few sacrifices had to be made. Haig did not allow his social life to become intoxicating; but neither was he ever too concerned with his studies. The two pursuits seldom clashed. His typical morning was spent 'drawing and reading in my rooms'; whereupon the rest of the day was his to enjoy. Studies were an unavoidable, though minor, nuisance.[17]

In addition to the required Greek, Latin and Rudiments of Religion courses, Haig read three 'Groups': French Literature, Elements of Political Economy and Ancient History – all of which were chosen, and read, with conspicuous detachment. There is no evidence that the material studied affected his subsequent outlook on life in any way. The same can be said for the influence of his tutors. The only tutor mentioned more than once in his diary is Walter Pater, with whom Haig studied Homer, and to whom he attributed his skill in writing English. But since Haig's written expression was hardly remarkable, Pater's effect could not have been profound. Contrary to the claims of Askwith (whose reliability as a witness is open to question), scholarly pursuits commanded Haig's attention when required, but seldom his interest.

In contrast, the Oxford social life had a much more important effect upon the development of Haig's character. In the words of Duff Cooper, he discovered a 'sense of his own importance'; social success caused his self-esteem to expand to monumental proportions. This was manifested in his decision (in February 1883) to begin a diary. Never an outlet for introspection, the diary was instead a useful place to record impressive achievements – a place where vanity was allowed to run rampant. Thus, on the first page of the diary, Haig wrote:

> Having oftentimes heard of the advantages to be derived from keeping a diary I determine to keep one. The difficulty is to have a good day to begin upon.

> I think it is well to start on the 19th day of last June upon which day I was twenty-one and put down as many events as I can remember with accuracy which happened from then until this day.

Having made this decision, he could not resist the temptation to start two days earlier, the occasion of a polo match with Cambridge, when 'I got the only goal on our side but we ought to have had several had our fellows backed me up.' When the teams met again

19

the following day, 'We got two goals, all of which I obtained.' This sort of entry was typical of Haig's diaries for the rest of his life. Though not introspective, the entries were private. They allowed him to grouse, gossip and boast in a manner otherwise unacceptable in polite society.[18]

The first diary covers only a portion of Haig's last year at Oxford. Admittedly incomplete, it is nevertheless immensely valuable, being the first written evidence of his self-image. It is also important because it covers a unique period of his life, a period of glorious irresponsibility. Pressure was at a low ebb; competition with peers was almost non-existent and the anxiety of earlier academic failures had disappeared. Haig thus found real relaxation for the first and perhaps only time in his life. He rode, played polo and cards, attended race meetings and luncheons, drank fine wines and discussed the 'important' issues of the day. A glimpse of this life is available from Askwith's account of his first meeting with Haig. Since the latter's 'wine had not arrived', they sat in Askwith's room and

> sipped a bottle of claret together. We laughed over our interviews held that morning with Dr. Craddock [the Principal] . . . To me he had finally ended by saying 'Drink plenty of port, sir. You want port in this damp climate.' To him he had remarked 'Ride, sir, ride. I like to see the gentlemen of Brasenose in top boots.'[19]

For Haig, Oxford was a brief but immensely enjoyable experience. Aspects of his character were allowed to surface which, later in life, were intentionally repressed. Thus, his ultimate rejection of the Oxford life is itself a clue to the man he became.

The diary reveals the naiveté of young gentlemen comfortable in their ivory tower. The important matters were club politics, sports, and the behaviour of fellow students. Outside issues, which rarely intruded, were discussed with contrived sagacity, with confidence borne of isolation:

> After dinner we have a great argument on the present evils of the Church, notably the narrow-minded views of Clergymen and their hypocracy [sic]. Mac talked loudly . . . in favour of the 'good works done by the Church' . . . Noll stammered out his views on 'Charity' which, he said, 'were never preached to the people'. I must say I

thought he had right on his side . . . Something does seem to be wrong in younger sons entering the Church because there is a living in the family and not because they have any inclination to it . . . I finished the argument amicably.[20]

As was usually the case, it was not the subject that was important, but the lively conversation it generated. The young men were play-acting: sitting on comfortable couches, puffing cigars, and sipping brandy, they discussed 'important' issues in imitation of their elders.

Club politics was conducted with far less civility. The jealous wrangling betrayed the youth of the politicians (though perhaps politics at any level brings out the boys in men). Haig played a central role in many of the political battles of the day, among them the selection of an officer for the governing body of Vincent's, Oxford's equivalent of the Victorian social club:

> Rather than have a split in the College, I said I had no intention of standing. Owing however to the pressure of all the other colleges and some of the members in B.N.C. Puxley and his committee decided to run himself and me – with Ascher as a third man. At 8 we went to Vincent's . . . Thanks to Noll everyone had agreed to vote for me! His endeavours were really wonderful, and excitement intense. The result was that I got 65 votes, Puxley 21 . . . Most of the papers were 'Old Committee and Douglas Haig'.

At Vincent's, members met to drink, smoke, dine, converse and be seen. Askwith wrote that Haig 'seldom came to Vincent's' but the diary indicates otherwise. In fact, he was an active member of many prestigious clubs, including the Vampyres (a Sunday luncheon group where the politics was as fierce as at Vincent's), the Octagon Wine Club, and the Phoenix. In all clubs, rules of etiquette were strictly observed. Members were required to act like gentlemen. Those who did not were punished, as when Puxley was fined for accusing Haig of making a wrong toast. A far more serious offence occurred when a member of Vincent's was caught cheating at cards. In his subsequent trial, 'Macdonnell laid down the case in a lawyer like fashion. Rather comic had not the occasion been so serious.' The jury (which included Haig) decided, after two days' deliberation, to ask for the individual's resignation.[21]

One club which Haig particularly enjoyed was the Bullingdon, concerned primarily with equine sports. Haig had, quite literally, grown up on a horse. Later in life, riding, hunting and polo were among the few distractions he allowed himself. He seldom missed an opportunity to participate in a hunt, though it was not a sport which he took seriously. He was mostly attracted to the relaxation and exercise the hunt afforded, and was not particularly interested in perfecting his technique. In addition, hunts, race meetings and polo matches provided valuable social (and later professional) contacts, though it was not on this basis alone that Haig found the activities attractive.

Polo was easily Haig's favourite sporting activity. After having abandoned rowing ('he could not bear the monotony of tubbings or the upbraidings of coaches'), he took up polo during his second year at Brasenose. His talents as a horseman made him an instant leader, a position to which he was naturally attracted. In addition to being the only sport in which he was truly expert, polo exposed him to uniquely valuable social contacts. In the Victorian Army, prowess at polo was seen as an important indicator of an officer's potential. But Haig would nevertheless have enjoyed the game just as much had no such advantages accrued. Polo was, in its order, precision and spirit, the peacetime equivalent of the cavalry charge, which, later in life, became for Haig the most sublime of human endeavours. Never just a game but a test of character, polo brought him immense personal satisfaction; providing levels of emotional intensity otherwise lacking in a life of restraint.[22]

Haig usually kept at least two horses in the college stables and spent considerable sums on the upkeep of his polo ponies. A full-time groom was paid 16s per week, while veterinarians were regularly consulted. Expenses like these constituted only a small part of the costs of his 'education'. Though not foppish, he appreciated fine clothes. He was usually seen 'scrupulously dressed . . . with his tails showing through a short cover coat, as was the fashion'. Similar quality was demanded in other areas. No expense was spared on food or wine. Menus and wine lists, like his dinner guests, were symbols of status proudly recorded in the diary. He preferred to dine out, having no stomach for the dismal offerings in the college hall. Parsimonious, even stingy, in most areas, he imposed few restrictions when spending on himself. The diary reveals his attitude towards personal frugality and the possible state of his own finances:

At dinner we discussed the meanness of some fathers to their sons up here in the hopes of making them acquire the knowledge of the value of money – such as the Duke of Westminster to Harry Grosvenor who is obliged to bet a little in order to get some money and Puppy Weymouth who is allowed £300 a year by the Marquess of Bath his father.

Haig, who shunned gambling, excused the practice when it was necessary to compensate for the 'meanness' of one's father.[23]

Within Haig's social circle was a number of men who attained subsequent distinction. 'Grey', a fellow office-holder at Vincent's, was Sir Edward Grey, later Viscount Grey of Fallodon. Lord William Cecil, later Bishop of Exeter, and his brother, Lord Robert, were also Oxford contemporaries. Haig, however, had little in common with them, finding their tastes rather curious. Lord William, 'the Fish', was a 'clever chap' who could 'talk away most amusingly'. But his dress was most unacceptable. 'His clothes, poor fellow, are not of the most swagger! In fact very seedy resembling the garb of a scholar!' Lord Robert failed on the same count. 'This Cecil like his brother does not waste money on clothes . . . Riding he does not care for.' In contrast to these social misfits, Haig was an accepted and widely admired member of the community who

> knew and was pleasant to everyone . . . but by no means court[ed] popularity. He liked to talk quietly to his neighbour and generally about a subject interesting to his neighbour or affecting the life or athletics of the College rather than his own interests. He was keenly desirous that the community should succeed, and loved to hear of a successful bump on the river or a win of the Cricket XI. He loved also a quiet joke, but I never heard him make one.

Askwith's description was echoed by most people who later came into contact with Haig. When crucial issues did not intervene, he could be an amiable, warm-hearted and kind man able to get on with almost anyone. Though he felt himself superior to those around him, this sense of superiority generally remained hidden in his diaries and letters. Quiet without being self-effacing, he preferred being an audience rather than an entertainer. Though he did not court popularity, he did pay close attention to his image, striving always to make himself worthy of respect. He dressed well, spoke properly and had impeccable manners. These attributes, refined at Oxford, proved immensely valuable later in life.[24]

Women were absent from Haig's social circle. The college and the clubs were obviously restricted to males, but he showed no eagerness to break out of this all-male cocoon. Though he was not uncommon in his avoidance of a serious relationship, he was unusual in his apparent disdain for casual affairs and his conspicuous abstinence from the seamier side of Victorian sexual proclivities. Whilst an encounter with a prostitute would probably not have been recorded in the diary, contact with one is as near to being inconceivable as is possible without concrete proof. Haig's avoidance of women seems to have stemmed from sexual repression, rigid morality and – later – professional practicality. Like his male contemporaries, he saw women as flippant, frivolous, mentally deficient, physically weak and morally unsound. When he finally married, at 44, the time, as much as the mate, was opportune. Before that time (and probably after) he saw women as inferior beings incapable of enlightening conversation. During an 1883 trip to Europe, he was dismayed because 'Women predominate. Such a cackle.' Their interests were 'most stupid, but evidently suited for those of childish dispositions'. They were, quite simply, a waste of a serious young man's time.[25]

Two women, his sister Henrietta and his wife Doris, were not subjected to Haig's irrational prejudices against females. His relationships with them were not based upon equality but rather upon respect. Though often condescending to them, he trusted them as he trusted no one else. His letters to them – the most candid of his correspondence – reveal a side of Haig which no one else saw. But his openness was a matter of degree; though Henrietta and Doris came into contact with a less inscrutable and controlled Haig, they could not penetrate his heavily armoured shell of self-reliance. Haig seems to have derived comfort and security from emotional isolation; he avoided true intimacy and the demands which it imposes. Henrietta and Doris may have brought him happiness otherwise unobtainable, but he was dependent only upon himself.

Henrietta and Douglas did not see much of each other prior to the death of Rachel. Ten years older than him, she had married and moved to Ireland by the age of 18. When Rachel died, she and Douglas were drawn together, each for different reasons. Henrietta had much in common with Rachel – most notably the superficial serenity which concealed a resolute determination and burning ambition. Her ambition for Douglas eventually became as monumental as Rachel's had been. Douglas, therefore, was probably drawn to his sister because she seemed able to fill the gap in his life which followed Rachel's passing. Henrietta, perhaps because she was childless, saw her orphaned brother as someone who still required support and guidance. Their relationship was more like mother and son than sister and brother.

The relationship brought happiness to both, but it was especially beneficial – socially and professionally – to Douglas. Henrietta's marriage, in 1869, to Willie Jameson (which linked two great whisky families) brought her into the inner circle of the English social élite. Jameson, the archetypal wealthy, fun-loving and 'manly' Victorian, was an active member of the 'idle' rich who gained some fame through his success as a transatlantic yachtsman – a hobby which also brought him into close contact with the Prince of Wales. The Jamesons were regular guests at Sandringham, Cowes and Balmoral. When Douglas came of age and his relationship with Henrietta blossomed, she introduced him into this élite circle. She was his contact, guide, tutor and mentor in the enchanted world of the privileged.

It is quite possible that Henrietta persuaded Douglas to enter the Army while the two were together on a trip through Europe in March 1883. Upon his return to university, his work took on a new seriousness. Most of his time was spent in diligent preparation for his coming exams. In order to find the desired privacy, he moved to lodgings outside the college. The diary was abandoned – whether because of a lack of time or a lack of events to relate is not clear. He passed his exams with no apparent difficulty and left Oxford at the end of the summer term 1883. Because he had missed one term earlier due to influenza, he was denied a degree since he had spent insufficient time in residence.

The peculiarities of the Army entrance procedure probably explain the urgency with which Haig approached his studies after his return from Europe. In his day, university graduates were not granted direct commissions. They had instead to go to Sandhurst where they were admitted on a par with young men fresh from the public schools. 'University Candidates' had to pass their final examinations, but did not have to earn a degree. They also had to be under 23 years old.

This may explain why Haig did not return to Oxford for the required final term. He turned 22 during June 1883. Had he returned for another term, he would not have had enough time to prepare for the Sandhurst entrance exam.[26]

Whatever the reason for his decision to leave Oxford before he earned his degree, there is no evidence that he regretted his failure to get one. Oxford had served its purpose. He had become, as his mother had wished, a gentleman. Nothing else remained to be accomplished. A degree was superfluous – certainly not worth the extra time required. His newly discovered resolve is evidence of how much he had matured in the previous four years. Though he had enjoyed the period of glorious irresponsibility, unlike many of his contemporaries, he placed strict limits on its duration. More serious pursuits lay ahead.

Though Oxford had been a stimulating experience (personally if not academically), Haig retained no fond attachment to the university. Later in life he displayed no profound devotion either to it or to its principles. Fellow students with whom he shared many pleasant times were quickly forgotten. Some he saw later in life but he did not seek their company. He took what he wanted from Oxford and turned his back on it. The main thing he took away with him was a sense of his own importance. Everything else was amusing while it lasted but did not concern him when it was gone. Throughout his life Haig displayed the same pragmatic detachment towards most institutions and almost all people. He was concerned mainly with his own progress, something from which he was never more than slightly distracted.

2

A Martinet

Haig's decision to become a soldier appears to have been made quite casually. A number of factors – social, familial, educational and personal – caused him to drift slowly but inevitably towards the Army, in a manner not uncommon among men of his background. Haig was, however, different in that he did not greet the prospect of a military career with the lazy complacency characteristic of his contemporaries. To many of them the regiment was just another gentleman's club. Haig's unique intensity and driving ambition was, according to an Oxford acquaintance, evident from the beginning: 'I said I thought the Army did not shew much of an opening. His chin went out squarer and more determined than ever as he replied "It all depends on a man himself how he gets on in any profession. If I went into the Church I'd be a bishop."' A similar incident was recalled by George Drummond, who met Haig while cramming for the Sandhurst entrance exam. Drummond and his friends ('the usual careless lot of youngsters') were playing roulette, and invited Haig to join in. He refused abruptly, saying, 'It's all very well for you fellows, you are going into the Army to play at Soldiering, I am going in it as a profession, and I am going to do well in it.' Haig's statements might, in both cases, be judged the typical bluster of a privileged young man. But he was never prone to idle boasting. What both incidents reveal is that Haig's confidence, self-righteousness and ambition were already at this stage in his life mixed in uniquely potent proportions.[1]

Like the vast majority of his contemporaries, Haig employed a crammer to prepare him for the Sandhurst exam. The crammer, Litchfield, was 'a sharp, well-read fellow about 50' who was impressed with Haig's 'look of determination'. A crammer was necessary because the examination was little more than a test of memory in subjects irrelevant to actual needs of the Army. Two compulsory subjects,

27

mathematics and English, had to be taken along with three options. Among the latter, the Classics paper was weighted three times more heavily than the others (3,600 points as opposed to 1,200). This meant that in order to score the requisite number of points on the exam, the candidate was virtually forced to choose Classics as an 'option'. A knowledge of the Classics, it was believed, was the mark of a gentleman. Gentlemen, in turn, made the best officers. Despite the fact that Haig found he 'had forgotten Latin greatly', with his crammer's help he was able to pass the exam on his first try. He entered Sandhurst on 12 January 1884.[2]

Just as the entrance exam was ill-suited to selecting officers, so the Sandhurst system was inadequate for training them. The public school's emphasis upon character over intellect, athleticism, and the Classics was repeated. This system, of questionable value to young schoolboys, was definitely ill-suited to the needs of a modern army in an industrialised age. The need for more professional training should have been obvious to Army educators after the Franco-Prussian War. But the Prussian system, in which the liberal arts were supplemented by extensive scientific and technical instruction, was considered too practical and plebeian by the British. The amateur ethic remained inviolable.

The bias against practical subjects meant that the training at Sandhurst was mostly irrelevant. Subjects such as logistics, communication, transportation and hygiene – of obvious utility to the young officer – were not taught. Little attempt was made to familiarise the cadet with the skills of commanding men, nor to introduce him to artillery or engineering problems. What was taught, on the other hand, was probably more relevant to senior officers. There were three required subjects: mathematics, fortification and surveying; and a list of options which included French, German, siege operations, landscape drawing, military drawing and the ubiquitous Latin. Because of their background, most cadets chose the latter as one of their two options. Military history was not offered.

Haig's record at Sandhurst was a remarkable departure from his earlier academic achievements. Eager to make a favourable first impression, he worked much harder than was actually required. General Sir Walter Congreve, who shared a room with him, remembered that 'after a lecture he would sit down and write out his notes, which few RMC cadets have done before or since'. But, aware that the

Army did not admire 'bookish' soldiers, Haig also concentrated upon mastering drill and parade routines, and the handling of arms. His efforts were rewarded during his second term when he was appointed Under Officer, a distinction which went to the most promising cadet in each division. He continued this success by later being awarded the Anson Memorial Sword as Senior Under Officer, and by passing out first in order of merit. But despite its success, the Haig approach had disadvantages. His attention was focused constantly inward – towards making himself into a model soldier. He cared little about his fellow cadets and, not surprisingly, they had little time for him. Congreve found him 'taciturn and rough'.[3] He left Sandhurst with no close friends. It seems unlikely that this bothered him.

Haig succeeded because his greatest attributes – determination, ambition, detachment, traditionalism and a penchant for order – were also ones which the Army prized. But his success is unimpressive because the quality of the Sandhurst education was poor. The short one-year course had three aims: (1) to supplement the cadet's general education; (2) to introduce him to military subjects; and (3) to teach him discipline, drill and routine. These aims were overambitious, therefore few were achieved. But the most serious failing of the Sandhurst system was that it constrained the young officer's intellect, encouraging him to be unimaginative and accepting. According to a Royal Commission, the officer was taught to 'regard with horror any deviation from a sealed pattern'.[4] Due to his social background, his education and his pedantic nature, Haig's intellectual horizons were limited even before he entered Sandhurst. Unfortunately, the Academy did nothing to broaden them. He became, at a very early age, a guardian of tradition.

After leaving Sandhurst in February 1885, Haig joined the 7th (Queen's Own) Hussars. As far as he was concerned, there was no other choice open to him but the noble and glorious cavalry. His devotion to the arm was steadfast and unquestioning. This devotion was not, however, entirely sentimental. Opportunism played its part. In addition to being the arm suited to his equestrian skills and social background, it also offered him the best prospects, since it was dominant within the Army. Untainted by the technological advance of warfare, it had been able to maintain social purity, resisting the invasion of middle-class technicians so noticeable among the engineers and artillery. It was the military equivalent of 'old money'.

With social status came power. Though the cavalry comprised, from 1870 to 1914, only 9 per cent of the total forces, its officers always held a disproportionate number of senior commands. Young cavalry soldiers were well looked after by the 'old boys' in the Army's higher echelons. Thus, though there is no reason to doubt Haig's loyalty to the cavalry, one should not ignore the fact that it was professionally advantageous for the young cavalryman to support his arm faithfully and unquestioningly.

The British cavalry remained dominant despite the fact that in military terms it had already begun a gradual decline into obsolescence. The small wars of the Victorian period shielded the cavalry and indeed the entire British Army from the need to adapt to new technology. The mounted arm remained a potent weapon against 'savages'. Since the Army saw itself (and was seen as) little more than an Imperial police force, there seemed little need to modernise along Prussian lines. Victorian society's attitude towards the Army reinforced this obscurantism. Officers were respected, but the Army as a whole was loathed. The British have, since Cromwell, feared a large, professional military. The Victorian Army was tolerated because it was small and unobtrusive.

With the Army secure in its isolation and reinforced by its colonial successes, there seemed little justification for altering the traditional distribution of power. But this hierarchy was also perpetuated because cavalry officers refused to surrender their élite status, for to do so was to accept eventual extinction. Technological advances such as smokeless powder, better rifles and improved artillery had severely limited the effectiveness of cavalry. In wars between industrial powers, its role had shrunk to auxiliary and protective services performed mainly behind the front lines. Reacting to this unstoppable tide of obsolescence, cavalry traditionalists stubbornly rejected evidence of the arm's decline. When, for instance, it was demonstrated in the American Civil War that cavalry was being superseded by mounted infantry (soldiers who used the horse as a means of mobility but fought mostly dismounted), the traditionalists argued that Americans were too uncivilised to carry out sophisticated cavalry manoeuvres. When the Franco- Prussian War reiterated the American lessons, British cavalrymen conveniently averted their eyes.

The traditionalists' campaign has been described as a 'last, desperate effort to withstand the depersonalisation of war'.[5] Whilst it is true that modern weaponry depersonalised war, the explanation for the cavalry attitude lies deeper. To men like Haig, cavalry was a 'moral' weapon. As Napoleon argued (and Haig repeatedly affirmed) 'the moral is to the physical as three is to one'. Moral factors could not, traditionalists maintained, be quantified scientifically. They were the unknown and important elements which separated two otherwise evenly matched sides. Moral fortitude, was, in turn, part of the soldier's character – something with which he was born. This was, in its most basic sense, a question of class distinctions. If technological skill became more important than moral qualities, intellect would become more important than character. This was in fact what was occurring. The traditionalists resolutely resisted this change because, if it was accepted that soldierly qualities could be learned, instead of being a birthright, it was conceivable that the pathways to power within the Army would be opened to the 'weaklings' and the 'cads' of the lower classes.

Haig played an immensely important role in the cavalry reaction. From his earliest days as a 7th Hussar, he sought to enhance the arm's image through strict discipline, efficient training and the emphasis upon chivalric ideals. Unfortunately for him, this enthusiasm did not at first coincide with a professional environment in which he could thrive. The boring routine of regimental duties was only occasionally broken by a polo tournament as when, in August 1886, he was selected to play for England against the United States. Though Haig was thrilled at the honour of playing for his country, he had joined the Army to be a soldier. Few real chances to be one came his way. Haig had to content himself with regimental life, capitalising on the infrequent opportunities for recognition which arose. The average young officer may have been satisfied with this arrangement, but the last thing Haig wanted to be was average.

When Haig returned from playing polo in America, he learned that the 7th Hussars had been ordered to Secunderabad. He welcomed the change, since India was still one of the more militarily active parts of the Empire. After a short visit to his family, he set sail on 25 November 1886, recording no sadness on his departure.

Haig's first year in India was a disappointing continuation of the monotonous regimental routine. His dissatisfaction was exacerbated by concern over his health. In March 1887, he contracted enteric fever and was ill for a month, his temperature sometimes rising to 106 degrees. Afterwards, the dreadful regularity of illness caused him considerable strain and much worry. Something of a hypochondriac, Haig may never have been as ill as he maintained; but what is important is how ill he believed himself to be. Worried that his health would not be the equal of his ambition, he at one point wrote, 'if I get any more fever I shall probably leave India at once'.[6]

In 1888, Haig was made adjutant of the regiment, an appointment which suggests that, despite the lack of evidence in the diary, he must have made a favourable impression during his first three years. As adjutant, he was given control over the training and discipline of enlisted men, a responsibility which he took very seriously. His diligence was recalled by Sergeant-Major H. J. Harrison, who served with Haig in India:

> On the drill ground, in the riding school, on the field, and in Camp or barracks, Haig was the same brilliant worker. At all times and in all weathers, Haig went about 'Soldiering', and Haig's soldiering was admitted by all who mattered to be unrelated to ordinary drills and tactics, but was embellished with a kind of finishing off process exclusively Haig.

Haig's zeal sprang from two sources. The first was his steadfast belief in the ideals of the cavalry and his conception of himself as the defender of the cavalry faith. The second source was ambition, his eagerness to be recognised and promoted. Five years older than the majority of officers of his same rank, he was determined to make up for lost time.

The ideals Haig cherished were made clear to Harrison at their first meeting. When the latter arrived in India as a new recruit,

> Lt. Haig in plain soldierly language made it clear to every member of the draft that every soldier in that famous regiment must be a man, and that effeminate or sentimental qualities would prove a menace, and a detriment to promotion . . . Exactitude, Promptitude, Smartness and strict veracity were a few of the virtues our adjutant strictly adhered to, and sympathy for a technical error was unknown . . . Procrastination, Slowness of Perception, untidiness and Nerves, were items calculated to make Lt. Haig spit fire . . . A dull-witted man was Haig's pet aversion.

Haig stressed that certain sacrifices had to be made for the good of the regiment. He had sacrificed a leisurely life, family contact, friendships and intimacies. The same was expected from his men. He wanted men 'blindly devoted to their duties . . . with . . . human sentiments totally eradicated'. The best soldier was the one able to 'ostracise the mind from everything soft or sentimental'. As Haig was wedded to his profession, he expected his men to be similarly attached. 'He was solidly against a soldier being married, and a man who approached him with an application to [wed] did so with fear and trembling.'

'Haig of the early nineties was a Martinet' whose obsession with soldiering at times drove him beyond the bounds of decency. Harrison remembered an instance when a signaller was pilloried after losing control of a temperamental horse during a parade. After accusing the unfortunate soldier of being an idiot, Haig ordered him to the infirmary, where he was to be checked for a mental disorder. On Haig's instructions, the soldier was given a draught of Croton Oil, a horrible tasting cathartic. Upon his return to the regiment, the signaller was confined to barracks for twenty-eight days.

The unfortunate signaller was a 'staff man' whose special duties occasionally excused him from drills, exercises and lectures. Haig loathed all such men (others included farriers, servants and cooks) and often singled them out for ill-treatment. Harrison, also a signaller, was once himself the victim of this prejudice when Haig was one of the judges examining him for promotion to sergeant. The other two judges felt that the necessary exercises had been completed perfectly, but Haig disagreed. Since the judges' decision had to be unanimous, Harrison was denied promotion. He appealed to the colonel of the regiment, who consulted Haig. The latter 'admitted that the move was perfectly done' but rejected Harrison because he felt that signallers and suchlike did not belong in positions of responsibility. The colonel reversed the decision, and, according to Harrison, 'Haig and I never afterwards were pals.'

It is no surprise that the incident is not mentioned in the diary; Haig was not in the habit of describing instances when he had been humiliated. But, though corroborative evidence is lacking, it is safe to assume that Harrison's account is genuine. His letter to Lady Haig (in which the events are recorded) was intended as a tribute to his former adjutant. In spite of the injustice done to him, he stressed that it filled him 'with pride on reading of [Haig's] exploits'. He had, he wrote, been impressed from the very beginning with the single-minded way in which Haig 'chose to renounce sentimentality, human inspirations, and affectionate feelings, to embrace a real hard, irrevocable task of producing soldiers for his country and Queen'.[7]

The diaries which follow Haig's appointment to adjutant reveal the intensity Harrison described. Instead of being concerned, as before, with insignificant day to day activities, the majority of entries pertain to important issues affecting the regiment or the Army in general. For example, in February 1889, after umpiring a cavalry manoeuvre, Haig used his diary to record comments which would have been inexpedient to include in his official report on the exercise. 'Col. Butler', he wrote, 'has no idea of manoeuvring an army.' Or, on another occasion: 'Our Cavalry under Walter was utterly useless. He has no 'method' in reconnoitring.' It is impossible to tell whether Haig's criticisms were justified. What is known is that they were inspired by a belief that the cavalry's continued viability (and therefore its survival) depended upon manoeuvres and exercises being properly executed. Therefore, any commander who was perceived to approach them with less than the requisite degree of seriousness was mercilessly (but privately) scorned.[8]

Manoeuvres and drills, Haig insisted, had to be relevant to actual battlefield situations. For instance, after a 'Divisional Field Day' on 29 November 1889, he commented:

> cavalry is quite out of place on such occasions as the opposing forces start so close to each other: how a man calling himself a General can think such field days of use for Cavalry I can't think? – They are quite a waste of time and do Cavalry harm in making the men ride loosely and get wild.[9]

The entry is additional evidence of Haig's sincere devotion to the cavalry. The 'man calling himself a General' was detrimental to the arm's precarious image. The cavalry could not afford fools.

It was not long before the energy which Haig applied to cavalry matters was noticed by senior officers. This was partially because he unashamedly courted commanders sympathetic to traditional methods. This often meant taking on tasks outside his regular regimental duties. One such example occurred when Haig, of his own volition, wrote a lengthy commentary on a proposed 'scheme for teaching cavalry reconnaisance'. This was sent to General Bengough, who replied that he was 'much interested in your remarks . . . all of which appear to me excellent'. He added that 'if all or most Cavalry officers took as much practical interest in instructing their men, we should have our Cavalry . . . equal to any in Europe'.[10]

Close contacts were also maintained with Colonel John French, at the time commanding the 19th Hussars. Haig met French in November 1891, the occasion of a large cavalry camp. Thereafter, their paths regularly crossed. French was considered worthy of Haig's attention because he was an ardent and well-placed cavalry traditionalist. Though of like mind as far as the cavalry was concerned, the two men otherwise had little in common. In social and political terms, they were poles apart. Haig was, for instance, especially disdainful of French's persistent womanising. Nevertheless, as will be seen, he went to extraordinary lengths to maintain close connections with French – that is, as long as those connections were beneficial to his own career and to the cavalry, and as long as he felt French's military thinking remained sound.

Army life varied little as the years passed. The promotion to adjutant brought new responsibilities and prestige, but once Haig became accustomed to these, he found the new routine not very different from the old. For reasons which remain unclear, he did not seek active special service in the colonies, an option favoured by many of his contemporaries who were hungry for action. He was therefore tied to the regimental route to promotion and dependent upon the recognition of senior officers. The slow progress of his career was naturally frustrating to a man of his self-assurance.

When Haig was recognised, it was more often than not for his administrative work – reports, training schedules, etc. In 1892, the commanding officer of a cavalry manoeuvre, Major-General Gatacre was so impressed with Haig's report that he had it printed for general circulation. Similar success came in August 1892 when Haig was selected for special service with the Bombay Army, at Poona. Paperwork had been allowed to pile up, so he was called to the rescue. The selection of Haig for duties of this sort was an acknowledgement of his remarkable ability to effect order out of chaos. His achievements, though hardly exciting, were widely admired. His superior officer at Poona remarked that 'whatever he

undertakes he puts his whole heart and soul into it and always . . .
makes things a success'.[11]

Though he yearned to be otherwise, Haig's lack of battle experience
and his proven organisational talents were combining to cast him in
the role of an office soldier. This gave rise to two problems. The
first, of which he was unaware, was that he began to look for an
organisational solution to every problem. Form, in his mind, became
as important as content. If a plan did not work, its processes, rather
than its aims, were suspect. The second problem, one which Haig did
notice, was that an office soldier was less likely to get recognised by
his superiors than an officer who had proved himself in battle.

The first problem will be discussed later, when its ramifications
become evident. As to the second, it is clear that there was no easy
way for Haig to be recognised as long as he stayed in India. The late
Victorian Army was divided into two factions: one controlled by Lord
Wolseley, the other by Lord Roberts. The latter's domain was India,
the former's Britain. While in India, Haig did not become a Roberts
man. One obvious reason was because the two men differed on the
subject of the cavalry: Roberts was a supporter of the mounted infantry
movement which Haig considered anathema. But more important
at this stage was the fact that 'Bobs' was an independent, practical
soldier with a distaste for theory; a fighter who believed that war
provided the only lessons of real value to a soldier. Haig, partly
because of circumstance but also because of his nature, was one of
the new breed of professional soldiers who stressed organisation,
efficiency, and education. The Army needed soldiers like Haig, but
many (including Roberts) did not realise this.

It was clear to Haig that he had to escape the Indian morass.
His lifeline, as he saw it, was the Staff College, which would allow
him to side-step the regimental route to promotion. He also hoped
that, back in Britain, he would come into contact with officers who
appreciated his talents. Having decided upon this option, he did not
delay in putting it into effect. 'As the exam for the Staff College is very
hard I think the sooner I come home the better,' he told Henrietta.
On 9 September 1892, he left India. The diary suggests that he did
not expect to return for a long time:

Find Regimental Sergeant Major Humphries waiting at launch for
me. We all go on board *Peninsular* – quite melancholy parting.

Humphries wrung my hand and said I was the 'best sort he had ever had to do with'. They all go down the ladder into a small boat . . . I watched them with my glasses until they were quite a small speck . . . I feel quite sorry at leaving them all.

He was probably not sorry about leaving India, where the promise he had demonstrated at Sandhurst had been allowed to stagnate.[12]

Haig was on leave until June 1893, time which he used to prepare for the Staff College entrance exam. Every day from early morning until 5 p.m. was spent with a crammer named James. 'What rubbish it is to say it is dull for me here,' he commented to his sister. 'I haven't time to think about much else than the subjects for examination!' Henrietta, on a yachting trip at the time, lent her brother her London flat and one of her servants so that he could study in comfort and privacy. Concerned about the illnesses he had contracted in India, she insisted that he undergo an extensive medical examination. He obediently reported the results to her:

In order to set *your* mind at rest regarding *my* health, I went and saw a Dr. after leaving James tonight at 5 p.m. One Hamilton Brown of a certain fame and certainly a most careful and painstaking Physician. He looked at me all over! My tongue of course, chalked with a pencil the size of my liver on my skin, put things in his ears and listened to my lungs and heart and so forth. He said he would pass me as a 'thoroughly sound man' *but* a *little* below par. So I hope you will be satisfied now. All I want is plain food and a certain amount of exercise.

Henrietta's cook, Mrs Baxter, provided the 'good plain cooking' which was 'just what my *digestion* requires'. Haig assured his sister that 'I'll be as fit as ever' in a short time'.[13]

After cramming with James until March, Haig went to Germany where he continued his studies alone. He had to leave London because, when the Jamesons returned, the social whirl in which they took part proved too distracting. 'I . . . was really sorry to leave you', Henrietta was told, 'but I fancy it is the best thing to do to come away by oneself in order to read up for this beastly exam.' She again made sure that her brother was properly looked after by lending him her butler, to whom she gave precise instructions. 'Metcalfe', wrote Haig, 'does first rate. Brings me beef tea, by *your* orders at 11 a.m.' In spite of his abundant comforts, he found the pressures of studying burdensome: 'You will see', he wrote sardonically, 'I have taken Easter holidays like the rest of the world!'[14]

Continued concern over his health did prompt Haig to take a short break at Schwalbach, one of the family's favourite spas. He described the cure to Henrietta:

> I am getting on nicely here, thank you, and am feeling all the better for the waters. My times are somewhat earlier than the ones you followed. I am out by 7 a.m. and get 2 half glasses drunk in time to have breakfast at 8 o.c. I then go out again about 10:30 take 1/2 glass and bath at 11 o.c. Walking about between drink and bath of course. Then another 1/2 glass and a bit of a walk and back here at 12. The lunch at 1:15. At about 4 I have some chocolate as I have a grand hunger here! . . . I get back about 7:30 and have dinner. I have omitted the afternoon drink which we take on the way for the walk.[15]

Haig's methodical nature was perfectly suited to the spa regime. Unlike many of his contemporaries, he was not attracted to spas because of their active social life, but rather because he sincerely believed that his ailments could be cured by rigidly adhering to the prescribed schedule of rests, waters, and exercise.

The Staff College exam was held from 29 May to 12 June and totalled forty-two hours. Though Haig finished among the top twenty-eight candidates (the statutory number to be selected via the exam), he failed mathematics, one of the compulsory subjects. In this section a total of 200 points (out of a possible 400) was required. Haig scored 182. The failure, perhaps the most bitter disappointment of his career, was kept a closely guarded secret for the rest of his life.

One avenue remained open to him. The Commander-in-Chief of the Army (the Duke of Cambridge) usually nominated four officers from those who failed to gain entry via the exam. The real choice, however, rested with the Adjutant General, Sir Redvers Buller, who forwarded the names to the Duke. Despite being provided with glowing recommendations of Haig from Generals Bengough and Graves, Buller refused to forward Haig's name to the Duke. He later explained his refusal by citing the fact that the Army Health Board had discovered that Haig was colour blind. The disability was slight (he could not distinguish pink from other shades of red) but was apparently enough to disqualify him. What is suspicious is that the eye test occurred prior to the entrance exam, but was not mentioned until after it – an indication that perhaps Buller's motives were not the most honourable.

In an attempt to appeal against Buller's decision, Haig prepared a lengthy petition arguing that he had been unfairly treated. The thrust of his argument was that the mathematics papers

> were *different* to those set in previous years – Now in every '*Official* Report on Examination for Entrance to the Staff College' the attention of the intending candidates is called to the papers previously set, and they are directed to make them as guides as to what is required of them. This year's candidates have been misled in the Mathematical Papers.

The fallacy in this argument – the fact that the exam was the same for everyone and no one else failed mathematics – apparently escaped Haig. He was, however, on firmer ground in his complaint about the colour blindness issue: 'Is it not rather late to fall back on the medical report now, because had I made 18 more marks on [the Mathematics] paper . . . I would have entered the Staff College without further question?' He pointed out that only a fraction of the candidates (those whose medical examination occurred in London) were actually tested for colour blindness. He even found a Professor Mohren ('the great German oculist') who testified that he was not in fact colour blind. How much this 'evidence' cost him is unknown.[18]

The petition failed, whereupon Henrietta intervened. She sent another plea, detailing her brother's academic and military qualifications to the Quartermaster General, Sir Evelyn Wood and to Sir Keith Fraser, the Inspector General of Cavalry. But this, too, was to no avail. Fraser's reply is revealing:

> It is most vexatious that this should have happened to your brother who is the very man the Cavalry require as a Staff officer, a man who has been an adjutant and a very good one.

I wrote to the Acting Military Secretary on the subject and he says that it is Sir R. Buller who submits names – and he does not raise any hopes saying there are others with higher claims . . . I fear as a cavalry man I have no influence whatever. If your brother was a Rifleman, he could have a better chance. I am so sorry.[17]

Buller, an infantryman, was taking full advantage of the opportunity to strike back at the usually dominant cavalry. Unfortunately, in this case, a deserving officer suffered.

His options exhausted, Haig had to return to his regiment. Before doing so, however, he attended, of his own volition, the French cavalry manoeuvres at Touraine. His decision to do so demonstrates his keen interest in the arm. The exercise was particularly enlightening because it was organised on a scale (two full divisions) unknown in Britain. Haig was especially impressed with the flexibility given to the brigade leader, who was allowed to adapt to conditions as he saw fit:

A cavalry division manoeuvred on such principles reminds one of a well-disciplined polo team . . . And are not the same qualifications desired for success in both cases? I mean that, just as the four players combine to get the ball through the goal – some by riding off or backing up, so as to enable one of their number to hit the ball, as much as possible unmolested, towards . . . the goal – so, according to French cavalry tactics, one brigade attacks the enemy at that point where the best result is likely to be produced, while the others support it as best they can, and do their utmost to ensure its success.

The techniques which caught Haig's eye were those which he found lacking in the British Army. The French staff were 'practical men . . . not merely a body of theorists' who 'go about their work with method and common sense'. They realised the need to be on good terms with regimental officers, in order to ensure efficient communication. Concluding his report on the exercise, Haig stressed that

The necessity for simple manoeuvres of all ranks if a force of cavalry is fit for what they will have to do in war seems most evident. Not only are many regulations and instructions which seem excellent in theory put to the test, but all ranks are made to take more interest in their work, and seem to acquire as their standard of efficiency 'readiness for war' instead of 'that amount of training which will pass muster before the inspecting General'.

'Readiness for war' would be the guiding principle in all Haig's subsequent training and organisational schemes.[18]

Feeling not unlike a defeated general, Haig returned to India after completing his report on the French cavalry. It is to his credit that the bitterness he felt over his recent failure did not alter his determination to carry out his regimental duties to perfection. The best evidence of this overwhelming sense of duty is a letter from his commanding officer, written on the eve of his second 'final' departure from the regiment:

My dear Douglas

I cannot let you go without saying that I appreciate what you have done for the Regiment. You came back to a position that a great many people would have disliked extremely . . . Instead of making a grievance of it all, I know what a lot of pains you have taken and how much improvement in [your] squadron has been owing to you; and up to the last moment when you were off, you have taken just as much interest in the preliminary musketry of the squadron as if you would be able to see the results. I cannot say how much you will be missed by all of us, officers, N.C.O.s and men. Your example to the regiment has been worth everything to the boys. You know I wish you every luck. You are, I think, bound to succeed because you mean to. I hate saying 'Goodbye' as I am sadly afraid I shall never soldier with you again, but only hope I may.

Yours very sincerely

Hamish Reid[19]

Haig returned to Britain in May 1894 to become Sir Keith Fraser's ADC – an indication that Henrietta's pleadings had at least had an indirect effect. Fraser, like Haig, was a cavalry traditionalist opposed to the mounted infantry movement yet cognisant of the need for structural reorganisation and practical exercises. As a result of their compatibility, Haig and Fraser were able to bring about wide-ranging (if short-sighted) reforms. For most of the rest of the year, Haig was kept busy darting from one cavalry regiment to another, setting exercises, inspecting, and reporting his findings to Fraser. On 20 September, he received notification that the colour blindness would no longer bar him from admission to the Staff College. Though the Duke's final approval was still required, Haig had essentially been admitted. Since the visual defect had obviously not disappeared, it seems that Haig's cavalry studies, his work with Fraser and perhaps pressure from other quarters had caused Buller to change his mind.

Haig was not due to enter the Staff College until January 1896. Having completed his work with Fraser in February 1895, instead of returning to his regiment, he spent the rest of the year in assorted pursuits, not all of a military nature. March and April were spent on leave, most of the time at Radway Grange in Warwickshire, lent to him by Willie and Henrietta. At the latter's urging, he underwent another extensive physical examination, this time from a Dr Weber who

> examined me with the greatest care, compared my present con-
> stitution with the last notes 1891 also the Gov'nr and Mama's
> constitution enquired into with the help of his books. He says
> that I must live carefully – meat only once a day and 1/2 bottle of
> claret as a maximum allowance for *a whole day*!!! etc. If I attend to
> this he says my constitution is similar to a large number of people
> who live to great ages! So you and I will be Methuselas together
> it seems! His present recommendation is Kissengen for a month,
> say after 4 or 5 weeks at Potsdam, then a month at Pontresina or
> Malaga 'without overexertion' . . . I am *quite sound*, no disease but
> liver enlarged and wants attention.

Haig found it difficult to follow the doctor's orders. Being limited to a half bottle of wine a day was tortuous. Also, the demands of his career, he told his sister, meant that 'I cannot well spend time for so much water curing as Weber recommends'.[20]

The water curing interfered with Haig's plans to attend German cavalry manoeuvres, an opportunity which was greeted with even more eagerness than his earlier visit to France. Whilst his fascination for Prussian efficiency and professionalism was justified, his interest in these manoeuvres was somewhat misguided. In 1870, the Prussians demonstrated their understanding of modern tactics by mauling the traditionally oriented French cavalry. The Prussians had accepted the limited role which technological improvements imposed upon the mounted arm. Yet in 1895 Haig was able to observe manoeuvres involving large forces of traditionally organised cavalry. The explanation for this apparent retreat into orthodoxy can be found in the character of Kaiser Wilhelm II who took the throne in 1888. The Kaiser loved pomp, and the cavalry was the arm best able to provide it. This revitalisation of traditional cavalry was misunderstood by British observers (like Haig) who assumed that the Prussians had returned to their senses. In reality, the expanded cavalry was simply a plaything for the Kaiser.

'I am getting on very well here,' Haig wrote from Berlin on 4 May 1895; 'all the German officers I have met do everything to make my stay agreeable and show me anything I want'. Armed with a letter of introduction from Fraser, he was given access to exercises usually closed to foreign observers. Dinner with the Kaiser was also arranged, an event which Haig proudly described in his diary:

> I found myself not among the foreign officers but at the end of the table opposite the Emperor . . . On my right was a Colonel Crosigh who commands the Fusilier Guards here – and a friend of the Emperor. After we had been a certain time at dinner the Emperor drank his health, then signalled to him that he wished to drink my health. So I stood up and emptied my glass to the Kaiser in the usual style – 'nae hieltaps'. He did the same . . .
>
> After dinner we went into the picture gallery and the Emperor came and asked about my regiment, about Keith Fraser and what I was anxious to do and the length of the leave which I had. Altogether he was most friendly.

Recognising the debt that he owed to his hosts, Haig asked Henrietta to purchase gifts for him to present to them upon his departure. 'You can spend £30 or more if you like,' he advised. 'But I must have genuine articles that will last: for of course it would never do to say to me next time I come back "what rubbishy things are made in England".'[21]

On the practical side, Haig's observations of the German cavalry proved even more valuable than his previous French experiences. His *Notes on German Cavalry* – an impressive sequel to the French report – emphasised the independence given to junior officers within the German system. The decentralisation of authority meant that the amount of staff work (and the flow of paper) was reduced. 'The office work, which is enormous in our army and which absorbs such a numerous staff . . . is absolutely reduced to nothing.' Though he admitted that the British were beginning to accept the wisdom of this policy, he criticised regimental colonels who were slow to adapt:

> in our army there are many men of sound judgement who cannot shake off the prejudices due to their old fashioned training . . . These officers of the old school maintain that the colonel should show his authority by a constant interference in the captain's sphere of activity.

The traditional method (the 'orderly staff system') had, Haig admitted, some advantages. By focusing obedience on a single individual (the regimental colonel) it was 'eminently conducive to the establishment and maintenance of discipline'. But, he argued, this was not sufficient reason to retain it:

> if the Army had been instituted merely for the purpose of working in a regular and symmetrical pattern in time of peace . . . we should be the first to recognise that the orderly staff carries out this task to perfection . . . But just the reverse is the case; not only was the Army not instituted with this particular object in view, but it has another, which is to prepare itself for active service.

Again there is evident the distinguishing feature of Haig's military thought: the first priority of every policy had to be the preparation for war.

Haig saw efficiency everywhere. Despite his usual reserve, he described one unit as 'the finest squadron I have ever seen – pace, direction, all perfect and cohesion always maintained'. Efficiency, he presumed, was a by-product of compulsory service:

> The military year begins with the enlistment of troops and ends with their discharge. Each year is a counterpart of the year before; month succeeds month and day succeeds day, bringing with them duties anticipated by and known to all concerned.

Order and regularity was also reinforced by the unique discipline of the Prussian system:

> it is not based upon fear of punishment but rather upon the general all around efficiency of the officers in whom the rank and file are taught from the day they join the army to place implicit confidence. It has been for years acknowledged in this army that no officer is able to command and instruct men unless by his personal worth and thorough knowledge of his duties he can impress upon his subordinates and inspire obedience. The discipline thus seems natural, and being so it is less likely to slacken on service than if it had punishment as its base.

Haig surmised that senior officers commanded respect because they 'are intellectually superior to those whom they command' and 'the way in which the Army is organised and duty discharged tend to show up the commanders at all times as superior beings to the rest'. Thus, the German Army demonstrated the importance of both character *and* intellect. Senior officers were invariably 'superior beings' in spite of the fact that national service meant 'the presence in the ranks of individuals from all classes of society'. Though Haig stopped short of advocating national service for Britain, he endorsed (and considered worthy of imitation) every other aspect of the German system.[22]

The visit to Germany was cut short by a summons from French, who was to command the cavalry in a staff tour on Haywards Heath. French selected Haig as his Staff Officer. Staff tours, manoeuvres without troops, provided the opportunity to test organisational methods without the encumbrance of large troop movements. Though Haig's appointment was a feather in his cap, even more importantly it brought him into contact with the Quartermaster General, Sir Evelyn Wood, who afterwards commented that, 'It gave me great pleasure to meet you . . . I think I may honestly say of you, what we cannot always say, that the expectation, though great, was even less than the pleasure you gave me by your conversation.' Haig commented (with what turned out to be remarkable accuracy) that 'Sir E. W. is a capital fellow to have upon one's side as he always gets his own way!'[23]

Shortly after the staff tour, Haig participated in a cavalry manoeuvre as a brigade major. His subsequent criticisms of senior officers recorded in the diary stem from his experiences over the previous two years. For example, recalling what he had seen in Germany, he again stressed the importance of decentralised command. Every commander, no matter how lofty his position, was taken to task for 'cut and dried' techniques in which 'nothing was left to the initiative of the individual leaders'.[24] Haig's comments were justified. The decentralised approach was appropriate to the handling of small cavalry forces. But what is important, as far as Haig's future is concerned, is the extent to which he thought he had discovered a cast-iron rule pertaining to any military command. As will be seen, what was good for the cavalry was not necessarily good for larger units. Decentralisation in a massive army could lead to a dangerous discordance.

It was in manoeuvres of this type that Haig's professional approach – the combination of detailed study, efficient organisation and relevant training – was most evident. What is ironic is that his enlightened methods were applied to an antiquated and dying institution. Haig's reactionary and progressive sides, which clashed throughout his career, are evident in his work on the *Cavalry Drill Book*, which he completed before going to Camberley. The knowledge which had been gained from the French and German tours, the work with Fraser, and the lessons of various manoeuvres was carefully incorporated into the new manual. But, no matter how modern Haig's methods, the drill book could never be more than a temporarily effective tonic for a terminally ill patient. The patient should have been left to die and the doctor should have devoted his very significant skills to more worthwhile pursuits.

When Haig entered the Staff College in 1896 the institution was just emerging from ninety years of obscurity and neglect. It had been plagued by insufficient funding, lazy students, unskilled teachers and the Army's general disdain for professional education – problems which obviously exacerbated each other. But the main obstacle to improvement was the Victorian preference for amateurism. 'Professionalism,' according to one historian, 'because of its association with Utilitarianism, seemed to . . . objectors to be a middle class phenomenon, the adoption of which threatened external recognition of the Army as an elitist organisation.' The Commander-in-Chief of the Army, the Duke of Cambridge, typified this class antagonism when he described Staff College graduates as 'very ugly . . . and very dirty officers'. It should, however, be noted that those who supported reform, Haig among them, were by no means egalitarian democrats.

They still believed that character was more important than intellect, but they felt that professionalism could be, and indeed had to be, grafted on to the élitist structure. This was why Haig could praise Prussian professionalism while stressing that the social superiority of the officer was at its core.[25]

By 1896, when Haig entered the Staff College, the Army was slowly emerging from its dark ages. The Duke had retired, and Wolseley had replaced him as Commander-in-Chief. A nascent spirit of reform was evident. At the Staff College reform meant better funding, a more experienced teaching staff and a more enlightened attitude towards professionalisation. A Staff College qualification became a worthy attribute for a young officer. But though the change was impressive, in retrospect it is clear that the college still straddled two eras. Outmoded attitudes had not been completely discarded. For instance, the distrust and fear of the middle-class technician survived, as evidenced by the quotas which admitted only six officers from the artillery and engineers each year.[26]

One very serious problem arose from the Army's uncertainty regarding the type of general staff it required. Did it need a general's staff or a staff of generals?[27] The former is a logistically oriented body which assists the commander in the handling of troops. The latter is the German concept of the 'brain of an army' – a 'think tank' concerned with grand strategy and tactics. The British were reluctant to accept the German model because of what could be called the 'cult of the omnipotent commander'. In Britain, victories (and defeats) were habitually personalised; they were seen as resulting from the genius (or otherwise) of a single individual. The inspired genius, propelled by natural forces to the top of the Army, was the source of grand strategy. In contrast, the German system held genius to be superfluous. Brilliant generals existed, but the system was not meant to depend upon individual brilliance. The staff formulated strategy; the leader carried it out. It was presumed that every general staff officer was able to assume control of the army without a decline in effectiveness.

Confusion over the type of staff required led to uncertainty over the proper function of the Staff College. At the college, students learned to be a general's staff. The thrust was towards logistics and administration, with grand strategy proportionately neglected. Paradoxically, however, whilst the college prepared its students to be a general's staff, they aspired to be a staff of generals. Those of Haig's class, for instance, were widely acknowledged to be the cream of the Army. Haig, from the beginning, set his sights on the top of his profession. Where was he supposed to receive the training commensurate with his ambition if the Staff College was the highest rung on the Army's educational ladder? It seems that leadership ability and strategical wisdom were still seen as attributes of character, the by-products of genteel birth.

This does not mean that the Staff College failed to attract men of impressive intellect. Haig's intake included some of the most able military minds of the generation, men like James Edmonds, George MacDonogh, Thompson Capper, and Richard Haking. Edmonds later described the careers of the 1896 class as follows:

> Of the batch of thirty-one, four (two generals) were killed in action or died of wounds . . . Of the remainder, two cavalrymen [Haig and Allenby] became Field Marshals and peers; fifteen became generals (of whom eight were knighted); one (the youngest) got no further than colonel; three retired for reasons of health before 1914; one resigned as he had come into a fortune; and one 'the bravest of the brave' shot himself, his mother-in-law and her lawyer in *une drama passionelle*.

Haig did not harmonise well with this group. As at Sandhurst he was aloof, taciturn and probably too openly ambitious. 'My fellow students', Edmonds wrote, 'were a cheery, sociable lot, with the exception of Captain Douglas Haig . . . who worked harder than anybody else, was seldom seen in the mess except for meals, [and] kept himself to himself.' When choosing a Master of the Staff College Drag Hunt, the students intentionally passed over Haig in favour of Allenby, even though the former was by far the better rider. George Barrow, a member of the 1897 intake, recalled that Haig was so unpopular that 'no one would sit next to him at mess if there was a place vacant elsewhere'.[28]

For most of these men the Staff College was a largely irrelevant prerequisite to high command. The courses included military history, strategy and tactics, fortification, staff duties and applied sciences. These were taught at a level which most students had already mastered. Edmonds described the usual scene:

> We sat at a few lectures – the good boys in the front row, the idle asleep in the back row – and heard what amounted to no more than the reading of some paragraphs of the regulation

books (mostly out of date) and some pages of military history . . . we did a great deal out of doors mostly making ordinary sketch maps . . . With our own fair hands, under an artillery instructor, we dug trenches, put up wires, made temporary bridges . . . and amid a scene of indescribable confusion we laid a few railway rails.

Edmonds remembered only one war game, which ended 'in a complete fiasco'. The education improved during the second year, but the scope remained limited: 'We worked on a number of "schemes" out of doors, comprising most of the small tactical operations of war, writing little appreciations and operation orders for a small force, not for a brigade or a division.' Edmonds wrote that he 'did not find it necessary to work very hard at Camberley'. He compiled a history of the American Civil War in his spare time, while MacDonogh used his to qualify as a barrister.[29]

The staff at the college, the most learned in its history, was still hopelessly inadequate. The Kriegsakademie, the Prussian equivalent, employed forty-four experienced professors and instructors. The Camberley group consisted of six military officers and two civilian instructors – one of whom Edmonds described as 'bone idle'. Only one instructor, Major C. R. Simpson, had served on a staff, an experience about which he was 'conspicuously silent'. To the college's credit, the Commandant, Colonel Hildyard, was a progressive teacher who tried to reverse the customary emphasis upon rote learning by abolishing the final exam. 'We do not want any cramming here,' Hildyard stressed. 'We want officers to absorb, not to cram.'[30]

Unfortunately, the difference between absorbing and cramming was too subtle for some officers, including Haig, to grasp – especially since cramming was what they had been encouraged to do since they were young boys. The urge to cram was especially irresistible in those subjects taught by the Staff College's most eminent scholar, Colonel G. F. R. Henderson, author of the classic *Stonewall Jackson*. Though Henderson was acknowledged to be an inspiring teacher, he perhaps unconsciously encouraged pedantry:

the method of study was one of excessive concentration on detail rather than an inquiry into the broad principles of the leader's art and comparison of that with the great captains of all ages . . . to be able to enumerate the blades of grass in the Shanandoah Valley and

49

the yards marched by Stonewall Jackson's men is not an adequate foundation for leadership in a future war where conditions and armament have radically changed.

Haig's exam papers reveal that the above statement is not entirely facetious. One paper, concerned with the strategic points in the valley of Viginia, was criticised because one bridge was omitted. Another was marked down because Haig neglected to mention that the sun sets earlier in Virginia than in England. While both of these points were obviously important to Stonewall Jackson, by 1896 they had become mere trivia.

There were some relevant lessons to be learnt from the American Civil War, namely, the effects of new weaponry on mobility. But, at the Staff College, the war seems to have been studied more in the sense that it reinforced old lessons than in the way it revealed new ones. This is partially because it was studied in conjunction with Napoleonic campaigns (particularly those of 1806 and 1815) which were considered to be at least as relevant. The Staff College placed enormous emphasis upon inveterate principles of warfare which, as Tim Travers points out, encouraged a belief in the concept of 'normal' war – 'there was only one "normal" kind of warfare – decisive, offensive, mobile but structured, won by morale and determined personal leadership'.[32]

The Staff College vision of war is worth examining in detail because, as will be seen, it was the type of war Haig tried to fight from 1914 to 1918. At Camberley, Haig learned that the main enemy army is always the principal objective, that victory is achieved by concentrating superior force at the decisive point, and that the aim, in all cases, is a decisive victory. Warfare was seen as 'structured, short, reasonably simple and predictable'. It was also, most importantly, mobile. Battles, he was told, conform to a neat sequential pattern of preparation, attack and exploitation. Phases follow upon one another like acts in a play; each is strictly limited in time.[33]

A structured war meant that the roles of the various arms were clearly delineated. Haig learned that infantry forces the decision, that artillery can play only a supporting role and that cavalry is the arm, the only arm, of exploitation. Because warfare is mobile and war a contest between human beings rather than machines, the role of the artillery would always be limited and that of the cavalry always paramount. Haig's belief that the capacity of cavalry to inspire terror had not been reduced by modern weaponry is evident in the emphasis he gave to the Frenchman Maillard's views on the mounted arm:

To believe that Cavalry can effect nothing against Infantry because the latter is now armed with a long range repeating rifle, is to suppose without proper reason, that surprises are no longer possible, that leaders will never again make mistakes, that troops will always be in good heart . . . that they will never be affected by fatigue or hunger nor by the results of an unsuccessful fight . . . Such conclusions are contrary to human nature because surprises, misunderstandings, mistakes and failures will constantly recur and Cavalry will be at hand to take advantage of them.

Cavalry remained important because war was seen as a moral contest in which one side imposed its will upon the other. The Staff College conception of war presupposed both sides being equal in men and material. In such a contest, noted Haig, victory went to the side with the most pluck: 'if it is not the only cause of victory, it is always the most essential factor and the one without which we cannot hope to succeed'.[34]

Related to moral factors was the importance of inspired leadership. The senior commander, Haig learned, had to be larger than life. He must never be seen to change his mind, nor to be lacking a solution to a problem. 'The authority of the CinC is impaired by permitting subordinates to advance their own ideas,' he noted. 'The chief duty of the higher command is to prepare for battle, not to execute on the battlefield. After having clearly indicated to subordinate leaders their respective missions, we must leave the execution to them.' Finally, reinforcing what he had recently seen in France and Germany: 'Interference of superiors with details really pertaining to subordinates, paralyzes initiative.'[35]

The Staff College conception of war became Haig's – he absorbed what he learned completely and unquestioningly. It is easy to see why Camberley had such a profound effect. First, the learning was traditional and so was Haig. It did not challenge his preconceptions, therefore he readily accepted it. Secondly, his ambition impeded his education. Success, in his mind, did not mean learning something but rather doing well on exams and exercises. This sort of success came through cramming, not questioning. Thirdly, Haig, as many sincere admirers admitted, did not have a critical mind. Barrow recalled how it was always obvious with Haig which military text he had last read. If a lecture or book accorded with his preconceptions, he accepted it; if it did not, he ignored it. According to Edmonds, Haig's mind was like a faulty telephone; one had to shake it to make it work. Unfortunately, the Staff College did little shaking.[36]

Since Camberley suited men with minds like Haig's, one might assume that his record there was excellent. In actual fact, he did well, but only well. His inadequacies are as revealing as his successes. On outdoor exercises, where he was required to think quickly without the aid of a text, he was, according to Edmonds, 'terribly slow on the uptake'. On one occasion, Edmonds refused to accompany Haig on a ride, explaining that 'I could not afford to be handicapped by you . . . any longer.' In written exams, on the other hand, his methodical, pedantic approach was rewarded. Nevertheless, it is significant that Henderson often cautioned Haig about spending 'more time than you can profitably spare to my problems'. Another examiner once remarked that Haig's essay was 'too elaborate . . . it is longer than intended'. Haig would often become so immersed in a question that he would lose sight of its original purpose. For instance, he spent days preparing responses to problems to which, had they arisen in an actual battle, he would have had only a few hours in which to react. This approach contradicted his usual emphasis upon practical and relevant training.[37]

By the 1890s, the Staff College had made some progress towards professionalisation. But much more was needed. The college's faults – the emphasis on learning by rote, the class bias, the confusion over the role of a staff, etc. – were deficiencies which characterised the Army as a whole. Camberley should have been at the forefront of progress; instead it reinforced obscurantism. It offered no secure bridge to twentieth-century technological warfare. In order to adapt to the warfare of the future, the officer would have to abandon completely what he had learned at the Staff College. This was unfortunate, since the students at Camberley included some of the best military minds of the day. Highly motivated and extremely dedicated, these men aspired to the highest echelons of the service. The college should have developed their enormous potential. Instead, they were left to learn the skills of their profession by themselves, while the college put them through a course of mundane and irrelevant training.

Haig is an excellent example of the college's failure. He had inexhaustible energy and dedication. But his 'power and habit of concentration', according to Barrow, 'was to no small extent accountable for the dwarfing of [his] imagination'.[38] His ambition had diminished the capacity of his perception. The Staff College did nothing to enlarge it. Because Haig mirrored many of the characteristics of the college – pedantry, distrust of technology, traditionalism, élitism, etc. – he was encouraged along the path he had long ago chosen. The college failed because it lacked the resources and dynamism to make Haig not simply an educated soldier, which he was even before Camberley, but a thinking soldier, which, in the broadest sense, he would never be.

3

A Taste of War

In early January 1898, Major-General Sir Herbert Kitchener asked the Adjutant General Evelyn Wood to send him three officers from the graduating class of the Staff College. The men were to join his campaign against the Dervish in the Sudan, a campaign inspired partially by a desire to revenge the killing of General Charles Gordon at Khartoum fifteen years earlier. Wood, without hesitation, selected Haig as one of the fortunate three. Wood's patronage came at a decisive moment in Haig's career. Had he returned to his regiment, he might have slipped quietly into obscurity. Instead he was given active service, and, as a result, was catapulted into the front rank of the Army.

On the surface, Wood's choice of Haig seems straightforward. Haig was, after all, an impressive soldier. But so were many of the other graduates who were not selected. Closer inspection reveals an element of devious intent; the Adjutant General was not simply rewarding an officer for whom he had high regard. Wood was suspicious of Kitchener, and was therefore eager to keep a close eye on him. This was where Haig came in; it was suggested that his opinions on how the war was being conducted would be welcomed. 'Write to me as frankly as you will,' Wood repeatedly told Haig, 'you may be sure I shall not quote you to anyone.'[1] While this was by no means a direct order, Haig, infinitely grateful for the appointment, responded as if it were one.

The Sudan campaign differed from most other Victorian wars in that it was a deliberate act of policy, not a sudden, rash reaction to a colonial threat. The desire for revenge was rationalised by the need to counter French encroachments around the upper Nile. The recent revitalisation of the Egyptian economy and the military made the expedition politically possible. In other words, British sensibilities were not aroused because it was clear that the Egyptian 'allies' would

54

bear the greatest burden. Little strain would be placed on the British taxpayer and few British lives would be lost.

In this war, the British supplied mainly the officers, the Egyptians mainly the men. British officers were seconded to the Egyptian Army for a fixed period of time, and rewarded with a rank directly above their own. Under British tutelage, the Egyptian Army had made remarkable progress since its defeat in 1882 by Wolseley. It consisted of 20,000 trained conscripts, mostly Egyptian fellahin, but including a large contingent of Sudanese. But, though vastly improved, the Egyptian Army remained an untested force. Many British officers feared that it would dissolve the moment it came in contact with 'raving Dervish hordes'. The Dervish, widely respected as fighters, were probably the toughest 'savage' enemy the British had to face. The weakest link in the Egyptian Army was felt to be the cavalry. Many British officers believed that the Egyptians, as an inferior race, could not be imbued with the moral qualities central to the *arme blanche*.[2]

Haig arrived in Cairo on 3 February. After formally enlisting in the Egyptian Army, he boarded a steamer to Wadi Halfa. While on the Nile, he recorded one of his characteristic observations of his fellow passengers:

> There are about 7 or 8 Germans . . . on board. At dinner one of them sent to have the saloon door shut. Some non-Germans insisted on its remaining open. The Germans at first retaliated by putting up their coat collars and the lady sent for her jacket which she slung vigorously around her expansive shoulders! . . . Many of us laughed and the Germans no doubt felt uncomfortable and got up en masse and left the table, like many petted children. No doubt, they felt as if they had withdrawn from the Concert of the Great Powers. So in due course they will receive a telegram from 'Wilhelm' to congratulate them on their spirited conduct in supporting his Kolonial Politik and 'Mailed Hand' theory on the banks of the Nile!

The passage, one of the rare bits of humour in Haig's correspondence, is perhaps an indication of his unusually high spirits at this time. 'The longer I stay here the more lucky I seem to be,' he commented to Henrietta. 'The crowds of fellows that have asked to be taken and refused is very great.' He was careful to assure Wood that 'I am *ever* mindful of how much I am indebted to you.'[3]

At Wadi Halfa, Haig met Kitchener for the first time and found him 'very cordial'. The Sirdar, mindful of Haig's reputation as an efficient organiser, at first intended to send him to Debbeh to train a squadron in 'bad order'. Haig was 'looking forward to going to Debbeh where I shall have a free hand and be able to train the squadron as I like'. He optimistically (but wrongly) predicted that 'if anything doing Debbeh will be the direction of the attack'. In fact, for no apparent reason, these plans never materialised. On 20 February, Haig was ordered to Berber. Impatient and disappointed, he commented, 'I don't know at all what he wants me to do.' The uncertainty was an indication of things to come.[4]

Before embarking for Berber, Haig asked his sister to send him '2 or 3 boxes of supplies, each box not to exceed 150 pounds in weight and to be *about* 3 ft long by 1 1/2 broad and 1 deep'. The boxes were to be packed with 'jams, tinned fruits, cocoa, vegetables, haddock in tins, tongue, biscuits, some hock and a bottle or two of brandy or any other sort of drink'. Soap, toiletries, blankets, sun shades, hats and silk underwear were also requested. The boxes were to be carried by camels, of which Haig had three, along with four horses, a donkey and a goat. (The latter supplied his milk.) To look after him and his animals, he engaged 'a cook . . . the black fellow "Suleiman" as a body servant . . . a syce for every two horses and a camel boy'. As the war progressed, additional servants and animals were added to his entourage. His 'requirements' were not, he thought, excessive. He pitied, but felt no guilt towards, the unfortunate officers of the British Brigade who were 'limited to 30 lbs of kit'. As for himself, Haig saw no reason to abandon gentlemanly habits simply because he was at war.[5]

Haig's arrival in Berber on 28 February coincided with the north-ward advance of a large Dervish force under the Emir Mahmoud. Kitchener responded to this threat by concentrating his force at the junction of the Atbara and the Nile – subsequently called Fort Atbara. In a letter to Henrietta, Haig provided a characteristically optimistic summary of the situation:

It would be great luck if they did come on because then they would bring the whole matter to a conclusion at once. For if they gave fight and are beaten we would probably pursue them right on to Khartoum. Certainly *over* 150 miles, but no doubt the tribes on the flanks of the dervishes would rise and assist in annihilating them as they fled.

A short time later, he gave great weight to rumours that the Dervish were on the brink of starvation. The rumours were typical of those which float around an army camp prior to battle, the product of imaginative minds eager for 'evidence' that the impending engagement will not be serious. The overly optimistic Haig was always susceptible to these fabrications, which he should wisely have ignored.[6]

Events did not in fact proceed as Haig predicted. Kitchener, preferring to err on the side of caution, called upon the British Brigade to strengthen his force. In order to reach Berber when he wanted it, the brigade had to march 100 miles across the desert in six days. The feat, widely acclaimed in the Sudan and at home, did not impress Haig. Damning criticisms were immediately sent to Wood. As Haig pointed out, a battle was not imminent. Aside from the worthless glory gained, the march achieved nothing. Most worrying was the effect it had on the morale and fitness of the men. 'The majority were very weary, and the feet of some of the officers and men were sore and bloody.' Haig wondered 'whether, if it had been necessary . . . to oppose the enemy on the Atbara, these men could have fought effectively'.[7]

The Egyptian Cavalry Brigade, which had also been moved to Berber, consisted of ten squadrons, seven of them commanded by British officers. One of these had been earmarked for Haig. On 13 March, however, he learned that the 'Sirdar does not want a change of Squadron leaders made at present while Dervishes still threaten to advance'. Haig's annoyance with Kitchener consequently increased: 'What does this mean? The Dervishes are certainly not threatening to advance! Is the Sirdar prepared to do so?' Almost six weeks after arriving in the Sudan he still did not have a formal appointment. He joined in patrols, but the work was hardly challenging. His talents, he felt, were being wasted. After one especially frustrating patrol, in which he was in the saddle all day but saw no sign of the enemy, he complained that, 'British officers [are] not necessary for this kind of patrol! A native might well have been sent!'[8]

Haig was not being singled out for ill-treatment. Instead, his dilemma was a manifestation of Kitchener's chaotic method of command. On the surface, things seemed to run smoothly. The large tasks, such as the building of a railway from Wadi Halfa to Berber, were completed on time and in order. Below the surface, however, anarchy reigned. Kitchener, who trusted only himself, tried to maintain complete control over all aspects of his command. 'He has 2 aides-de-camp . . . but beyond them he employs no staff at all,' Haig told his sister. As a result, the minor tasks usually handled by staff officers were often left in disarray. 'It might be better for the comfort of the troops if he had a staff.' Worse still was the fact that 'the Sirdar is most silent and no one has even the slightest notion what is going to be done until he gives his orders!' The situation prompted another denunciatory letter to Wood, who replied that he had 'pointed out to [Kitchener] . . . that however well he may be able to command large bodies of troops without any intermediate links . . . he is not immortal, should a bullet or sickness strike him down, it would be hard on his successor'.[9]

While waiting for an appointment, Haig carried out informal inspections of the Egyptian Army, recording his observations in letters home. Unlike many of his colleagues, he did not discount the fighting value of the average soldier. With good leadership, the Egyptians and Sudanese could be turned into a fine fighting force. But, in order to achieve this, more responsibility had to be given to the junior officers, especially (of course) the British ones. 'The real pity is that so many valuable and keen young officers are not more used to train the men.' Though he was obviously referring to himself, he knew of others who 'find it difficult to find work to do'. The Egyptian cavalry officers were, on the other hand, 'duffers'. As he told Wood, 'We play polo with them twice a week, to make them ride and be a bit more manly, but the majority don't improve much. They sigh after a life of ease at Cairo, and want "medaille d'or" to wear with the ladies.'[10]

An opportunity for Haig to test his conclusions came on 21 March, after the Cavalry Brigade had scouted the Atbara south of the fort. On its return, it was followed by a small Dervish force, which had cleverly eluded the advanced outposts and was in position to harass the main body of troops. Revealing only a small portion of their force, the Dervish enticed a squadron of cavalry to pursue them into the scrub. An ambush resulted, causing ten killed and eight wounded among the Anglo-Egyptian force. After the successful ambush, the Dervishes quickly withdrew. Their losses were slight.

As this was Haig's first experience of combat, it received more emphasis than it probably deserved. Nevertheless, the conclusions which he drew, in a letter to Wood, are significant:

1. The outpost service, tho' theoretically right, was carelessly done. When I passed the picket in question, many were lying down, apparently asleep.

2. The eyesight of the Egyptian vedette can't be relied on. For the dervishes passed the front line of vedettes.

3. The pluck of the Egyptian cavalryman is right enough in my opinion.

4. The Horse Artillery against enemy of this sort is no use. We felt the want of machine guns when working alongside of scrub for searching some of the tracks.

The third point was directed at the critics of the Egyptian Cavalry. The reference to machine-guns is also significant, since Haig has been accused of not appreciating the value of the weapon. Yet just prior to his departure for the Sudan, he took a special trip to Enfield to study the Maxim gun and during the campaign commented repeatedly on its indispensability.[11]

After this clash with the enemy (though not as a result of it) Haig was finally given a formal appointment. On 25 March, the commander of the Cavalry Brigade, Kaimakam (Lieutenant-Colonel) R. G. Broadwood, made Haig his staff officer. Broadwood, as perturbed with Kitchener as Haig was, realised that Haig's enormous potential was being wasted. The position was prestigious, but it meant that direct command of a unit in battle – experience which Haig desperately needed – would again be denied him.

Throughout March, Mahmoud retreated southwards, the aim being to lengthen the Anglo-Egyptian line of communication and to entice Kitchener into making mistakes. Haig, in his new role as staff officer, took part in patrols which scouted the Dervish position. During one of these a serious clash with the enemy occurred. On 5 April, the entire Cavalry Brigade, accompanied by horse artillery, two Maxim batteries, and camel corps, reconnoitred the Dervish position at Nukheila. While retiring, it was attacked. A detachment of Dervish cavalry moved upstream against the Anglo-Egyptian flank, while another blocked the line of retreat by advancing from a position downstream. Simultaneously, the Dervish infantry left their trenches in a frontal assault. 'The situation was a difficult one', Haig admitted, 'and to add to it a strongish north wind prevented our seeing clearly the moment a squadron moved.'[12]

Since Haig's subsequent letters are the only detailed account available, he naturally takes centre stage in the action:

> I had just been to Baring to get him into position on the right of the guns to cover them during our withdrawal when I noticed our left rear (Le Gallais) attacked. Broadwood was at the left of the guns retiring at a trot. I galloped to him and told him the left rear was strongly attacked. He could not see this from where he was because of the dust. Broadwood attacked with the two squadrons (Le Gallais), and fortunately the enemy (infantry and cavalry mingled) gave way before us.

After the initial disaster had been averted, Broadwood sent Haig to look after the horse artillery, which Haig found 'trotting gaily to the rear'. In the same vicinity he encountered Captain Mahon, in charge of three cavalry squadrons:

> Mahon . . . said 'I can't see what has happened, what do you suggest?' I at once said 'Place one squadron on flank of guns and support Le Gallais with your other two on *his* left. I will then bring Baring and remaining three squadrons on your left as a third line.' Mahon advanced. I gave Baring his orders, putting all three squadrons under him . . . I thought there was no time to lose to ask for orders so I went direct to the maxims and told them they must come into action against the most threatening of the enemy (which I indicated) as soon as the cavalry cleared the field of fire.

Haig returned to Broadwood, apprised him of the situation, and suggested a flank attack. Broadwood agreed. His men cleared the field, whereupon the Maxims poured a deadly fire on the Dervish lines. The plan worked perfectly. 'We were able to fight our way out of the infantry fire.'[13]

Leaving aside the inevitable embroidery, there is no doubt that Haig played a major part in averting a rout. 'Broadwood was much obliged to me for my assistance and told the Sirdar so,' he wrote. Kitchener, in turn, awarded him with a Brevet Majority. Haig's steadiness amidst utter confusion was most impressive. This was not the sort of conduct expected of an officer in only his second action. Haig, however, was not surprised by his performance. The aplomb apparent in his letters indicates that he acted exactly as he thought he would. Nor did the danger of the situation affect him. 'You say that you are anxious,' he commented to his sister. 'That is all nonsense, because neither the Dervish horseman nor the bullets of their infantry worry me in the least.'[14] Though this sounds like false bravado, it was probably genuine. Haig could disregard danger because he sincerely believed that he was destined for greatness. A serious wounding or ignominious death in the Sudan was inconceivable.

The Egyptian cavalrymen were immensely proud of their performance. This time, however, Haig was not impressed:

> The Gyppie Cavalry acted *steadily* on the whole, but there was no glorious charging home, as some of the tales I have heard would have us believe. Moreover, if the Dervish horsemen had *really* come on, I feel sure that few of the Brigade would have escaped. Indeed General Hunter gave it as his opinion just before the maxims opened fire, he thought 'suave qui peut' must be the only ending. However all's well that ends well and the Gyppie Cavalry are considered heroes. That is rubbish . . .

The only performance which Haig praised was his own. His commander, on the other hand, had nearly caused a catastrophe. 'He, Broadwood, was wrong to charge as he did with the front line, for the whole Brigade then passed from his control.' This was one of Haig's pet aversions: the cavalry officer so keen for glory that he loses sight of his responsibilities as a leader. But Broadwood was forgiven this momentary lapse: 'He is a very sound fellow and is excellent at running this show.'[15]

From Haig's account, it seems clear that the Maxims stabilised the situation long enough to effect an orderly retreat. If this was indeed the case, he did not emphasise the fact. Instead, for him, the action demonstrated the lightning effect of a cavalry charge. The Dervishes 'ran away the moment we showed a bold front'.[16] The doctrine of the *arme blanche* had thus been vindicated in a single action lasting less than an hour. First impressions of this magnitude are highly significant. What effect, one wonders, would an outright disaster have had on Haig's faith in the cavalry?

The Battle of the Atbara followed two days later. After extensive reconnaissance, the Dervish position had become well known. Kitchener moved his force to within 600 yards of the enemy, whereupon the Dervish reacted like a cornered animal. Their cavalry attempted, rather haphazardly, to harass the Anglo-Egyptian lines, but were cleared away by Broadwood's men who then retired, having done their bit. The Maxims and artillery then softened the Dervish trenches. After a suitable interval, the infantry advanced. Mahmoud's men, confronted by a force superior in numbers, arms and organisation, took the wisest course and bolted. Anglo-Egyptian casualties numbered 650, the Dervish over 2,500. Among the captured was Mahmoud.

Haig dutifully sent Wood a critique of the action. Having finished his fighting early, he had 'a very good view of what took place'. He was not impressed. 'Why', he wondered, 'was the attack frontal?' An attack on the right seemed to offer more advantages. The Dervish 'would have been forced to retreat across the open desert to the Nile without being allowed time to fill water skins, etc.'. He also had serious doubts about the effectiveness of the artillery. 'Our side says the guns did tremendous damage! Mahmoud and over 30 men (Enemy) . . . say "We did not mind the guns, they only hurt camels and donkeys."' Finally, he disagreed with the Anglo-Egyptian formation which was 'extraordinarily deep'. 'This may have accounted for our severe losses.' Had he been in Kitchener's shoes, he would have placed the neglected cavalry, an infantry brigade and some guns on the opposite side of the river. This force would have enfiladed the enemy lines and cut off their escape route. The main attack, by only two brigades ('as many as the frontage admitted'), would have been concentrated on the enemy's right.

Haig admitted, however, that, 'I calculate as if I had troops that can shoot and manoeuvre! It would be unwise to rely on the blacks doing either *well*.' Therefore, he accepted (with uncharacteristic charity) that 'all the more credit is due to the Sirdar for limiting himself to a more moderate victory instead of going for annihilating the Mahmoud's army'. It is nevertheless safe to assume that Haig would have opted for annihilation. His letter to Wood reveals a fundamental difference between Kitchener and himself. Kitchener, the engineer, was basically a siege commander. Aware that he faced an erratic enemy who did not fight according to classical patterns, he manoeuvred his army to a safe position from which he could handle any eventuality. Victory came easily but not brilliantly. Haig's plan, more in accord with classical patterns, was the product of a cavalry mind and a Camberley education. It called for the rolling back of flanks and the release of a vigorous and destructive cavalry charge. The enemy, demoralised, would never fight again. The plan had as much to do with romance as with reality.[17]

Kitchener, immensely proud of his victory on the Atbara, called for an appropriate celebration. 'The order is to "decorate Berber"!' Haig told his sister. 'A lot of mud walls and dust and only palms available for the job!' Always contemptuous of excessive pride or coarse jingoism, Haig ridiculed the Sirdar's desire for a 'triumphal entry into Berber – a sort of Roman triumph with Mahmoud tied to his horse's tail'. The eventual ceremony was even more vulgar than he had expected. Five squadrons of cavalry and a guard of honour of 100 men accompanied Kitchener, who rode into town on a white horse. He was followed by Mahmoud (who was collared and chained) and other Dervish prisoners. 'In front of Mahmoud was a calico screen with [the] inscription: "This is Mahmoud, the commander of the Army which said it was going to capture Berber."' Natives were instructed to throw stones at the Emir. Haig was sickened at the sight.[18]

He was equally scornful of the Press. Bennet Burleigh of *The Daily Telegraph*, the most famous of the war's correspondents, was a 'loathsome creature'. Haig was astonished by the 'rubbish the British public delights to read. The exaggeration of some of the reports almost makes a good day's work appear ridiculous. The headings of the D. T. are so overdrawn that instinctively one says "Waterloo Eclipsed".' In a letter to Henrietta, Haig described the 'class of creature which represents the press in this part of the world':

> The class of correspondent is very low indeed (only one man, Stevens of 'Daily Mail' at all *educated* as a gentleman) . . . the work performed by all newspaper correspondents is most degrading: they can't tell the whole truth even if they want to do so. The British public likes to read sensational news, and the best war correspondent is he who can tell the most thrilling lies.

This was Haig's first real encounter with the Press. His revulsion was as great as when he later began to have dealings with politicians. In both cases, the process of time did not soften his disdain.[19]

During the four months following the Battle of the Atbara, Kitchener's force prepared for the final assault, which was to be directed towards Khartoum and Omdurman, where the Khalifa's main army was situated. Cashing in on the prestige he had gained, Kitchener demanded (and received) additional support: four British battalions, a cavalry regiment, an engineer company and additional artillery and auxiliary corps. The reorganisation of the force meant that Haig was finally assigned a squadron of his own. He was given 150 horses, many of them young and raw, to train and make battle-ready. The work brought him immense satisfaction and enjoyment. 'You would be surprised at how quickly the time passes here,' he told Henrietta. Hard work was combined with much relaxation and entertainment, including shooting, fishing, racing, and polo. For Haig, life continued to be as comfortable and enjoyable as he could make it. He concluded that 'war' was good for him:

> they all say I look far better than I ever did in England. The days are hot, but the nights are cold. That is to say, from 6 p.m. to 6 a.m. the climate is excellent. I have the squadron to play with in the morning and three days a week play polo. At present we have not got our fizzy water yet and the soda water machine has broken down. Still the Nile water is excellent at this date. We filter it and cool it. This with sour claret is excellent.

Even better was the champagne (three cases) which arrived in July with the parcels from Henrietta.[20]

During the build-up to the final battle, Haig continued to put unwarranted store in rumours of the enemy's condition. On 21 April, he speculated that an insurrection in Omdurman was imminent, a belief which he repeated a month later. On 5 June, he told Henrietta:

> Some deserters arrived here yesterday direct from [Khartoum]. They [tell of] murders in the streets and fighting among the Emirs. But of course one can't say whether they are speaking the truth or not. Still there is just a chance of the Khalifa's power breaking up entirely.

Though Haig admitted that the Dervish would probably fight to the last, he should not have let idle gossip sway him at all. What is ironic is how critical he was of the Press for exactly the same fault.[21]

The respite also gave Haig plenty of opportunity to expand upon his scathing criticisms of Kitchener. When the Anglo-Egyptian force was moved to Wadi Hamed, seventy miles from Omdurman, Haig found a 'muddle' which had resulted, he told Wood, because the Sirdar 'insisted on doing every detail himself, in place of trusting a staff officer'. The problem itself is relatively unimportant. What is interesting is how enthusiastically Haig was fulfilling his role as the eyes and ears of Evelyn Wood:

> You must not think that I am finding points to criticise. (I'll tell you much more when I get back!) But as I owe my presence here to your kindness, it pleases me to write to you and tell you of any odd event which may not otherwise reach you except with the accompanism [sic] of an official colouring.

The letters to Wood served two purposes: they allowed Haig to return a favour and they relieved his frustration with the situation in the Sudan. What cannot be ignored is the way the image of Haig they provide contrasts sharply with the usual one of him as the straightforward, honest dealer. There is no doubt that he relished the role Wood had assigned to him.[22]

The Battle of Omdurman was launched on 2 September. The Dervish, situated on a plain north of the city between the strategic heights of the Kerreri Hills and Jebel Surgham, were divided into two groups, the southern led by the Khalifa and the northern by his son, Osma Sheikh ed Din. The Anglo-Egyptian force was situated between the Dervish and the river, supported by a number of gunboats. As had been the case on the Atbara, Kitchener manoeuvred his force into a strong position and then waited for the Khalifa to act. Responding as the Sirdar wished, the Dervish threw themselves first in one direction, then in another. The attacks were well ordered, but lacked strategy. Astounded at the enemy's courage, Haig wrote that he 'could not have believed it possible for human beings to advance in the way they did against such a fire'. They 'seemed to come in countless numbers and in rank after rank . . . their order and manoeuvring power was wonderful'. Nevertheless, the battle soon deteriorated into a sequence of mindless, suicidal assaults each successfully repulsed by the stiff Anglo-Egyptian defence. The Sirdar's superior firepower gradually dissolved the Dervish strength.

Faced with complete annihilation, the Khalifa's men wisely chose to run.[23]

Had the Khalifa been able to concentrate both parts of his force in a simultaneous attack, the situation would probably have been much more difficult. Haig made this point in his letter to Wood. The battle, he felt, had been lost by the Khalifa, not won by Kitchener. The Dervish leader erred by not seizing the two strategic heights: 'What losses would we have suffered in turning him out?' Haig also criticised Kitchener for failing to capitalise on the enemy's divided force:

> the Sirdar's left should have been thrown forward . . . and gradually drawing in his right and extending his left south-westwards, he might have cut the enemy off from Omdurman and really annihilated the thousands and thousands of Dervishes. In place of this, altho' in possession of full information, and able to see with his own eyes the whole field, he spreads out his force, thereby risking destruction of a Brigade. He seems to have had no plan, or tactical idea, beyond allowing the latter to attack the enemy.

What Haig and others saw as Kitchener's excessive caution seems to be vindicated by the relatively low casualty figure of forty-eight killed and 434 wounded. Haig's plan, another example of his preference for the aggressive offensive (and of the influence of Camberley), may indeed have 'really annihilated . . . thousands and thousands of Dervishes'. But at what cost? As it was, 11,000 Dervish, over a quarter of their force, were killed.[24]

Haig was especially disappointed with the handling of the cavalry. Though the arm did not figure in the main action, after the Dervish force dissolved, Kitchener, eager to reach Omdurman before nightfall, called upon the cavalry to make a dramatic charge into the city. A frontal assault was ruled out, since the battlefield was littered with individual Dervish who were still fighting. The Cavalry Brigade instead attempted to skirt the resistance by approaching the city in a wide arc from the south. Haig took off in a group of three squadrons but soon found the task impossible. Bullets came from all directions. Dervish soldiers who had apparently surrendered shot at the cavalry after it had passed. 'My men seemed to bend their heads as one does to escape a storm of rain!' Cut off from the rest of the brigade, the three squadrons retired to the river where they spent the night. A number of horses died of exhaustion; others had to be shot. No supplies were available until late the next day when a cargo boat was finally able to reach the shore. Haig did not arrive in Omdurman until 4 September, by which time the excitement of victory had abated. Tired, hungry and disappointed, he was furious at those who had ordered the charge. 'It was a ridiculous idea for three squadrons to attack some 10 or more thousands of armed and resolute men scattered all across the plain.'[25]

The cavalry's reputation could not afford such a fiasco. Nor could it afford fools like Colonel Martin, commanding officer of the 21st Lancers, who, in the pursuit of glory, left behind his common sense. The Lancers had joined the campaign after the Battle of the Atbara. As they were a new regiment, they were eager to claim some distinction in this their first major test. Unfortunately, they chose the wrong occasion to do so, with disastrous consequences. One of the Lancers, Winston Churchill, described how Martin, on the basis of intelligence which was obviously faulty, decided to charge a Dervish position:

before [the distance] was half-covered, the whole aspect of the affair changed. A deep crease in the ground . . . appeared where all had seemed smooth, level plain; and from it there sprang, with the suddenness of a pantomime effect and a high-pitched yell, a dense white mass of men nearly as long as our front and twelve deep . . . the collision was prodigious.[26]

The charge of the 21st Lancers rivalled that of the Light Brigade at Balaclava in magnificence and futility. Sixty-five men and 119 horses were killed or wounded attacking a position which was of no strategic significance. As if to encourage such idiocy, three Victoria Crosses were subsequently awarded.

Whilst Haig had unquestioning faith in the moral effect of a cavalry charge, he always emphasised that the charge had to have an objective other than simply excitement, prestige or award. Venting his anger in a letter to Wood, he wrote

You will hear a lot of the charge made by the 21st Lancers . . . We onlookers feared this all along, for the regiment was keen to do something and meant to charge something before the show was over. They got their charge, but at what cost? I trust for the sake of the British cavalry that more tactical knowledge exists in the ranks of the average regiment than we have seen displayed in this one. Yet this C.O. [Martin] has had his command extended . . . I cannot think that the Promotion Board fully appreciates the responsibility that rest with them when they put duffers in command of regiments.[27]

In his anger, Haig failed to notice two very important tactical lessons to emerge from the fiasco. The first was the devastating effect of the antiquated Dervish rifles. The way in which British cavalrymen were so easily shot down should have alerted him to the effect which *modern* rifles would have when fired by European professional soldiers. The second, and equally important lesson, was that the Lancers had extricated themselves from the predicament by dismounting and using their own rifles. Thus the charge of the 21st Lancers reiterated that traditional cavalry tactics were obsolete. But this was a lesson which it was impossible for Haig to comprehend. To him, the catastrophe was the fault of a single 'duffer' and, if anything, an affirmation of what wise leadership could still accomplish.

On 4 September, a moving service was held for Gordon in Khartoum. The dignity of the event was tarnished two days later when Kitchener ordered the destruction of the Mahdi's tomb. The great leader's corpse was exhumed, the body burned and thrown in the Nile, and the skull presented as a trophy to the Sirdar. Someone suggested mounting it in silver or gold; others thought it would make a fine drinking cup or inkstand. Kitchener himself was so impressed by its enormous size that he considered sending it to the Royal College of Surgeons. The subject caused both horror and delight in Britain. In the end, the Sirdar bowed to pressure and had the skull secretly buried in a small cemetery near Wadi Halfa.

Due to his late arrival in Omdurman, Haig missed the memorial service. He only briefly mentioned the issue of the skull, as if to show his distaste for the whole affair. As far as he was concerned, the war was over. He ridiculed officers who wished to stay in the Sudan with the Egyptian Army, in the hopes of decoration or promotion. 'To me there were no such fancies.' With characteristic clumsiness, he described his feelings to Wood, who had recently offered him a position at the Horse Guards:

I think that in spite of the feeling in this Army against new arrivals that they will give one credit for training my squadron and doing my best *always* for the show, *not for myself.* I don't want credit for it because it pleased me and kept me well during the trying heat at Berber all summer. Now I think this show is pretty well over and though I am ready to remain if the Sirdar requires a Squadron leader, I think your kindly advice about slackness in hot countries very much to the point and I am ready to come home in any minor capacity.

In a subsequent letter to Wood, Haig emphasised the experience he had gained. 'For all this I have only you to thank.' He left Omdurman on 17 September and arrived in London eighteen days later.[28]

Haig had indeed gained valuable experience. His first taste of combat proved, to himself and others, that he could maintain his composure in a crisis. But this ability would not have surprised him. The war, in fact, provided few surprises. There were some unexpected experiences: the behaviour of the Press, the foolishness of men eager for glory, the performance of Kitchener – the 'great leader'. Otherwise, Haig found that the war confirmed old lessons, but did not introduce new ones. Any new lessons which might have arisen were by this time beyond his comprehension. The war did not deflect him from the path he had long ago taken.

4

Chasing Boers

Though the Sudan campaign was a disappointment for the British cavalry, Haig's faith in the arm did not diminish. He was able to explain every mediocre performance without having to question the basic premise that the arm remained an indispensable moral weapon. This extraordinary faith was rewarded in South Africa – or so it seemed to Haig. The post-mortems which followed the Boer War revealed considerable disagreement regarding the cavalry's contribution. But what is important as far as Haig is concerned is how he and his soul-fellows interpreted their role in the war. To them, the war proved beyond doubt the value of cavalry traditionally trained and armed with lance and sword. Their experiences in South Africa inspired them to resist efforts to modernise the arm prior to 1914.

Since the promised position at the Horse Guards did not materialise, Haig instead rejoined his regiment at Norwich in the autumn of 1898. His stay was short, as he left the following May to become Brigade Major of the 1st Cavalry Brigade, Aldershot. Again there was an unseemly side to his selection for this coveted appointment. French, the commander of the Aldershot Brigade, was on the verge of bankruptcy, due to unwise speculation in South African mining shares. Bankruptcy would have ruined his career. Fortunately, Haig came to the rescue. Shortly before his appointment to Brigade Major, he loaned French £2,500. The loan was perfectly legitimate (a formal contract was signed and interest charged) but it undoubtedly tied Haig to French in an unorthodox manner. Haig was quite candid about his reasons for loaning the money: 'It would be a terrible thing if French were made a Bankrupt – such a loss to the Army as well as to me personally.'[1] Rescuing French was in no sense a kind act for a friend. The £2,500 turned out to be a profitable investment in Haig's own career and in the cavalry.

On 14 September, French was selected to command the cavalry in the force preparing for war in South Africa. Six days later, Haig was confirmed as his Chief Staff Officer, or Assistant Adjutant General (AAG). Thus, hardly a year after the battle of Omdurman, he was again on his way to war. In a letter to Henrietta written on his departure, he reflected that, 'You and I always seem to be saying "Goodbye" to each other, and yet practice does not seem to make the process easier but rather more trying.'[2] This rather banal statement was apparently enough to purge himself of inconvenient emotions. Haig soon settled into the voyage, which was unique in the fact that his fellow passengers included Boer soldiers, among them two nephews of Paul Kruger, the President of the Transvaal. The irony of men travelling together for seventeen days in order to fight each other on the other side of the world apparently escaped Haig's notice.

Upon his arrival in Cape Town on 10 October, Haig learned of a Boer ultimatum demanding the withdrawal of all British troops by the following day. 'It is generally agreed that even Lord Salisbury cannot knuckle under to this piece of Boer swagger.' Haig was itching for a fight, but was frustrated by annoying delays. The overland route to East London, where the cavalry was gathered, was closed, thus forcing him and French to wait for sea transport to Durban. Haig blamed the delay on 'the actions of Govt. officials, i.e. a general want of *foresight* all round!'. News of British troops trapped in Mafeking compounded his annoyance.[3]

While waiting for the war properly to begin, Haig prepared a paper suggesting possibilities for the employment of the mounted troops. In it he demonstrated a keen perception of Boer strengths and strategy. He accepted that the enemy would have a number of advantages: they knew the terrain, they were prepared for war and they were committed to their cause. As men who shot game for food, they were natural marksmen. Frugal and tough, they were able to live for days on meagre rations. These factors, when combined with their adequate horsemanship, made them highly mobile. Though Haig considered the Afrikaner an inferior being, he had complete respect for his fighting abilities. He therefore considered that it was best to pursue a cautious policy for the first few months. The available troops should be used on a 'passive defence' aimed to 'have as many horses . . . fit and in hard condition when the moment for the general advance arrives'. This advance would have to be delayed until British reinforcements arrived and were trained.[4]

The source of this insight was a study of the Boer problem which Haig carried out prior to the war. In his 'Notes on the Transvaal', he examined past campaigns in South Africa, in order to discover lessons applicable to the present conflict. In the first action he examined, the Battle of Boomplatz, 'The Boers fought well, but against them was a general [Sir Henry Smith] of great experience having the capacity of infusing his spirit of energy into the men he commanded.' Awkward expression aside, Haig was emphasising the importance of leadership and moral factors. Smith's inspiration was missing in the 1880–1 Boer War. The Commander, General Sir George Colley, was 'very clever' but he could not instil confidence in his men. His dispirited army was defeated at Majuba, demonstrating that 'even an English force becomes demoralised after . . . defeat'. Though Haig was correct in his criticism of Colley's leadership qualities, the defeat at Majuba had more to do with Boer marksmanship than low British morale.

The same campaign also demonstrated how 'Both the civil and military authorities . . . remained in absolute ignorance of the Enemy . . . No one took the trouble to consider the conditions of the problem.' Determined not to make the same mistake, Haig examined Colley's force and discovered that it lacked mobility, being grossly deficient in cavalry. This lesson was confirmed by the third action he examined, the Jameson Raid. In response to Jameson's tactics, the Boers 'kept prolonging their line'. Their greater mobility meant they could not 'readily be outflanked'. In response to similar problems, Moltke at Koenigsgratz, Blücher at Waterloo and Napoleon at Baritzen had divided their forces in order to hold and compress the enemy front while the cavalry manoeuvred for the flank. Whilst admitting that it was dangerous to divide one's force in this way, Haig thought it worth the risk. 'Otherwise our tactics will merely drive the Boers back from position to position and a series of rearguard actions will result.' This had to be avoided at all costs. The British would have to be in a position 'such as to insure the annihilation of their field force'.

Having conducted this study, Haig felt qualified to advise on the composition of the British force. He did not think that the Boers would field more than 10,000 men. The British, in response, would need to maintain only a slight infantry superiority, as a very large force would reduce mobility. Since the cavalry would bear the burden of the offensive, it had to be proportionately larger than usual. Artillery, in contrast, would be useless: 'A Boer enemy is not a suitable objective for artillery' since 'he fights as an individual' – meaning he would not hold a position under artillery bombardment. As Haig did not expect sieges or counter-attacks in this mobile war, he predicted that the need for engineers would also be minimal.

Though many of Haig's suggestions were relevant, many others were wide of the mark. The Boers fielded a larger force than he anticipated, the British required much more than a slight infantry superiority, and sieges occurred at Mafeking, Kimberley and Ladysmith. Moreover, Haig was wrong in his appraisal of the 'objective':

> *The Boer Army*: Defeat that and the country is at our mercy. How is that to be got hold of? Aim at a strategic point, which the Army is sure to cover.
>
> The strategic point is *Pretoria*.

Haig's errors resulted from applying conventional military thought to situations where it was irrelevant. Thus, the Boer War was an 'abnormal' war. But its abnormality arose because the British were at war with the Boer people, not just their Army. Victory would come by destroying the people's will, not by capturing a strategic point or winning battles. In this sense, the war resembled the twentieth-century concept of total war much more than the ancient contests upon which Haig based his thinking.[5]

Haig's first action came shortly after his arrival in Durban on 18 October. After the declaration of war, the Boers moved into Natal and seized Elandslaagte. Further north, 4,000 British soldiers were retiring towards Ladysmith after an inconclusive battle at Dundee. Unfortunately, Elandslaagte lay in their path. Lieutenant-General Sir George White, commander of the garrison at Ladysmith, assigned French the task of clearing the Boers away. French was able to call upon units from the 1st Manchesters, the Devonshire Regiment, the Gordon Highlanders, the 5th Lancers and 5th Dragoon Guards, in addition to two field batteries, and local volunteers under the banner of the Imperial Light Horse. He had, in all, 3,000 troops – a three to one superiority over the enemy.

At 3 p.m. on 21 October, the Devonshires pushed forward in a frontal attack on the Boer position. The men came under heavy fire, but, as Haig had hoped, were able to keep the enemy front concentrated. This enabled the Manchesters and Gordons to turn the flank. Hand-to-hand fighting ensued. Terrified of the bayonet, the Boers chose to run, at which point French released the cavalry. The first charge caused utter confusion; the return trip completed what Haig appropriately called an annihilation.

'The Boers fought to the end with extraordinary courage.' Haig put this down to 'the fact that the commands . . . were entirely composed of high class Boers, who had more or less organised the present revolt and so must sink or swim by the result of the campaign'. While interviewing prisoners, he was surprised to learn of their reaction to the cavalry charge. 'They were wild at the way the fugitives were killed with the lance! They say it is butchery not war.' This abhorrence was widespread; some Boers vowed in future to shoot captured Lancers. As it turned out, an Elandslaagte-type charge was not repeated for the rest of the war, probably because the memory of it was sufficient to produce the desired effect. In other words, in future, a British readiness to charge was enough to provoke a quick Boer retirement.[6]

After Elandslaagte, and a similar success at Rietfontein, the British force arrived safely at Ladysmith on 26 October. But, having escaped the frying pan, they quickly found themselves in the fire. Ladysmith was more a trap than a sanctuary. As October ended, the Boer stranglehold on the town tightened. British attempts to break out were notable only for their bungling. Haig, who daily found examples of incompetence about which to complain, began to ponder the possibility of a long, demoralising siege – hardly a situation suited to a dashing cavalryman.

The siege of Ladysmith lasted until 28 February 1900, but neither Haig nor French – to the obvious advantage of their respective careers – had to endure it. At 11 a.m. on 2 November, White received a telegram instructing him to release both Haig and French, so that the latter could assume command of the cavalry division shortly arriving from Britain. Two hours later, Haig and French departed on the last train to leave Ladysmith for four months. 'The railway authorities doubted our getting through,' Haig recorded. After travelling for half an hour, the train came under heavy fire. 'We all lay down on the seat and floor! Not a very dignified position for the Cavalry Division Staff to assume – but discretion is sometimes the better part of valour!' A 2.5–inch shell passed through one of the vans, causing damage to Haig's luggage. 'I did not mind', he told Henrietta, 'for if this shell had hit a wheel or the engine boiler, we would certainly now have been on our way to Pretoria instead of Durban!'[7]

Upon arrival in Cape Town on 8 November, Haig was told that the reinforcements from Britain had yet to arrive. While waiting for these troops, he again took up his pen, recording his reflections on two weeks of fighting Boers. In his 'Notes on Operations', he drew conclusions not only about this conflict, but about modern war in general. For instance, he had learned from prisoners taken at Elandslaagte that the 'shells bursting over their positions . . . killed no one!' This demonstrated that 'the effect of artillery is more moral than physical' (even the moral effect was 'negligible') and, therefore, 'peace manoeuvres and text books must be modified'. This dangerous assumption had a shaky foundation. It is true that few, if any, Boers were killed by artillery at Elandslaagte. But Haig seems to have ignored the fact that early in the battle British seven pounders destroyed the outbuildings of the station, a defensive stronghold which would have been difficult to secure by any other means. It is also significant that whilst Haig questioned the effectiveness of shrapnel against entrenched Boers, he did not consider the possibility of using high-explosive shells. Instead, he advocated reducing artillery units to a minimum, in the interests of greater mobility.

A proportionate reduction of the infantry was also in order. In defence, infantry were valuable, but Haig was certain that the British would not be on the defensive for long. Otherwise,

> the value of the Infantry . . . is small, owing to the superior mobility of the Boers. Sufficient only is required for the assault of a position which the Boers hold with guns . . . The remainder of the attacking force (say the half) must be mounted troops to oppose the Boer turning movements.

Haig's demand for more cavalry arose from his belief that the arm's offensive capacity had been shown to have greatly increased. '*That Cavalry*,' he argued, 'armed as it is now, with a good firearm *is a new element in tactics* was abundantly proved by these operations.' Even more important, Elandslaagte had demonstrated that the charge was still a viable tactical option. Haig was correct to stress the importance of the cavalry in South Africa. The peculiarities of this war – open spaces and a highly mobile enemy – did give unusual scope to the mounted arm. But where he was wrong was to interpret this fleeting renaissance as a revelation of twentieth-century tactics.[8]

In his 'Notes on Operations', Haig emphasised the need for extensive dismounted training. This was not, however, an endorsement of the mounted infantry, which he continued to ridicule, for example in a letter to Henrietta:

> The one thing required here is 'Cavalry'! I think the country ought to be alive now to the fact . . . that we don't keep enough of the arm in peacetime! This mounted infantry craze is now I trust exploded. So far they have proved useless and are not likely to be of use *until they learn to ride*! You had better not give these views to Sir Evelyn, for both he and Lord Wolseley are the parents of the Mounted Infantry.

According to Haig, there was nothing mounted infantry could accomplish which well-trained cavalry could not do better. Cavalry, unlike MI, had the added advantage of being able to fight mounted – still the most important function. Haig's attitude was best expressed in his praise for the Imperial Light Horse after Elandslaagte: 'When for a moment there was a check in the advance . . . the ILH first went forward again.' This was because the 'ILH are cavalry, not M.I. being organised as cavalry'.[9]

Continued delays in the arrival of reinforcements increased Haig's annoyance with the British government. The politicians, he decided, were too eager to rely on locally raised (and 'useless') mounted infantry. 'The Sec'y of State for War must be strongly condemned for not sending ample cavalry in *fast* ships to this country.' He was certain that, 'If we only had sufficient cavalry with *fit* horses, we could do anything we liked with these Boers.' The poor quality of troops and horse dictated continued caution. The disasters of Black Week – the blundering reverses at Colenso, Magersfontein and Stormberg between 10 and 15 December – came about 'because self-advertising men . . . push on without realising the value of well-formed Cavalry'. The prospect was not entirely bleak; the war, Haig thought, 'will do the country a lot of good: already many, who held reputations for skill in *savage* warfare, have been found useless'.[10]

In stark contrast to the disasters of Black Week were French's operations around Colesberg, where a Boer force of 5,000 men was poised ready to invade Cape Colony. French, though heavily outnumbered, contained the threat until February by keeping constantly on the move, thus cleverly deceiving the enemy about British strengths and intentions. Haig, always at French's side, wrote with characteristic aplomb that, 'It is very satisfactory to have kept so many . . . of the enemy to their positions near Colesberg.'[11] By containing the Boers the British were granted the time necessary to train the newly arrived reinforcements. For French and Haig, the success meant a further rise in their stock. So far, they had shared in most of the successes, and avoided all the disasters of the war.

In mid-January, French left the Colesberg area to take command of the now battle-ready Cavalry Division. At this time, Roberts (the new Commander-in-Chief) ordered that Colonel the Earl of Errol, recently arrived from Britain, was to replace Haig as French's AAG. Haig was to become DAAG. Protesting to Roberts, French pointed out that the position of AAG had been promised to Haig by Buller before Roberts took command. Furthermore, Haig's 'services [had] been invaluable'. Kitchener, Roberts' Chief of Staff, replied that though 'the very excellent services rendered by Major Haig' were beyond dispute, the position had to be filled by an officer senior to Haig. In truth, Roberts was simply promoting the career of an officer who was a member of his 'ring' at the expense of another who was not.[12]

Realising that he owed much of his success (not to mention a good deal of money) to Haig, French sent an ADC, Captain J. F. Laycock, to GHQ to persuade Roberts to change his mind. Laycock argued that Haig knew the country, Boer tactics and the men of the Cavalry Division better than Errol. Roberts, however, did not budge. 'On the third time of making my appeal', Laycock recalled, 'I was so seriously shut up that it was impossible to carry the matter further.' Thus, Errol assumed his assigned position and Haig his. Haig, though 'very annoyed', maintained, according to Laycock, 'a most correct attitude'. This is indeed revealed in a letter to Henrietta: 'Everyone I meet down here consoles with me on being superseded . . . As a matter of fact I think less about this appointment than my friends. But of course it is gratifying to think that one's work is appreciated in the Division.'

The nonchalant attitude was easy to assume because the change was only a formality. Haig remained French's trusted adviser, with Errol left in the cold.[13]

Soon after Errol replaced Haig, the British offensive began. By containing the Boer force at Colesberg, the British were able to move northward virtually unimpeded as far as Modder River Station. Here Roberts concentrated 30,000 men of all arms. He aimed his first strike at the besieged town of Kimberley, where 50,000 inhabitants were surrounded by a small but well-fortified force of 4,000 Boers. One of the captives was Cecil Rhodes whose De Beers group owned valuable diamond mines in the area. He had fallen foul of the commander of the garrison, Colonel R. G. Kekewich. Kekewich controlled the military, but Rhodes, as the town's principal employer, had the citizenry in his pocket. As the siege dragged on, fears grew that Rhodes would convince the townspeople to capitulate.

The tension in Kimberley ruled out a prolonged battle. The bulk of the Boer force, under General Piet Cronje, was situated due south of Kimberley, in the direct line of Roberts' advance. In order to side-step this obstacle, Roberts decided to abandon his line of communication, march east and then north through the Orange River Colony, and approach Cronje from the east, his left. The plan was risky, but because this was where an attack was least expected, Cronje was weakest here. If the long march could be completed without disaster, the final assault promised to be relatively easy. By attacking in this direction, Roberts also hoped to cut Cronje off from retreat into the Orange Free State or north into the Transvaal.

Since speed was essential the attack depended upon the cavalry. On 10 February, Kitchener impressed upon French 'the difficulty of the situation, not merely in South Africa, but the risk to the Empire generally if Kimberley was not relieved'. French replied that if he was still alive on the 15th, he would be in Kimberley. Roberts reiterated the urgency of the situation when he addressed cavalry officers later on the same day:

> I am going to give you some very hard work to do but at the same time you are going to get the greatest chance cavalry has ever had. I am certain you will do well. I have received news from Kimberley from which I know that it is important the town should be relieved in the course of the next five days, and you and your men are to do

this. The enemy have placed a big gun in position and are shelling the town, killing women and children, in consequence of which the civilian population are urging Colonel Kekewich to capitulate. You will remember what you are going to do all your lives and when you have grown to be old men you will tell the story of the relief of Kimberley . . . The enemy are afraid of the British cavalry, and I hope when you get them into the open you will make an example of them.

The advance began the following morning. French's cavalry set a gruelling pace. Nearly five hundred horses collapsed from exhaustion and had to be shot. In the early evening of 14 February, French siezed Klip Drift, twenty miles from Kimberley. All that lay between him and the town was an enemy force consisting of 900 men and two guns situated on two converging ridges a short distance away. The position had to be taken before Kimberley could be freed. The British had at their disposal 8,000 cavalry, 6,000 mounted infantry and 56 guns.[14]

The assault began early the next morning. Contrary to Boer expectations, French drove his men through the two fortified ridges. Captain C. Boyle, a galloper on the cavalry staff, submitted a stirring account of the action to *The Times*:

The moment was one I can never forget. There was a pause during which we all looked at each other. I watched the General, wondering what he would do. It would have been simple enough to manoeuvre and fight, had we nothing to do but fight the enemy in front of us. But we had to get to Kimberley that night or fail. Suddenly the General decided to make a dash . . . He sent for the Brigadiers, ordered three batteries up to play on the enemy, and the 16th and 19th Lancers to make a dash at once . . . a terrific fire opened up on them and as they disappeared into the dust one wondered how they could have fared. As the dust cleared the General decided to ride for it himself . . . We sat down and rode all we knew, expecting the same fire on us. To our great surprise not a shot was fired. The moral effect of the cavalry charge across their front and the fear that we should work round their flank had been too much for the Boers and they had bolted. Still more remarkable was the little loss they had inflicted – a few dead horses and some wounded was all I saw on the plain.

The whole thing was a marvellous example of what a cavalry dash can do.

French quickly ordered the cavalry on to Kimberley. He and Haig followed at a safe distance and were greeted by the mayor and Rhodes as they entered the town. They celebrated their famous victory that night at Rhodes's table, dining on horsemeat, washed down with 'plenty of champagne'.[15]

The relief of Kimberley, the last legendary charge of British cavalry, was the high point of the war and arguably the most impressive spectacle of Haig's career. Not only was the charge dramatic and successful, but success had been achieved at a low cost. Only seven men were killed. But the 'charge' should not have succeeded. A cavalry force, no matter how morally inspired, should not have been able to overrun a well-fortified position. It was not the charge, but rather the four-day march that preceded it, which saved Kimberley. Roberts had manoeuvred to the Boer weak spot. French had then pierced it with an overwhelming force. This is not to discount the spectacular nature of the attack or the bravery of those involved. But it must be emphasised that the relief was a testimony to wise preparation rather than to moral inspiration.

These qualifications escaped the notice of the men involved. To them, the charge was all that mattered. As Roberts had predicted, these men remembered what they had achieved for the rest of their lives. Every year on 15 February, until long after the Great War, they gathered in London to recall their day of glory. Whilst Haig certainly enjoyed this glory, he was more interested in what Kimberley demonstrated and in how it could be used. 'You will I think agree with me', he commented to Lonsdale Hale, 'that the Cavalry – the *despised* Cavalry I should say – has saved the Empire.' Hale was urged to 'insist on a large and efficient Cavalry being kept up in time of peace'. '*At least two Divisions complete*' was essential.

You must rub this fact into those wretched individuals who pretend to rule the Empire! And in any case, before they decide on reorganising the Army let them get the experience of those who have seen the effect of modern firearms and have learnt to realise that the old story is true, viz. that 'moral' is everything, and not merely guns but men who can use them is what is wanted to defend the Empire.

The dust of Kimberley would blur Haig's vision for the rest of his career.[16]

Despite the stunning victory at Kimberley, Cronje somehow eluded the trap which had been set for him. As a result, the cavalry again had to come to the rescue. French scraped together a brigade from his beleaguered force and raced it to Koedoesrand Drift, which lay directly in Cronje's path. This was enough to slow the Boer retreat long enough for the infantry and artillery to arrive. The Battle of Paardeburg followed. Cronje and his 4,000 men were forced to surrender.

This impressive result was not enough to soothe the bitterness which cavalry officers increasingly felt towards Roberts and Kitchener, who had demanded monumental efforts without providing proper rest and rations. Valuable horses had either been run into the ground or subjected to slow starvation. Men like Haig would have been able to tolerate this treatment had they felt that the infantry was making an equal sacrifice. Unfortunately, it seemed that the cavalry had repeatedly been forced to rescue pathetic and dilatory foot soldiers. 'Personally I think there is something far wrong with our infantry from the Generals downward,' Haig told Hale. He was furious about 'the state of muddle and confusion existing at Roberts' headquarters'. Roberts, like Kitchener, had not paid proper attention to the importance of efficient staff work. His staff consisted of 'old Simla warriors, grey with the experience of years of office work' and numerous 'lordlings and social lights [sic]'. Buzzing around them were 'Kitchener's youths from Egypt' – a barbed reference to relationships which seemed beyond the professional. 'I was at Head Quarters 7 days', Haig added, 'and if I described all that was going on, you would say I was a "croker".'[17]

Around this time, Henrietta warned her brother that the Prince of Wales was concerned that he (Haig) was 'too fond of criticising . . . senior officers'. Haig's criticisms, the Prince thought, 'may be correct, but it does not do'. Taken aback, Haig answered:

I never criticise people except privately, and what a stupid letter it would be if I did not express an opinion. Besides, I think we would have better Generals in the higher ranks and the country would not have to pass through such a period of anxiety had not honest criticism, based on sound reasoning, been more general in reference to military affairs during the last twenty years.

Haig's criticisms may have been honest but they were never open. This was not necessarily his fault but that of a society which encouraged Jekyll and Hyde qualities. Within every successful gentleman there lurked a fox. Those who made the most of this duality prospered. For this reason, Haig was never likely to heed the Prince's advice.[18]

Continued uncertainty over his position *vis-à-vis* Errol undoubtedly fuelled Haig's contempt for Roberts. The issue was resolved in Haig's favour after the Battle of Paardeburg, but not before another confusing game of military musical chairs. On 21 February, Haig was given command of the 3rd Cavalry Brigade, a promotion brought about after French had moved aside one Brigadier-General and ordered another home. In a letter to Henrietta, Haig reflected, 'It is a great piece of good luck being given command of this Brigade, for of course we have any number of old fossils about – full Colonels, etc.' But, within a few hours, the old fossils were back in their positions, on the authority of Roberts. At the same time, Laycock was complaining to Kitchener that as CSO Errol was 'potentially dangerous and definitely harmful'. Kitchener immediately reinstated Haig in his old position and sent Errol to a mounted infantry unit where he presumably would do less harm. Haig undoubtedly derived some wry pleasure from his Lordship's fate. As for himself, he confessed that the change 'will suit me very well'.[19]

After Paardeburg, Roberts aimed for Bloemfontein, the capital of the Orange Free State. The Boer defence under Christiaan De Wet was organised south of the city at Poplar Grove, where a long string of kopjes provided a tactical advantage. Roberts decided that the cavalry should work around to the rear of this position, whereupon the infantry would attack from the right. It seemed a good plan, but it depended upon the Boers sitting tight while a massively superior force annihilated them. Understandably, they did not cooperate. With the Cavalry Division thundering ever closer, it dawned on them that if they ran away they might fight again another day. The Boer defence in tatters, Bloemfontein fell, anticlimactically, on 13 March.

It was becoming increasingly obvious that this war was not about capturing capitals but about destroying armies. Bloemfontein had fallen, but De Wet's force had indeed escaped to fight again. Unfortunately, the two Boer presidents, Paul Kruger and Marthinus Steyn, escaped with it. According to Roberts, they could have been captured (and the war presumably ended) if only French had given chase, 'instead of wasting valuable time going after small parties of the enemy'. To his dying day, Roberts blamed the fact that the war dragged on for another two years on the cavalry's failure at Poplar Grove. The judgement was unjustified. True enough, the cavalry had failed to give chase. But they did not do so because they had been forced to dismount by a small number of cleverly concealed riflemen left as a rearguard. 'We lost fairly heavily in turning some Boers out of a farm and off a ridge,' Haig admitted. Thus, the lost opportunity was not really an opportunity at all. Roberts had expected something which the cavalry was no longer capable of delivering. Poplar Grove demonstrated how a few resolute men with rifles could frustrate thousands of equally resolute men on horses. It was a lesson which should by now have been familiar.[20]

And it was a lesson which Haig and his friends ignored. They blamed the failure at Poplar Grove on the deplorable condition of their horses and therefore, by implication, on Roberts' mismanagement. 'I have never seen horses so beat as ours,' Haig commented. Restricted to 'only 8 lbs. of oats a day', they were 'practically starving'. To his disgust, the cavalry was forced to share meagre rations with the 'Colonial Skallywag Corps' – locally raised mounted infantry units which were 'quite useless'. 'They can't ride and know nothing about their duties as mounted men. [They] are good only for looting . . . [and] disappear the moment a shot is fired.' Haig's explanation for Poplar Grove was plausible because the situation he described was indisputable. Horses *were* starving. Those brought from Britain could not survive on the rough and indigestible South African grass, and, due to Roberts' economies, there was not enough good forage to go around. Furthermore, Roberts *had* mistakenly assumed that large numbers of inferior, ill-equipped and poorly trained mounted infantry would suffice as a mobile force – in other words, that quantity was as good as (and cheaper than) quality. Unfortunately, Roberts' mistakes obscured a basic fact: even quality cavalry on well-fed horses could not have dashed past those riflemen at Poplar Grove. It was physically impossible.[21]

Roberts rested for seven weeks in Bloemfontein, time which the Boers used profitably to rethink their strategy and recover their morale. Meanwhile, British troops suffered from Roberts' incompetent management, the most tragic effect of which was an epidemic of typhoid which could have been easily controlled with better billeting arrangements. 'The Field Marshal', Haig told his brother, 'has fairly made a mess of things since we reached Bloemfontein. Instead of organising his Army into three of four parts he tries to command every little detachment and to command each little part by himself by telegram!' Haig was most disturbed by Roberts' 'sideshows' around Bloemfontein which wasted valuable men and horses but did not benefit the eventual northward advance. 'We are continually on the move and our horses are quite done up,' he told his sister. 'Whenever there is an alarm, Lord Roberts at once orders out French and the Cavalry. I don't know what we will do for horses.' On one such sideshow a cavalry brigade under Broadwood was sent to Thabanchu to search out a Boer force of 6,000 men. Haig thought it 'a mistake to engage in a secondary operation in that direction'. He was right. The Boers easily side-stepped the brigade. Then, on his return to Bloemfontein, Broadwood led his men into a trap at Sannah's Post which De Wet had actually set for a smaller British force also in the area. Over 500 men were forced to surrender. Seven guns and eighty-three loaded wagons were also lost. A contemptuous Haig commented, 'One almost thinks Lord Roberts likes losing guns, judging by the way he received B. on his return.'[22]

To add insult to injury, the cavalry had been called upon to distribute letters urging Boers to surrender in exchange for a general amnesty. This was part of Roberts' 'velvet glove' strategy for a quick, economical and humane victory. Scornful of this policy, Haig described how

At Thabanchu many poor creatures brought in their guns and swore an oath not to fight us again. Then we withdraw our troops and the Transvaalers burn all the farms!!

Such conduct merely brings us into contempt, altho' Roberts no doubt expected to gain popularity with the British Public by being generous and merciful to the conquered.

Haig suggested an alternative:

It seems high time we treated these people with greater severity. Up to the present we have made the war too pleasant for the Free

Staters, and so they allow it to continue. If we were only to loot and burn a few farms, the inhabitants would wish to get us out of the country soon and at once sue for peace.

As the passage of time would prove, Haig was unfortunately right. Leniency did not impress the Boers.[23]

The march to Pretoria began on 22 April. The British marshalled an impressive force of 100,000 men divided into five groups, with another 50,000 guarding the rear. The advance was uneventful and largely unimpeded. Its ease, Haig was certain, was due entirely to the cavalry. In fact, he commented,

> the Infantry are *quite jealous* of the successes of the Cavalry. The poor creatures merely carry their guns without loosing off! In fact they simply wear out their boots to no purpose!! All the same, but for the Cavalry . . . many of them would now be below ground.

But, in his own way, Haig was equally jealous, especially of the credit Roberts insisted on claiming for himself. 'We came on here with the Cavalry and Roberts marched in at the head of the Infantry!', he wrote from one captured town. 'I am afraid he is a silly old man and scarcely fit to be C. in C. of this show.'[24]

On 5 June, the 'silly old man' raised the Union Jack above Pretoria. General Louis Botha had, the day before, escaped unmolested with his army.

Haig had earlier predicted that the capture of Pretoria would spell defeat for the Boers. He did not immediately change this view when he arrived in the town. 'I fancy that if Buller would only come on, and if an able man was sent to sweep up the N.E. corner of the Free State this war would soon be finished.' Buller did eventually move north, but the war continued. Haig nevertheless remained optimistic. With the coming of warm weather, 'a good many [Boers] will try to get back to their farms. I am therefore inclined to believe a report that the war will be practically over by the . . . beginning of September.' In a sense, the war was over by September, but a new war, a guerilla war, began in its place.[25]

When it became clear that the capture of Pretoria would not end the war, Haig decided, 'What is wanted now is to form detachments all about the country so that movable columns can sweep the country without having to take waggons with them.' Furthermore, since 'there is now no enemy in formed bodies to be dealt with but merely a lot of bands of marauders', it made sense for the Cavalry Division to be 'broken up . . . and the regiments spread out with various columns'. Rather belatedly, these were the measures taken. In November 1900, the Cavalry Division was disbanded. French was given command of a force of all arms which was to police the Johannesburg district. Haig, remaining as his Chief of Staff, predicted that 'there won't be a great deal of active work to be done by General F. and his staff', since they had merely to monitor the situation and, when disturbances occurred, despatch an appropriately sized force. He decided that 'Johannesburg is quite the best part of the country to stay in, so we can't complain.' It was hardly war. 'We are living in luxury now' in 'a grand house on the top of a hill overlooking Johsburg, two bath rooms with hot and cold water . . . I play polo 3 days a week.' Haig urged his sister to come and enjoy the good life with him, assuring her that he could entertain her in the style to which she was accustomed. In any case, the war would probably be over by the time she arrived: 'At present all is at a standstill waiting for Lord Roberts' . . . departure!! Lord Kitchener will then take up the command and no doubt will quiet the country very soon.'[26]

In common with most British officers, Haig had again underestimated the Boers' commitment to their cause. Quieting the country did not turn out to be as easy as he predicted. As a result, the Elysium in Johannesburg did not last long. In December, Haig and French were sent to Bloemfontein to try to stop De Wet, who threatened to invade Cape Colony. Though headed off, De Wet was not captured. The experience convinced Haig that the war was likely to last a long time. Henrietta was advised to cancel her trip: 'I am afraid this country is so disturbed that I shall have . . . to ask you to delay.' But, in spite of the setbacks, Haig remained as confident as ever of eventual victory. 'Every day shows a little progress and brings us nearer the end,' he assured Henrietta. It was an attitude which would come in handy in a future war.[27]

In January 1901, Haig was given a column of his own (consisting of 2,000 men) and sent to Cape Colony, where Boer raids had escalated. Maintaining control of the population proved difficult, since 'all the magistrates nearly are disloyal and 3/4 of the population: indeed I may say *all* farmers are dutch'. He nevertheless found that commanding a column was 'much more interesting than a Cavalry Brigade' mainly because he was able to 'move as I think best in pursuit of the Enemy'. 'I enjoy myself well,' he wrote after one particularly frenetic period. 'We are having a tremendous hunt after these wretches.'[28]

For Haig, the war was a daily fox hunt. 'From my point of view', he remarked on one occasion, 'nothing would have pleased me and my column better than a good hunt after De Wet . . . the next best fox is Kritzinger.' But the thrill of the chase was marred by Kitchener, who was prone to 'fits of funk':

> He (K) occasionally gets alarmed without real cause and hurries troops to this or that point without sufficiently considering, what the effect must be of denuding certain places of troops. So one is forced to conclude that the Sirdar is not the large minded man capable of taking a *broad* view of the *whole* situation which the papers would have us believe.

During February, Haig was in Cape Colony chasing Commandant Kritzinger, a particularly wily raider. After a few weeks Kitchener transferred him to Thabanchu and put French in his place with a larger force. By April, Haig was back in Cape Colony on Kritzinger's trail again. The continual shifting of troops was a measure of Kitchener's frustration. Haig found it exasperating: 'Lord K seems to meddle rather and does not give French quite a free hand.' The lack of a 'broad view' made chasing Boers infinitely more difficult.[29]

Commanding a column did not just mean chasing Kritzinger or De Wet across the veldt. Haig was also responsible for burning farms, executions, rounding up women and children and similar measures which gave the war its grisly notoriety. On these, he took a somewhat paradoxical view. In the case of farm burnings, for instance, he admitted that it 'is ridiculous to think that the Boers can be starved into submission when they have such a vast area from which they can draw supplies'. But, this was no reason to abandon the policy. It was valuable simply because it was punitive. The Boers had to be punished for continuing the war; when the punishment became intolerable, the war would end. The measures were especially applicable in Cape Colony because 'It is fully more difficult hunting Boers in this colony where all farmers are secretly their friends, and the Govt. almost seems to assist the invader, than in the Free State or Transvaal where one can trust everyone as the enemy.' Unconventional war called for unconventional policies. Questions of morality were immaterial. Suffering was, to Haig, simply proof that his measures were working.[30]

Despite the increasingly severe measures, Haig occasionally still felt that his hands were tied by namby-pamby officials. When he was prevented from hanging two rebels caught in June, he complained that, 'There is too much "*law*" and not enough rough and ready justice in this land.' Two months later, however, he was delighted to report:

> The authorities are all for blood now I hear! This will have a good effect. There were three men shot at Colesberg when I was there. I did not care to go and see the spectacle but all the local dutch magnates had to attend and a roll was called to see that they were present. I am told the sight was most impressive and everything went off well.

Measures of this type all contributed to eventual victory. 'Every day the situation here improves,' Haig repeatedly emphasised. 'Improvement' did not solely mean bringing peace nearer. He was certain that 'the more Cape Colony farmers who get ruined the better it will be for the country . . . I feel sure that S. Africa is deriving good from the continuance of this war.'[31]

The purgative effects of war were a constant theme. 'The Dutch own the best farms and the English farmers are beneath contempt! So *both ought to be cleared out*.' On another occasion, he remarked:

> The Dutch are so terribly indolent, that it is not to be wondered at that the country is so backward. The average English colonist too seems to have been (in the past) inferior to the Dutchman! Hence the secondary position which our colonists were content to occupy in the presence of the Dutch element.

Thus, farm burnings and the forced movement of people cleared the way for a new tide of righteous English imperialism. Haig accepted that part of his role was to make South Africa safe for the English to exploit its vast riches. He in fact urged Henrietta to invest her 'millions' in the 'new' South Africa.[32]

Ever since the fall of Pretoria, Henrietta had become increasingly concerned about post-war rewards for her brother. Though hostilities would drag on for another nineteen months, the bee having entered her bonnet, her meddling seldom ceased. Having consulted a sympathetic Wood, she decided that Douglas deserved a number of decorations. He, however, was politely dismissive, warning his sister that he did not want to be likened to 'these self-advertising people like B.P. [Baden Powell] and family'. He boasted that, 'There is not a single officer on this staff from French down who has a single decoration!' – a good thing since 'decorations and small wars ruined the French Army before 1870: the same causes have done much to render our own inefficient'. As he repeatedly insisted, he was 'not at all anxious for rewards which after all mean very little'.[33]

Haig was much more interested in the subject of promotion. When the possibility of commanding a regiment became increasingly likely, he told his sister, 'If it is necessary I'll do it, but there is no cachet in going to command some regiment which has to be wheeled into line a bit.' In August, Wood directed French to find Haig a regiment. The cavalry, Wood felt, was terribly deficient in leadership and needed to encourage men with potential like Haig. According to Haig, French replied

> that I had once been appointed to a Brigade, and that I might now be in command of one were it not to the interests of the service that I should remain in my present billet. My present appointment of Chief Staff Officer of a Cavalry Division of 4 Cavalry Brigades is superior to any regt. appointment.

With conspicuous insincerity, Haig concluded, 'I don't care much what happens to me.'[34]

Henrietta did care. When French did not heed Wood's wishes, she reacted angrily. In December 1900, Haig found it necessary to cool his sister's temper:

> don't think for a moment that French has not done his best for me. He is only too anxious to help me on, but I think, in remaining as his Chief Staff Officer, I did the best for the Cavalry Division, for him and for myself . . . So don't make a fuss about my being now in the same position I started in. Recollect also many have gone lower down!

This logic had little effect. Henrietta refused to leave the matter alone. In November 1901, Haig had again to correct his sister's misconceptions:

> By the way the General [French] mentioned to me that you had written to him some time ago and apparently conveyed the impression given you by old Evelyn that he (General F) had not done all he could and might have done to push me on. Now as I have told you often, the General wrote to Evelyn several times about me, and to others recommending me for all sorts of things, so you are quite under a misapprehension.

According to Haig, blame for the fact that 'I have not been made Commander-in-Chief, K.G., K.T., etc. etc.' rested with '*the late* lady killer of Pall Mall and not poor French!'[35]

Henrietta may have had grounds for complaint as far as French was concerned. There is no doubt that he thought Haig worthy of promotion, as he indicated to Hugo Haig early in the war:

> I cannot tell you what a comfort and assistance Douglas has been to me here and throughout the whole campaign. He is a perfect Staff Officer – and my great hope is that I may live to see him rise to the highest position in the service. The further and higher he rises the better for the country and its Army.

Likewise, on 20 May 1901 French told Haig, 'I feel they have treated you very badly.' But he seems to have done suspiciously little about this injustice. Claims that he took the matter up with 'Evelyn Wood, Ian Hamilton and even Bobs himself' are not supported in his private papers. When the command of the 17th Lancers fell vacant, Roberts and Kitchener suggested Haig for the post but French rejected the idea. Though Haig was 'in every way fit', French thought the regiment should go to Herbert Lawrence who 'has more claim'. (Lawrence's claim was based on seniority and the fact that he was already a member of the regiment.) What is clear is that French did not go out of his way to push Haig forward. For most of the war, this was probably due not to malice but rather simply to self-interest: French was not eager to part with a valuable assistant.[36]

French's advice was ignored. After the 17th Lancers had been promised to Lawrence, Roberts reversed the decision in May 1901 and gave the regiment to Haig. Roberts decided that Haig was 'the more [sic] capable and distinguished of all the younger cavalry soldiers'. Lawrence, in a fit of pique, left the Army and took up a career in the City. Haig was delighted with the appointment. Since the 17th Lancers were on active service in South Africa at the time, he was able to combine the duties of regimental colonel with those of column commander:

> I can easily look after the regiment in addition to directing the other columns. I know the country so well now that it does not bother me much to make up my mind where to send the latter to hunt the Enemy. Besides, I am giving the Squadron Commanders a chance of having a little show occasionally on their own account. There is nothing so good as responsibility for making good officers.

One 'little show' ended in disaster. On 17 September, 'C' Squadron was ambushed while defending a difficult position. The Boers, wearing captured British khaki, had been able to approach virtually unsuspected. Of the 130 British soldiers, 29 were killed, another 41 wounded. Haig was anguished at the loss: 'It made me miserable to see what had taken place . . . the wounds were terrible, the brutes used explosive bullets.'[37]

As the war dragged on into 1902, progress was measured in the increased ruthlessness of British tactics. Then, in April, came indications that those tactics were finally having an effect. Botha, Steyn, De Wet and others met at Klerksdorp to discuss peace terms. An initial offer was rejected by Kitchener because it did not include the essential surrender of independence by the Boer states. The Boer leaders, however, could not countenance such a surrender without consulting the commandos in the field. It was decided that a larger meeting would be held at Vereeniging, where the issue would be debated. Since the commandos were scattered over the country and were often cut off from communication with the Boer leaders, it was not a simple task to inform them of the meeting. In some cases, the British were called upon to assist. Haig, for instance, had to locate and escort Jan Smuts to Vereeniging. Having accepted this responsibility grudgingly, he consoled himself with the knowledge that Smuts 'was

91

State Attorney at Pretoria, and was at Cambridge, so is more or less civilised'.38

Haig ridiculed the 'meeting of the people' scheduled for 15 May at Vereeniging. The Boers could not be trusted. Their desire for peace was a front; they would use the truce to plan a new military response. This was no time for leniency: 'I hope that there is no question of giving terms to these rebels. It would be much better to go on fighting for 10 years than to give way on anything to them.' Politics had superseded force, therefore Haig was out of his element. All he could offer as means towards a settlement was more brutality: 'If Lord K were to put [the delegates at Vereeniging] on half rations in the rest camps for a week or two they would all vote for surrender!' When a treaty was signed on 31 May, he decided that it was 'right enough provided Martial Law is maintained in this Cape Colony for another three years'. The British had to be given time to weed out the inferior and dangerous elements and to remould the country.39

Waging war gave way to keeping the peace. Haig was directed to oversee the surrender of arms in a large district of Cape Colony. The task was approached with his usual severity: it was made clear to Smuts that access to stocks of food would not be granted until all arms had been surrendered. As usual, he underestimated the time required to restore order. In June, he predicted that 'a month or two should see me on my way to England'. But, as the winter wore on, progress slowed. He became increasingly despondent. 'Martial Law will soon be a dead letter,' he complained to his sister. He added that 'they have no police in sufficient numbers to keep order, and I fear the loyalists and those who have helped us will have a bad time'.40

In February 1900, Haig blamed the government for the humiliations of the early part of the war. 'I would disband the politicians for 10 years,' he suggested to his sister. 'We would all be better off without them!' The precarious peace after Vereeniging reinforced this attitude. He doubted

whether the Govt. in England know the real state of feeling in this Colony . . . I am certain that the Govt. of Cape Colony know very little about the feeling in the Districts . . . The govt. here seem like a lot of schoolboys, quite happy and thoughtless of the future.

Politics was, oh, so much more complicated than war. Haig found it difficult to understand that the military solution is never a complete one, that force might change sovereignty, but it did not change people's minds. Thus, he was incredulous when the Bond – the traditional party of the Dutch Afrikaner – continued to gain a majority in Cape Colony. When he finally accepted that farm burnings, executions and concentration camps had not significantly altered political alignments, he reacted in a characteristically simple-minded way. Suspend the constitution and allow the military to build a proper South Africa, he argued. He warned that, 'If the Politicians are allowed to have their way in this country . . . [it] will be entirely Dutch and natives in 20 years time and England merely will *exist* at Capetown.' Disillusion predominated in his last letter from South Africa:

> Things seem to be turning out badly in this colony. Fancy a rebel member of the Parliament (Te Water) who fled the country on account of his fear of punishment for his misdeeds being received by the Prime Minister with open arms and allowed to sit on the Treasury Bench with him. I went to the House of the Legislative Assembly the other day: It almost makes one ill to see the brutes and to hear them talk.

At his wits end, Haig suggested 'a general smash up of all political parties and arrangements in the hopes of gathering together the least hurtful elements'. It was time for him to go home.[41]

As the 17th Lancers were slated to be one of the garrison regiments in South Africa, Haig expected to stay in the country for another two years. In August, however, the Scots Greys replaced the Lancers, and the latter were sent home. Haig left with them, on 23 September – three years to the day since he had left England. The period saw his career flourish. He began the war as a staff officer of a small cavalry force, and ended it a local Brigadier-General in command of a large area and a massive force of all arms. He served in every part of South Africa and found success everywhere. Whilst the careers of many officers were destroyed by the war, Haig's prestige soared. He became one of the men destined to shape the Army of the new century. The lessons he had learned in South Africa would determine that shape.

5

A Cavalry Counter-Reformation

The Boer War was the pivotal point in Haig's career. The reputation that he had gained would open doors for him. But, whilst establishing Haig as a soldier of the future, the war also ironically confirmed for him the cavalry doctrines of the past. His development as a soldier was virtually complete: no subsequent events would negate the 'truths' which had been confirmed on the veldt. The period up to 1914 was, therefore, one in which Haig rose in the Army, but did not, in any other sense, progress.

Haig's rise was fuelled by an all-consuming sense of patriotic duty. A child of the British Empire, he was driven resolutely forward by a perceived debt of service to King and Country. This was by no means unique; contemporaries of similar social background felt similarly obligated. But a distinguishing feature in Haig's case was a peculiar egotism: his self-assurance led him to believe that his contribution was by definition more valuable than that of his contemporaries. The conception of duty and the sense of superiority were both evident in a letter written to a nephew in 1902. Hugo Haig had considered leaving the Army in order to become a member of the landed, and presumably idle, gentry. His eventual decision not to do so was applauded by Uncle Douglas:

> It would be absurd for a lad of your years and without any real experience of the Empire and its inhabitants to settle down into a turnip grower in Fife. Leave these pursuits until you get into the doddering age! Meantime do your best to become a worthy citizen of the Empire . . . It has been your *good fortune* not only

to become a soldier, but to have served and risked your life for the Empire – you must continue to do so, and consider that it is a privilege . . . The gist of the whole thing is that I am anxious not only that you should realise your duty to your family, your Country and to Scotland, but also to the whole Empire – 'Aim High' as the Book says, 'perchance ye may attain.' Aim at being worthy of the British Empire and possibly in the evening of your life you may be able to own to yourself that you are fit to settle down in Fife. At present you are not, so be active and busy.

The distinguishing feature of Haig's sense of duty is revealed later in the letter:

Don't let . . . mediocrities about you deflect you from your determination to belong to the few who can command or guide or benefit our great Empire. Believe me, the reservoir of such men is not boundless. As our Empire grows, so is there a greater demand for them, and it behoves everyone to do his little and try and qualify for as high a position as possible. It is not ambition. This is *duty*.[1]

Doing one's duty for the Empire did not, in Haig's case, always imply an unselfish and uncomplaining acceptance of assignments. After the Boer War, Kitchener wanted Haig as Inspector General of Cavalry in India, whilst French had him in mind for the commander of the Aldershot Cavalry Brigade. Though Haig thought the Indian appointment 'a fine [one] . . . with great opportunities of keeping one's hand in handling mounted troops', he made no secret of his desire to join French. But, since the decision was up to Roberts, Haig doubted that his wishes would be granted. 'I fancy the excellent house at Aldershot . . . will oblige Lord Roberts to select the husband of "Dear Mrs. So and So" because the nursery rooms will exactly suit the family!' In the end, Haig's scepticism was justified (though his reasoning may not have been). When Roberts decided to send Haig to India, the latter remarked 'so no doubt Roberts' pals (or ? Lady R's pals) have been chosen . . . [for Aldershot]'.[2]

Since the incumbent's term in India did not expire until October 1903, Haig had to spend a year in relative limbo with his regiment in Edinburgh. Not overjoyed at this return to his birthplace, he complained that the city was 'a bad place for Cavalry – no drill ground and half the regiment on detachment'. He tried, through French, to arrange a transfer to Aldershot or York, but French could do nothing. Haig dutifully went to Edinburgh where he found life exceedingly dull. Having never been enamoured of the regimental routine, he did not change his attitude when he became a commanding officer. After leading 2,500 men in war, leading 800 in peace was drudgery.[3]

The year did provide two notable diversions. In July, Haig participated in the Inter-Regimental Polo Tournament as captain of the 17th Lancers. In the final, which took place on the 11th, the Lancers faced the Blues before a royal audience at Hurlingham. In the Royal Box with Queen Alexandra was her lady-in-waiting, the Honourable Dorothy Maud Vivian, the future Countess Haig. Years later, she described the match in her biography of her husband:

> To the surprise of all, the game did not progress as expected. The Blues did not seem to be getting on well. Their play became wild, whilst the team of the 17th Lancers continued a steady, combined game. Everyone noted that the strong player who never missed nor sent a crooked shot, and who kept the whole team together, was *Colonel Douglas Haig*, playing back. Many comments were made in the Royal Box about the Colonel's remarkable play and his alert, smart appearance.

The Lancers won by five goals to one. Miss Vivian did not get an opportunity to speak to the colonel who, she noted, was at that time reputed to be a 'woman-hater'.[4]

The second important event came in October when Haig was presented with the CVO while staying at Balmoral. The King gave him the honour 'in recognition of the services which I had rendered in the past and would render in the future as IG of Cavalry in India, and also as "a mark of HM's personal esteem"'. The CVO was seen by Haig in a different light from ordinary military medals. It, and the attention of the King, was symbolic not only of past achievements but also of future social standing. He was undoubtedly delighted to note that 'His Majesty has desired me to write to him when I go to India.'[5]

Haig delayed his departure in order to work on *Cavalry Training*, which was being revised in the light of the South African War. Work on the manual aggravated the long-running conflict between the cavalry traditionalists and the reformers – among the latter Roberts and

Kitchener. Generally speaking, the two groups disagreed about the relative merits of mounted and dismounted action. The traditionalists naturally believed that the offensive potential of the arm, and especially the efficacy of the charge, had not been affected by technological advances. In consequence, they insisted that mounted training should receive the primary emphasis in the manual. The reformers, on the other hand, were certain that 'knee to knee charges in future will be few and far between'. They did not advocate abolishing the arm, but rather only modernising it. Reformers wanted the rifle to be the cavalry's main weapon. Since cavalrymen could not shoot accurately from a galloping horse, offensive action would, by necessity, have to take place dismounted. The horse would become simply a means of mobility rather than a tactical weapon in and of itself. The *arme blanche* would likewise diminish in importance. 'Instead of the firearm being adjunct of the sword', Roberts argued, 'the sword must henceforth be adjunct of the rifle.'[6]

Reformers and traditionalists alike cited experiences in South Africa to bolster their cases, thus further complicating the argument between them. Neither side questioned that the war had been a mobile one in which cavalry played an important role. Disagreement instead centred on the quality of the cavalry's performance. Roberts attributed many of the failures of the war to cavalry leaders who were unwilling to recognise the need for new tactics. His displeasure was expressed in his dismissal of twenty-one senior cavalry officers (including eleven of seventeen regimental commanders) during his eleven months in South Africa. Erskine Childers, a reformer with whom Roberts was in complete agreement, wrote:

> It was the Boer dash based on the rifle alone that cost us so many smarting reverses . . . and it was lack of dash on our side, caused largely by the old, inveterate, ingrained reliance on the arme blanche with a consequent reluctance to take a bold, logical grasp of the immense possibilities of the rifle, that prevented our Cavalry from setting the example of effective retaliation by tactics similar to those of the Boers.[7]

To the cavalrymen who had fought in South Africa, the arguments of Roberts and Childers felt like a knife in the back. All they could remember were sublime sacrifices and insufficient support. The few flaws in the cavalry's performance which Haig would admit to were stubbornly blamed upon senior officers (particularly Roberts and Kitchener) and politicians. Poor planning had meant that the supply of quality horses and feed was inadequate. Well-trained horses had been starved to death or run into the ground. Instead of bolstering the professional cavalry, the authorities had tried to improvise with second-rate mounted infantry. In spite of its lack of support, the cavalry had, at Elandslaagte, Kimberley and Paardeburg, 'saved the Empire'.

Roberts' memories of South Africa convinced him that *Cavalry Training* should be made into a primer on dismounted action. For Haig, on the other hand, it was essential that the manual should reflect the 'lessons' of Kimberley. Roberts described the disagreement in a letter to Kitchener:

> Haig, I am surprised to find, still clings to the old *arme blanche* system, and in the chapter for the Revised Edition of the Drill Book, which was entrusted to him to write, on Collective Training, there is not one word about Artillery or Dismounted Fire. Haig, supported by French and Scobell, insists on Cavalry soldiers being taught to consider the sword the chief weapon, and the rifle as a kind of auxiliary one . . . I am all in favour of cavalry soldiers being bold riders, and endeavouring to overthrow their enemy's mounted men, but I am convinced that in 99 cases out of a hundred this will be done more effectively by Artillery and dismounted fire in the first instance.

The wrangle over the manual continued into the autumn of 1903. Roberts' efforts were undoubtedly made easier by Haig's eventual departure for India, as he indicated to Kitchener: 'The revised *Cavalry Training* is getting on, and I hope it will be published next month. A good deal of it was started by Haig . . . and consequently much of his work has had to be re-written.' Roberts had won, but it was a meaningless victory. He did not, by any means, change Haig's mind. And a revised manual was worthless in the hands of a cavalry determined to ignore it.[8]

Roberts and the traditionalists also clashed over the lance. Reformers argued that arming cavalry with carbines rendered the lance superfluous. The weapon, therefore, had to be abandoned. This did not mean the complete abolition of the *arme blanche*. The sword would be retained for the same reason that infantry still required bayonets. The lance, on the other hand, was a clumsy weapon which impeded the cavalryman's ability to use his rifle effectively. Traditionalists naturally did not agree. Since they did not believe that the charge was a thing of the past, they could not accept that the lance was obsolete. Elandslaagte had, after all, demonstrated its awesome and frightening power. And, though the reformers promised that they did not want to dispense with swords, the traditionalists saw the abolition of the lance as the thin end of a wedge. If they lost this argument, the sword would eventually also go.

Traditionalists often cited esoteric reasons for the retention of the *arme blanche*. Arguing before the Elgin Commission in 1903, French stated that 'if the Cavalryman is taught to rely mainly on his rifle, his moral is taken away from him, and if that is done his power is destroyed'.[9] Cavalrymen deprived of steel weapons were like Samson shorn. Without the *arme blanche*, the cavalry spirit would evaporate. This spirit was not a chimera. Cavalry fought at close quarters – man to man. The combination of speed and proximity to the enemy which characterised cavalry combat made it unique. Artillery or infantry engagements did not inspire the same emotional intensity as occurred when two lines of thundering horsemen collided. But the fact remained that modern weaponry had rendered this collision virtually unthinkable. With the charge a thing of the past, the *arme blanche* became functionally obsolete and the cavalry spirit little more than a quaint piece of nostalgia.

In a letter to an MP and former 17th Lancer, Haig argued that 'half the cavalry should have swords; the other half lances. *I don't think it is wise to abolish the lance* ... Strategical reconnaissance must culminate in a tactical collision if the enemy possesses Cavalry; we want the lance for this.' The argument at one time made sense. By 1903 it was a *non sequitur*. The traditionalists' case rested on the assumption that a future war would begin with a great classical cavalry engagement. But the fact remained that no such engagements had occurred during their careers. As Roberts correctly maintained, 'Haig ... inclines to the lance though he can have had no experience of its use in war.' Nor would the future provide this experience. It required foresight to recognise that not only would future cavalry have little use for the lance, future armies would have little use for cavalry. Foresight was not Haig's strongest point. For him, studying war meant prostrating himself at the temple of Napoleon, Wellington, and Blücher. His head stuck in the sands of time, he could not see the future that lay ahead. Like French, who claimed that 'nothing can make me alter the views that I hold on the subject of cavalry', Haig refused to accept that long-range rifles, deadly machine-guns and powerful artillery would annihilate Lancers before they could even attempt to prove the worth of their cherished weapons.[10]

The roots of Haig's obscurantism can be traced to Kimberley. Even before the dust had settled, that 'charge' had been neatly incorporated into the cavalry mythology. It was, to Haig, a vindication of everything the cavalry held dear. Its effect upon him can be seen in the following statement:

> it is not the weapon carried but the moral factor of an apparently irresistible force, coming on at highest speed, in spite of rifle fire, which affects the nerves and the aim of the rapidly dismounted rifleman . . . I ask those who have felt the elation of a successful charge or who have known the despondency which attacks those who have been ridden over by the horseman whom they have fired at in vain, whether magazine fire; which makes the shooting so erratic, hurried and much less easily controlled, and spends the ammunition so quickly, has really so much changed the conditions of thirty years ago?[11]

Yes, conditions had changed radically. These changes had occurred before Haig entered the Army. He could vividly describe a scene which he himself had never experienced because it was a part of the cavalry dogma. Its constant repetition over the previous thirty years had worn a groove in his mind.

Despite Haig's opposition, Roberts was able to abolish the lance in 1904. This second success makes his reformist campaign seem impressive. But the changes were short-lived. When the post of Commander-in-Chief was abolished in late 1904, Roberts lost the authority to impose his will upon the traditionalists. With his attention increasingly focused upon the campaign for universal service, Haig and his friends were left alone to conduct what became an impressively successful cavalry counter-reformation. In 1907, a new *Cavalry Training* was published with the heretical elements of the 1904 manual excised. In 1909, the lance was reintroduced. By 1910, 80 per cent of the training schedule of the Aldershot Cavalry Brigade was devoted to shock tactics.

Cavalry reform was repeatedly frustrated because of the prestige and power of Haig and French. The reputations they had gained in the Boer War obscured their antiquated ideas. Haig, in contrast to French, had the added advantage of being in other areas a genuine progressive. Within the Army, he was recognised as an educated professional, a soldier of the future. Thus, with Haig as the cavalry's leading spokesman, the arm's image was naturally enhanced. This combination of traditionalism and progressivism seems contradictory, but before 1914 the two elements did not in fact conflict. Haig was progressive in the sense that he wanted to make the Army a more efficient institution. Thus, he campaigned for improvements in organisation, training and education. He was certain that the fundamental principles of the Army – its traditions – were perfectly sound, and therefore worthy of preservation. To attack those traditions (chief among them the cavalry spirit) was to erode the ideological core of the Army. The implications of Haig's attitude can be seen in his effect upon the cavalry: under his guidance, it became extremely proficient at obsolete practices.

The idiosyncratic blend of the progressive and the traditional was reflected in Haig's approach to his duties as Inspector General of Cavalry in India. According to Charteris:

The Indian Cavalry under the influence of many of its officers who had served in South Africa with mounted infantry units was permeated with the new doctrines and looked for the approval of the new Inspector General. There was a rude awakening. Haig would have none of it. Both at his inspection of regiments, and still more by means of his training memoranda and staff rides, he taught unceasingly to his cavalry in India that warfare still offered scope for horse and man and bare steel.

The Indian cavalry under Haig became a functionally efficient but tactically obsolete unit. An indicator of his priorities can be seen in his schedule of inspection, itself an impressive piece of administration. Top of the list were the traditional subjects: drill, order, wheeling, charging and squadron versus squadron mock battles. The eleventh and final item was shooting and dismounted drill.[12]

Kitchener, Commander-in-Chief in India, endorsed cavalry reform. Though not as committed a reformer as Roberts, he did support the abolition of the lance and the revised edition of *Cavalry Training*. As he indicated on 30 June 1903, Roberts was grateful for Kitchener's support: 'I am glad to get your opinion about the lance, it will help me with the King, who was somewhat regretting the weapon having been done away with, after he had some conversation with Haig at Edinburgh.' Having recently experienced the intensity of Haig's cavalry fundamentalism, Roberts was anxious that Kitchener should be aware of what was in store. The latter was urged to 'keep Haig in the right line'. 'Haig is one of the strongest supporters of the sword and charging. You will have to be very firm with him.'[13]

Four days after his arrival in India, Haig had his first meeting with Kitchener. Cavalry issues dominated the conversation. Haig, who often heard only what he wanted to hear, recorded that Kitchener was 'quite at one with me regarding method of cavalry action, namely *offensive* tactics'. In a letter to Roberts, Kitchener told a different story:

> Haig . . . seems to have a wrong idea that the morale of the cavalry will be injured by dismounted training. I have told him I disagree with this, that while I do not wish in any way to injure the dash and power of shock tactics of cavalry they must understand that whereas in the old days the carbine was the adjunct to the sword or lance, now the sword or lance must be the adjunct to the rifle.

In reply, a sympathetic Roberts wrote that it was 'quite a misfortune that Haig should be of the old school in regard to the role of the Cavalry in the field' since 'he is a clever, able fellow and his views have a great effect on French'. He hoped that Kitchener would 'be able to get Haig to change his mind, or as Inspector General of Cavalry he may do a great deal of mischief'.[14]

Subsequent meetings seem to have gone better. Kitchener even went so far as to suggest to Roberts that 'someone must have given you the wrong impression about Haig'. This apparent harmony was shattered in mid-May, when the old points of conflict suddenly re-emerged with a vengeance. The workings of Haig's mind became very clear to Kitchener:

> I have had a long talk with Haig. It was not quite satisfactory because though he agrees with my views he always seems to hark

back as if something more was intended or that he was afraid that more was intended than was said . . . The cavalry are I think evidently very nervous that . . . [by] training for the role they can now perform with their rifle, they may lose the power or spirit to attack the enemy's cavalry when it is necessary and they have the opportunity of so doing. I can see no reason why they should not do both equally well.

Haig's defence of the traditional cavalry had become a paranoid obsession. He feared that if he made even the slightest concession to the reformers the complete disintegration of the cavalry would eventually result. Thus, he began to distrust even the relatively moderate Kitchener. Had the two men continued along these opposing courses, a serious conflict would undoubtedly have developed.[15]

In fact, after May 1904, the cavalry issue almost completely disappears from Haig's diaries and Kitchener's letters. Further conflict was avoided because Kitchener's attention was distracted elsewhere. A major row with the Viceroy, Lord Curzon, had arisen over the role of the Military Member of Council. The Military Member was junior in rank to Kitchener, but, due to his position on the Council, he could intervene in the Commander-in-Chief's affairs. Since the Viceroy controlled the Council, the Military Member was essentially a tool of Curzon. Objecting to this interference, Kitchener threatened to resign. Haig, faced with a clash between a politician and a soldier, naturally sided with the latter:

The C. in C. in India has really very little power, as all the Supply, Transport, Remounts and finance are under an individual called the 'Military Member of Council'. This is to say that Lord Kitchener may order men to Thibet [sic], but he does not know whether they will starve or not because he has nothing to do with the supply arrangements. Such a system is obviously ridiculous. It is like a pair of horses in double harness *without* a coachman. The latter ought to be the Viceroy, but he has too many things to attend to already, even if he were capable of discharging such duties which the majority of Viceroys are not.[16]

The argument over the role of the Military Member was simply the focal point of an inevitable conflict between two imperious individuals whose orbits unfortunately intersected. For Haig it was a godsend. With Kitchener distracted, he was given free rein to manage the cavalry as he wished.

An element of give and take may also explain Kitchener's apparent tolerance. He may have been aware of the valuable help Haig could provide; likewise Haig may have sensed the advantage he could derive from being supportive. Just before Haig was due to go on leave to England, Kitchener 'spent over two hours explaining the whole case . . . so that I might be quite au fait when I get home and able to give his case without difficulty'.[17] It is not clear to what extent Haig influenced the outcome. Nevertheless, while on leave, he did visit the King, and must have raised the Kitchener Curzon issue. Not long after, the King expressed his displeasure with the affair. The eventual resolution was favourable to Kitchener.

Left to himself, Haig was able to mould the Indian cavalry into a highly efficient unit. To this end, he criss-crossed the country in exhausting tours of inspection. He tried to make himself a familiar figure, a focal point for improvement, and saw himself as more a teacher than an inspector. 'Every day of inspection must be a day of training,' he wrote. 'The troops should feel . . . not merely that their efficiency has been tested but that they have learnt something.' He claimed that, in judging performances, he was '*most* considerate as it is better to carry people with one, than to stifle keenness by mere criticisms, without explaining what improvements and . . . changes are required'. It is probably best to take Haig at his word regarding his success in India. Leaving aside his traditionalism, there is no reason to doubt that he made an excellent Inspector General.[18]

The effect which Haig had was enhanced by the close attention he paid to the image he presented. He was keenly aware that it is largely superficial qualities which inspire the ordinary soldier to respect a senior officer. Thus, he was always careful to make a positive first impression: 'You would be surprised at the amount of baggage and stuff I have to go about with – horses and clerks and office boxes and orderlies . . . so l'arrivée is most impressive . . . especially for the regiment as they are not quite certain what to expect.' Additional evidence of the image-conscious Haig is found in a letter written from South Africa: 'I hear our staff is always considered well-dressed and clean,' he told his sister. 'This has a good effect on all ranks.' Cleanliness implied efficiency and thus supposedly inspired efficient performances. It also suggested honesty, courage and reliability. Haig's natural affinity for cleanliness and his obsession with order were therefore reinforced because they were useful tools of leadership.[19]

Haig's active cultivation of his image was at this stage quite harmless, and in many ways beneficial. But images are apt to be misconstrued and, as such, can be an insecure basis for authority. Whilst it was perhaps correct for Haig to inspire obedience among the ranks by projecting himself as the perfect cavalry officer, he had to be careful not to apply the same technique in dealings with junior officers, particularly staff officers. The staff must be allowed to see through the mask; its loyalty must be based on respect for more than just superficial characteristics. If staff officers are in awe of the commander, there is a danger of loyalty becoming blind.

In order to function properly, the staff must be composed of able and intelligent men possessing the courage to question their commander. As Haig himself often stressed, a premium must be placed upon independence. It is up to the leader himself to ensure that these requirements are satisfied. Few succeed. The failure to choose staff officers with independent minds is often an indication of weaknesses in the commander's own character. He may want the staff to be a convenient counterweight to outside criticism and may, as a result, seek officers with whom he feels comfortable. Likewise, he might feel threatened by intelligent subordinates, high fliers who could be potential successors. Consciously or subconsciously, he might select intellectual inferiors in order to reduce the threat subordinates pose. Being surrounded by inferiors also boosts the ego of the commander, providing him with confirmation of his ability to lead.

Haig was, in 1905, at a critical point with regard to his attitude towards the staff. Whilst he recognised that modern war demanded efficient and outspoken staff officers (men like himself), when he began for the first time to choose a staff of his own, he displayed many of the weaknesses outlined above. This is revealed in a letter to Henrietta:

Alan Fletcher is to go to Cairo with the 17th before he comes out here . . . I am sorry you don't think much of his brain power as you doubt whether he is 'clever enough for the job'! The so called sharp people very often disappoint us or cheat or have some other draw back such as being disagreeable, bad-tempered, etc. All I require is people of *average* intelligence who are keen to do their work properly. Alan is well up to this standard and is most unselfish and tactful, so that I find it a pleasure to go about with him.

Fletcher typified the staff officers Haig, with few exceptions, preferred for the rest of his career. Obsequiousness was a predominant characteristic among those closest to him. In choosing a personal staff, Haig stressed harmony; he wanted a 'band of brothers'. Honesty and integrity were less important than an amiable temperament. He had little patience for men with the same qualities which had characterised him during his days as a staff officer. It was of no concern (and some positive attraction) if subordinates held him in awe. These weaknesses negated his otherwise progressive attitude towards the staff and staff training.[20]

During the summer of 1905 Haig was on leave in England. It was for him a long-delayed 'coming out'. Social columnists chirped on about this 'very soldierly looking fellow' – a hero in South Africa and the Sudan – who was regularly seen at race meetings and parties in the company of society's brightest. The abandonment of his normally quiet habits was probably deliberate. Haig had reached a watershed in his career. As a young officer, he had concentrated upon proving himself a serious determined professional, a task which precluded anything approaching frivolity. By 1905 his reputation was secure, and joining the social round henceforward became not only possible but advantageous. As a Major-General, he was expected to attend and to give parties – parties at which a properly directed wink or nudge could do one's career no end of good. Haig went about shaping his social profile with the same calculated resolve as he had his military one. Moderation and discretion ruled. He cultivated contacts with the Royal Family and with other individuals of good background, acceptable habits and traditional ideals. Politicians and other dangerous types were as far as possible carefully avoided.[21]

It was in a similarly calculated way that Haig chose to marry during his leave. The inveterate 'woman-hater' suddenly realised that it was advantageous to have a wife. Once his mind became open to marriage, he did not dally over the choice of a suitable partner. A long, perhaps disastrous love affair did not accord with his plans. After a whirlwind courtship, he proposed to the Honourable Dorothy Maud Vivian, the first woman to whom he paid more than passing attention. A social columnist accurately called it 'A wooing not long a-doing':

> Major-General Douglas Haig . . . received with his bride, the Hon. Dorothy Vivian, the honour of being married in the private chapel of Buckingham Palace. A good deal of romance surrounds the betrothal, for it is said General Haig and Miss Vivian only met for the first time on Monday of Ascot Week, were engaged the following Saturday, and married within a fortnight.[22]

In fact, the couple met over golf on Thursday of Ascot Week. They spent the next day together at the races, and played golf again in the evening. Haig proposed on the links on Saturday, after telling the caddies to make themselves scarce. Since no bench was available near to the hole they were playing, he unfortunately had to pop the question while remaining on his feet. The absence of the romantic touch did not, however, cause Miss Vivian to deliberate. The wedding followed on 11 July. When questioned about his haste, Haig is said to have replied that he frequently spent far less time contemplating more important decisions.

Despite the lack of deliberation, the marriage was, according to the standards of the day, successful. Love, given little time to propagate, nevertheless became robust in time. But, initially, emotions were less important than the fact that Doris (the name she preferred) suited Haig's professional and social requirements. Of good family (the daughter of the 4th Baron Vivian), she had served as Queen Alexandra's lady-in-waiting. Most importantly, she was fully suited to the role of the dutiful, discreet and supportive military wife:

> Lady Haig fulfilled to perfection the difficult role that falls to the lot of the wife of a great man. She never interfered in official business, yet she was always there to help her husband. Her tact and intuition never failed. She was a discreet and sympathetic confidante and she strengthened his faith in his own power to overcome difficulties. She devoted every moment of her married life to her husband.

Charteris also claimed that Doris 'brought to Haig completeness'.[23] Whilst to an extent true, it is nevertheless important to note that the marriage permanently altered Haig's relationship with his sister.

Letters to her became less frequent and dealt with more mundane topics. On her part, Henrietta, though remaining interested in her brother's progress, ceased to meddle in his career. Doris, less scheming, self-confident and shrewd than Henrietta, could never adequately fill the gap which had been created. Thus, while the marriage may have satisfied an emotional need, in other important ways, it left Haig more alone.

For reasons which were professional rather than personal, Haig was reluctant to return to India after his wedding. In Britain, anxious eyes were being focused on the need to reform the Army. Wanting desperately to monitor these reforms (particularly those affecting the cavalry), Haig made it known among his friends that he fancied an appointment at the War Office. After consultations with Haig, the King asked French to press Arnold-Forster, the War Secretary, to appoint Haig Director of Staff Duties. But, on 6 August, French informed Haig that there was no chance of success, because

> A.F. thinks that the King is trying to push you into that appointment simply on personal grounds, and because you and your wife are friends of his. Like all political intriguers, he is always suspicious, and thinks people are acting as he would probably act in similar circumstances.[24]

Arnold-Forster argued that the incumbent DSD, General Hutchinson, still had two years to serve, and had done nothing to warrant his replacement by Haig. The King's influence seems ironically to have hindered Haig from landing a position to which, as time would prove, he was ideally suited.

Though Haig returned dutifully to India, his heart was no longer in his work. Goings on at the War Office became an obsession, while Indian affairs took a back seat. Haig would not have seen his lack of enthusiasm for his responsibilities in India as a contradiction of his customary devotion to duty, since he believed that he possessed special talents for which there was a critical need in London. His friends at home were of like mind. Prominent among the schemers on Haig's behalf was Viscount Esher, who became particularly persistent after the Liberal victory in 1906 brought in a new War Secretary, Richard Burdon Haldane. Haig told Henrietta how he received a letter from Esher 'cracking up Haldane'.

Then towards the end . . . he writes: 'There is only one change, not yet made, which Haldane *must* make. It is to put you in Hutchinson's place. I have never let him alone for a day since he took office on this subject. If *you* get back here in that place for two years – the whole tone of Army officers and their Education will have undergone a change, which will recast the Army.'

Whilst Haig claimed that 'personally I am quite happy in India', in truth he feared that every day he spent there increased the risk of ill-considered Army reforms. Eventually, he got his wish, escaping India on 12 May 1906, five months prior to the completion of his term.[25]

Haig's interest in the modernisation of the Army contrasts sharply with the antiquated tactical lessons he stressed in India. His approach is best illustrated by the staff tours he organised. Each tour was based upon a cavalry action of the all-too-distant past, culled from dusty cavalry manuals. No attempt was made to hypothesise upon the nature of the arm's future employment. For example, one exercise was summarised as follows:

> A 'Decisive Battle' – the real object in war – Strategical Preparation – Selection of a 'Primary' and a 'Secondary' Theatre of War, and use of Entrenched Depots, illustrated by 1809. – Measures to be taken with regard to a 'Buffer State' – Employment of the Cavalry Divisions and of the Army Cavalry up to the 'Decisive Battle'.

A second tour, concerned with 'The Operations of a Containing Force in a "Secondary" Theatre of War', was modelled on 'Prince Eugene's Campaign in Italy, 1809'. Likewise, a third tour focused upon 'The Strategical Employment of Cavalry covering the Concentration of the Main Army to one Flank' as demonstrated in the Ulm Campaign of 1805. In contrast, cavalry actions in the Franco-Prussian, South African and American Civil Wars – of far more relevance to the future – were ignored. The technological revolution in warfare of the previous century had apparently escaped Haig's notice.

The tours mentioned above were described, along with two others, in *Cavalry Studies*, written by Haig in 1907 with the help of Lonsdale Hale. In the book, Haig argued that since war was growing larger in scope and more technical, the cavalry's role would change accordingly.

He predicted that cavalry would in future take three different forms: Independent Cavalry: intended mainly for reconnaissance; Protective Cavalry: medium-sized units designed as a first line of security for the army behind it; and Divisional Cavalry: designed specifically for decisive offensive action (in other words, the sort of function that cavalry was least likely to perform in the future). The first two formations were not new; the functions were ones which cavalry had fulfilled throughout its history. Divisional Cavalry was, however, a unique concept, at least in Britain, where the mounted arm had never been organised on a scale larger than brigades. It will be recalled that after Kimberley Haig advised Hale that the British cavalry should be expanded to 'at least two Divisions complete'. He reiterated this demand in his book, justifying the enlargement by arguing, '*The war of masses necessitates mass tactics.*' Thus, while many were arguing for the limitation of the cavalry's role, Haig advocated its dramatic expansion. Any other policy was sure to be 'vain, uncertain and harmful'.

In drawing the above conclusions, Haig paved his way with two basic assumptions: the first that cavalry was indispensable; the second that war was becoming larger in scope. The latter assumption was obviously correct, the former overstated but not wrong. Cavalry was, after all, still valuable in reconnaissance, flank protection, rearguard actions, and wherever mobility was paramount. But, from these two basically correct assumptions, Haig concluded that the role of the cavalry would increase, that 'large armies entail large numbers of cavalry'. It is here that he entered the clouds. He did not understand that, though time had not altered cavalry's basic indispensability, it *had* drastically changed the functions it could perform. It did not require extraordinary insight to realise that the rifle and the machine-gun had revolutionised warfare. War had become not only larger, it had also become more deadly, more technical and more impersonal. Haig may have noticed these changes, but he did not perceive their implications. Only an ostrich could have failed to sense which way the wind was blowing.

The qualities of the ostrich were even more evident towards the end of the introduction to *Cavalry Studies*. In response to the claim that the 'day of the cavalry is past', Haig argued as follows:

The role of the cavalry on the battlefield will always go on increasing because –

1) The extended nature of the modern battlefield means that there will be a greater choice of cover to favour the concealed approach of cavalry.

2) The increased range and killing power of modern guns, and the greater length of time during which battles will last, will augment the moral exhaustion, will affect men's nerves more, and produce greater demoralisation amongst the troops. These factors contribute to promote panic and to render troops (short service soldiers nowadays) ripe for attack by Cavalry.

3) The longer the range and killing power of modern arms, the more important will rapidity of movement become, because it lessens the relative time of exposure to danger in favour of the Cavalry.

4) The introduction of the small bore rifle, the bullet from which has little stopping power against the horse.

The points are too absurd to deserve detailed rebuttal. Safe in his own dream world, Haig went on to claim that because of its moral effect, cavalry would continue to play a part 'in the prologue, the principal act and the *dénouement*' of every battle. Finally, he reasserted his belief in the continued viability of the charge, the *arme blanche* and the cavalry spirit: 'All great successes can only be gained by a force of cavalry which is trained to harden its heart and charge home.'[26]

Cavalry Studies has been used by Haig's critics as a noose by which to hang him for the carnage of the Great War. Facile and sensationalist commentators have too often attempted to explain Haig's tactics by referring to his apparent lack of faith in the killing power of modern rifles. The issue, unfortunately, is not so simple. As will be seen, the passage of time caused Haig to rethink his misguided notions about the ineffectiveness of rifle fire. But this is where his progress stopped. He never lost faith in the continued ability of horse and rider to play a dramatic offensive role in future campaigns. Thus, he never questioned the logic of a cavalry oriented strategy.

The statement that 'the role of the cavalry . . . will always go on increasing' implied a belief in the immutability of the type of battle which Haig experienced at Elandslaagte, a battle which was an anomaly when it occurred. Elandslaagte was in the tradition of the great military engagements which Haig had studied throughout his career. It was a battle of frontal assaults, breakthroughs, rolled-up flanks and cavalry charges. But the machine-gun, modern artillery, unlimited battlefields, huge citizen armies, barbed wire, gas, and other developments negated many of the sacred military truths which underlay this type of battle. Haig's stubborn insistence on their continued relevance seriously hindered his understanding of the monumental changes in military science which were in progress. The era demanded an open mind, not one clouded by the tenets of Napoleon and Blücher, nor one paranoid about the disintegration of the cavalry ethos. While Haig was by nature slow to adapt to progress, his mind had been slammed shut at Kimberley.

6

Politicians and Paperwork

Before the Boer War, Haig had established himself, in certain significant circles, as a competent administrator – one of the new breed of professional soldiers. After 1902, as a result of his war record, his reputation widened. Meanwhile, the war had revealed the need for fundamental reform of the Army. Thus, at a time when the need for change was widely recognised, Haig was seen as one of the few men qualified to advise on its nature. But, it must again be emphasised that Haig was both progressive and reactionary: when he arrived in Whitehall he brought with him some very conservative ideas about tactics which inevitably imposed limitations upon the reforms he was prepared to implement.

A major defect revealed in South Africa was the Army's lack of coherent planning; whilst the initial mobilisation was well organised, there was no blueprint for wartime expansion. This meant that the local commander had virtually sole responsibility for making operations run smoothly. If he failed or if the task grew too large for him, there was no safety valve in the form of a General Staff to provide assistance. The faults of this system were revealed in the commands of Roberts and Kitchener during the Boer War. Though both men provided more energetic leadership than Buller, there were nevertheless serious shortcomings in planning and supply.

It was one thing to create a new institutional framework, another entirely to find men to staff it. A shortage of well-trained staff officers had been exposed in South Africa. On the surface, the solution seemed simple. The Staff College had only to expand its output and improve its product. But the persistent prejudice against the college, its graduates and the whole idea of professionalisation made this task complicated. Thus, the problem of creating an efficient staff system was as much a question of changing attitudes as institutions.

Even more frightening was the fact that Britain required, at the peak of the war, 450,000 men to defeat the Boers. This had exhausted available reserves and had left the homeland essentially undefended. The threat of a massive European war made the need for a dependable reserve army, capable of expansion upon mobilisation, imperative. In France and Germany, huge armies had been created through conscription and short service. For two reasons, Britain could not copy the continental practice. First, the Liberal government was reluctant, due to the conflicting demand for expanded social services, to spend more than £28 million per year on the Army. A second, more significant, reason was the traditional British abhorrence of standing armies. Lord Roberts' fruitless campaign for universal service only demonstrated that conscription was unacceptable in peacetime. Thus, the size of the reserve force was limited by the government's willingness to fund it and by the population's willingness to volunteer.

All these problems were accentuated by the threat of war on the Continent. The Anglo-French accord of 1904 and the continuing naval rivalry with Germany made British involvement almost certain. Since Britain could not hope to match the military power of the German Army, the help of the Empire became essential. This requirement revealed additional administrative problems, including the standardisation of weaponry and the necessity for agreement on strategy, tactics, training and channels of command. Uniformity was imperative. But uniformity required cooperation, and the institutions for fostering this cooperation did not exist.

All the deficiencies described above had been acknowledged by the various committees of inquiry which studied the British effort in South Africa. The conclusions reached prompted Lord Esher, with the support of the Conservative government, to form a committee to advise on specific reforms. Esher plunged enthusiastically into this task, producing three massive reports in four months. His main recommendation was the replacement of the Commander-in-Chief by an Army Council composed of the four military heads of department (Chief of the General Staff, Adjutant General, Master General of Ordnance and Quartermaster General) and three civilians (the Secretary of State for War, Parliamentary Under-Secretary and Financial Secretary).

Below the Army Council, each separate department would be divided into specific directorates. For example, under the CGS would be the Director of Military Training (DMT), Director of Staff Duties (DSD) and the Director of Military Operations (DMO). The committee also recommended the establishment of a General Staff on the German model, designed to be not simply an administrative but also a policy forming body. Finally, Esher recommended a drastic pruning of top Army commanders, men whom he feared would otherwise obstruct reform.

Esher's recommendations were accepted by A. J. Balfour, the Prime Minister. On 3 February 1904, the Army Council was set up and the post of Commander-in-Chief abolished. It was then up to the Army Council to implement Esher's other proposals. But here progress ground to a halt. The War Minister, Arnold-Forster, lacked the political muscle needed to push reform further. In addition, though Esher's suggested reforms were undoubtedly wise, his selection of men to implement them was not. The first Army Council consisted of weak men ill-suited to the gigantic tasks which faced them. By the time the Conservatives were defeated in 1906, few of Esher's plans had been realised.

The reform agitation was initially greeted by Haig with cautious optimism. Though nervous about the prospect of politicians fiddling with the Army, he was nevertheless impressed with Esher's intention to 'approach all reform from the point of view of *War* . . . We want to make it an organisation for War, adaptable to Peace.' Esher recognised, and Haig agreed, that this was 'a novelty in War Office procedure'. Haig's confidence must have increased still further when he learned of Esher's plan 'to sweep out the old lot and put in new men', especially since it was likely that he would be included in the latter group:

of thoughtful, broad-minded soldiers there is a singular dearth. Perhaps you have no conception how barren is the land here! And without good men, the machine – however you construct it – is bound to creak. I believe that you, more than any, have *thought* out problems. If ever you falsify the hopes you have raised in all those who care for the Army, woe betide you![1]

The malfunctioning Army Council and Arnold-Forster's weaknesses did not at first dampen the enthusiasm which Esher's letter inspired.

When Henrietta described the new system as chaotic, Haig quickly corrected her misconception. 'Of course there must be some confusion in the War Office . . . after such a thorough shaking up . . . But I feel sure that the *system* of Army Control which has been started is a good one.' All that was needed was a period of 'settling down'. But, after Arnold-Forster refused to countenance his transfer to the War Office, Haig soon began to deride the reform programme and to distance himself from it. 'I don't think a sedentary life would altogether suit me.' The grapes had suddenly turned sour.[2]

Haig's spirits were quickly revived when the Tories left office at the end of 1905. His reaction is somewhat surprising, since the Liberals were traditionally seen as the more pacific party and Haldane, the new War Secretary, had no experience or apparent interest in military affairs. Nevertheless, probably because of good reports from Esher, Haig was able to conclude, 'Haldane cannot be worse than Arnold-Forster and he must have some pluck to take over the post of Secretary of War.' In February 1906, he was pleased to report to Henrietta:

> Every one I hear from in the soldiering line at home, speaks well of Haldane, so the advent of the radicals is certainly of great advantage to the Army . . . French seems to like him very much; and the 'Army Councillors', Hubert Hamilton writes me, 'have now the spirits of schoolboys home for the holidays'. So for now at any rate things seem to be going well for the Army.

Haig became even more hopeful when he learned that he would be taking over the Directorate of Staff Duties when Hutchinson left in October 1906. 'This . . . will be a very good arrangement for Doris and me,' he commented. After pressure from Esher, however, Haldane decided to recall Haig earlier than planned and install him in the Directorate of Military Training. Haig was even more ecstatic. 'Although called "Training" the department also deals with "War Organisation" and "Home Defence" so that now it is the most important Directorate in the General Staff at the present time.' He thought it 'a very great honour to be sent for at this critical time to help to decide the future organisation of the Empire's forces. So I ought to be thought very lucky.'[3]

Thus, Haig returned to Britain confident that he was to play a major role in the Army's and the country's future. His belief in his own illustrious destiny was reinforced by the revelations of a spiritualist visited on 20 September 1906:

> At 3 p.m. went with Henrietta to see a medium, Miss McCreadie . . . [She said that] I had come recently from abroad and was now settling down. Seemed to be drawing a great force around me which would be of assistance in the new Scheme . . . She thought a 'company basis' better than a 'battalion basis' for expansion of Territorial Army. Then I gave her a letter from Mr. Haldane (the S. of S.). She said he was a 'very clever man'. Honest and far-seeing and would fight to bring people around to his opinions. Asked by Henrietta about me (before she went under control) she said she felt I wanted magnetism and had been unwell but was getting better. It seemed as if I would go abroad for some special object of a wide and important nature. Much would depend on me. Then when under control by a little native girl 'Sunshine' she said that I was influenced by several spirits: notably a small man named Napoleon aided me. That it was in my power to be helped by him for good affairs but I might repel him if his influence was for bad, tho' he had become changed for the better in the spirit world. I was destined to do much good and to benefit my country. Asked by me how to ensure the Territorial Army Scheme being a success, she said *thought governed the world*. Think out the scheme thoroughly, one's thoughts would then be put in so convincing a manner that the people would respond (*without any compulsion*) and the National Army would be a reality. She could not bring Napoleon to me when I wanted but I must think of him and try and get his aid as he was always near me. My mother too was close to me and a sister . . . My mother threw a light around me and Henrietta and placed on my breast a star which illuminated all about me.

Haig and the rest of his family mirrored the Edwardian fascination for spiritualism. Henrietta regularly communicated with her dead brother George on important topics such as whether her 'pet doggies – Creenie and Bogie' were present in the spirit world. Though Haig did not have the time to visit Miss McCreadie as often as his sister, those visits he did make were too frequent to be explained as idle curiosity. He did not doubt the ability of some mediums to communicate with spirits. Whilst he dismissed one as 'a great fraud', others, including

117

Miss McCreadie, were trusted implicitly. He was impressed when, on another visit, the spirit of Hector MacDonald, the hero of Omdurman, was raised and 'a guitar was played in mid-air'. But the sessions he enjoyed most were those in which he was given a glimpse of his own future. They were undoubtedly attractive because they invariably revealed glorious successes. Psychic or not, Miss McCreadie had the sense to tell her subject exactly what he wanted to hear.[4]

On 3 February 1907, Henrietta warned her brother that she had learned from a medium that the 'Germans intend to invade England and that letters pretending to be English but really emanating from Berlin will appear in the Press, accusing Haldane of aiming at conscription'. An alarmed Haig concluded, 'The object . . . [is] to prevent England from having a national Army.' Haig passed the information on to Haldane who, betraying his rationalism, 'thought it most interesting, but not of the spirit world'.[5]

Spiritualism was one of the many subjects upon which Haig and Haldane – two very different individuals – diverged. They nevertheless got on splendidly. Their harmonious relationship resulted in part from their similar goals regarding reform of the Army and their realisation of the assistance each could provide to the other. Haldane felt that Haig possessed a 'first-rate General Staff mind' – a not inaccurate appraisal when it is considered that the British conception of the General Staff was traditionally that of a purely administrative body. 'When he arrived in London', Haldane later wrote of Haig, 'he grasped the situation completely and gave invaluable advice.'[6]

Haig was likewise immediately impressed with Haldane. 'He is a big fat man with a kind genial face. One seemed to like the man at once.' Haldane conflicted with Haig's preconceptions regarding politicians; in fact, he seemed 'a most clear-headed and practical man. Most ready to listen and weigh carefully all that is said to him.' But, rather than accepting that his preconceptions might perhaps be wrong, Haig chose instead to see Haldane as an exception to the general rule. His disdain for the men in frock coats survived unscathed. But it is ironic that what Haig admired most in Haldane was his ability to get things done, usually by manipulating, courting favour or cleverly finding a way around opponents. By any objective definition, these were the skills of the politician. But Haig would not have seen it that way. Politicians were sordid, self-seeking and ungentlemanly. If they used some of the same shady techniques as Haldane or even himself, the difference, in both his and Haldane's case, was that these techniques were employed for noble purposes and were therefore sanctified in the process.[7]

Haldane has, with justification, been called Britain's greatest War Minister. But great though he may have been, there is a danger of exaggerating his accomplishments and therefore of Haig's contribution to them. The issue is complicated by the fact that Haldane became a popular scapegoat for the British failures in the Great War. Post-war criticism inspired Haldane's two polemical autobiographies which were clearly attempts at self-justification. In other words, Haldane should not be taken at his word. What he failed to achieve and what he left alone are almost as important as his actual accomplishments. For instance, his primary objective was never to prepare Britain for war, despite post-war claims to the contrary:

> I became aware at once that there was a new army problem. It was, how to mobilise and concentrate at a place of assembly to be opposite the Belgian frontier, a force calculated as adequate . . . to make up the inadequacies of the French armies for their great task of defending the entire French frontier.

Haig also encouraged this misconception. After the war, he dedicated a volume of his despatches to Haldane, 'in grateful remembrance of his successful efforts in organising the Military Forces for a War on the Continent'. Though this may have been the effect of Haldane's efforts, it was not their intent.[8]

Haldane's first priority was to make the Army as efficient and professional as possible within the confines of a low budget and the popular abhorrence of compulsory service. These restrictions, not the requirements of a continental strategy (as Haldane later claimed), shaped the reform. Had he really intended to prepare for war, he would have pushed for larger Army estimates and a compulsory service law. He would also have paid closer attention to strategy and tactics, areas which, it will be seen, he virtually ignored. Had he pursued these wider goals, he would probably have failed. The country would not have accepted the massive militarisation of society which a continental strategy implied. Thus, Haldane achieved the maximum possible. His reform programme was a political solution to a military problem. As such, it was incomplete and inadequate.

119

The Haldane reforms can be grouped into three general areas. The first encompasses the structuring of Army commands, the creation of a reserve army and the formation of the British Expeditionary Force. The second area includes the measures leading to the development of a General Staff, the third that of an Imperial General Staff. Of the three areas the most important and the most difficult was the first. What was needed was a force that could be easily mobilised and quickly expanded on the outbreak of war. Esher had provided few guidelines. Haldane's predecessors had stumbled in this area, and consequently proceeded no further.

On the question of a reserve army, Haldane benefited considerably from the failures of his predecessors. Both Arnold-Forster and St John Brodrick had tried to create a reserve by increasing the terms of service (the time spent with the colours and the reserves) of the Regular Army. This meant a very long-term commitment; the individual had essentially to make soldiering a career. Without compulsion, the number of men willing to do this was bound to be small. A reserve force, no matter how the terms of service were juggled, could not, therefore, grow to an adequate size. Haldane decided that another source of manpower had to be tapped, namely the auxiliary forces (Militia, Yeomanry and Volunteers) which were composed of men who, though unwilling to become career soldiers, were eager to serve their country on a part-time basis.[9]

The idea appears remarkable in its simplicity. The existing, some-what ramshackle collection of forces would be neatly converted into a two-tiered system of Regulars and Territorials. But though the auxiliaries were a ready source of manpower, they were not a dependable one, being deficient in leadership, training, organisation and supply. Their size was prey to the whims of national conscience, and they were neither intended nor prepared for service overseas. Raised in separate localities, the standards of each auxiliary unit varied widely. From this very raw material Haldane had to create a force capable of mobilisation at the outbreak of war and ready to fight abroad after a short period of preparation.

The auxiliary forces had, therefore, to undergo a drastic transformation into a single military unit complete in all arms and services. This entailed the surrender of each force's original identity. It was here that the real difficulties, ones which Haldane failed to anticipate, arose. The auxiliaries had a distinguished reputation which, though disproportionate to their actual military value, carried weight in the political arena. Officers were very often members of the landed gentry and were either MPs or had other means of exerting political pressure. The Militia, a force older than the Regular Army, was especially reluctant to surrender its identity. The Volunteers and Yeomanry, though neither as old nor as adamantly opposed to amalgamation, were nevertheless determined to be difficult. Their reluctance was based partly on the proposed structure of the Territorial Force. Haldane planned to create uniform county associations which would handle administration but not command. The latter would be shifted to the crown and the General Staff. The officers of existing auxiliary units correctly perceived that what the government intended was to leave them with the dreary responsibility of recruiting, organising and administering their units, whilst depriving them of the glory of command.

Probably because he was too ready to delegate authority to others, Haldane did not at first understand the feelings of those opposed to reform. He especially did not appreciate that the opposition was not of one mind. For this reason, his initial attempts to negotiate on a bilateral basis with auxiliary representatives failed miserably. Solutions which were acceptable to the Yeomanry or Volunteers were vetoed by the Militia. Finally, in August, he tried a different approach. Abandoning the large and unwieldy committees, he decided to meet auxiliary representatives individually, the aim being to fragment the opposition into distinct groups and to deal with the interests of each separately. It was expected that Haig's reputation as a distinguished cavalryman would enable him to play an influential part in the negotiations. Unfortunately, Haig, the proverbial bull in a china shop, did not make the best negotiator, being impatient with contrary opinions, and ironically, intolerant of traditionalist views. But, in spite of his deficiencies, agreement was somehow reached with the Yeomanry, the weakest of the three forces. The Volunteers, however, were another matter entirely: 'They won't have the associations constituted as proposed at any price,'[10] Haig complained to Esher. He could not understand and was quite disgusted with the objections to what he saw as a workable system for a modernised Army.

These were frustrating times for Haldane and his aides. The unexpected intransigence of the opposition caused a great deal of ill-temper in the War Office. When, on 12 November, the Military Members of Council complained about proposals for reorganising the Militia, Haig speculated that the issue was 'only an excuse to show they are really angry because S. of S. does not consult them enough!' A similar explanation might apply to the rather petty complaints which the CGS (Lieutenant-General Sir William Nicholson) made to Haig later in the day:

> He very shirty. Tells me not to be absent on Saturdays without his approval! and wants all papers from S. of S. to be given him at once. This not my affair as these papers go to him before coming to me, but shows how angry he is. The result of someone stirring him up, no doubt Douglas backed up by Miles!

Two months later, Haig described how 'Fleetwood Wilson comes into my room during the operation and criticises severely the way in which he has been ignored in the matter of the new scheme. Miles also finds fault.' It was, on the whole, 'A terrible day of criticism.' Around every corner there were bruised egos. Miles (Director of Organisation and Recruiting) and Wilson (Director General of Army Finance), among others, objected to Haig because of his closeness to Haldane. The latter, no admirer of protocol, gathered around him those men with whom he felt he could work best, and ignored the others. Haig was delighted to be one of the chosen, but would undoubtedly have been as upset as Miles and Wilson had he been in their shoes.[11]

The struggle with the stubborn auxiliary commanders continued until mid-February. Haldane, demoralised and disoriented, at one time considered abandoning the entire scheme, but, due to some timely encouragement from the ever-confident Haig, decided to soldier on. He could have forced the new programme upon the local commanders through legislation, but in so doing would have encountered considerable resistance in Parliament. Also, the success of the Territorial Force depended on the willingness of ex-auxiliary members to join it. There was a risk of that willingness evaporating if legislative coercion was used.

The Volunteers and Yeomanry, through a series of intricate agreements, finally accepted the Haldane scheme. The Militia, however, remained intransigent. Legislative force therefore became inevitable.

Haldane decided to abolish the Militia, but placated its members by proposing the establishment of a Special Reserve to act as an immediate reinforcement to the Regular Army. The Special Reserve was to be the exclusive refuge of the displaced Militiamen. The Militia would lose its name, but not, it was argued, its identity.

This was the exclusivity which the Militia coveted. Though some diehards remained, the Special Reserve idea substantially weakened the opposition. Haldane's proposals were explained to the Commons during his speech on the second Army Estimates on 25 February. The speech was well received, and thus gave him the mandate to proceed with the Territorial and Reserve Forces Act. The parliamentary opposition to the act which Haldane had expected did not in fact materialise. Most MPs found the bill excessively dull, and debates were not well attended. The bill was passed by 286 votes to 63 on 19 June 1907. It went into effect on 1 April 1908.

The passage of Haldane's bill brought to an end the first phase of Haig's service at the War Office. His work on the Territorial Force scheme had not been ideally suited to his talents. He abhorred the 'smoke filled room', was uncomfortable among strangers and had little patience for opinions different from his own. Whilst his assistance in formulating the mechanics of the scheme was valuable, his tactlessness at times impeded effective negotiation. Haldane admitted as much when, after Haig's departure from the War Office in 1909, he remarked, 'Haig always infuriated Miles by his manner, and it may be easier now.'[12] Haldane nevertheless continued to support Haig, probably realising that, with the passage of the Territorial Forces Act, negotiation would give way to administration, a task to which Haig was more suited.

While the wrangling over the reserve army was proceeding, the reformers were also engaged in the much easier task of creating the British Expeditionary Force (BEF). Before 1907, a proper expeditionary force did not exist. The Army was little more than a collection of regiments with only one suitably organised corps at Aldershot. The Army Order of 1 January 1907 provided for the coordination of this disorganised mass into one cavalry and six infantry divisions. This force (totalling 120,000 men) was intended for rapid mobilisation on the outbreak of war. With the subsequent passage of the Territorial Forces Act, the two-tier system which Haldane had envisaged was in place.

The BEF which was created by the Army Order of 1907 was essentially the force that went to war in 1914, with the rapidity that had been intended. But it must again be emphasised that neither the size nor the composition of this force was dictated by a continental strategy. On the contrary, the Army Order was mainly a pragmatic response to the financial restraints imposed by the Liberal government. In its pre-1907 form, the Army was wasteful and inefficient. By consolidating into seven major commands, waste could be reduced and the Army could reach its maximum possible size within the limits of its budget. It is important to note that this consolidation meant having to reduce the numerical strength of the Army (some field batteries and infantry battalions were retired) in order to balance the books. The cavalry, perhaps because of Haig's influence, was, significantly, left untouched.

The creation of the BEF did not magically provide Britain with a force of 120,000 men ready to fight on the Continent within fourteen days. This was the intent; the actuality would follow years of hard work. It was to this problem that Haig directed his attention after the fight for Haldane's bill. Among a wide variety of tasks, his work included organising staff tours, formulating mobilisation plans, inspecting troops, devising training schemes, and carrying out mock embarkations and disembarkations. The emphasis was upon uniformity, efficiency and preparedness, thus Haig was particularly well suited to the work. Though technically Director of Military Training, his duties were never confined to those formally within the purview of that directorate.

In analysing the Liberal response to the problem of Army reform, one cannot ignore the fact that it was mainly a political problem assigned to a master politician. Haldane's main objective was to implement the Esher Report, to push the changes outlined in that report past opponents in Parliament, the Army and the country. Once basic approval was secured (as with the passage of the Territorial Forces Act and the Army Order) the details were left to others. Haldane, as has been argued, 'came to rely upon officers who sympathised with his own objectives, who could think clearly and who grasped the detailed implications of Army Reform: he came to rely, above all, upon Douglas Haig'.[13] In this arrangement, Haldane was a passive, and at times not very attentive, overseer. This meant that the detailed contents of his reforms reflected not so much his thinking as that of his closest advisers.

It also meant that Haldane ignored and even ostracised those who disagreed with him. The War Office became dominated by Haldane men, men implicitly loyal to their chief and his plan. Others, because they disagreed with the Territorial Force scheme or other reforms, were not asked to contribute. These included men like Plumer, Roberts and Henry Wilson who, especially in the field of tactics and strategy, had much to offer. (Though Wilson, as DMO, was influential in BEF mobilisation planning.) The loyalists, on the other hand, were rewarded by being given a free hand to shape the Army as they saw fit within Haldane's broad outlines. In Haig's case, this meant that War Office funding was provided for an extraordinary number of cavalry staff tours similar (in the traditionalist sense) to those he had conducted in India. The cavalry reaction of the pre-war years, including the reinstitution of the lance and the publication of the revised *Cavalry Training*, was tacitly encouraged by Haldane's non-involvement. In this ideal environment, Haig's conservatism flourished.

The implications of Haldane's approach were particularly evident in the case of the Territorial Artillery. It had been intended that the Territorial Force would be complete in all arms — a nice idea, but difficult to achieve. The country did not possess the modern guns to equip the reserve army properly. In addition, modern artillery tactics required a degree of expertise which was impossible to attain within the short training period of the Territorial Force. Frightened by the prospect of ill-equipped and ill-trained batteries, Lord Roberts came to the conclusion that it would be better if the Territorial Force had no artillery contingent at all. Reserve batteries, he argued in the Lords, would not 'in spite of their numbers, be of the slightest use in the field'; instead, they would be a 'positive danger'.[14]

For Roberts, the question came down to whether quantity was desirable if quality was absent. He, of course, thought it was not, Haldane and his cohorts were equally certain that it was. In his campaign for Universal Service, Roberts had tried to establish a system which ensured both quantity and quality – in other words, a large force and the time to train it properly. But the Territorial Forces Act dealt his campaign a mortal blow. The act provided the large force but skimped on the training. Roberts, the soldier, abhorred this half-baked system. Haldane, the pragmatic politician, saw it as the only possible solution to the nation's requirements. He was not overly agitated if the force he created was technically deficient: the important point was that it existed. The technical aspects were the concern of the Army proper, not his Ministry. He had done the best he could, in spite of a parsimonious government and a weak-willed nation.

It is difficult to argue with Haldane's pragmatism. A more principled man might have achieved less. On the question of the Territorial Artillery, however, Roberts was right. Gunnery was not an area in which one could profitably cut corners. Roberts' advice was ignored because he was not one of the 'chosen'; his campaign for Universal Service had made life difficult for Haldane. The Secretary of State instead relied upon the loyalists, some of whom had little knowledge of artillery matters. One such was Haig.

Haldane's pragmatism is understandable, Haig's less so. He, it seems, should have insisted upon higher standards, especially since, as DMT, he witnessed for himself the low level of expertise of both reserve and regular artillery units. In June and July 1907, he staged a number of field firing exercises in which the Regular Artillery, Royal Horse Artillery and batteries from the auxiliaries practised together, in the hope that the part-timers would learn from the professionals. It soon became evident, however, that the standards of the latter were not worthy of imitation. One exercise was described as 'rather a farce'. None of them inspired praise. But what is surprising is Haig's apparent lack of concern at what he observed. The diary suggests a man out of his depth who was simply going through the motions – a cavalryman who did not really understand the technical nature of modern artillery. His old bugbears were evident: he complained about meddling commanders, the lack of independence given to subordinates and 'cut and dried schemes'. But hardly any comments were made on the technical aspects of the firing: the aim, range, accuracy, cover, organisation, etc. Whilst he may have been right about the points he stressed, it is questionable how valuable his inspections and advice were if his Boer War experience and the teachings of the Staff College left him with little respect for the arm's potential.[15]

As Director of Military Training, Haig was concerned with preparing the BEF and Territorial Force for war. With regard to the latter, this initially meant deciding upon the size of the force and the quotas required from the various county associations. Ignorant of political and financial limitations, Haig at first envisaged a force of 900,000 men. Haldane settled for a more realistic 300,000, but did not, ultimately, even achieve this. Haig was better suited to the more straightforward administrative details of the Territorial Force such as the formation of a transport section and the coordination of infantry training procedures. The immense amount of work and its elementary nature demonstrate how very raw was the raw material of the Territorial Force.

These somewhat mundane tasks were put aside when Haig moved from the DMT to the DSD in November 1907. With the transfer, both directorates were redesigned to suit his abilities. As he explained, 'all education (except Staff College) pass[es] to DMT and war organisation go[es] to DSD'. This meant that 'DSD will have sufficient officers to work out "Principles of employment of troops" and other fundamental questions which have hitherto been ignored'. He did not elaborate on what these 'fundamental questions' were, but one supposes that he hoped Britain would edge closer to the ideal of the German General Staff.[16]

An examination of Haig's accomplishments as DSD lends credence to this supposition, but it also reveals that he did not understand the enormity of the task. On the surface, his achievements are impressive. As DSD, Haig was at last able to address himself to the obstacles to professionalisation. This meant reforming the staff training programme and the policies governing employment of staff officers. For instance, he attacked patronage by forcing through a ruling whereby commanding officers were required to take the staff officers assigned to them (in other words, Camberley graduates), rather than being allowed to choose their own. Haig also established a system for allocating staff positions with the Territorial Force to Camberley men, thus extending the areas in which valuable experience could be gained. He also tried to create 'War Schools', where senior staff officers could study higher strategy and tactics, but, through no fault of his own, the schools unfortunately were not fully operational prior to the Great War.

Though wise in theory, these changes are examples of Haig's limitations as a military reformer. If, as seems to have been the case, he was interested in establishing a 'brain of the Army' on the German model, as opposed to a purely administrative staff, not simply new institutions, but an even more radical and widespread change of attitude across the entire Army was required. Promising young soldiers had to be taught to think creatively about tactics and strategy. Senior officers open-minded enough to teach them had to be found. And 'old soldiers' had to be shown that the days of Britain's omnipotent commanders were past.

There are two main reasons why Haig was not the man to bring about such a fundamental change of attitude. The first was his mixture of administrative progressivism and tactical conservativism. He had been chosen for Haldane's team because his organisational abilities were relevant to an Army in need of structural modernisation. But whenever an open mind to progress in tactics and strategy was required, Haig's limitations were revealed. His cavalry mind was out of touch with the new age of military science. Thus, whilst capable of establishing institutions or formulating policies necessary to a 'brain of the Army', he could not inspire it to think nor benefit from its thought.

A second, equally important, reason for Haig's inadequacy was that he was not altogether different from those men whose minds he sought to change. The ideals of leadership which he had been taught at the Staff College conflicted with those inherent in the German system. In addition, on a personal level, though Haig professed a belief in the value of highly trained, independent staff officers, as has been seen, with regard to his own staff, he admitted that he preferred loyal men of average intelligence. Thus, Haig in many ways resembled the traditional omnipotent commander who surrounded himself with sycophants while he continued to do things his way. Though he may in principle have sympathised with the ideals of the German system, his basic nature prevented him from understanding its ultimate implications.

One of Haig's most important achievements as DSD was his success in forcing the publication of *Field Service Regulations*. The manual, the first of its kind in British military history, was designed to provide staff officers with detailed directions covering every conceivable wartime contingency. As such, it stressed a degree of efficiency and standardisation which had previously been lacking. 'Without these manuals', writes Corelli Barnett, 'the colossal expansion of the British and Dominion Armies during the Great War must have resulted in military chaos.'[17]

Haig has, on occasion, been given too much credit for *FSR*.[18] It was not his creation. His main contribution came in forcing the manual past hesitant senior officers, primarily by organising staff tours which demonstrated the viability of its principles. As to the content, Haig's influence is most evident in the sections covering cavalry action. Though the manual reveals an appreciation of the wisdom of arming cavalry with rifles, there is no concomitant acceptance of the relative obsolescence of the *arme blanche* or of the primacy of dismounted over mounted action. Cavalry's ability to 'combine attack and surprise to the best advantage' is stressed in a way which gives one the impression that the machine-gun was yet to be invented.[19]

With regard to dismounted action and the *arme blanche*, Haig's attitude had not changed at all. At the same time that he was working on *FSR* (the 'modern' manual), he was also completing *Cavalry Studies* and pushing for the reinstitution of the lance. During his time as DSD he staged a large number of cavalry manoeuvres which were of a decidedly traditional bent. Though the supervision of these exercises was not one of his stated duties, he attended them, as is clear from the following, so as to be certain that heretical doctrines would not be practised:

> attended meeting at 10:30 a.m. of Brigadiers and C.O.s with Inspector General (Sir J. French). Latter very complimentary to me – said I had nothing to gain from the extra work I had undertaken in training the Cavalry Division etc. etc. but gave vent to some real heresies such as chief aim of Cavalry Division in battle is their rifle fire: led horses to be moved and men need not be close to them.

Haig disagreed, emphasising that 'Cavalry should *always* go for its adversary.' The prospect of these two men clashing over cavalry doctrine was a novel one It will be recalled that French wrote in 1903 that nothing could make him alter the views that he held on cavalry. Yet something had changed his mind, however slightly. Haig's mind, meanwhile, remained closed.[20]

The final area of concern during Haig's service at the War Office was the formation of an Imperial General Staff. The intention was to expand the organisation of the General Staff so as to make it applicable to the rest of the Empire. Towards this end Haig did what he could do best: he prepared studies and formulated plans for the unification, standardisation and cooperation of Imperial forces. Haldane confessed that he 'could not have had finer help' in this area than he had from Haig. As the War Secretary pointed out, previous attempts at Imperial unity had failed because of the 'desire of the old War Office to centralise authority'. Under the plan formulated by Haig (with the assistance of Nicholson), the Dominions were allowed greater autonomy. 'All we asked of them was that they should organise on our pattern local sections of their own of the General Staff, and should appoint to them officers who had a General Staff training at headquarters and in the Staff College.'[21]

The scheme was approved at the Imperial Conference on 21 April 1909. This completed Haig's major tasks at the War Office. He spent the rest of the year on mundane chores which he would probably have preferred to leave to someone else. When the opportunity to become Chief of the Indian General Staff was offered, he gave the appointment due consideration and eventually accepted.

The years in London had been hectic. Haig's days were spent busily at the War Office, his nights at social gatherings or in consultation with Haldane into the wee hours. Haldane thrived on the long nights, rich food, strong drink, huge cigars and endless debate. Haig did not. His fitness declined as his physical activity dwindled and he put on weight. It was not an environment conducive to the abatement of his hypochondria. He rushed off to continental spas in search of elusive cures and consulted quack doctors, including a 'magnetic health giver' who was seen every other day for a month. Anxious inquiries were made to spiritualists about the state of his health. During 1908, a mysterious illness confined him to bed for over a month. He recovered completely, but was left with a firm conviction that this was not the type of life for him.[22]

In February 1909, Haig and Haldane had a conversation about the future. 'We discussed objects for which [the] Army and Expeditionary Force exist. He is in no doubt – viz. to support France and Russia against Germany and perhaps Austria. By organising war may be prevented.'[23] On first reading, this may seem to contradict the argument that Haldane made up his foresight in retrospect. In fact it does not. The continuing Anglo-German naval rivalry and other disagreements had, by 1909, convinced Haldane and most others in the know that Germany would be the enemy in an impending war. This knowledge may have influenced the tempo of reform, but it did not determine its shape. The size of the Army which Haldane created – a small fraction of the German force – is adequate proof that the German threat was not, as he claimed in his autobiography, the primary influence in determining the nature of his reforms.

In the end, war was not prevented. But neither Haig nor Haldane ever doubted that they had done their best to prepare the country for war. The picture which Haldane presented in *Before the War* is of a noble and heroic crusade. Similarly, Haig claimed in 1918 that 'the organisation of the Army *for War*' originated from the time he and Haldane were together. Before then, 'no one knew for what purpose our Army existed!'[24] But, as is understandable, neither man was an unbiased judge. The struggles in the War Office caused them to exaggerate their perspicacity and their achievements. They did indeed do their best, but their best could never have been good enough.

The achievements of both were incomplete because of their respective limitations. Haig was limited by his blinkered approach to strategy and tactics; the cavalry traditionalist could never be an open-minded reformer. For instance, though he accepted the value of the machine-gun and modern artillery, he believed that both could be incorporated into a strategy in which the cavalry's role remained unaffected. He recognised the likelihood of a European war and was familiar with the size and sophistication of European armies, but this did not lead him toward a realisation that the clash of these great armies would result in a completely different type of war. Haig did not understand that the science of war is fluid. As a result, the Army he helped to create, though superficially more efficient, still stressed Victorian, small war, tactical principles. Furthermore, Haig was limited as a reformer because he saw an administrative solution to every problem. He did not understand that reforming men's minds, or his own mind for that matter, was far more difficult than setting up a new institutional framework.

Haldane, on the other hand, was limited by his pragmatic acceptance of what he could and could not achieve. He reformed only what he could reform. What he could not change, or was not bothered to change, he left alone. And it is significant that much of what he left alone he left to Haig. It was an effective political partnership. Haldane and Haig exchanged loyalty to each other for assistance in implementing their respective pet projects. Their achievements were above all political ones, born of compromise, and therefore incomplete.

Haig's period at the War Office was in keeping with the new focus to his career which began after the Boer War. His position in the Army was further consolidated. He had demonstrated his devotion to the Army and his acceptance of the need for reform. Despite three years working with politicians, he successfully avoided being labelled a political soldier. Thus, his prospects were enhanced. In other respects, however, the period had little effect upon him. He did not himself undergo reform. There was in fact a negative side to the years in the War Office. Ever since his work with Fraser in 1894 – with the sole exception of a brief and unspectacular period in the Sudan – his duties had been predominantly administrative. His service with Haldane was a continuation of this trend and thus a reinforcement of the attitudes it inevitably engendered. Haig had, quite unintentionally, become an 'office' soldier. For too much of his career he was far too removed from the command of men. The gulf between him and the common soldier was dangerously wide.

7

Many Important Questions

By 1909, Haig was certain that a European war loomed and that Britain had little time to prepare herself. It is therefore curious that he chose at this point to leave the centre of military activity for an assignment at its outer reaches, namely, Chief of the General Staff in India.

Indian military administration had changed in the three years since Haig's departure, but it was hardly less chaotic than it had been. As a result of Kitchener's victory over Curzon, the posts of Commander-in-Chief and First Military Member were henceforth occupied by one man. This was an inadequate reform since the administrative apparatus connected to each office was left virtually untouched. The posts were fused, not amalgamated, with the inevitable result that 'all important cases came before the Commander-in-Chief twice, each time submitted by different subordinates, who probably each advocated different and often contradictory solutions to the same problem. Cases were not unknown of the Commander-in-Chief disagreeing with himself as Army Member.'[1] Ordinarily, this was the sort of tangle which Haig would have delighted in unravelling. But, as CGS in India, Haig would not have the power and authority he had had under Haldane. He would be able to suggest changes but he could not initiate policy. Essentially, he would have to tolerate the chaos and try to soldier on in spite of it.

Memories of past problems and an apprehension of future ones caused Haig to decline the post of CGS when the Commander-in-Chief, Sir O'Moore Creagh, offered it on 15 March 1909:

> I declined at first saying that I was so fully engaged on the Imperial General Staff and other important matters – besides the Simla people

133

were such a crooked lot I could not work with them! He replied that he would like to join with me in ousting the rascals! and I could think the matter over for a week!

The excuse Haig gave to Brigadier-General Launcelot Kiggell, his assistant at the DSD, was that he 'would rather stay at home' because going to India would mean 'leaving the children here, and my wife coming out with me and visiting them each winter etc'. Creagh, however, persisted and Haig finally relented. Taking into account all his reservations, it seems curious that he accepted the post.[2]

The best explanation is probably the standard one: duty. As he explained to Kiggell on 24 April, 'on thinking the matter over, and looking at the importance of starting a General Staff in India, weeding out Simla and developing the Imperial General Staff, I thought it best I should go'. He elaborated three days later:

> As regards meeting 'the storm' which we all foresee, it seems to me that it will take a long time, we'll win by wearing the enemy out, if we are only allowed three more years to prepare and organise the Empire. And it is of vital importance to have the machinery available in India trained as soon as possible to turn out Staff Officers who may be of use when the time comes, and the resources of that country organised for *Imperial* needs, instead of only for India's at present.

Haig loyally accepted what was for him an unpleasant assignment because, as he told Kiggell, 'I honestly believe that I can do more good [in India] than here during the next three years.'[3]

Haig delayed his departure in order to find a suitable replacement for himself at the DSD. He had in mind someone who could be trusted not to tamper with the system he had established. After some deliberation, Kiggell (who was, conveniently, a traditional cavalryman) emerged as the obvious choice. 'If I can only arrange to get you here, while I am C of S in India', Haig told Kiggell, 'we might do much towards creating the beginnings of an Imperial General Staff.' Kiggell seemed malleable enough to control from faraway India. 'I am very eager that you should succeed me here in order to ensure continuity,' Haig wrote; adding, almost as an afterthought, 'not to mention that you are the best man for the job'. It took some effort to convince Kiggell, a man of low self-esteem, that he was indeed the right choice. 'I don't agree with your views on Brigadier Kiggell, nor do you correctly value the importance of "continuity".' In the end, it was impossible to resist Haig's powers of persuasion. When Kiggell agreed, Haig called it a 'triumph for ability and honesty over incapacity and intrigue'. With virtue triumphant, he had 'great hope for the future of the General Staff'. It was safe to go to India.[4]

Haig arrived in Bombay on 22 October 1909. Though far removed from the War Office, his attentions did not stray from matters there. Fortnightly letters were sent to Kiggell, who treated Haig's suggestions as if they were commands – probably in the way they were intended. Advice was proffered on changes to the Staff College curriculum, on promising candidates for Camberley and on others deemed unworthy. When reforms of the entrance exam were being considered, Haig recommended dropping the mathematics portion, a suggestion undoubtedly inspired by the still acute pains of 1893. 'It seems to me almost impossible to set a simple mathematics paper without having catch questions in it.' Despite his failure, he had not 'found any need for a more thorough knowledge of mathematics than [I] already possess!' Where possible, Kiggell put these recommendations into effect. When, in July 1910, it became apparent that his lackey was considering accepting the post of Commandant of the Staff College, Haig's reaction was swift. '*On no account* should you go to the Staff College. The development of the General Staff will be thrown back for many years if you leave your present job now.' He elaborated:

Besides with as many *talkers* at W.O. – Aldershot – Camberley and elsewhere who know not what war really is, nor Clausewitz' Fundamentals, the whole show may be wrecked unless you are in a responsible position and able to put a stopper in the windbags' mouths! I already see from your discussion of the Staff College Conference a tendency to split hairs, and a desire for *precise* rules to guide officers in every conceivable situation in war. This wants watching. Only a man of character like yourself can produce the right corrective . . . but you must remain where you can insist on *principles of employment* of the Army being thoroughly sound.

Kiggell eventually went to the Staff College in March 1914, but for the time being did as he was told.[5]

Haig's complaints about the 'talkers' at the War Office referred to the attacks upon the *FSR*, which had been renewed in his absence. It was necessary to stiffen Kiggell's resistance to this dangerous meddling:

> As regards the Adjutant General's attack on Field Service Regulations . . . Taken as a whole the book is in my opinion excellent, and . . . the principles being absolutely sound can easily be applied without friction! . . . it would cause a great deal of trouble if any change in principles were started now, and any change ought not to be made without full discussion and the general concurrence of all concerned.[6]

According to Haig, *FSR*, though perhaps imperfect, was better than no manual at all, and its complete abandonment would mean chaos in wartime. He was right on this score. The Army did not have time to begin anew.

The argument over *FSR* boiled over into the pages of *The Times*. Charles A'Court Repington, the paper's military correspondent, judged the manual a failure because it did not set forth clear guidelines for the employment of the BEF in a European war. In his report on the 1911 Indian Staff Tour, Haig made a thinly veiled reference to Repington and his followers:

> Certain critics of the British General Staff and of our regulations have recently argued that a doctrine is lacking . . . the critics urge that the British General Staff hesitates to teach and to publish a clear line of action. The reason[ing] seems to be that unless some such definite doctrine is decided and inculcated in time of peace, action in war will be hesitating and mistakes will be made. The critics seem to lose sight of the true nature of war, and of the varied conditions under which the British army may have to take the field. It is neither necessary nor desirable that we should go further than what is clearly laid down in our regulations. If we go further, we run the risk of tying ourselves by a doctrine that may not always be applicable and we gain nothing in return.

Haig repeatedly stressed that 'with our normal Army of 6 Divisions we must try to have a little generalship'. The British response, he wisely realised, would be determined largely by Germany and

France. His advocacy of tactical flexibility is indeed impressive. But it must be remembered Haig was prone to divorce principles from practice. Tactical flexibility, easy to preach in peacetime, was less easy to achieve in war. One must therefore take care not to assume that, simply because Haig advocated 'a little generalship' in 1911, he demonstrated the same during the Great War.[7]

Nor should a few hints of insight in an Indian Staff Tour report be taken as evidence of a successful twenty-six month tour of duty.[8] Haig's diaries and his letters to Kiggell reveal that the period was primarily one of disappointment and failure. He went to India, as he had indicated, with two well-defined goals. First, he wanted to develop the Indian General Staff along the lines agreed at the Imperial Conference. Secondly, he wanted to prepare the Indian Army for its responsibility *vis-à-vis* the rest of the Empire in a future European war by directing the focus of attention away from its customary internal peacekeeping function. As it turned out, he failed to achieve either of these goals. His failure was due not to personal shortcomings, but because it was impossible to achieve significant progress within the disorganised system of Indian military administration and because the internal threat to stability could not be wished away.[9]

The diaries are full of examples of Haig's frustration. When he tried to devise plans for mobilising the Indian Army in the event of a European war, the Viceroy, Lord Hardinge, intervened and ordered him to destroy the plans. With regard to his efforts to set up a cavalry staff school, he commented that he was 'much annoyed by the way in which all work is held up, and keenness of staff dampened by delay'. Conditions surprisingly seemed worse than during his previous tour in India. He was particularly annoyed with the organisation of the cavalry; standards had fallen drastically from when he was Inspector General. Angered at finding officers often in the same rank as when he last saw them six years earlier, he complained how 'difficult [it is] to have efficiency in the I.A. with such slow promotion'.[10]

Most frustrating of all was how little he could do to alleviate these problems. Despite his earlier experience, Haig underestimated the monolithic obstructions built into the Indian military bureaucracy. The system did not lend itself to rapid reform; nor did diehards in the Army welcome zealous outsiders bent upon change. Even Creagh, who had promised to help Haig 'oust the rascals', had himself rascally tendencies. A veteran of forty years' service in the Indian Army, he did not welcome disruption of his comfortable niche. Since any changes in the Indian system were bound to come up against the opposition of the meddlesome Hardinge, it was essential that Haig be supported in his work by Creagh. Haig was, however, disgusted to find that 'the C. in C. wishes to oblige the Viceroy because the latter is so agreeable to him, and says that he (the Chief) should not pay house rent but that his residence should be furnished and kept up like that of a Lord Governor of a Province!' Just before his departure from India in late 1911, Haig predicted that

> the Viceroy and the C. in C. will be glad when I cease to be CGS here. The Viceroy is not at all pleased with the lines taken in the G.S. memo . . . and the poor C. in C. is under the influence of us both, and has consequently given contrary opinions from time to time!

In Britain, Haig's work on the General Staff system had been aided by a number of men who shared his goals. With the opposite the case in India, with obstacles around every corner, he failed. Since the administrative reform of the Indian General Staff was central to Haig's plan of preparing the Indian Army for war, his inability to achieve anything significant was all the more worrying.[11]

Equally worrying was the precarious loyalty of the Indian soldier and the country as a whole. The possibility of insurrection was always on Haig's mind, as evidenced by some random notes which he recorded not long before he left:

> We have reverted to the conditions which prevailed when John Lawrence spoke of *safety* rather than *power* as the primary requirement of the Army in India . . . At present Army's special function is as a reserve of the forces of law and order. It being a mercenary Army its loyalty must be bought and cannot be presumed.

Haig warned of the 'danger of *sweating* the Indian Army in the cause of military efficiency' and the concomitant 'danger of giving Sikhs a partial monopoly of military service'. The cause of internal stability was not helped by the fact that 'the ignorance of some of the old officers regarding the various Indian societies and what has been going on for some years is very remarkable'. In a letter to Kiggell, Haig explained what he was doing to correct this deficiency:

We are . . . arranging for a certain number of regimental officers to tour in the districts from which they recruit to get to know the Indians of importance and also the civil officials. The latter must work hand in hand with the soldier now in order to combat the enemy who is already in the field you may say. I think the General Staff here has made a good beginning in organising to meet the internal enemy.

But Haig's efforts could never be more than a drop in a bucket. If it is considered that one of his goals was to redirect the focus of the Indian Army from the internal to the external function, his diaries and letters are proof that he was unable to do so. By the end of his tour questions of internal stability occupied the greatest part of his attention.[12]

The disappointments of India caused Haig to become preoccupied with affairs in Britain and alert to the possibility of an early return. In his mind, a confrontation with Germany was inevitable. He had no desire to be caught in India when it began. Aware, however, that it was not proper to appear too eager to return home, he was cagey in his reply to Kiggell's suggestion that he might soon be given the Aldershot command:

I much appreciate the friendly remarks about myself and what you want me to become in the near future . . . As to going to Aldershot there are too many applicants I expect for that billet for the powers to [sic] be to think of me. In any case I have never asked for an appointment and I don't intend to begin now – besides I am full of work here and could not leave those who have most loyally supported me in difficult times for another year at least. I should then have done three training sessions out of my allotted four!

It is true that Haig never asked for an appointment. His technique was more subtle. He would send letters like the above to friends expressing interest in a post while simultaneously insisting that his only concern was to do his duty. This usually had the desired effect. It certainly did in this case. Haldane offered the Aldershot appointment to Haig five weeks after the above letter. He left India on 23 December 1911. It was apparently easier for him to leave his 'loyal supporters' than he had anticipated. 'The situation at home is more important at the present time than India,' he explained to Kiggell. 'I shall be glad to be close at hand to discuss personally, the many important questions which may be under consideration by the General Staff.' He was equally glad, no doubt, to be leaving the Indian backwater.[13]

Haig arrived at Aldershot in March 1912 accompanied by two members of his Indian staff: Captains H. D. Baird and John Charteris. The regular I Corps staff referred to these two unwelcome outsiders as the 'Hindu Invasion'. Haig's action was indeed worthy of scorn. The man who had struggled, while DSD, to turn the staff system into a meritocracy was here engaging in patronage pure and simple. Neither Baird nor Charteris had been to Camberley; their staff experience was minimal; and the greater part of their careers had been spent in India. Their main qualification for this impressive promotion was their ability to please their master.

The relationship with Charteris, which had a controversial effect upon Haig's command in the Great War, is worthy of detailed examination because of the light it sheds on Haig's character, methods of command and attitude towards subordinates. It is at first difficult to understand Charteris's appeal, since he was brash, outspoken, impolite, unkempt and of considerable intellect – the opposite in every way to the quiet malleable gentlemen of 'average intelligence' usually preferred by Haig. The answer might lie in the circumstances of their first meeting: Haig, on one of his tours of inspection as CGS, encountered Charteris, a Royal Engineer, supervising the construction of a pontoon bridge. Always fascinated by technical processes, Haig was immediately impressed by Charteris's expertise and by his lucid explanation of the work. (Eloquence always struck a chord with the inarticulate Haig.) Shortly afterwards, Charteris was found a place on Haig's personal staff. A very curious relationship grew. Charteris was a companion but never a friend; their relationship was symbiotic but not close. Haig came to rely heavily on Charteris in both personal and professional affairs, but does not appear to have confided in him.[14] Charteris was loyal, supportive and, perhaps most important, respectful of Haig's superiority. He fed Haig's ego. In return, he was allowed to bask in the reflected glow of his hero. There was room for only one Charteris on Haig's staff; he was the 'principal boy' – court jester, man Friday and fag. The schoolboy teasing which he had to endure was accepted as confirmation of his subservience and his exclusivity.[15]

Aldershot was the proverbial calm before the storm. Haig, at the age of 50, had risen to the highest field command in the British Army. Despite his relatively late start, he had been promoted past all his contemporaries in age. The satisfaction which this gave him was complemented by domestic bliss. According to Charteris:

For the first time in his married life he was settled in a real home. Government House, if not palatial, was spacious, and in those pre-war days it stood in country surroundings. Happy in the reunion with his family, Haig set himself to the just admixture of the life of the serving officer and country gentleman.[16]

This was true fulfilment. The usual pleasure that Haig derived from his work was combined with more frequent opportunities for relaxation – hunting, fishing, tennis and golf – and leisure time with his wife and two lively daughters. His was a prominent name on guest lists at society parties. Fortune-tellers and mediums predicted nothing but continued success and glory. Haig was self-satisfied and serene.

The Aldershot command was composed of the 1st and 2nd Divisions and the 1st Cavalry Brigade. Upon mobilisation, this force was to become I Corps of the BEF. While still in India, Haig heard from Haldane that 'there was a good deal to be done at Aldershot'. He nevertheless confessed that he was 'glad at this as I should feel nervous at taking over the command in "absolute efficiency"'. 'Absolute efficiency' became Haig's goal. It was a task for which he was naturally suited, and one in which he was eventually enormously successful. He was interested in every aspect of the command including, significantly, the budding air arm. But, as always, a disproportionate amount of attention was paid to his beloved cavalry.[17]

The Aldershot Corps received its first significant test in a massive war game held in East Anglia, in the autumn of 1912. Haig's I Corps, the 'Red Force', was pitted against the 2nd Corps, or 'Blue Force', commanded by Lieutenant-General Sir James Grierson. The addition of Allenby's Cavalry Division gave Haig's force, in the role of the European invader, numerical superiority. According to the prearranged plan, Grierson was to fall back for the defence of London. Through superior use of his air arm, he managed to outmanoeuvre Haig, and was generally agreed the winner. After the manoeuvres, the senior officers involved met in the Great Hall of Trinity College,

Cambridge. Haig and Grierson were asked to explain their actions and to outline the lessons to be learned. Haig, whose numerous gifts did not include oratorical skill, foolishly abandoned his prepared speech. He became, according to Charteris, 'totally unintelligible and unbearably dull. The University dignitaries soon fell fast asleep. Haig's friends became more and more uncomfortable; only he himself seemed totally unconscious of his failure.' As if to confirm Charteris's last point, Haig noted in his diary: 'I think my remarks well received.'[18]

It is probably unwise to read too much into Haig's failures at a single manoeuvre. To the senior officers involved, the exercise was proof that the Army was finely tuned and ready for war – that Haldane's reforms had resulted in a more streamlined and efficient force. A similar manoeuvre the following year gave further cause for optimism. This sense of well-being was shattered when the Curragh Crisis exploded from the Ango-Irish troubles in March 1914. Home Rule, passed in January 1913, was to come into effect in June 1914. Protestant Ulster, opposed to the bill, had gathered together a paramilitary force which numbered 100,000 men, half of whom were armed. It became increasingly apparent that the military would have to be called upon to enforce Home Rule. Since many senior officers had Unionist sympathies (especially those from Ulster), serious questions of loyalty arose. Though willing to serve in a peacekeeping capacity, almost all officers rejected anything which smacked of forcing Home Rule upon the Ulster loyalists. This explosive situation was discussed at meetings in London, on 18 and 19 March, attended by the Secretary of State for War, J. E. B. Seely; the CIGS, Sir John French; the Adjutant General, Sir Spencer Ewart; and the commander of the forces in Ireland, Lieutenant-General Sir Arthur Paget. The meetings ended with no clear policy being agreed upon with regard to the potential conflict of loyalty. Unclear as to what to tell his subordinates (and by this time out of his depth), Paget went back to Ireland and took the extraordinary step of telling his officers that, in the event of a clash with the Protestants, those from Ulster would be given leave of absence for the duration. All other officers, however, would have to fight or resign.

Paget's foolhardy and reckless ultimatum had the effect of setting a match to emotions which were tinder-dry. Brigadier-General Hubert Gough, commander of the 3rd Cavalry Brigade stationed at the Curragh camp, who was of a southern Anglo-Irish stock, had for some time agonised over the question of having to fight his countrymen. Pushed to the brink by Paget, he chose resignation. Sixty of his subordinate officers followed his example. Suddenly, with war on the horizon, the British Army seemed in danger of disintegration.

Haig was golfing with Lady Haig at Littlehampton when the crisis broke. News of it reached him via a letter from his Chief of Staff, Brigadier-General John Gough, who wrote, on 20 March, that his brother was intending to resign. 'You know my views which mean everything to me,' he told Haig. 'I wired back to Hubert "I will not fight against Ulster if you are dismissed, my resignation goes in at once."' He intended to visit the War Office the next morning in order to find out what decisions had been made 'and then act according to my conscience'. An alarmed Haig sent the following telegram to Gough: 'Hope you will not act precipitately I feel equally strong on the subject as you there is no question of Army fighting against Protestants or against Catholics our duty is to keep the peace between them.' Haig aimed to save the Army, his command and his own career – all of which were threatened by the events in Ireland. In order to do this, he had to assume an intentionally vague stance, the first indicator of which came with the above telegram. He could in no way have felt 'equally strong on the subject' as Gough, who was willing to sacrifice his career. Nor could he really have been confident that the Army would be able to 'keep the peace' without 'fighting against Protestants or against Catholics'. This intentional equivocation (a talent perhaps learned at the War Office) eventually enabled him to glide through the crisis completely unscathed. On this particular occasion it had the desired effect, as Gough replied that he intended to delay his formal resignation until the future was more certain.[19]

Having stabilised the situation, Haig rushed to London on the morning of the 23rd in order to lend his hand to the search for a solution to the crisis. His energetic efforts, mainly in conjunction with Haldane, had, however, little effect. Meanwhile, Ewart, after extensive consultations, had drafted a document designed to soothe the temper of Gough and his fellow officers at the Curragh. This document, approved by the Prime Minister (Asquith) on the afternoon of the 23rd, declared the incident a misunderstanding and decreed that the resignations would not be accepted. It was disingenuously added that all British officers had 'to obey lawful commands given to them . . . by the Army Council, for the protection of public property and the support of Civil power'. Seely, fearing (with justification) that this would not be enough to satisfy Gough, subsequently added (without Asquith's consent) two paragraphs stating, basically, that the government's rights to use the Army to enforce law and order would not be used 'to crush political opposition to the policy or principles of the Home Rule Bill'.[20]

Asquith was furious when he learned of the amendment, which essentially implied that his ministry was so weak that it had to negotiate with its Army officers on the conditions of their service. More important, the deal struck with Gough was a slap in the face to the Irish nationalists, who naturally concluded that the government was not committed to the enforcement of Home Rule. Asquith therefore repudiated the document on the 25th, whereupon Seely offered to resign, with French and Ewart following suit. The government at first refused to accept these resignations. A frantic search for a compromise agreeable to the triumvirate and Asquith followed, but none could be found. On the 30th, the resignations of Seely, French and Ewart were accepted. Meanwhile, the original issue (that of Gough's resignation) was settled with a new Army Order which set out, in terms as vague as possible, the responsibilities of officers with regard to following orders. Gough went back to the Curragh satisfied that he had won his point.

While French, Seely, Asquith and others were arguing, Haig was working behind the scenes to calm his officers. On the 25th, he called together his division and brigade commanders and pointed out the 'danger of disruption in [the] Army to [the] Empire'. He 'begged them to induce regular officers to give up dabbling in politics. We were all united to do anything required short of coercing our fellow citizens who have done no wrong.'[21] Haig did not explain how his men could avoid coercing their fellow citizens without (by definition) dabbling in politics. The contradiction was probably deliberate. A continuation of the calculated vagueness taken with John Gough, Haig's soothing words were intended to satisfy subordinate officers but were not meant to be tested. Meanwhile, Haig undoubtedly prayed that his bluff would not be called.

On 30 March, French sent a circular to senior commanders announcing his resignation. He claimed that, 'The issue was purely a personal one, absolutely unconnected with any political consideration whatever.'[22] This was not enough to mollify Haig, who had become extremely contemptuous of French's handling of the affair. Throughout the crisis, Haig had been intent upon shielding the cherished reputation of the British officer corps from the odium which devious (and blameworthy) politicians attempted to cast in its direction. Unfortunately, the task of protecting the Army became impossible when French resigned. As Haig correctly perceived, the resignation would not be seen as a 'purely personal matter' (as French had hoped) but as an acceptance of blame. In Haig's eyes, French had agreed to shoulder a burden of guilt which rightfully belonged to Asquith.

The way in which French had besmirched the integrity of the Army was, according to Haig, so serious that he never forgave him. On 13 October 1916, the occasion of a visit by French to the Western Front, he wrote: 'Many of us do not forget . . . how he sacrificed the whole Army during the Irish crisis before the war.'[23] Haig's attitude is revealed by a comparison of his treatment of French and that of Hubert Gough. Gough resigned over a matter of principle and honour, an action which Haig respected. He subsequently harboured no ill-feeling towards Gough, nor to his brother, who remained a valued assistant until his death in February 1915. French, on the other hand, had shown himself to be weak and easily manipulated, and was therefore scorned.

Tremors from the Curragh quake continued into the summer. In other respects, both Army and country experienced an eerie serenity. The strange calm, noted by so many from the 1914 generation, is evident in Haig's diary. The entries from the end of March to the advent of mobilisation are short, uninteresting and mostly concerned with matters outside the military. It was as if the serious preparation for war was complete, and the combatants were content to wait patiently for an issue over which to fight.

Few actually recognised 'the issue' when it arose. The assassination of the Archduke Franz Ferdinand escaped mention by Haig in his diary. Nor do the entries after 28 June demonstrate any of the same concern displayed during the Agadir Crisis or the Balkan Wars. But before long, events assumed a momentum of their own, and their significance could no longer be ignored. On 1 August, France and Germany mobilised. Britain did likewise three days later.

On 4 August Haig, alarmed by news that Kitchener was to be appointed Secretary of State for War (a post assumed by Asquith after

Seely's resignation), appealed to Haldane to 'return to the War Office for as long as war lasts and preparations are necessary. No one knows the details of the problems of organisation as you do!' A man of Haldane's experience was necessary because

> This war will last many months, possibly years, so I venture to hope that our only bolt (and that not a very big one) may not suddenly be shot on a project of which the success seems to be quite doubtful – I mean the checking of the German advance into France. Would it not be better to begin at once to enlarge our Expeditionary Force by amalgamating less regular forces with it? In three months time we would have a quite considerable Army, so that when we do take the field we can act decisively and dictate terms which will ensure a lasting peace.

Haig felt the concern of a father whose only son was going off to war. The BEF, his child, had been placed in the hands of men neither familiar with it nor sympathetic to its spirit. His knowledge of Kitchener's faults convinced him that he was not the man to lead the Army at this critical time.[24]

Haig's experiences in the Boer War are plainly visible behind his exhortations to Haldane. In South Africa, the early momentum had been sacrificed to the Boers because the British took the field unprepared. But Haig did not immediately realise that circumstances were decidedly different in 1914; his letter reveals an astonishing blindness to political and military realities. The British were not dealing with a small, untrained Boer army, but with a massive, professional force – the match of any in Europe. This force had to be met immediately; there was no time to improvise. The idea of waiting until the Army could expand, though perhaps wise in theory, was formed in a political vacuum. He presumed 'that France can hold out even though her forces have to fall back from the frontier for the necessary time for us to create an army of 300,000',[25] but he failed to consider the effect which bearing the brunt of the German attack alone would have upon the French Army and people. An occupying force deep within the French frontier could have quickly destroyed the morale of the population. Though the British force would admittedly be small, its presence would be massive; psychological factors were at this stage more important than physical ones. While Haig was prescient in predicting a long war, he did not seem to realise that its duration in many ways depended upon the British response.

Haig soon returned to his senses. Over the next ten days, he in fact emerged as one of the few wise men. The outbreak of war brought to the surface an astonishing lack of preparation amongst military and political leaders. Britain was superficially ready – the BEF (as manoeuvres had shown) was finely tuned – but the deeper complexities of a war on the Continent in alliance with the French had not been sufficiently explored. The depth of British ignorance became apparent at the first War Council meeting on 5 August. Details of French and British staff talks (which had been going on for many years) were explained, for the first time, to the generals whose actions they governed. Yet in spite of the plans agreed with the French, the immediate consequence of war was chaos. It had been decided that the British would concentrate behind the French left at Maubeuge and subsequently take up the left flank. Mobilisation plans had been formulated accordingly. Unfortunately, because the British mobilised three days later than the Germans and the French (something which the planners had not foreseen), a concentration at this point became too dangerous. There were no contingency plans.

It was up to the War Council to devise one rapidly. Unfortunately, confusion reigned. Ideas for the employment of the BEF – some of them quite ludicrous – flew across the table like shuttlecocks. French, the newly appointed Commander-in-Chief of the BEF, was responsible for some of the more alarming suggestions. He and Henry Wilson, in contrast to Haig, thought the allies would require no more than three months to defeat the Germans. Acting more like a little boy eager to get a punch in before the head teacher called a halt to the playground brawl, French proposed that the British should take on the full might of the German Army by an immediate landing at Antwerp. Here, he surmised, reinforcement would be provided by the Belgian and Dutch Armies (he mistakenly assumed that the latter were allies). Haig, stunned by French's apparent lack of fitness for his lofty command, later recalled, 'I trembled at the reckless way Sir John French spoke about "the advantages" of the B.E.F. operating from Antwerp against the powerful and still intact German Army!'[26] The First Lord, Winston Churchill, fortunately vetoed French's proposal by stating that the Royal Navy could not guarantee the safe passage of the BEF to Antwerp.

There is considerable disagreement about what subsequently transpired. After the war, French claimed (in his book *1914*) that Haig, when asked to give his opinion, 'suggested postponing any landing until the campaign had actively opened'. It is not inconceivable that such an idea was mooted by Haig since it would have been in keeping with the letter written to Haldane the day before. But Haig, upon hearing of the allegations in *1914*, was furious. He immediately asked the Cabinet Secretary, Colonel Maurice Hankey, to correct French's inaccuracies. Hankey's notes of the meeting do indeed provide a fuller and more flattering picture of Haig's contributions to the meeting. But French was not the only one guilty of repainting the canvas of war. Haig's enmity towards French caused him to rewrite his diary entries for the period 4–12 August 1914, in so doing enhancing his own perspicacity whilst casting French in the worst possible light. Needless to say, his recollections must in this case be taken with generous pinches of salt.[27]

The most accurate account of Haig's contribution would therefore seem to be Hankey's notes. According to the Cabinet Secretary, Haig asked a series of questions designed to alert those at the meeting to the complexity of the situation.

> Is it possible to delay and take time to organise, or will the French be beaten if we do not go at once? If the French are already falling back when we arrive, will our small Expeditionary Force be sufficient to turn the tables? What is the state of the French Army? How do their numbers . . . compare with the Germans? Have we enough troops, with the Belgians, to wage an active campaign, or do we run excessive risk, at the moment, of defeat in detail? Where can we act with most effect and when? Would it be of value to send a small force, at once, say, two divisions and a cavalry brigade? What do the French wish?

Many of these questions need not have been asked had British preparation been more complete. Nevertheless, Haig's inquiries were directed towards encouraging a consideration of delaying full British mobilisation. French's accusations were not, therefore, wide of the mark. But, Haig's most important question was his final one, one which French conveniently ignored. As Hankey confirmed, 'The trend of [Haig's] remarks was that our best policy at the present time was to do as the French wished us.'[28]

In his diary, Haig claimed that he went on to outline four additional considerations. First, since Britain and Germany would be fighting for their existence, 'neither would acknowledge defeat after a short struggle'. It was essential, therefore, to 'organise our resources *for a war of several years*'. Secondly, he emphasised that Britain had to begin building a huge army – of at least one million men. Thirdly, in order to train the huge force, it would be necessary to withdraw some officers and NCOs from the BEF. Finally, Haig claims that he advised sending 'as strong an Expeditionary Force as possible and as soon as possible, to join the French Forces and to arrange to increase that Force as rapidly as possible'. It is significant that the first three points were subsequently confirmed by Hankey. The fourth was not.[29]

The dispute over Haig's contribution aside, it is obvious that he was more clear-sighted than many of his colleagues. He had, however, only been asked to give advice, not to formulate policy. The War Council members could, and did, ignore his suggestions at their peril. After 6 August, his assistance was no longer required. He in turn concentrated upon preparing himself and his corps for mobilisation. On the 9th, he travelled to Southampton to inspect embarkation arrangements and noted that 'the Naval Officers were not fully up to what was expected of them' – a remark probably inspired more by inter-service rivalry than actual fact. The following day brought news that the Turks and Bulgars were mobilising. 'Everything now points to the whole of Europe becoming involved in this Great War.' In view of this fact, Haig was dumbfounded to find, two days later, that 'no decision had yet been arrived at regarding our concentration area in France!'[30]

On 11 August, Haig saw the King and Queen at Aldershot. The King 'seemed delighted' that French had been given command of the BEF. Haig, in response,

> told him at once, as I felt it my duty to do so, that from my experience with Sir John in the South African War, he was certain to do his utmost to carry out orders which the Government might give him. I had grave doubts, however, whether his temper was sufficiently even or his military knowledge sufficiently thorough to enable him to discharge properly the very difficult duties which will

149

devolve upon him during the coming operations with the Allies on the Continent. In my own heart I know that French is quite unfit for this great command at a time of crisis in our Nation's history. But I thought it sufficient to tell the King that I had 'doubts' about the selection.[31]

Like the War Council entries, the above was written after the war. It is therefore possible that Haig embroidered his account so that unsuspecting historians would judge him especially sagacious. If a conversation along these lines did take place, Haig's motives are open to serious question. What he called duty might justifiably be called opportunism.

It is difficult to gauge Haig's motives due to the confusion over what he thought at the time and what he wrote after the fact, and, indeed, what he did or did not say to the King and others. Granted, he did have 'grave doubts' about French in August 1914: the two had disagreed over cavalry tactics, the Curragh affair and the question of mobilisation. But his diary entry for 13 August (revised, of course, after the war) includes references to other complaints about his former friend which were not as securely founded:

I have an uneasy feeling lest we may be thoughtlessly committed to some great general action before we have had time to absorb our recruits . . . This uneasy feeling which disturbs me springs, I think, from my knowledge of the personalities of which our high command is composed. I have already stated somewhat briefly my opinion of Sir John French's ability as Commander in the Field. His military ideas often shocked me when I was his Chief of Staff during the South African War . . . With all this knowledge of the Chief . . . behind me, I have grave reasons for being anxious about what happens to us in the great adventure upon which we are now going to start this very night. However, I am determined to behave as I did in the South African War, to be thoroughly loyal and do my duty as a subordinate should, trying all the time to see Sir John's good qualities and not his weak ones.

It will be recalled that during the South African War Haig often criticised Kitchener, Roberts and other senior officers – at times so openly that he was mildly reprimanded by the King. French, on the other hand, received nothing but praise. When French was appointed CIGS in 1911, Haig applauded the selection. It is clear, therefore, that the above entry was simply the retrospective fabrication of a malevolent mind. Leaving aside the intriguing but unresolvable issue of whether similar fabrications were given a wider hearing in 1914, there remains the question of what it was Haig was trying to accomplish in writing in this vein after the war. A simple answer might be that the events of the war had so poisoned his feelings for French that Haig could not resist an opportunity to villify him whenever it arose. Alternatively (and more deviously), Haig may have worried that future historians would accuse him of usurping French's position in 1915 and might therefore have taken the opportunity to provide 'evidence' of French's unsuitability for supreme command, not to mention of his own loyalty. Similarly, it is possible that Haig, already sensitive to criticism of his command in the war, might have wanted to present himself as Britain's wisest military leader in 1914.[32]

Continuing in the same rather curious tone, Haig wrote that 'in all my dreams I have never been so bold as to imagine that, when . . . war did break out, I should hold one of the most important commands in the British Army'.[33] This, too, was pap intended for the digestion of historians. Haig never wore humility well. He had not risen to his lofty position by selling himself short or underestimating his own potential. During his thirty years in the Army, he was never surprised at his accomplishments. It is inconceivable that he was, for the first time, on 13 August.

On the 14th, Haig embarked for France. His departure was in harmony with his approach to life and to war. Henrietta and Willie Jameson motored from London with a case of champagne. Haig and his personal staff joined them in the drawing room of the Dolphin Hotel, where toasts were drunk to 'success and a safe return'.[34] It was all very genteel and restrained. There was no sadness, no tears, no fear of the turmoil which would follow. No one seemed to sense that the next four years would bring about the destruction of the society that had produced Douglas Haig, the gentleman-soldier. That night, Haig boarded the *Comrie Castle* and went to war.

Part II

At All Costs

8

An Abnormal War

On the day Britain declared war on Germany, Haig received a letter from Henrietta, written while she was under the spirit influence of their brother George, who had died in 1905. Henrietta, certain that Douglas would play an important role in the war, perhaps felt that some inspiring words from a deceased relative would be of benefit to him. Its actual source aside, the message was certainly prophetic:

> Tell Douglas with my love and blessing to go forward without fear because God will watch over and guide him and he will return covered with glory . . . Douglas must not forget to ask for the blessing of God on his great campagne [sic] because nothing ever happens by accident and God blesses those who ask him for it . . . I am not deceiving you or Douglas. He will come back with honour.[1]

Fascinating as the communication may be, it probably did not have much of an effect upon Haig, whose self-assurance was already monumental. Nor did he have to be told that God looked after those who asked for His blessing.

Despite the encouragement of his dead brother, and his own remarkable self-confidence, Haig embarked for France with some trepidation. If his retrospective diaries are to be believed, he was extremely concerned about French's fitness for command, concerns exacerbated by the fact that Sir John's staff officers seemed to mirror the deficiencies of their chief. Equally frightening was the behaviour of the politicians in those first ten days of war. Not only were they woefully unprepared for war, they seemed unable to put aside their petty squabbling or to grasp fully the threat posed by Germany. It is perhaps true to say that the self-righteous Haig was unfair in his

155

judgement of others, that he had little patience for ordinary human frailties. Nevertheless, the standards he applied were ones which he was certain he himself could satisfy. Those standards, and his experiences during the first fortnight of war, shaped his approach to the next four years. In other words, he became extremely wary of trusting anyone other than himself.

Haig's experiences after embarkation did not cause him to extend this trust. The best naval officers were apparently with the fleets; those on the docks and on the *Comrie Castle* failed to meet Haig's standards of efficiency. He was annoyed that no meal was available on the ship and that the cabin accommodation was poor. Conditions did not improve when he landed in Le Havre. Since the Base Commandant had gone 'gagga' with the pressure, 'no arrangement for billeting had been made and the rest camp was flooded'. Through perseverance, Haig managed to find a hotel in the city, but then suffered the indignity of getting stuck in the lift on the way up to his room. A hot bath and a warm meal soon soothed raw nerves.[2]

Just prior to embarkation, Haig had finally been informed of the decision to concentrate near Le Cateau and Wassigny. 'In view of the ignorance still existing regarding the enemy's movements, the rate of his advance into Belgium, and his intentions, it seems to some of us somewhat risky to begin our concentration so close to the enemy.'[3] Though correct in this judgement, Haig was unaware of the complicated background to the decision which made it somewhat inevitable. In July 1911, Henry Wilson (the DMO), after secret talks with General Dubail and Adolphe Messimy (the French CGS and War Minister, respectively), agreed that the British would concentrate on the left flank of the French Army and that the French would decide where that flank would be. By 1914 the French had settled upon Plan XVII which entailed concentrating their troops for a vigorous offensive into Alsace-Lorraine. The other side of this plan was, naturally, a somewhat depleted defence in the north. This placed the British in a rather precarious position, bearing in mind the miniscule size of their force and the widely acknowledged German intention (the Schlieffen Plan) to advance in strength through Belgium. Kitchener, like Haig, objected to the proposed point of concentration on the grounds that it was further south and east than a more sober appraisal of the German threat would have dictated. Wilson, however, maintained that since the original agreement was irrevocable, the British were honour bound to comply with French wishes.

The very weak position in which the British thus found themselves as they began to march north from their concentration area caused Haig profound unease. Early intelligence reports indicated that the Germans were 'marching as fast as possible round our left flank and as far as we know are unopposed'. A potentially disastrous battle seemed imminent. To Haig's considerable alarm, those in authority seemed ignorant of the danger. An atmosphere of unreality prevailed at French's GHQ, located as it was at Le Cateau, thirty miles from the advancing force. 'It is impossible to command a small force of 4 Divisions *successfully* from a H.Q. so far in the rear.' Haig also criticised the 'very large number of officers' at GHQ. 'They must get in one another's way, and at any rate impede the rapid transaction of business.' But most worrying of all was the excessive optimism of Sir John and his cohorts. Virtually ignoring the German juggernaut, on the 20th French ordered the British force to 'advance beyond Maubeuge and prolong the French left'. A justifiably wary Haig wondered, 'Are we strong enough?'[4]

French, mesmerised by the oversanguine Wilson, had no doubts that the British were sufficiently strong. At a meeting on the 23rd, Haig was shocked to find that Sir John seemed concerned only with the three German corps facing him in the vicinity of Mons:

> Little attention seemed to have been paid to the reports which have been coming in for several days that the enemy is moving large masses on Tournai. The C. in C. had apparently not discussed the situation with his Intelligence Officer (MacDonogh) [who]...told me after the conference that all the roads running West from Brussels to Ath and Tournai were thickly covered with masses of German troops of all arms marching very rapidly westwards. This was indeed an alarming situation. Yet the C. in C. ordered my Corps to press on![5]

The source of French's optimism was Wilson, who chose to ignore intelligence reports which did not accord with his wishes. Wilson was certain that the situation would be saved by an enormous attack by de Castelnau in the Ardennes. In other words, a French breakthrough there would force the Germans to withdraw their troops from the Belgian front. Haig was understandably sceptical.

Euphoria gave way to panic by the end of the day. At 4 p.m. the two advancing forces collided like automobiles in heavy fog. By nightfall, it appeared that the German blow had been miraculously contained. Haig went to bed reasonably confident, only to be awoken at 2 a.m. on the 24th with a telegram from GHQ ordering an immediate retreat towards Bavai. French had, in the nick of time, realised the danger facing him. So began the longest day of the war. Haig spent the next eighteen hours rushing about in a vain attempt to establish a secure line of defence. His war came close to ending ignominiously when his driver took a wrong turn in the dark and headed for the enemy lines. 'We soon detected our mistake,' he commented rather phlegmatically. Previous experience had hardly prepared him for this type of war. Everything happened so quickly, 'in a way which would have been impossible before the days of motors'.[6]

It was immediately obvious to Haig that the position established around Bavai would not be strong enough to stall the German steamroller. Unfortunately, events had not yet shaken French out of his stupor. At GHQ on the evening of the 24th, Haig found everyone 'much excited, but with no very clear plan beyond holding this wretched Bavai position'. Alarmed at this prospect, he 'pointed out to Sir John that if we halted for a day at Bavai the whole force would be surrounded by superior numbers. He agreed and ordered the force to continue its retreat'.[7]

The story of the retreat from Mons has been told too many times to repeat it in detail here. On the night of the 25th, a German advance guard broke into Landrecies, surprising Haig and his men in their billets. Haig's subsequent reaction was not in keeping with his characteristic calm and has thus been overemphasised by historians eager to exploit even the slightest chink in his armour. He did panic, but it is well to remember that the retreat caused even the best of men to shake with terror. A more notable feature of the retreat was its order – for thirteen days, and 200 miles, I and II Corps were in almost constant flight, most of the time cut off from each other. The fact that both Corps survived largely intact is a testimony to steady and competent command.

The' strains which the retreat imposed caused Haig a great deal of anxiety. 'Staff officers as well as troops were so dead tired it was most difficult to get orders . . . carried out. The men were daily becoming weaker from want of rest, and from not having sufficient time properly to prepare their food.' Haig resorted to the 'extreme measure' of cutting the ammunition carried by the column in half, thus freeing waggons to carry soldiers' kits and exhausted men. He could, however, do little to lighten the spiritual burden. 'The strain of daily skirmishes and of the continual retirement was . . . severely felt.' He tried to maintain a confident exterior, even though confidence 'was more than I felt often, but I dared not show all that I knew and felt. It was a most anxious time. The Regular Officers and indeed the Brigade and Divisional staffs knew very little, or did not understand how nearly surrounded we were.' Whilst Haig's presence did inspire his men, they had mainly to rely on their own inner strength. Their endurance taught Haig how remarkable were the men he had the privilege to command.[8]

In contrast, the retreat also taught him – rightly or wrongly – how unreliable were his allies. The troubles began on the 27th when the French announced peremptorily that they would be using the roads which Haig himself had planned to use that day. Though he by no means had exclusive title to the roads, it was the Allies' dictatorial attitude which left him with a bitter taste. To make matters worse, they also refused to assure Haig that they would delay their retreat long enough to protect the British troops on their flank. As the days progressed, evidence of French fallibility (much of it rather dubious) flowed Haig's way. On the 31st, he noted his annoyance 'that the French are not able to stand up better against the German advance'. Three days later, he described the Allies as 'so unreliable. One cannot believe a word they say as a rule.' These first impressions did not undergo a subsequent reassessment; the complaints would be repeated like a broken record over the next four years.[9]

The two lessons of the retreat – the resilience of his men and the unreliability of the French – caused Haig to favour a radical change in the strategic purpose of the small British force. On 3 September, he commented to his wife that

It is too sad losing so many good fellows without materially affecting the result of the campaign. I should like to see the whole of our Expeditionary Force moved entirely around to Ostend where we could operate on our own against the German lines of communication which pass through Belgium.[10]

The importance of this brief suggestion cannot be exaggerated. It will be recalled that at the War Council on 4 August, Sir John French put forth a similar plan calling for independent action against the German Army near Antwerp – an idea which Haig condemned as 'reckless'. Conditions had not changed so radically as to justify such an operation one month later. What, then, is the explanation for Haig's extraordinary suggestion? It probably arose from two strains of thought. The first was Haig's chauvinism: he may have feared that his wonderful army risked annihilation if the link with the unreliable French was maintained. Alternating with this nightmare was a dream that the superior British might achieve something magnificent on their own. At the very least, operating on the coast offered an easy escape route if the French were defeated. The other strain was Haig's cavalry mentality. Frustrated by continuous retreat, the cavalry officer in Haig dreamt of a dramatic action redolent of *Boys Own* magazine. But what is most important about Haig's suggestion is that it was the first mention of a desire which would burn in him over the next three years. It was a desire unaffected by reality.

At this stage in the war, dreams remained dreams; Haig had to cooperate and keep in close contact with the French. Despite his doubts about their willingness to attack, it was Joffre who decided on 5 September that the time had come to go on the offensive. Haig was somewhat incredulous when he received 'a note from Sir John French . . . to the effect that the French were really going to stand and attack! This time there was to be no mistake about it, they would fight to the death!' It was agreed that the British would take a position between the Fifth and the Sixth French Armies. 'The whole are to advance North, North East and Eastwards and crush the German Corps now in our front between us!' Ironically, the day before, Haig had advised French that his troops, though in a 'determined mood', were incapable of attacking without a week's rest. These doubts were quickly swept aside. According to Haig, 'no words could have been more welcome to the troops than those announcing the advance'. On 6 September the march to the Aisne began.[11]

Forward movement quickly erased the anxieties which had plagued Haig over the previous fortnight. If anything, the advance was not fast enough; subordinates, like General Maxse, were criticised for a lack of 'fighting spirit'. 'I thought our movements very slow, in view of the fact that the enemy was on the run!' Haig commented on 7

September. The euphoria of the chase even caused him to rethink his predictions of a long war. He thought 'that a little effort now might mean the conclusion of the war!' In a similar vein, Haig criticised Joffre's decision (taken on the 11th) to wheel to the right: 'Personally I think it was a mistake to have changed direction now, because the enemy in our front was close to us last night and was much exhausted. Had we advanced today on Soissons, with cavalry on both flanks, large captures seemed likely.' Three days later, the advance lost its steam. The decision to wheel to the right may have sapped its energy and therefore limited the gains, but an eventual loss of momentum was inevitable. Neither an end to the war nor a glorious role for the cavalry were realisable on the Aisne in 1914.[12]

The retreat to the Marne and the advance to the Aisne increased the contempt which Haig felt for Sir John French. First he had been too bold, then he was too cautious. In contrast, French had nothing but praise for the men of the 1st Corps and their commander. On 15 September he wrote as follows to Haig: 'I feel very strongly that the favourable position we are in (on the whole), and the good chance we have of ultimately throwing the enemy back, are due to the splendid advance which has been made by you and the First Army Corps.' Haig agreed. His troops had been magnificent; 'what a splendid action they had fought, after so many trying weeks retreating and marching! They had indeed given their lives to save their Fatherland! It will be hard to find a finer example of endurance and discipline in all the annals of British arms.'[13]

By 15 September the front stabilised. The war began to take on the character which it would assume for most of the next four years. Mobility was replaced by stalemate, impulsive reactions by methodical preparations. Guns were carefully positioned in permanent emplacements, screened from aerial observation. For the men, the shovel became as important as the rifle, barbed wire as valuable as bullets. But, as with constant marching, stalemate imposed terrible strains upon the soldier. Betraying his inexperience of this type of war, Haig wrote on 20 September that 'Our troops have been a week in the trenches . . . It is well nigh impossible for many to have a hot meal and the weather has been very wet and cold.' In common with his men, he found it difficult to adjust to trench warfare: 'The situation is quite unlike what was anticipated by our regulations.' Most annoyingly, it limited the independence of the British, as Haig discussed with French on 23 September:

> The C. in C. . . . asked our views as to whether we could advance or not. I said we ought not to advance until the French on our right had come up level with the front of the 1st Corps; then it would be possible for us all to go on together. But all must engage enemy and try to advance at the same moment, because otherwise the enemy would enfilade my troops and guns.

It was an easy solution to prescribe, a difficult one to effect.[14]

As the autumn wore on, the belligerents tried unsuccessfully to outflank each other in the north. Each flanking movement was quickly countered until, eventually, the armies ran out of room. A static line from Switzerland to the sea resulted. On 30 September, Sir John French suggested moving the British forces around to the left flank, thus placing them closer to the supply ports on the Channel. Haig approved of the proposal but feared that the proximity of the enemy would make withdrawal difficult. As it turned out, it was not the Germans but the French who caused difficulties. Due to what Haig saw as a lack of cooperation on the part of the Allies, the transfer of I Corps was repeatedly postponed. The delays, of course, did nothing to improve Haig's already low opinion of the French, likewise of Sir John, who was criticised for not asserting himself. After weeks of threats and wrangles, Haig's corps finally moved to its new position on 15 October. In the end, 'The only objection raised was that the trenches were too deep for the little Frenchmen to fire out of them comfortably.'[15]

After I Corps was installed in its new position, Haig visited French at St Omer, the new GHQ. Though the troops had by this time spent over a month in static positions, there was still hope of a return to a war of movement. Haig recorded that French 'seemed quite satisfied with the general situation and said that the enemy was falling back and that we "would soon be in a position to round them up"'. Misguided as this attitude obviously was, it did not seem so to Haig at the time. He, in fact, had expressed an equally sanguine opinion to his wife a few days earlier, when he wrote that the Germans had 'given up any idea of breaking through here now, and as soon as they are pressed . . . they will have to fall back or risk having their line of retreat cut off'. Because Haig shared French's opinions on the war, he did not question the latter's ambitious objectives for the First Battle of Ypres when they were revealed on 19 October:

> Sir John stated that he 'estimated that the enemy's strength on the front Ostend and Menin, at about one Corps, not more'. I was ordered to march via Thourout and capture Bruges. 'Defeat enemy and drive him on Ghent.' My right 'would pass through Ypres'. After passing that place, I was free to decide whether to go for enemy on the north of me, or that part of him which was towards Courtrai.

Haig was absolutely certain that he could achieve a great victory. Though the cost would be high, the price would be worth paying. 'The results of failure in this war', he reminded Rawlinson (the 7th Division commander) 'would be so terrible for England, that we must all be prepared to submit to severe losses.'[16]

What neither Haig nor French had realised when planning the battle was that German objectives around Ypres were at least as bold as those of the British. Consequently, for one of the few times in this war, a battle began with both sides attacking. On the morning of the 19th, the two armies met in a ferocious head-on collision which quickly shattered dreams of an overwhelming advance and an end to the war. As Haig wrote on the 22nd:

> the enemy was in considerably greater strength than had originally been anticipated by Sir John French when he gave me my instructions at St. Omer. Further it seemed certain now that the enemy's action was going to take the form of a determined offensive, and not, as had been anticipated, that of a rear guard. Reports which now reached me . . . indicated that the enemy was . . . preparing to make a considerable effort to reach Ypres.[17]

A desperate contest between two punch-drunk fighters resulted. Haig, originally sharing French's buoyancy, began to assume a more measured outlook. Unfortunately, Sir John, safely distanced from the fighting, did not abandon his ambitious objectives. British troops were pushed mindlessly forward at a time when prudence dictated a consolidation of the defence.

Haig was astonished at the way soldiers on both sides reacted to this extraordinary war. On 25 October, he was told of

the gallant action of two half companies of Gloucesters. They went forward on west of Langemarck Village to occupy some trenches hurriedly vacated by the Coldstream Guards. Enemy's fire was very hot, and soon the officers were killed or wounded. The N.C.O.s and Section Leaders arranged for ammunition to be passed up, a matter of great difficulty. About 500 rounds a man were fired and they counted 140 dead Germans on their front after they beat off the attack. Out of 180 men, only 60 unwounded remained . . . The Germans, quite young fellows, came on with great gallantry. One mounted officer kept encouraging his men to go forward, until within 400 yards of our firing line, when he was killed.

Elsewhere, heroism (according to Haig) seemed in short supply. The fifty casualties suffered by Byng's division on the 20th, were 'a small number considering the nature of this war and all that is at stake!' On the 26th, Haig was 'astounded at the terror-stricken men coming back' after heavy fighting in the vicinity of Kruseik. But in both cases, he was careful in apportioning blame. At Kruseik, 'fine troops' had been 'reduced to inefficiency through ignorance of their leaders . . . [who] placed them in trenches on the *forward* slopes where enemy could see and so effectively shell them'. The old adage about there being no bad men, only bad officers, apparently still applied in this unique war.[18]

One profound lesson pertained to the range and power of modern artillery – the arm so often discounted by Haig before the war. Haig learned of how Langemarck had been shelled with 'Black Marias': 'the bombardment was terrific, with the result that the town does not exist'.[19] Even the high command, ensconced well behind the lines, was at risk. On the 31st shells fell on Hooge Chateau, the headquarters of the 1st Division. Three senior officers were killed instantly, and the commander, Major-General S. H. Lomax, died of his wounds the following April. Two days earlier, Hooge had been Haig's reporting centre, but, feeling sorry for the 1st Division staff who were crammed into a two-room cottage, Haig had given it to Lomax.

At the end of October, the German commander Falkenhayn embarked upon a fresh effort to break the Allied front and turn the flank near Ypres. Fresh troops were brought in, supported by 250 heavy guns. A portion of the attack was to be concentrated upon Haig's front – facing his three divisions was a German force nearly twice as large. Early on the morning of the 30th, Haig, with some trepidation, noted that though the 'direction of enemy's move [is] uncertain . . . there is no doubt that some big operation is in execution'. By 8 a.m. the situation was 'serious'; Haig was 'most anxious about the communications which ran through Ypres'. But, by nightfall, despite colossal casualties on both sides, the position remained (or seemed) miraculously secure.[20]

The following day has been described by the Official Historian of the War as 'one of the most critical . . . in the history of the British Expeditionary Force, if not of the British Empire'. The hyperbole aside, Haig's corps did come desperately close to an overwhelming defeat. At daybreak, Haig was told that

> the troops are very exhausted! The two Brigadiers (Landon and Fitzclarence) assure me that if the enemy makes a push at any point, they doubt our men being able to hold on. Fighting by day, and digging by night to strengthen their trenches has thoroughly tired them out.

The push came with the shock and the force of a broken dam. German artillery poured the heaviest fire yet seen onto the British positions around Gheluvelt. The infantry surged forward, driving Haig's men from their trenches and capturing the town. A despondent French visited Haig at his headquarters at 3 p.m.:

> Sir John was full of sympathy and expressed his gratitude for what the Corps, as well as myself, had done since we landed in France. No one could have been nicer at such a time of crisis. But he had no reinforcements to send me, and viewed the situation with the utmost gravity.

At worst, the situation seemed to point to a German breakthrough; at best, a hasty British retreat. A desperate Haig decided that his troops had somehow to be rallied. Mounting his charger, he readied himself for what was intentionally designed to be a dramatic ride through the crowds of frightened soldiers in headlong retreat on the Menin Road. But, before Haig set off, a messenger arrived with news that Gheluvelt was being recaptured by a single battalion, the 2nd Worcesters. Though its purpose had evaporated, the ride went ahead, much to the delight of Haig's future biographers.

Falkenhayn interpreted the counter-attack by the Worcesters as evidence that the British were still strong, which they were not. The German commander therefore called off the attack when he was inches away from a dramatic victory. The incident was subsequently seen by Haig as providing one of the most important lessons of the war: that being that victory went to the commander who pushed, pushed, and then pushed again.[21]

With undisguised glee, Haig commented that 'the attack was one to which the Germans attached the greatest importance'.[22] A psychological victory had been won; a massively superior German force had been contained. But, had less sentimental, more pragmatic minds analysed the situation, it would have been apparent that British forces now found themselves in a precarious position into which they could (and should) have forced the Germans. The decision to hold on to Ypres at all costs – taken because senior commanders had learned to equate retreat with cowardice (not to mention their abhorrence of surrendering ground won by British blood) – meant that British soldiers had to remain in a deathtrap salient for most of the rest of the war. It could have been the Germans. A subtle strategic British withdrawal could have left the enemy stuck in a perilous bulge. The obstinate refusal to surrender a worthless piece of ground gained the British a moral victory, but the inspiration derived from it would be quickly eroded as German shells rained incessantly down.

The argument is made, admittedly, with the privilege of hindsight. Neither Haig nor French would have imagined that the British would remain in and defend the Ypres salient for the next three years. Though they recognised its danger, they were more concerned with its value as a launching pad for future (certain to be successful) offensives. The loss of Ypres was inconceivable to the British; its capture essential to the Germans. Consequently, the action of the 31st did not bring an end to the fighting. Both forces continued to hammer each other. Each day produced another crisis. The terrible sacrifices which had been suffered gave justification to their continuance. On 5 November, Haig noted in his diary:

Our troops have been in the trenches the last ten days and have . . . had terrible losses! But we have to stick it! I rode to the 1st Division Head Quarters . . . and told them the position must be held. There was no possible second position. In the event of the enemy piercing our line, supports must counter attack at once. There must be no retirement.

The constant pressure naturally caused men to crack. On the 7th, soldiers from the Lincolns, Northumberland Fusiliers and Bedfords left their trenches in frightened flight. Haig later learned that the bombardment at the time had been 'mild'. In this precarious state, he found no room for leniency. He ordered 'all men who have funked . . . to be tried by Court Martial and the abandoned trenches to be reoccupied at once'.[23]

On 11–12 November, the enemy made one final attempt to break through. Fifteen fresh Guards battalions were brought to the line. Most of Haig's men, in contrast, were exhausted after ten horrible days in the trenches. Haig warned GHQ that without French help there was a great risk of being cut off in the salient – 'an irreparable loss to England at the present time'. Reinforcements were not forthcoming, but the line somehow held. By the 12th, I Corps' original establishment of 18,000 men had been reduced to 68 officers and 2,776 other ranks. Responding to this desperate situation, Sir John French suggested that II Corps should take over Haig's front. Doubtful of the quality of II Corps and of the abilities of its commander, General Sir Horace Smith-Dorrien, Haig was unenthusiastic. The 'best solution', he thought, was to 'get the French to take over all our line, in any case they must relieve us of a considerable portion of it'. Totally immersed in the Ypres battle, Haig could not easily see beyond his front. The French were clearly 'not doing their fair share in attacking the enemy'.[24]

Eventually, Sir John, who was determined to give I Corps the opportunity to rest and refit, proposed that half of Haig's line be taken over by II Corps and the other half by the French. After encountering a 'good deal of trouble' in getting Foch to agree, French finally elicited a promise from him that the relief would commence by the 15th. 'I have every reason to be sure', Sir John assured Haig, 'that he will keep his word.'[25]

Haig remained sceptical. By the 18th the relief had still not taken place, and it became increasingly likely that the 2nd Corps, ill-equipped as it was, would have to take over the entire front. The implications of this were, Haig thought, very serious:

> I wired GHQ that unless the number of the British Forces in this theatre were greatly increased it would be madness for the British to take over such an extended line. To do so would mean that our troops could not be given proper rest, and the Expeditionary Force would cease to be of fighting value. With the disappearance of this force, the voice of Great Britain in European strategy would be much diminished. It will be many months before the new forces forming in England can take the field. Our policy ought therefore to be to husband the strength of our present field army as much as possible and get the French to treat us fairly! Because ever since we landed in France they seem ready to drain the last drop of blood out of the British Force!

The situation, according to Haig, was exacerbated by the fact that Henry Wilson seemed 'quite ready to acquiesce and fails to uphold the interests of the British Forces. He seems to pander to Foch and is more French than the French!'[26]

As it turned out, the relief was completed on the 21st. Haig's alarm, albeit overdone, was understandable. The constant pressure of the previous month had severely frayed his patience with the allies. He had a genuine grievance, but his chauvinism prevented him from understanding its true cause. It was easy for him, believing as he did that the Frenchman was a lower life form, to apportion blame. The French were not gentlemen, therefore they could not be trusted. But in reality, their apparent lack of cooperation was the fault of the system: the British and French were allies only in the loosest sense of the word. There was no unity of forces or command. No organs for collective decision-making had been established. It was natural, therefore, that in a desperate situation national self-interest (the protection of one's own forces) was the rule. The French undoubtedly delayed in coming to the aid of the British at Ypres, as they did at many other times in the war. But they never denied assistance when doing so would have meant a serious British defeat. To do so would have been to cut their own throats. In other words, they came in the nick of time, but seldom earlier. Emergency, not compassion, spurred them to action. Therefore, though the claim that the French wanted to 'drain the last drop of·blood out of the British' is an overstatement, they understandably preferred when the British bled instead of themselves. The British, the other half of this haphazard alliance, did not act altogether differently.

The problems with the Allies and the crisis at Ypres temporarily drew Haig and French closer together. Sir John was appreciative of the way Haig tackled the crisis 'with the same grim determination, steadfast courage and skilful forethought which had characterised his handling of the operations throughout'. He recommended Haig for immediate promotion to full General. Haig's attitude in turn mellowed; French, he decided, was 'really most kind and grateful for my help'. After a meeting on the 21st, a genuinely concerned Haig commented on how French 'had had a severe attack of heart, and doctors had ordered him to take things more easily . . . He looked rather pulled down'. French was worried that 'people at home were despondent and knew little of what tremendous operations we had encountered and what had been done here'. He thus decided to send Haig home in order to enlighten public opinion. At the same time, Haig was to consult Kitchener about plans for restructuring the BEF into two armies, a change which Haig admitted would have the beneficial effect of relieving the burden on the Commander-in-Chief.[27]

'London', Haig commented when he arrived on the 23rd, 'looked much as usual except that many of various ages were wearing officers' Khaki uniforms'. At the meeting with Kitchener, agreement was quickly reached on the plan to divide the BEF into two Armies, each to consist of six divisions. Kitchener was, however, less willing to make promises regarding when the extra men would be made available, preferring instead to steer the discussion towards munitions issues. On the 24th, Haig saw the King, who unfortunately seemed not to understand the manpower problem:

[He] said that more Territorials could not be spared to join us because they had (until now) no trained troops at home to resist invasion. I remarked that the surest way to prevent the enemy from attempting to invade Great Britain was to engage and press him hard on the Continent.

At this stage, Haig was mainly concerned with questions of quantity. But, as was revealed in a conversation with General Sclater, the

Adjutant General, quality was also a problem. Sclater complained that, 'Latterly the special reservists had neither the will nor the physique for fighting.' Haig replied that what was needed was 'patriots who knew the importance of the cause for which we were fighting'. The German people, unlike the British,

> have been impregnated from youth up with an intense patriotic feeling so that they die willingly for their country. There are not many of our men at the present moment who will do this unless well led. Now we are short of officers to lead them. I said send out young Oxford and Cambridge men as Officers; they understand the crisis in which the British Empire is now involved.[28]

It was obvious to Haig that character (as defined by the Oxbridge standard) remained important even if war itself had changed almost beyond recognition. Without character there could not be good leaders. To Haig's annoyance, this simple fact seemed to have escaped the King who, during a visit to the front in early December,

> seemed . . . inclined to think that all our troops are by nature brave and is ignorant of all the efforts which commanders must make to keep up the 'moral' of their men in war, and of all the training which is necessary in peace in order to enable a company . . . to go forward as an organised unit in the face of almost certain death.[29]

At the root of this complaint and the advice to Sclater was Haig's personal philosophy of war. The Napoleonic maxim of the moral being to the physical as three is to one had lost none of its relevance. This was, after all, at the heart of Haig's religious devotion to the cavalry. In addition, it was behind his belief that the British were destined to triumph in this war. The elixir of victory was the English character distilled at Oxford, Cambridge and the public schools. This character made the British Army by definition superior to the French or the German. Thus, the morale of the British troops, once sufficient leaders were found, would not be broken. Victory, in the long run, was certain.

When Haig returned to the Western Front, he found that Sir John 'looked fitter than when I last saw him, but, there seemed an air of depression about the whole establishment'. The depression lifted the next day, when reports (rather spurious) indicated that the 'German Army outside Lodz is fighting desperately to save itself from annihilation'. On hearing this, French commented

> 'this will be the end of the war, about a month more!' The gist of his remarks to Battalions today was that all the hard fighting was over, and that the Germans could not continue much longer to withstand the combined attacks of the British and French Armies.

These predictions were repeated when French addressed some of Haig's troops on 1 December. It is surprising that Haig, who should have been aware of the effect which raising false hopes could have on the morale of troops, was not more critical of French's fantasies. His silence was probably due to the fact that he held similar views. On 13 December, he told his wife that 'the war is going well'. Though he did not predict when victory would come, he insisted that 'We probably have only a "shell" opposed to the French and ourselves, so that if we succeed in cracking it, we may be able to push the enemy back a very long way – say to the Rhine.'[30]

What is fascinating about Haig's optimism is its extraordinary resilience. Adverse results from the battlefront hardly affected his spirits. When, for instance, the 2nd Corps was unsuccessful in an attack on the Messines–Wytschaete ridge on 14–15 December, Haig refused to interpret the failure as additional proof of the difficulty of movement on the Western Front. Instead, as far as he was concerned the failure demonstrated two deficiencies in the British Army which, when corrected, would restore mobility. The first problem pertained to the overall direction of the war; the 'general instruction' from the GHQ staff and French seemed to Haig 'rather vague'. A sense of determination was lacking; staff officers were 'rather slovenly in their methods of carrying on war'. This casual approach in turn affected the men in the trenches. According to Haig, the troops were bound to interpret the failure at Messines as proof that 'They (GHQ) did not mean business.'[31]

On 18 December, Haig spoke candidly to French about his lack of confidence in the GHQ staff, but stopped short of criticising Sir John directly. French 'seemed grateful for my telling him what was going on' and admitted that there were serious problems with his staff. He told Haig that he had asked Kitchener to replace Murray (his

CGS) with Wilson, news which prompted Haig to suspect that the 'cunning' Wilson 'has been intriguing to get poor Murray moved on'. Haig, who thought Wilson 'had no military knowledge', suggested to French that William Robertson (the Quartermaster General) would make a better CGS. As it turned out, Kitchener was thinking along similar lines, as Murray was shortly afterwards replaced by Robertson, with Wilson remaining sub-CGS. This was an improvement, but as far as Haig was concerned a more radical change remained to be made. He wrote that he 'felt sorry for [French] being in his present plight', which, translated, probably meant that Haig thought him hopelessly inadequate as Commander-in-Chief.[32]

The second fault which Haig noted at this time pertained to the strategic direction of the war. After over four months of war, he had concluded that

> there are only two ways of gaining ground either (a) a general offensive all along the front with careful preparations of artillery at specially chosen points in order to dominate the enemy's artillery and use of trench guns, mortars, hand grenades, etc. to occupy the enemy's attention everywhere, and press home in force at certain points where not expected. The other method (b) is to sap up, as in siege warfare. This is a slow business, especially in wet ground.[33]

Both methods would be used by Haig in the years that followed. But it was the first method, with some embellishments, upon which he pinned his hopes for eventual victory. The implication behind this method was that movement, and particularly a breakthrough, remained possible. But, in order for this to be achieved, the first fault had also to be corrected. In other words, a commander had to be found who had the courage and the resolve to sustain the heavy losses which would eventually lead to a breakthrough. The beauty of Haig's theories was that they allowed him to remain optimistic and to shield himself from the disturbing realities of the war while he waited for the two deficiencies to be corrected. In his mind, the depressing stalemate in which the British Army had been stuck since the first month of the war was not an unalterable condition, but, instead, evidence of inadequate leadership or unwise strategy.

For the moment, Haig was not able to test his theories. The end of the year brought an end to the campaigning season. But the war did not mean a moratorium on Christmas festivities. Leopold Rothschild sent out fifty pairs of fur-lined gloves for his friend Haig to distribute among his staff. Lady Haig also sent a present for each member of the staff, including the servants. 'What an amount of pleasure it gave me to distribute [the] Xmas gifts in the midst of all my anxiety.' After a satisfying Christmas dinner which included turtle soup and 1820 brandy (supplied by Rothschild), Haig and his personal staff

spent a cheery evening in spite of the uncertainty of the future. Doris's Xmas presents had reminded us that my corps staff was a 'family party' and had greatly touched us all at this high season. I felt truly thankful to the Higher Power for having been permitted to command the First Corps during the whole period of the past four critical months of the war, and to have done so with conspicuous success.

The war which was to be over by Christmas entered a new year.[34]

9

The Search for a Way Forward

The reorganisation of the BEF into two Armies went into effect on Boxing Day 1914. Haig was given command of the 1st Army, consisting of I, IV and the Indian Corps; and Smith-Dorrien the 2nd Army, comprising II and III Corps. The new structure was intended not only to relieve French of some of the pressures of commanding a large force on an extended front, but also to facilitate the incorporation of the New Army units being trained in Britain.

Haig immediately set to work organising his new staff. John Gough was made CGS and Charteris was placed in charge of Intelligence. Haig also retained his two I Corps ADCs – Straker and Fletcher. The choice of a new headquarters was left to the staff, but it soon transpired that agreement was not easily reached:

> A nice chateau . . . on the road to St. Venant would not suit . . . Charteris said the house was very damp and so unhealthy . . . Then the staff selected houses for us at St. Venant. That place would not suit me as it is too far from the main routes to Corps H.Q. and G.H.Q. So now a chateau at the north end of Lillers has been chosen. Charteris says it is satisfactory and Alan F. says it is too damp! Ryan now says I ought to turn the Maire out of his house and occupy it. He has a very fine house. But there is a Mrs. Maire, who is 'full of determination'. Personally I think an empty house best. We then have a kitchen to ourselves and the servants' big military boots won't cause annoyance to the owner of the carpets![1]

The problem was complicated because neither Haig nor his staff saw any reason to sacrifice peacetime comforts. Central heating was therefore a must. In the end, the headquarters had to be moved three times before a chateau, suitable in every way, was found.

More serious matters soon diverted Haig's attention. As an Army commander, his concerns widened from tactical questions to strategic ones. On 29 December, he and French discussed the role which the British would play when Kitchener's New Armies began to take the field. The British, Sir John thought, should

> take over the front line from La Bassée to the sea, and so free the French Army under D'Urbal. Sir John's intention is then to work as a separate Field Force independently of the French. He (Sir J.) proposes to cooperate with the Navy and use his reinforcements as far as possible for work along the coast, instead of employing them in the trenches.[2]

The idea was attractive to Haig, being not dissimilar to the one he had earlier proposed to his wife. Kitchener had also begun to favour this plan, mainly because the government and the Admiralty had lately become anxious about the depredations of German submarines based at Ostend and Zeebrugge. The French, however, understandably concluded that a coastal operation favoured British interests, and did little to rid the French countryside of the Hun invader. General Joffre therefore began to put pressure on Sir John to cooperate in a combined operation further south, in the region of La Bassée.

Aside from the obvious one of countering the submarine threat, Haig could see three reasons in favour of a coastal operation. First, it promised independence from the unreliable French. Secondly, it offered (he thought) the best possibilities for breaking the German line and turning the flank. Finally, because the area was strategically important to the Germans, they would defend it at all costs, which meant that any British action was bound to result in heavy enemy casualties. Haig conveniently ignored the contradiction between point two and point three: a line could not be both heavily defended and easily breached. The third point was important because it served as a handy counter: if, in action or in argument, the second point was refuted, Haig could always justify a coastal campaign on the basis of attrition.

Behind Haig's thinking was a conviction that victory could only be won by defeating the German Army on the Western Front. He was,

therefore, understandably alarmed when, in early January, Kitchener
hinted

> that the New Army might be better used elsewhere than on the
> French frontier. A suggestion had been made of cooperating with
> Italy and Greece. I said that we ought not to divide our Military
> Force, but *concentrate on the decisive point* which is on this frontier
> against the German main Army. With more guns and ammunition
> and more troops, the allies were bound in the end to beat the
> Germans and break through.

Revealed above are two beliefs from which Haig did not drift during
the entire war: the first that the British must concentrate on the
Western Front; the second that, given adequate supplies of men and
arms, a breakthrough remained possible. Both beliefs were echoed
in a conversation with Repington on 22 January:

> He was most anxious to know whether I thought we could ever
> advance on this front. He thought the German front impregnable
> and much doubted whether we would ever get a General suffi-
> ciently fearless of public opinion to incur the losses which must
> be suffered in any attempt to pierce the enemy's front. He thought
> the British people would not stand heavy casualties. I replied that,
> as soon as we were supplied with ample artillery ammunition of
> high explosive, I thought we could walk through the German lines
> at several places.

It is ironic that at this stage it was Repington who perceived the need
for a General 'fearless of public opinion' and it was Haig (eventually
that General) who seemed to think the victory could be achieved
without extraordinarily heavy losses.[3]

The future looked very simple to Haig: everything (as he had learned
at Camberley) depended upon the offensive. If it was strong enough,
it was bound to succeed (i.e. break through). What was required was
vast quantities of ammunition, especially high explosive shell. The
value of HE had lately been confirmed when

> a man in our trenches brought as a souvenir to show his officers,
> the arm of a German soldier which had been thrown into our

trenches by the force of the explosion of one of our shells. The enemy's trench is some 150 yards from ours; this shows that the high explosives used in our shells is very powerful.

On 28 January, Haig met the MGO, Sir Stanley Von Donop, and demanded 'an unlimited amount' of high explosive, in addition to siege howitzers and trench mortars. Von Donop promised Haig that 'every round that was possible to make is being sent out' and that 'by April we would have an ample supply'.[4]

In view of his earlier doubts, Haig's acceptance of the value of modern artillery was significant. But it is important to point out that Haig usually forced weapons to conform to preconceived ideas rather than changing his ideas to exploit the weapons. Such had been the case with the cavalry's rifle, and so it was with the artillery. New guns firing high explosive shells were incorporated into Haig's psychological battlefield; they were valued not for their ability to destroy positions or kill men, but primarily for their capacity to demoralise. War remained, after all, a moral contest. Artillery frightened men who could then be run over by infantry. Into the breach would ride the cavalry. As Haig indicated to Rothschild in early February:

This trench warfare is much more severe on the nerves than the old type of warfare, because the troops are living under shell and rifle fire whereas formerly a battle took place once or twice in 3 or 4 months . . . So it seems that when we do begin to fire our big guns in earnest the enemy won't be able to stand the bombardment as he did at the beginning of the war.

Support for his predictions was easy for Haig to find. 'The enemy was greatly demoralised by our fire,' he assured himself on 9 February. 'With more heavy guns and howitzers and more ammunition he will be still more demoralised!' It did not matter where or how the guns were fired, only that they were fired incessantly.[5]

The well, however, soon threatened to run dry. On 11 February, Robertson cautioned Haig about his prodigious use of scarce ammunition. The scarcity, Robertson explained, was due to munitions production in January having dropped to 'only half of what was expected'. 'This', Haig was quick to explain, 'is doubtless due to the

New Year's holidays which . . . our unpatriotic workmen insisted on taking at home.'[6]

News regarding the supply of men was also worrying. On 4 January, Haig was alarmed when Kitchener announced that

> six armies will be formed each of about three Corps. We all think these new formations, with rather elderly Commanders and inexperienced staff officers, a great mistake . . . It is folly . . . to send out the 'New Army' now by Divns. and Armies. Much better to send it out by Battalions or even by Brigades, for incorporation in our existing Divisions and Corps.

French consulted his senior commanders on the issue, who agreed that the 'New Armies which are insufficiently trained might readily become a danger' unless incorporated into seasoned units. Aware, however, that there was little chance of changing Kitchener's mind, French took the extraordinary step of going directly to the Prime Minister. Kitchener, furious at being circumvented, never forgave French. Haig, though agreeing with French on the original issue (on which they were right and Kitchener was wrong), took a conveniently sanctimonious line. The argument, he thought, was 'unnecessary, because we ought all to have but the *one object* namely beat the Germans'.[7]

Despite Asquith's intervention, Kitchener had his way. French took solace in the fact that the New Armies would probably not take the field until June, 'by which time, he thought, the war would be over'. This belief was based upon information that the Germans had been forced to withdraw a substantial number of troops to the Eastern Front. It was therefore clear that one massive Allied offensive would overwhelm the weakened enemy. To this end, French and Joffre met in early February and agreed upon a joint action consisting of French attacks in Champagne and Artois, and a subsidiary assault by the British around La Bassée. French subsequently assigned the task to Haig because, as the latter recorded, 'he could never be certain of getting satisfactory results from Smith-Dorrien' and 'my troops were better'.[8]

Haig immediately began preparing for an attack near Neuve Chapelle which he hoped to launch on 15 February, depending on the state of the ground. But, as was the case with every action in this war, the battle was long delayed in preparation. After giving initial approval to Haig's plan, French qualified it by revealing that the government was still keen on a coastal operation. Excited by the prospect of a quick victory in conjunction with the French, Sir John had lost interest in an operation on the coast, as had, momentarily, Haig. 'We have neither troops nor guns in sufficient numbers, and . . . the enemy has carefully prepared that front against attack from sea.' Haig was equally critical of the politicians' enthusiasm for the idea of sending troops to Salonika, a move intended to bring Greece, Rumania and perhaps Bulgaria into the war on the side of the Entente, with obviously disastrous effects upon Austria-Hungary. Though he agreed that the plan was politically sound, 'from a *Military* point of view, it is a mistake to scatter our small army and to have more than one objective'.[9]

It was not until 19 February that approval was finally given to Haig's plans. He now hoped to launch the attack by mid-March, weather permitting. Suddenly, however, the French threw in a spanner when they asked the British to take over trenches in the Ypres area. Haig and French sensed that the problem arose because, 'in consequence of the fiasco of Smith-Dorrien's attack by the Second Army on Messines last December, the French don't believe we mean business!' After a heated argument with Joffre, French was able to delay the relief indefinitely. But, in order to pre-empt any more inconvenient requests, Sir John insisted that Haig's offensive be 'on a big scale' and be launched as soon as possible. Haig agreed, but emphasised that, owing to the weather, 10 March was the earliest possible date to start.[10]

Haig's immediate aim in the Battle of Neuve Chapelle was to capture the Aubers Ridge – an important observation point. But, more ambitiously, he aimed for a dramatic breakthrough, through which the cavalry could rush and then run riot behind the German lines. This objective seemed simple, therefore he looked for a 'simple common sense way' to achieve it. In his search, he clashed with Rawlinson, the IV Corps commander, who wanted to attack the village 'by "halves"; one half one day followed by the other half next day'. Such a plan was too complicated and unambitious; Haig wanted instead to push through to the ridge on the first day. For similar reasons, he disagreed with his artillery commander who proposed to bombard the area 'by compartments' over a period of four days. Haig preferred to 'compress the fire into a terrific outburst for three hours . . . and follow it by a sudden rush of our infantry. This will take advantage of the element of surprise'. The difference between Haig and Rawlinson was the difference between the infantryman who aimed for a deliberate, localised tactical success and the cavalryman who hoped for a profound strategic victory. As Haig explained to Rawlinson on 2 March:

> Our objective [is] not merely the capture of Neuve Chapelle. Our existing line [is] just as satisfactory for us as if we were in Neuve Chapelle. I aim at getting to the line . . . of the La Bassée road to Lille and thus cut off the enemy's front. It seem[s] to me desirable to make our plan in the chance of surprising the enemy and with the definite objective of advancing rapidly (and without any check) in the hope of starting a *general advance*.

Haig placed a cavalry division in readiness behind the lines.[11]

The battle began as Haig had hoped on 10 March. Due to the shortage of ammunition, the planned three-hour bombardment was limited to a mere thirty-five minutes. When the guns fell silent at 8.05 a.m., four British divisions advanced. Since secrecy had been well maintained, they were confronted by a force half their size. By 10 a.m., the British had broken through on a front of 1,500 metres, and had captured Neuve Chapelle. Everything had so far gone according to plan. Haig ordered the cavalry forward, but by early afternoon the advance ground to a halt. Undaunted, he was certain that movement would be quickly restored in the morning.

It wasn't. Aubers Ridge remained inviolate. During the night, the enemy had rushed extra men and machine-guns into the lines. The bombardment of the second day had little effect upon them. On the 12th the Germans counter-attacked, but with little success. After three days of incessant fighting, the battle came to an end and the new line established as a defensive position. Rawlinson's comments on the battle are revealing:

> I think D. H. would have been better advised to content himself with the capture of the village instead of going on with the attack on the 11th, 12th and 13th for the purpose of trying to get the cavalry through. I advised him to do this in the first instance but he and Sir John were so obsessed with the cavalry idea that he would not listen. Had he been content with the village we should

have gained just as much ground and reduced our casualties by three quarters.

On a front of about 3,000 metres the British had penetrated to a depth of 1,000 metres, at a loss of over 12,000 men. The latter figure, Haig admitted, 'make[s] me quite sad. So many good fellows no more; but it can't be done without incurring loss.' German casualties were about equal.[12]

French quickly penned a letter to Haig, congratulating him on 'the magnificent gallantry and devoted tenacious courage displayed by all ranks whom you have ably led to success and victory'. Haig, however, was more concerned with opportunities lost. His plan, he was certain, had the potential for success, but success had not been realised in the execution. A post-mortem revealed that at the crucial moment after the capture of Neuve Chapelle, British forces had not pushed forward quickly enough to exploit their gains. Haig asked Rawlinson to explain this delay and was told that 'Joey' Davies, the 8th Division commander, had not pushed his reserves forward. In consequence, Haig asked French to recall Davies, who then revealed that he had been acting on Rawlinson's orders. When Rawlinson finally confessed that this was indeed the case, French threatened to sack him. Haig then stepped in, arguing that since he had 'many other valuable qualities for a commander on active service', he should escape with a severe reprimand.[13]

The incident involving Davies is complicated by a web of personal animosities which makes an objective assessment of guilt impossible. It was not, by any means, simply a case of moral cowardice on Rawlinson's part – though elements of such do exist. Rawlinson had for long been dissatisfied with Davies, and had been searching for an issue to justify his removal. Unfortunately, he grabbed in haste at the wrong issue. As a result, as he admitted, 'it makes things look as if I had been trying to sacrifice him in order to save myself and this I do not like at all'. Regrettably, the incident also obscured some disturbing realities about the Neuve Chapelle battle. On a crucial part of the front, the wire (contrary to Haig's assumption) had not been destroyed. Thus, a conflict of purposes with regards to the bombardment was revealed (to those who cared to notice). The storm of shells had frightened the wits out of the Germans, but had not prepared the way everywhere for the infantry. Battalions from the Scottish Rifles and the Middlesex had been mowed down in front of uncut wire. Rawlinson saw no reason to pour more men into the bloodbath and had instructed Davies to hold back the reserves. As he remarked in his diary:

> Douglas Haig was disappointed . . . but I think he looked for too much – he expects to get the cavalry through with the next push but I very much doubt he will succeed in doing more than lose a large number of gallant men without effecting any very great purpose. I should be content with capturing another piece out of the enemy's line of trenches and waiting for the counter attack.

The difference between Rawlinson and Haig was again revealed. But, despite the former's claims to the contrary, objections to Haig's plans were never properly aired. Though Rawlinson knew that the wire had not been cut, he did not tell Haig. He did not do so because he was too much in awe (and indeed too afraid) of the Chief. The fact that Haig had saved Rawlinson from a sacking made candour even less likely in future.[14]

Whilst he did not consider the battle a success, Haig was nevertheless proud of his achievements. He was therefore annoyed to find on 27 March that he had been ordered to rewrite his report of the battle so that it 'reads as if the action taken was on the orders of the GHQ!' He let off steam in his diary:

> The whole thing is so childish, that I could hardly have credited the truth of the story had I not seen the paper. The main thing, however, is to beat the Germans *soon*, and leave to the British public the task of awarding credit for work done after peace has been made.

French tried to soothe Haig's temper the following day by telling him that he had recommended him for a GCB. Haig, however, would have none of it. 'I told Sir John that my one thought was to finish the war as soon as possible, that the decorations did not enter into my mind, all I wanted was responsible work; decorations always come to people along with old age.' Though he was probably not as disinterested as he made out, Haig did feel that it was important that credit be given where it was due. As he wrote on another occasion, 'It seems unmanly to wish to take the credit which really belongs to others!'[15]

The little Battle of Neuve Chapelle had a massive effect upon Haig's tactics during the rest of the war. As far as he could see, a brilliant victory had nearly been achieved. He was especially impressed with the bombardment on the first day: (for all he knew) the enemy wire had been destroyed, and machine-guns largely silenced. A breakthrough – albeit of a very limited nature – had been achieved. The apparent mistakes made in the execution convinced Haig that there were no flaws in the design. Comfortable in his ignorance, he could assure himself that it would be relatively easy to correct these errors and therefore to expand upon the small successes of his first independent engagement. As he told Rothschild, 'I think the main lesson of Neuve Chapelle is that given sufficient ammunition and suitable guns we can break through the enemy's line whenever we like! . . . but of course the losses on both sides must be considerable.'[16] In other words, Haig concluded that if Neuve Chapelle was a partial success, a complete success would result from an expansion of all of its elements. Longer bombardments, more men, wider fronts, longer battles and more casualties would bring about the real breakthrough which Haig was certain he could achieve. But the emphasis on things big clouded his comprehension of things small. Nor had he apparently heard of the law of diminishing returns.

Two weeks after the Battle of Neuve Chapelle, Haig learned that it would be some time before he would be able to put into practice the lessons he had learned. On 20 March, Robertson informed him 'confidentially that ammunition is likely to be just as short next month as at present'. Haig was predictably annoyed:

In my opinion, given sufficient High Explosive gun ammunition we could drive the Germans out of France in six weeks. Instead of having thirty rounds a day per gun and howitzer, we will only have seven. It is a disgraceful state of affairs to be in this situation after over 7 months of War. How can we order Officers Commanding Corps to 'press on with vigour' and at the same time say 'mind you must not expend more than 7 rounds a gun in a whole day!'

Ten days later, Robertson announced that a general offensive was to be launched by the French and the British in the first week of May. In the meantime, Haig was to conserve as far as possible his ammunition, without endangering the safety of his men.[17]

The shortage of ammunition was a problem of some political complexity. For this reason, far removed from the scene, Haig did not entirely understand it. Eager for simple explanations, he settled upon the industrial workers as an easy target for censure. In February, he had accused them of being too eager to take holidays. Two months later, they were criticised for drinking too much. Haig explained the problem and suggested a simple solution:

> As re the workmen who are said to get drunk now. I expect that the New Army has taken away a very large number of the best workers, so that many who were only occasional workers (because of their taste for Drink) have now to work full time. Their presence or absence was hardly noticed until the need for a full output of work was rendered necessary by the war. I don't suppose it would be possible to make such people sober by any regulations. The best thing, in my opinion, is to punish some of the chief offenders . . . Take and shoot two or three of them, and the 'Drink habit' would cease I feel sure. These sub-people don't care what the King or anyone else does – they mean to have their drink.

The recommendation was echoed in a letter to Rothschild. But, afraid that he might be misconstrued (and perhaps worried that the Rothschild well of vintage brandy might consequently run dry), Haig insisted that he had no truck for total abstinence. 'Personally, I believe in moderation and have little confidence in the water drinker! It is usually a sign of weakness in some respect.'[18]

The munitions problem was complicated by the attempt, in mid-February, to force the Dardanelles straits. When Haig first learned of the plan to gain access to Russia via the Black Sea, he thought it basically sound. The problem, as he indicated to Rothschild, was that the politicians (particularly that fool Churchill) had no idea how best to achieve their objective:

> it was madness to attempt a landing on an open beach in the Gallipoli peninsular [sic], with the enemy fully prepared and waiting for the operation to begin . . . Why not land in Herzegovina and advance via Sarajevo to the support of the Servians? Anything would

be better than a check at the Dardanelles. Moreover every attempt at a landing which did not succeed would be regarded as a defeat.

At this stage, Haig was not as censorious of alternative strategies as he would later become. Though he could accept the theoretical justification for the Dardanelles expedition, he thought it an unnecessary distraction since it was clear that the Germans were being beaten with little difficulty on the Western Front. Proof of their imminent defeat was, after all, abundantly available. Letters which Charteris took from prisoners captured at Neuve Chapelle indicated that 'Germany has begun to feel the effects of the war greatly and [is] despondent'. From this and similar information, Haig was able confidently to predict that 'by the end of July she will show signs of wanting peace'. There was a danger that the troops sent to the Dardanelles were the very ones capable of pushing the Germans over the brink.[19]

The combined Allied offensive scheduled for early May was to consist of a French thrust in the Vimy area and another British effort against the Aubers Ridge. The enemy, however, upset the calculations by again attacking on the Ypres front on 22 April. The battle was notable for the German use of poison gas which took the French by surprise. The occasion prompted a now customary tirade against the French, whose

surprise . . . should never have happened. It seems to have been a distinctly bad performance, and the possibility of its happening was never realised by Foch and Co. These French leaders are a queer mixture of fair ability (not more than fair) and ignorance of the practical side of war. They are not built for it by nature. They are too excitable and they never seem to think of what the enemy may do. And they will not see a nasty situation as it really is, and take steps to meet it.

Haig's perceived superiority over French commanders had been encouraged a few days earlier when Ferdinand Foch ('regarded in the French Army as their most capable General!') had visited him in order to 'study the method of attack adopted by the British' at Neuve Chapelle. 'Hitherto they have rather looked upon us as "amateurs" rather than "professional soldiers".' A similar boost to the ego came when Esher relayed information from a third source that the Kaiser judged the '1st Army Corps under Douglas Haig . . . the best in the world'. Haig feigned humility, but nevertheless took considerable pride in this rather dubious piece of information.[20]

French also had good words for Haig, telling him, on 30 April, that 'he could not express what he felt for the staunch support and help I had been to him throughout the war. He had never had any anxiety about my command.' This was an indirect reference to Sir John's very serious worries about Smith-Dorrien, who 'was quite unfit (he said) to hold the Command of an Army'. French had never forgiven Smith-Dorrien for disobeying orders during the retreat from Mons. His apparently ineffective command during the previous week on the Ypres front was the last straw; French persuaded Kitchener to send him home. The Second Army went to Plumer, with Allenby taking command of Plumer's V Corps. Though a cavalry officer, Allenby was no favourite of Haig's, since he allegedly believed that the war would 'continue and end in the trenches' and that 'cavalry would cease to exist as such'. Haig rejected these heretical views outright, insisting that the cavalry's day would soon come. He railed against the 'short sighted policy to put Cavalry [soldiers] in the trenches', pointing out that 'it will be impossible to replace them when wanted later on to reap the fruits of victory'.[21]

While the German attack on Ypres dragged on, Haig was left in relative peace to prepare his Aubers Ridge operation. His initial intention was simply to multiply the ferocity of the Neuve Chapelle assault in the hope of extending its success. It gradually became clear, however, that this would not be possible – at least not to the extent Haig wished. The necessary quantities of men and ammunition were not available. As a result, by 30 April, he was doubtful of success:

> I . . . told the C. in C. that in my opinion we had not enough troops and guns to *sustain* our forward movement, and reap decisive results . . . In my opinion, three more good divisions are required (in addition to my eight divisions) . . . Sir John said Lord K. would not send out his new Army because he was afraid they might be wanted at the Dardanelles or elsewhere. He wished me to attack and do the best I could with the troops available.[22]

Haig had, in effect, exonerated himself from failure even before the battle began.

The Battle of Aubers Ridge, finally launched on 9 May, was even less successful than the temporarily pessimistic Haig had predicted. The preliminary bombardment was slightly longer than that at Neuve Chapelle (forty minutes) but much less effective, primarily because German defences were much stronger. Plodding forward at 5.40 a.m., the infantry crashed headlong into virtually uncut wire and machine-guns which had not been silenced. The first wave was completely annihilated; the second, pushed stubbornly forward in the afternoon, met a similar fate.

'Our losses yesterday are *estimated* at *145 officers and 9,400 men*,' Haig recorded on the 10th. These figures, he thought, were 'probably 25% too high'. (In fact, there were about 2,000 more casualties than he had been told.) In a letter to Rothschild, Haig attempted to explain the British failure:

> Possibly I ought to have insisted on the Enemy's trenches being bombarded for a longer time; but the commander of the Division and Corps considered the nature of the enemy's entrenchments which they were going to attack and they got all the heavy artillery support which they asked for.

This was an uncharitable assessment of the reasons for the failure, and not unlike Rawlinson's evasion of responsibility after Neuve Chapelle. Haig never hesitated to correct subordinate commanders if he disagreed with their plans. That he did not do so on this occasion is evidence that he agreed with them, and that blame for the failure was rightly his.[23]

Meanwhile, the French were attacking Vimy Ridge. Whilst initially more successful than the British, they had, due to the greater scale of their effort, suffered losses of a magnitude which the British had yet to experience. For this reason, they expected the British to continue their assaults. Haig, however, preferred a short delay, because

> in view of our failure to get the Aubers ridge by a rapid rush, it was necessary to proceed methodically to break down the enemy's strong points and entrenchments . . . We are confronted by a very

carefully prepared position, which is held by a most determined enemy with numerous machine guns.

Thus, a 'fairly long artillery bombardment will be necessary'. Haig insisted upon 'accurate observations of *each shot*', so as to 'make sure of flattening out the enemy's "strong points" of support, before the Infantry is launched'. The bombardment would be sustained day and night, in order to 'shatter the nerves of the men who work [the] machine guns'. 'This bombardment, at a slow rate of fire, should be continued . . . till the hostile defences are really destroyed. The assault is to be postponed till this is reported, and until our guns have also mastered the enemy's artillery.' This was a significant change from Haig's previous tactics, and certain to be more effective. But there remained a fundamental contradiction between what Haig wanted to achieve and what artillery could achieve. Artillery was dominant, but it could not blow holes in enemy lines or so demoralise German soldiers as to lead to the breakthrough which he confidently expected. This was a war of attrition, and Haig

did not understand the *tactical* difference between a breakthrough battle and the . . . battles of attrition in which he engaged . . . The *modus operandi* [in a battle of attrition] is the orchestration of firepower. By its means limited objectives may be gained and the defender destroyed when he attempts to regain vital ground. Ground is important only if it enables the killing business to be more efficient. To quote a distasteful and unfortunately discredited phrase, the body-count is what matters.

Dominick Graham's point is that instead of trying to destroy the enemy (all that was possible in this war), Haig tried to capture strategic objectives, as classical lessons dictated. The attempt to capture ground rendered the 'killing business' less efficient.[24]

Attrition battles, unlike attempts to capture strategic objectives, should be launched where conditions favour the attacker. The area around Aubers Ridge, with the enemy on the high ground, was not such a place. Heavy rains rendered the soil which had been churned by a three-day bombardment into a vast and slimy pit of mud. Shell craters filled with water, turning the landscape into a scattering of tiny lakes. It was across this horrible terrain that the infantry slogged at 11.30 p.m. on 15 May, in the first night attack. There was sporadic success. In places, the German front line trenches were overrun. Elsewhere, men were mown down in the mire of no man's land. The British continued to ooze forward over the next ten days, whereupon the exhaustion of ammunition supplies forced a halt. From 15 to 25 May (technically, the Battle of Festubert) an advance of 1,000 metres (on a front of 4,000) had been bought at the cost of 16,000 casualties. German losses numbered perhaps 6,000.

Prior to the push on the 15th, Sir John told Haig not to be discouraged in the event of failure since 'by simply attacking we helped the French greatly . . . we thereby drew German troops upon ourselves which would otherwise be used on their front'. According, then, to French's criteria, the Battle of Aubers Ridge was a success. The Germans were forced to use reserves which would otherwise have been employed against the French. Haig, however, was not content with this limited definition of success. He sought and easily found other reasons for optimism. Evidence from the front indicated that 'the enemy does not . . . have many reserves to bring up against us'. A breakthrough was therefore imminent. On the 17th, he commented that 'things are going well and the enemy on our front shows signs of breaking up'. Rothschild was told how the longer bombardment made it 'fairly easy' to overrun German trenches. Furthermore, 'the prisoners captured are very inferior to those taken at Neuve Chapelle'. Inferior prisoners were taken as evidence that the cream of the German Army had been annihilated and that the enemy was on his last legs. Haig neglected to explain how these inferior specimens had, on two occasions within the space of a fortnight, prevented the British Army from reaching any of its primary objectives. As this fact did not accord with his fantasies, it was conveniently ignored. Gazing dreamily back on the previous month's fighting, Haig concluded:

We have broken the enemy's front for a distance of over three miles and have advanced at one point over a mile from our old line. If this is compared with what the French have done near Arras it will be found that our progress is considerably greater . . . But the most satisfactory result [is] the state of demoralization into which we succeeded in throwing the enemy . . . We kept firing . . . with such good results that many surrendered because they had not slept for several days and had no food. They said they were starving! . . . for the first time it is noticeable that German Private soldiers are of the opinion that 'Germany cannot win.'

This ability to turn black into white enabled Haig to withstand four depressing years of war.[25]

French was less euphoric. Though indicating otherwise to Haig, he was certain that British efforts had failed because of the gross scarcity of ammunition. The frustrated Sir John found himself in a horrible predicament: Kitchener stood on Scylla urging him to conserve men and munitions for the Dardanelles, while from Charybdis Joffre cried persistently for British attacks to continue. Losing his patience, French leaked news of the shell shortage to Repington at *The Times*. Reporting on the Festubert operation, Repington wrote: 'The need of an unlimited supply of high explosive was a fatal bar to our success . . . It is certain that we can smash the German crust if we have the means. So the means we must have and as quickly as possible.'[26] Though the article was a direct attack upon Kitchener (who was responsible for the 'means'), French appears to have had a wider objective, namely, the destruction of the Liberal government. He sent two members of his personal staff to London to discuss the shell shortage with Conservative leaders and Lloyd George, Asquith's main rival. The morning after Repington's exposé, Lord Fisher, First Sea Lord, resigned because of his doubts about the Dardanelles expedition. The combination of the shell scandal and the Fisher resignation led to the fall of the Liberal government on 19 May. The Conservative leaders were brought into a coalition, but the most significant change as far as the war was concerned was the establishment of the Ministry of Munitions under Lloyd George.

Haig, perhaps even more so than French, had had to endure the frustrating effects of the shell shortage. But despite his annoyance, when the scandal finally broke, he was quick to come to the defence of Kitchener. 'I do think the attacks on Lord K. are most disgraceful,' he wrote on 24 May. 'I hope that the government will suspend all Harmsworth's papers.' To Colonel Fitzgerald, Kitchener's Military Secretary, Haig wrote:

> I must send you a line to tell you how thoroughly disgusted we all are here at the attacks which the Harmsworth reptile press have made on Lord K. It is most unfair and most unpatriotic at the

present time. That 'Times' has published several articles for which the editor would have been shot in any other country but England.

The last sentence was obviously not written in praise of British civil liberties.[27]

On the 26th, Haig received a letter from Clive Wigram, the Assistant Private Secretary to the King, informing him of 'an organised conspiracy in the Press controlled by Lord Northcliffe against Lord Kitchener' in which 'Sir J. French's personal Staff are mixed up'. Wigram apparently thought Haig could use his influence to restore calm. Haig, however was doubtful:

> I have always put in a word, when I get a chance, advising that we all, especially at this time, should pull together, and think about nothing else but beating the enemy. I fear such advice from me had no effect. The truth is that Sir J. is of a very jealous disposition.

Despite Haig's impotence, Kitchener managed to pull through the crisis. Haig was 'glad to see that he has come out of it stronger than ever'.[28]

Though Haig claimed that he did not have any influence with French, it is more likely that he did not want to get involved. In a reference to Wigram's letter, he told his wife that 'I have really no spare time to meddle in such squabbles!' His choice of words indicates the disdain which he felt for the whole affair and the danger which he sensed. When Lady Haig advised that he should do his duty but otherwise not get involved, he replied:

> I entirely agree with what you say: namely, that as long as I am serving under Sir J. French my duty is to loyally carry out his orders and help him to beat the enemy, to the best of my powers. This I am trying to do, and I put my own personal feelings out of the matter altogether.

Unfortunately, Haig's 'personal feelings' were in conflict. Whilst he disagreed with Kitchener over the supply of men and munitions, he clashed with French on many, more fundamental, issues. In Haig's opinion, French was unbalanced, petty, jealous and easily manipulated by the evil Wilson. He had again brought the Army

191

into disrepute by meddling in politics. Simply stated, he was a danger as Commander-in-Chief. Haig still respected Kitchener, but had no remaining respect for French. He found it impossible to take the latter's side, even though, on this occasion, he sympathised with his motives. Haig probably also sensed that French's days were numbered, and nothing could be gained by allying with him. He therefore kept his distance, and 'loyally carr[ied] out his orders' – a different matter entirely from loyally supporting French.[29]

Haig's desire to protect the Army (and thus to ensure the most efficient conduct of the war) also influenced his decision not to meddle in the affair. Aware as he was of Kitchener's faults, Haig still believed that the Army could not do without him, simply because he was the only soldier powerful enough to stand up to the politicians. Without Kitchener, Haig feared, the conduct of the war would be left entirely to the men in frock coats. The Dardanelles expedition was an example of what was at risk if the politicians were allowed to meddle unchecked. As the folly of that expedition became increasingly clear to Haig, his contempt for amateur strategists grew. 'Indeed there seems to us here (soldiers) to be no real direction of the war in London,' he told Rothschild on 30 June. 'It is certainly absolute folly to go on pouring troops and ammunition into [the] Dardanelles, a point of secondary importance, while this, the decisive point, is starved.' Kitchener had, ironically, done very little to counter this folly. Haig accepted this fact but supported the War Secretary regardless. Matters would be much worse without him, as was intimated later in the letter to Rothschild.

> I attribute all this mismanagement to the fact that the General Staff *in London* is practically non-existent! It is the duty of that body to give a seasoned opinion for the assistance of the government. Instead we see talkative politicians like Winston controlling the strategical operation of the military forces of the empire. What qualifications have such men for work of that nature?

To further the irony, it was again the War Minister who was partially responsible for this state of affairs. Contemptuous of trained staff officers throughout his career, the dictatorial Kitchener had done much to hasten the demise of the General Staff during the war. Haig could not have been unaware of the damage done to the institution he and Haldane had carefully nurtured. But, when the choice came down to a flawed Kitchener or a potentially disastrous Churchill and company, Haig had no difficulty deciding where his loyalties lay.[30]

Finally, Haig refused to support French because he disagreed vehemently with the way Sir John went about his attack. In such a situation, Haig would have whispered in the ear of Esher or the King. French had instead enlisted the assistance of the Press, which Haig likened to carrying on with a whore. (Speaking of which, this was another cause of Haig's disapproval of French.) Ten months of war had done nothing to improve Haig's low opinion of newspaper correspondents, originally formed during the Sudan campaign. As he indicated to Rothschild on 17 April, the control of the Press was 'not satisfactory':

> The 'Times Military Correspondent' deduces military lessons (or tries to do so) from gossip: soldiers' letters are published, and Sir J. French's dispatches sometimes also give away military information of value to the enemy. All this might be stopped by having military correspondents of the Bennet Burleigh type – who will write highly coloured descriptions which are of no real military value, but would please 'Arriet and sell the newspaper! In my opinion it is a mistake to employ anyone who has had military training to write for a newspaper while the war is going on: such a one cannot help reporting events from a military standpoint and so divulges secrets.

Whilst pleading national security, Haig was also making a very personal attack upon Repington, a thorn in his side for a number of years. He found the knowledge and influence of *The Times* correspondent threatening. In addition, it was especially galling for the Army to be criticised by this particular scoundrel, a man whose fondness for London society and for other men's wives was notorious. Haig's consuming hatred inspired the rather spurious claim on 21 May that the shelling of an observation post at La Couture arose from the fact that Repington had mentioned its existence in *The Times* three days earlier. 'We in the First Army have a grudge against Repington,' he confessed, 'it was quite wrong to allow such a deceitful fellow to come to the front at all.'[31]

Thus, French's liaison with Repington caused Haig's opinion of both men to plummet even further. He noted with disgust that 'French

seems to have that scoundrel Repington staying with him as his guest!'
It was 'most unsoldierlike . . . to keep one's own advertising agent'.[32] In
effect, this is exactly what French was doing. He had discovered that it
was safer to have the Press on his side than to have correspondents
sneaking around behind his back asking embarrassing questions. And,
if French was having trouble getting his way with politicians, where
better to turn than to the newspapers – the moulders of public
opinion? Haig, however, had yet to make these discoveries. In the
meantime, his anger with Repington prompted him to rule that no
correspondents were to be allowed within the fighting zone under
his control.

On 7 June, Robertson announced that French and Kitchener were
on better terms and suggested that Haig should invite the latter
to the front in order to further the reconciliation. It subsequently
transpired that Sir John would not agree to the visit 'on the grounds
that French Commanders would lose confidence in [him]'. Haig
concluded: 'Apparently French is still afraid that K.'s presence with
the Army might undermine his own position as C. in C. in the field!'
Haig, determined that Kitchener should learn 'at first hand what the
needs of the Army are', nevertheless persisted, and was finally able
to arrange the visit.[33]

When Kitchener arrived on 8 July he astonished Haig with his
ignorance of the situation on the Western Front. 'The general system
of our lines of defence caused Lord K. anxiety', but he 'did not really
know a great deal about our system.' This judgement was reinforced
when Haig again met Kitchener in London six days later. 'K. seemed
to me very ignorant of what is being done, and how trenches are
attacked and how bombarded. He admitted that the nature of the
modern lines of defence was quite new to him, and he said he felt
"quite at sea" on the subject.' Haig, still intent on being charitable to
the War Minister, simply remarked that he 'respected him for being
so honest!'[34]

Haig was at this stage more interested in Kitchener's attitude
towards French. The latter was apparently still being difficult, and
was of late completely ignoring Kitchener's advice. 'However, he
(K.) was ready to do anything "to black French's boots" if need be,
in order to obtain agreement and win the war!' Haig was implored
'to assert myself more, and to insist on French proceeding on sound
principles'. Doubtful of succeeding, he told Kitchener 'it was more

his affair to control Sir John French than mine. I had really to do as I was ordered by Sir John, and French had much more self-confidence now than when I was with him in South Africa.'[35]

As far as Haig was concerned, French was beyond redemption. His misgivings multiplied as the days passed. It was not a single incident, but rather the dreadful regularity of petty annoyances which exhausted Haig's patience. French was like a tap that dripped in the night. His worst fault was his inconsistency: on one occasion orders from GHQ apparently changed three times in as many days. Equally annoying were his views on the future of the war, which swung wildly with his mercurial moods. Opinions expressed during a meeting on 9 July especially rankled Haig, for obvious reasons:

> Sir J. . . . gave out as his opinion that 'the German line would never be broken and Cavalry pursue, as some thought'. 'He believed that the line would be bulged and after the Germans had suffered heavily, the war would end more or less where the Armies were now in Western France!' Neither I nor the CGS quite believed this, nor did Sir J. give any 'reasons for the faith he holds'.

Though obviously accurate, the prediction was, to Haig, evidence of an unbalanced mind. It was clear to him that French did not have the temperament to lead a massive army which would soon bear the brunt of the fighting on the Western Front. Haig's contempt is revealed by a remark made later in the month, after French had predicted that the army would have to spend another winter in Flanders. 'To the minds of many', Haig commented, 'this was hailed as a good sign that the war would end fairly soon, because Sir John has never until now held this opinion . . . Indeed, *last November*, he told regiments that "all the hard fighting was over".' Meanwhile, Haig's own views were solidly consistent, if invariably wide of the mark.[36]

Haig nevertheless tried, according to his own definition, to remain loyal to French. Open disagreements would, he feared, only hamper the British cause. Therefore, when discussing his plans for an upcoming leave, Haig told his wife on 28 June:

> I don't want to go to London, unless I am ordered to appear at the War Office or elsewhere. French goes there this week, and if I went I should probably say something quite opposed to what

he has advised! This would only lead to friction which must be avoided at all costs . . . I sent him a line . . . and said 'my one object was to help him to end the war as soon as possible'.

Meanwhile, various influential people were urging Haig to speak his mind. Kitchener, as indicated above, wanted him to 'assert' himself. In a letter to Lady Haig, Wigram intimated that the King had similar hopes:

> if it was possible for H.M. to see Sir Douglas, I think from an Imperial point of view it would be helpful as events are moving very fast these days, and important decisions have to be taken at a moment's notice. The King, moreover, has a very high opinion of Sir Douglas's views of the situation, and it is so important at this crisis that H.M. should have the benefit of the opinion of those who can be trusted to say what is worth hearing.

Considering the pressure upon him, it is perhaps understandable that Haig soon began to transgress his own code of loyalty.[37]

Though he had no desire to go to London, Haig could not ignore the wishes of the King and Kitchener, who were eager for his views on French. After giving Haig the GCB in a private ceremony at Buckingham Palace on 14 July, the King quickly dispensed with formalities and struck straight at the issue at hand. He noted how, in the Grand Fleet, 'all the Admirals were on most friendly terms with one another' and concluded:

> the Army would be in the same satisfactory state . . . if the officer at the head of the Army in the Field . . . was fit for his position! He (the King) criticises French's dealings with the Press . . . All most unsoldier-like and he (the King) had lost confidence in Field Marshal French. And he had told Kitchener that he (K.) could depend on his (the King's) support in whatever action he took in dealing with French.

Haig replied that he thought the time to get rid of French had been immediately after the retreat, adding, rather curiously, that 'Now the Army was stationary [it] could practically be controlled from London.' Before leaving he was urged to write as candidly as he wished, with the assurance that whatever he wrote would be kept in the strictest confidence. Kitchener echoed this message during a meeting after lunch, assuring Haig that 'He would treat my letters as secret, and would not reply, but I would see my proposals given effect to and must profess ignorance when that happened!' Haig reflected that

> At both my interviews to-day, I was urged to write regarding the situation and doings of the Army in Flanders to Lord K. The King quite realised the nature of such conduct on my part, because he told me that he had said to Lord K. with reference to it 'If anyone acted like that, and told tales out of school, he would at school be called a sneak.' K.'s reply was that we are beyond the schoolboy's age![38]

Haig could play a sneak as well as anyone, but he always preferred 'straightforward gentlemanly dealing'. The influence which politics and politicians had in this war was abhorrent. Small men meddling in great issues rendered a broad view impossible. Concurring with Lady Haig that the political direction of the war was chaotic, Haig remarked: 'I agree that a Dictator is wanted, but the difficulty is to find one.' On another occasion, he commented rather cryptically (but somewhat alarmingly): 'I have little to do with the political direction of the war, but if necessity arose I would, of course, "do what my conscience dictates to be the right thing" regardless of my personal advancement.' His overriding emotion was one of impatient disdain and detachment. Exhausted with the incessant squabbling, he was, he told his wife, 'just waiting till this war is over, [so that] we can live our own quiet life together again'. This prospect, and 'the consciousness that we possess the sympathy and affection of *one* being', enabled him to withstand the strains of war. But, until peace came, the two of them should, he advised, ' "Look not mournfully into the past it comes not again," but "wisely improve the present, it is thine" and "go forth to meet the shadowy future without fear, and with a manly heart!!" '[39]

Behind Haig's disdain for those above him and his contentment with himself was his belief that the 1st Army was a model of military management, worthy of copy. His diaries are full of self-congratulation, for instance after a visit by Asquith:

> Sir John stated that the Prime Minister had expressed himself as greatly pleased with his visit to the 1st Army, and (for my own

information) had drawn comparisons between the 1st and 2nd Armies greatly to the disparagement of the latter! Sir John attributed the difference to the way in which Smith-Dorrien interfered with his Brigadiers and others under him, so that no one knew exactly what was wanted. I said I thought I had an advantage in having had 2 Divisions complete under my command for over two years at Aldershot . . . This was the 1st Corps which set the standard for the 1st Army both in discipline, in system of command, and Staff Duties.

Praise came to Haig from all directions. On 15 July 1915, Lieutenant-General Sir Aylmer Hunter-Weston, recently back from the Dardanelles, described the appalling state of organisation there. He suggested that the solution was to move Haig to the War Office, where he could keep Kitchener 'right if he goes wrong'. Elaborating, Hunter-Weston wrote:

Your power of clear thinking, your power of organisation, your study of your profession in the past, your experience of modern war, above all your strength of character make you the man for the military head of the War Office (CGS) under Lord Kitchener . . . You are needed to organise the nation for war.

Though Haig probably agreed with the description of his own abilities, he had no intention of going to the War Office, there to deal everyday with the dreaded politicians. Praise such as this did, however, reinforce his belief that he had special gifts to offer the nation and that he was unduly restricted by the incompetents above him.[40]

The ever-growing confidence that he alone knew the right way to victory is revealed in the pronouncements Haig made upon the future course of the war during the lull in the fighting between 30 June and 25 September. In a by now customary fashion, his conclusions were based on a less than charitable appraisal of the contributions of the French. For instance, on 14 June he noted with considerable derision 'the peaceful appearance of the villages and buildings on the front occupied during the winter by the French'. He concluded that the French had pursued a policy of 'live and let live', which in turn explained why the British casualties in the same area were proportionately higher. On the same day, Haig was perturbed but not surprised when one of General Joffre's staff officers announced that 'the French people are getting tired of the war'. The tremendous cost of the war, the occupation of a very wealthy part of France by the enemy and the cessation of trade and farming operations were affecting them. Everything was practically at a standstill and the whole of the manhood of the nation was concentrated on this frontier. *There was a general wish that a vigorous effort should be made to end the war by autumn.*

Quite paradoxically, a few days later another of Joffre's staff officers told Haig that the French public and the military were in 'doubt as to the real determination of the British Government to bring the war to a successful conclusion'. Confused as to the Allies' true feelings, Haig commented that 'the important point seems to me to be to prevent the peace party in France from gaining the upper hand, otherwise they will make peace in the autumn'.[41]

In order to achieve this, the French had to be prevented from finding any cause for complaint about a lack of British resolve. As Haig candidly admitted, French fears were not without foundation. 'One factor which had cause[d] much misgiving was the despatch of 4 Divisions of the "New Army" with much ammunition to the Dardanelles while the British Force in France is being starved for ammunition!' In a letter to Wigram, Haig argued that

it is fatal to pour more troops and ammunition down the Dardanelles sink. The whole British Expeditionary Force here if added to the Force now there cannot clear the two sides of the Dardanelles so as to make the Straits passage safe for ships and ensure the fall of Constantinople. By going on in the way the Cabinet is now acting great risk is run of the French making peace by the winter.

Haig again emphasised that the Western Front 'is the decisive point'. The duty of the government was to 'bring all the strength of the Empire to this point and beat the enemy. Then all else will be ours for the picking up.'[42]

In his letter to Wigram Haig reiterated a point which he had stressed almost since the beginning of the war:

To the onlooker here there seems to be no supreme control over the war as a whole. I attribute this to the failure to make use of

199

the General Staff in London. You allow our policy to be directed by whoever is the ablest speaker. Fundamental principles of strategy seem daily to be ignored.

Haig could discern no consistent policy for the direction of the war. The politicians simply flitted from one madcap scheme to another. When one of these failed, as appeared to be the case in the Dardanelles, panic resulted. As Robertson revealed on 26 June, 'They (the Cabinet) are in a funk.'[43]

The details of this 'funk' were alarming. 'The inclination is to send more and more troops to the Dardanelles,' Robertson warned. Since this would inevitably reduce British strength on the Western Front and increase the susceptibility to German attack, the Cabinet had, according to Robertson 'asked for our plans and lines of retreat!' He, in reply, had advised ministers of the importance of maintaining contact with the French Army, and of pre-empting the Germans by cooperating in an attack as soon as possible. Under no circumstances should the British abandon contact with the Allies in order to protect the Channel ports. On this point he differed with French, who maintained that, as the first priority was to preserve the British Army, defending the ports was of absolute importance. Haig, on the other hand, agreed with Robertson. On 23 June, he told a now morose Sir John that 'by joining the French and defeating the enemy, he would cover the channel ports more effectively than if our troops acted on the defensive!' Alternatively, 'If . . . the British were to separate . . . it would certainly mean defeat in detail, because the enemy could contain us with a comparatively small force, while he massed in great strength and defeated the French.'[44]

Whilst it was clear to Haig that the British could not carry on without allies, he was at the same time certain that 'the British Army is gradually becoming the most important factor': 'the situation is different to last autumn. Then the British had only five or six divisions in the field. Now we have 25 Divisions or more, and are daily getting stronger, whereas by October the French will have exhausted their trained reserves.' Haig exaggerated a process which was indeed occurring, but which would not lead to the circumstances he described for some time. It was a case of the wish being the father of the thought. Haig yearned for more British influence over Allied military strategy, therefore he discounted the importance of the French whilst he magnified that of his own Army. For instance, he predicted that the main German attack in the coming months would be directed against the British, probably with the aim of capturing Calais. 'England is the real enemy of Germany. It is even possible that Germany may seek to placate France, and get terms of peace.'[45]

Haig could at this time also discern other changes in the nature of the war. For instance, on 22 June, he admitted:

> The enemy's defences are now so strong and sufficient ammunition lacking to destroy them, they can only be taken by siege methods – by using bombs, and by hand to hand fighting in the trenches. The ground above is so swept by gun and machine gun and rifle fire that an advance in the open, except by night, is impossible.[46]

Taken by itself, the above passage seems to imply that Haig had come to terms with a static war, that he had shifted decisively from a strategy of penetration to one of attrition. But the key to this statement is the reference to the lack of sufficient ammunition. With enough heavy artillery, the German line could, Haig believed, still be broken and mobility restored. In other words, more guns would open the way for the cavalry.

The course which Haig's tactical thinking had taken since the beginning of the war is evident in some advice he gave to an assistant from the Ministry of Munitions:

> We discussed the nature of guns and ammunition most required. I said large numbers of *heavy* guns and howitzers because enemy's defences had become so strong. We ought to aim at having enough guns to engage enemy on a front of 25 to 30 miles, while retaining in addition a strong central reserve. After wearing down the enemy the Reserve should be sent in to attack at whatever point the enemy appeared to be weakened. By this means the decisive attack would come as a surprise. This can never be the case if an attack is made on a narrow front. Owing to the present strong defences, the enemy is able to hold up any attack long enough to enable his Reserves to arrive before the line is pierced.

Shortly afterwards these ideas were incorporated into a memo to the General Staff. Specific recommendations were made regarding the scope of future offensives and the men and material necessary for their implementation. The British, Haig emphasised, should attack on a front of twenty-five to thirty miles with a force of at least thirty-six divisions supported by 1,150 heavy guns and twice as many field guns. In a conversation with Lord Haldane, Haig revealed that he had come upon his ideas by 'applying old principles to present conditions'. In the past, a breakthrough had been achieved when an attack of sufficient strength was made on a wide enough front. Nothing, Haig thought, had altered this basic military truth. The new conditions – massive armies, massively armed – simply magnified the proportions of the attack (its size and its time-scale) without changing the principles. The Battles of Passchendaele and the Somme were born.[47]

It cannot be emphasised enough that the 'big' battles which Haig had in mind were not meant to be battles of attrition. He did not intend to use the prodigious supplies of munitions and men to wear down the enemy, but rather to defeat him with a bold, decisive and overwhelming stroke. As he indicated to his wife on 10 August, this sort of victory was possible because 'the enemy is further through his resources in men than our papers make out. He can't go on after January and I would not be surprised to see him give in by November.' Eager as he was to find evidence of a German collapse, he not surprisingly found it around every corner. For instance, he made great capital out of reports that German soldiers were forbidden to write home about their recent heavy losses in Bavaria. In fact, these restrictions were probably no different from the censorship which applied in the British Army. On another occasion, he commented that the new British junior officers, despite their lack of 'practical knowledge' were nevertheless 'much better than anything the German Army can now produce'. Daily intelligence reports produced a drug-like euphoria. Peering through the haze, Haig concluded: 'I don't think it will be many months before the Germans are reduced to make peace *on our terms*.'[48]

A commander must be optimistic about the future, otherwise he will not be able to maintain his resolve or inspire his men. But optimism and fantasy are two different things. The wild statements such as those cited were not odd aberrations in an otherwise balanced view – they were Haig's perception of the war. It is therefore correct to speculate on the extent to which his tactics and strategy were a product of that perception. In other words, had Haig realised that victory was not 'just

1. Rachel Haig, 1867.

2. Rachel with *(left to right)* Douglas, George, John (Bee), 1867.

3. Haig at 20 – a rare photograph of him in a kilt.

4. Phoenix Club, 1882 (Haig is seated on the left).

5.   Henrietta Jameson
(née Haig) 1886.

6.   Dorothy Maud Haig
(née Vivian), 1910.

7.   On the eve of war – Haig a
Aldershot, 1914.

8.   Mud.

9. Haig, reviewing troops, 1918.

10.   Captain G. S. Duncan, C.F.

11.   Brigadier-General John Charteris

12.   Haig with his Army commanders and assorted staff, GHQ Montreuil, 1918.
Front row *(left to right):* Plumer, Haig, Rawlinson. Second row: Byng, Birdwood, Horne.

13.   A rare moment of relaxation –
Haig golfing in Canada, 1926.

14.   Haig inspecting the Richmond
poppy factory on the day before he
died, 27 January 1928.

15. Bemersyde, 1925. *Left to right:* Alexandra (born 9 March 1907, later Lady Dacre of Glanton) Lady Haig, Lord Haig, Victoria (born 7 November 1908, later Victoria Montagu Douglas Scot).

16. Dawyck (the present Earl Haig, born 15 March 1918) with Irene (born 7 October 1919, later Lady Astor of Hever). Bemersyde 1925.

around the corner' but rather years away, would he have suggested a different way of fighting the war?

Haig's unbridled optimism aside, the Allied commanders had little cause for cheer in the summer of 1915. The Dardanelles expedition had become bogged down in a manner depressingly similar to the offensives in the West. Italy had joined the Allies in time to suffer a series of humiliating defeats on the Isonzo. In contrast, Bulgaria (due, in Haig's opinion, to the failure of the diplomats) had joined the wrong side. The worst news came from the Eastern Front, where, after a million casualties, the Russian Army was forced into a humiliating retreat.

These concurrent disasters, and the need to relieve the pressure on the Russians, prompted Joffre to press for a massive Allied offensive, with the British attacking next to the French Tenth Army in the vicinity of Loos. The area, open ground with numerous slag heaps and chalk pits providing excellent defensive cover, was an attacker's nightmare. Upon learning of Joffre's wishes, Haig commented that the position was far too dangerous and that he preferred another assault upon the Aubers Ridge. French agreed but felt it was important to comply with Joffre's wishes. He hoped, however, to attack mainly with artillery, using the infantry only to hold the Germans on their front. Thus the needless sacrifice of British lives in an attack upon a virtually impregnable position could be avoided.

Anxious at the prospect of a half-hearted British effort, Joffre complained to Kitchener, who then instructed Sir John to comply with French requests. Needless to say, serious misgivings remained. Robertson thought the 'attack was not a satisfactory matter from any point of view'; while French maintained that 'we must have big losses in order to achieve any result'. (Big apparently meant much bigger than anything previously.) Kitchener, who shared these views, explained to Haig on 19 August that it was essential to go ahead with the plan because the Russians 'had been severely handled, and *it was doubtful how much longer their Army could withstand the German blows*'. Referring to Joffre's fear that Sir John would not attack in earnest, Kitchener emphasised that '*we must act with all our energy, and do our utmost to help the French even though, by so doing, we suffered very heavy losses indeed*'. When Haig replied that his Army was ready to attack, but that more ammunition was required, Kitchener answered that 'we could get all he had!' – an amount nevertheless much smaller than Haig wanted.[49]

Kitchener, Robertson and French expected that very little, aside from massive losses, would result from the Battle of Loos, scheduled to begin on 25 September. Whilst Haig at first shared this pessimism, the preparations for the battle resulted in a characteristic flood of enthusiasm. On 24 August, he cautioned his wife not to 'be in too great a hurry to decide upon a winter campaign being a certainty'. The Germans, he had heard, were having difficulty raising men and money. 'An early peace is advised as the only way to save the country.' Delighted with this prospect, Haig nevertheless hoped that 'the end may come as a direct result of a victory on this front and I have great expectations from our next effort'. Nor were these simply the words of a man trying to raise his wife's spirits. Two weeks later, Haig explained to his corps commanders why the British were obliged to attack before they were entirely ready, but emphasised that it would still be possible to 'get on the enemy's rear and cut his communications'. When Foch, concerned about the British willingness to attack, visited the First Army front on 12 September, Haig told him with complete sincerity that his men 'were never in better heart and were longing to have a fight'.[50]

Closer to the front, the situation did not look as rosy. Six days before the attack was to be launched, Rawlinson wrote that he was 'not altogether happy about the coming attack, there is too much being left to chance and it is evident from the immense amount of work that the enemy are putting in to their trenches that they are ready for us'. The British had a significant numerical superiority but little else to cause cheer. The breakthrough which Haig envisaged depended upon surprise, but the bombardment was insufficient, in weight and duration, for this to be achieved. Only 110 of the 850 pieces of artillery were heavy guns and howitzers. Worse still, the ammunition was sufficient for only a four-day shelling. Haig planned to supplement the artillery by employing chlorine gas for the first time, but was told on 26 August that only about half the supply which he had requested was available due to manufacturing delays. He wanted to postpone the attack for a week or ten days until sufficient supplies were available, but French vetoed this idea.[51]

To add to the difficulties, there were disagreements with French regarding the placement of the GHQ reserve, which consisted of the

21st and 24th Divisions of XI Corps. On 18 September, Haig met French at St Omer and 'urged the importance of having the general Reserve . . . with the head of its two divisions at Noeux-les-Mines and Verquin, respectively, by *the morning* of the 25th. Sir John seemed to think that was too close up.' Sure enough, GHQ confirmed the next day that the reserves would be south of Lillers on the 24th, in other words, too far for them to reach the point Haig desired by the following day. Haig, through his CGS (Butler), immediately protested to Robertson, who promised to comply with Haig's wishes. The matter appeared to have been resolved satisfactorily. But, as will be seen, while the argument raged as to where the reserves were to be placed, insufficient attention was given to arrangements for their transport to and employment in the actual battle.[52]

The disagreement over the reserves was part of a wider difference of opinion between Haig and French regarding the prospects for the battle. Rawlinson thought that Sir John despaired of the plans, and was, contrary to assurances, not intending to push them through resolutely. In contrast, Haig, as has been seen, was planning a decisive victory. It is indeed possible that French's reluctance to surrender control of the reserves to Haig arose from his fear that they would be squandered in hopeless attacks. French certainly cautioned Haig about pushing the cavalry forward too soon, much to the latter's annoyance. But the disagreements were not confined to Haig and French. As was the case at Neuve Chapelle, Rawlinson preferred a battle of attrition in which the Germans would be forced into costly counter-attacks, an idea which Haig abhorred. On the other hand, Hubert Gough, the commander of I Corps (on Rawlinson's left), was like Haig a cavalry commander and a 'thruster'. Though the overall plan was Haig's, it was inevitable that the contrasting temperaments of these men would be reflected in what occurred at the front.[53]

French also infuriated Haig when he instructed him not to talk to Kitchener about the battle plans because 'If Lord K. were to know . . . he would tell the others in the Cabinet, and then all London would know! and the Germans would also get to hear of the proposed attack.' Haig ignored the directive on the grounds that 'when the Secretary of State for War asks a commander for certain information the commander is bound, I consider, to give it to the best of his ability'. Besides, talking to Kitchener was a useful tonic in preparing for battle:

he told me that it is of very great political importance to gain a success at the present time . . . I felt what an advantage it is to the Army that K. should frequently visit it in the field and get first hand knowledge of its needs. Personally, I also felt the advantage of having a talk with him and getting to know at first hand what the Government really expects of the Army. I can give my orders with much more confidence when I know that efforts on a large scale are really needed of us at the present time.

The night before the attack Robertson provided an extra lift to Haig's spirits when he confided that 'he was glad for England's sake that the fighting of the coming battle was in my hands'.[54]

During the early hours of the 25th, Haig nervously studied meteorological reports in anticipation of the planned gas attack. Though there was virtually no wind at 3 a.m., he was told that at sunrise (5.30) it would probably be stronger. Choosing to trust this prediction, he fixed zero hour for then. The main attack was to be launched an hour later. At 5 a.m. he and Fletcher found:

Almost a calm. Alan . . . lit a cigarette and the smoke drifted in puffs toward the NE. Staff Officers of Corps were ordered to stand by in case it was necessary to counter-order attack. At one time, owing to the calm, I feared the gas might simply hang about *our* trenches. However, at 5:15 a.m. I said 'Carry on'. I went to the top of our wooden lookout tower. The wind came gently from SW and by 5:40 had increased slightly. The leaves of the poplar trees gently rustled. This seemed satisfactory. But what a risk I had run of gas blowing back upon our own dense mass of troops.

Apart from a few places, the gas drifted slowly over the German trenches, where it took the enemy completely by surprise. The subsequent infantry assault was initially successful, except on the extreme left, where the 2nd Division found uncut wire and gas blowing back upon them. By noon, the first objectives of Loos and the Hohenzollern Redoubt had been captured, but the German second line remained everywhere intact. Nevertheless, by evening Haig was able to conclude that the attack had been 'a very satisfactory one on the whole'. The advance, he claimed, was 'the largest . . . made on the Western Front since this kind of warfare started'.[55]

But, as Haig had feared, the reserves were not available at the crucial moment. The leading units did not arrive at the front until after 2 p.m., in other words, too late to be used that day. Determined to extend the very limited gains he had made, Haig decided to throw XI Corps into the mêlée on the 26th. It is doubtful whether, at their best and at the most opportune time, these men could have made the dramatic contribution which Haig envisaged. In fact, the time was *not* opportune and the men *not* at their best. They had arrived in France two weeks before, had never been in battle, and were commanded by inexperienced and ill-prepared officers. Worse still, they had covered over fifty kilometres in three successive night marches and were, quite understandably, hungry, tired and demoralised. They nevertheless went forward with, under the circumstances, incredible gallantry. Expecting to find broken defences and open countryside before them, they marched headlong into securely defended positions and were promptly gunned down in their thousands.

'Experience', Rawlinson wrote on the 28th, 'teaches us that in these attacks one does not make much progress on the first day and [Loos] is no exception to this rule.'[56] The efforts to extend the advance continued for two more weeks, to no avail. The battle sputtered to a halt in mid-October with over 50,000 British casualties.

In Haig's view, the failure of the battle could be traced to the first day when the enemy second line had been 'quite undefended'. 'It is thus certain that even with *one* Division in Reserve, we could have walked right through.' Unfortunately, during the night, the Germans had been able to reinforce their positions. The opportunity was consequently lost, and it was French who had squandered it. 'When the C. in C. remains blind to the lessons of war in this important matter (handling of Reserves) we hardly deserve to win.' But an annoying detail obstructed the case against French. As Haig admitted to his brother Bee on 5 October, the 'poor devils' of XI Corps had 'just landed in the country and . . . had never seen a shot fired in earnest. Consequently they were not much good.' (And, presumably, they would not have been much good had they arrived in time.) This fact was, however, quickly and conveniently forgotten. On 2 November, Bee was told that Sir John had retained the reserves 'under his own hand so long that they did not arrive in time to be of use'. To make matters worse, it seemed that French had of late quite clearly lost his will to fight. On the 28th, Sir John 'seemed tired of war, and said that "in his opinion we ought to take the first opportunity of concluding peace otherwise England would be ruined!'" Haig, of course, could not agree. The time to act had come.[57]

In a letter to Kitchener dated 29 September, Haig outlined the case against French. Basically, Sir John was guilty of: (1) not putting the reserves close enough to the line, and (2) not placing the reserves under Haig's command. After bombarding Kitchener with details of times and distances, Haig concluded:

> I think it is right that you should know that the lessons that have been learnt in this war at such cost have been neglected. We *were* in a position to make this the turning point in the war, and I still hope we may do so, but naturally I feel annoyed at the lost opportunity.

It was an argument which Haig would repeat and repeat, like a parrot with a small vocabulary, over the following weeks. His case, superficially sound, was in fact riddled with holes. He told Kitchener that Loos had been captured at 6 a.m. 'and reserves should have been at hand then'. Leaving aside the fact that the capture did not occur as early as that, it remains a mystery why Haig delayed requesting the reserves until 8.45 a.m. (And, contrary to another of Haig's claims, French released them almost immediately – by 9.30.) The point at issue is not when the reserves were released, but where they were released from and the time it took them to reach the front. The first units took over six hours to arrive. Clearly, as Haig claimed, they had been positioned too far from the front. But, as it turns out, they were on the line Noeux-les-Mines–Verquin, in other words, exactly where Haig had requested. Therefore, the fact that they had to march eight kilometres before they reached the front was as much Haig's fault as anyone's. Furthermore, the march itself was delayed unnecessarily by congestion on the roads and at level crossings – a fault of the 1st Army staff, and, ultimately, Haig. Whilst Haig was perhaps correct to maintain that the reserves should have been placed under him much earlier (say, before the battle), the above factors do not give one confidence that he would have handled them more effectively had he had such control.[58]

Haig was probably genuinely ignorant of the weaknesses of his case. Relations with French had reached such a hiatus that it was impossible for him to see any good in Sir John or admit to any errors himself. Nor were the holes in Haig's reasoning apparent to others; his vehemence and sincerity made his case seem watertight. French, meanwhile, made matters worse for himself by insisting to Robertson that 'the second day of the battle was the correct time to put [the reserves] in and not the first'. This was an indefensible position, tantamount to admitting that he was responsible for XI Corps not being ready on the 25th. Haig was prompted to remark, not without justification, 'It seems impossible to discuss military problems with an unreasoning brain of this kind.'[59]

As the days passed, a further consideration of opportunities lost fuelled Haig's ire. On the 11th, he learned that captured enemy officers could not understand why the British had failed to push forward on the first day of the battle, when German lines were broken. Reports indicating that the Germans had begun to register the 1918 class (in other words, men who would not ordinarily have been drafted for two years) led Haig to conclude that 'the situation for the Allies is more favourable than at any previous time in the war'. Echoing this point in a letter to Rothschild, he argued: 'The German Army is only a shadow of its former self . . . it is certain we can break the German line provided we attack in sufficient strength. Indeed we have broken it every time we have set out to do it: Aisne, Ypres (1914), Neuve Chapelle, Loos.'[60]

Haig's message was that victory was ripe for picking. Unfortunately, cads and cowards stood in the way. French was one obstruction; Westminster was full of others. Referring to the recent Allied landings at Suvla Bay and Salonika, Haig complained to Colonel Lee, MP on 15 October that the government's penchant for hare-brained schemes was inhibiting progress in the West. 'We will win the war by killing and beating Germans, not by killing Bulgarians and Turks!' When Lady Haig accused the government of cowardice for not introducing conscription, he agreed. 'We must rely on the manhood of England to win the war, not of any continental people!' One important change which Haig suggested was to make Robertson ('a good sound practical fellow') CIGS. 'The present man (Sir A. Murray) seems to modify his views to suit Lord K's orders. The war will be lost or won *in London*. So let us have our best military advisers there.'[61]

It is probably no coincidence that Haig praised Robertson at the same time that 'Wully' was proving a very useful witness in the case against French. Robertson, having been asked by the King (through Lord Stamfordham) whether it was time for French to go, sought Haig's advice before replying. On 17 October, Haig told him that

> up to date I had been more loyal to French and did my best to stop all criticisms of him or his methods. Now at last, in view of what had happened in the recent battle over the reserves, and in view of the seriousness of the general military situation, I had come to the conclusion that it was not fair to the Empire to retain French in command on this main battle front. Moreover, none of my officers commanding Corps had a high opinion of Sir J's military ability or military views; in fact, *they had no confidence in him*.

Robertson, in reply, said that 'he knew now how to act and would report to Stamfordham'.[62]

Robertson's conversation with Stamfordham prompted the King to raise the issue when he saw Haig during a visit to the front. Haig, still maintaining that he wished to avoid intrigue, nevertheless did not pull his punches. Until now, he told the King, he had been under the impression that trench warfare presented 'no great scope for French to go wrong'. It had seemed pointless to remove him and Haig had, in consequence, remained a loyal subordinate. Of late, however, he had changed his mind. In words which echoed the message given to Robertson, Haig argued that 'French's handling of the reserves in the last battle, his obstinacy, and conceit, showed his incapacity', therefore, 'for the sake of empire, [he] ought to be removed'. Haig stressed that he was 'ready to do my duty in any capacity, and of course would serve under anyone who was chosen for his military skill to be C. in C'.[63]

French was no match for the machinations of Haig's powerful friends. At first, he was blissfully unaware of the conspiracy against him. When he finally realised the seriousness of his predicament, it was too late. Caught like a fly in a spider's web, he was capable only of frantic, but ultimately ineffective, movement. He tried to answer his critics by publishing in *The Times* of 2 November a despatch in which he maintained: 'At 9.30 a.m. [on 25 September] I placed the 21st and 24th Divisions at the disposal of the GOC First Army, who at once ordered the GOC XI Corps to move them up in support of the attacking troops.' This was technically correct, but gave the impression that the reserves were ready to go into battle at that time, when in fact they were eight kilometres from the front. Haig, though hopping mad, was satisfied that these 'distortions' would be French's undoing. 'The truth is bound to come out in time, when no doubt he will be despised in the way he deserves.' In order to support his case Haig sent French the telegrams from the day of the battle and challenged him to correct his despatch. French replied that no correction was necessary, and, in a separate official letter, ordered all correspondence on the matter to cease. Haig, for perhaps the first time in his life, disobeyed an order.[64]

On 10 November the two antagonists met at GHQ. Haig described the meeting to his wife:

> I could see Sir John was most uncomfortable at meeting me . . . *He is to send all my letters to the War Office* and he said I could see what he writes in his forwarding letter before it went. I am afraid I am of too forgiving a nature, and of course said 'No'. He must write whatever he considered 'right and just' on the whole question without any interference on my part . . . You may think it was weak of me to have acted in this friendly way to Sir John – but I feel that I have no time for carrying on these discussions which are so petty in comparison with my real work as GOC 1st Army . . . Besides, as long as I am under Sir John, the Army will only suffer if there is friction between us. So I said 'as long as the *true facts* of the case are sent to the War Office, I shall be satisfied' and so I hope the controversy is closed as far as I am concerned.[65]

Technically speaking, Haig was right; the controversy was over as far as he was concerned. People in high places had been supplied with evidence of French's guilt. It remained for them to pass judgement.

For the time being, the problems with French faded into the background. Haig was instead preoccupied with the government's apparent eagerness to throw troops into the Balkan dustbin. A bewildered Robertson had recently returned from London to report that 'the higher conduct of the war seems to be getting more complicated, and hopeless every day'. It was in this atmosphere that Haig met his old friend Esher on 15 November. (Esher had around this time predicted that Haig would be made Commander-in-Chief 'because of his blue eyes and knowledge and Scottish coolness'.) He listened intently to (and promised to pass on) Haig's recommendation that Robertson be appointed CIGS, on the understanding that he would then advise the War Cabinet directly instead of through the War Secretary. This, in addition to other more complicated changes, would, Haig thought, bring into being a stronger, more independent General Staff. It could then devote itself entirely to the strategic direction of the war, advising the Cabinet and GHQ accordingly. Such a function was more in line with the duties of the General Staff as originally intended. Haig also hoped that, as a result, closer contact with the French could be mantained, and the Allies would together pursue sounder policies than those characteristic of late – namely, the adventures in Salonika and the Dardanelles. Finally, under Haig's scheme, the War Office would take on a predominantly administrative function, supplying men and material according to the lines set forth by the General Staff.[66]

During his conversation with Esher, Haig made no attempt to hide his disappointment with Kitchener who was, he felt, largely responsible for the sorry state of affairs in London. Though Haig's admiration for Kitchener had not diminished, he had come to the conclusion that he was not, and could never be, an effective War Secretary. When Esher asked what should be done with Kitchener, Haig suggested appointing him Viceroy of India, where 'trouble is brewing'. Though regrettable, 'some blood letting [was] . . . necessary for the health of the body politic!'

> If Lord K. won't go to India, then let him be the business manager at the head of the War Office, with a seat and vote on the War Committee. In my opinion, it is important to remove Lord K. from the Mediterranean and Egypt, because wherever he is, by his masterful action he will give that sphere of the operations an undue prominence in the strategical picture.

Haig's last sentence struck at the heart of the Kitchener problem. His ability to impose his will in any situation had ensured success in the Sudan and South Africa. But, in a decidedly different war, it had become a liability.[67]

The recommendations given to Esher were repeated during a meeting Haig had with Asquith on 23 November. 'The matters which we discussed were of such vital interest to the Empire that I never alluded to my own affairs, and the differences which I had had with Sir J. French.' A similarly unselfish approach was taken on the following day when Haig met Bonar Law and the Conservative Whip, Lord Edmund Talbot. On both occasions, the need for Robertson to be made CIGS was pressed. Bonar Law's support and sympathy did not prevent Haig from scorning him as a 'feeble man' who 'failed to realise the urgent need for immediate and energetic action'. His weakness, and indeed that of the entire government, was an inability to 'look beyond' the situation in the Balkans and in Egypt.[68]

On 25 November, Haig rather nonchalantly mentioned in his diary a rumour from Robertson that French was to be recalled as part of a general restructuring of the high command. According to Haig, Robertson 'added that the selection [of a successor] . . . lay between me and him, but that he of course was out of the question and that there was no one in it but me!'[69] Haig's surprise was as genuine as a politician's smile. Over the previous weeks, he had whispered the right things to the right people, while patiently waiting for events to take their natural course. (It is indeed difficult to believe that he refrained from mentioning French in his conversations with Asquith and Bonar Law.) Whether his actions constitute intrigue or merely advice depends a great deal upon whether one is sympathetic to Haig or to French. Haig maintained that it was his duty to give advice when asked. Nevertheless, he could not have been unaware of the fact that he was French's logical successor, and that by undermining his former friend he also promoted himself. Whilst he repeatedly claimed that his only interest was the greater good of the Empire, it is difficult to believe that the resolute ambition which fuelled his earlier career was at this stage absent. Rather, as in the past, the realisation of ambition and the fulfilment of duty became for Haig one and the same.

It took some time for rumour to turn into reality. The official news of Haig's appointment was released by Asquith on 10 December. Among the hundreds of congratulatory messages Haig received was an especially welcome one from the King: 'I know you will have the confidence of the troops serving under you, and it is almost needless to assure you with what implicit trust I look forward to the successful conduct of the war on the Western Front under your able direction.' According to Hankey on 14 December, the King 'told me all about the forthcoming changes, Haig for French in France and Robertson as Chief of Staff, and rather hinted that he had done the whole thing'. To Haig, the King expressed the hope that 'you will from time to time write to me quite freely', adding that 'I shall consider your letters in

213

the strictest confidence'. Thus the liaison which had helped to bring about French's demise would be continued for other purposes useful to Haig.[70]

Haig's appointment coincided with Robertson replacing Murray as CIGS in a restructured and revitalised General Staff. Though the changes corresponded (not coincidentally) to those he had suggested to Esher and Asquith in November, Haig nevertheless had reservations about Robertson

> I am sure that it is good for the government and the country to have such a man in authority at the War Office at this time. But 'he talks too much about "I" and "I'll 'ave to get rid of 'im later, etc."' He means very well and will succeed I am sure. How much easier, though, it is to work with a gentleman.[71]

Robertson had risen from the ranks. For this reason, though he and Haig agreed on most military issues, a wide gulf always divided them.

The change of command naturally sent ripples through the upper echelons of the Army. Haig was immediately hounded by rival cliques eager to secure important posts for their men. In a conversation with French's Military Secretary, Brigadier-General H. Lowther, Haig claimed that he was determined to avoid factionalism: 'I had only one idea, namely to do my utmost to win the war, that in my eyes only those who had proved their fitness for advancement should be promoted. I had no "friends" when it came to military promotion and I would not tolerate a "job" being done.' The words sound very noble; the reality was very different. As Haig's own career abundantly demonstrates, promotion in the Army had always been based as much on personal ties as on real ability. It would have been a monumental feat of self-control for Haig suddenly to change the habits of a lifetime and exorcise himself of favouritism. In actuality, he seems to have made very little effort to do so. Haig's favourites (most notably his acquiescent staff officers and 'thrusters' like Gough) did very well out of his accession to chief command. In April 1916, General Sir Aylmer Haldane was approached by Haig's Military Secretary, the Duke of Teck, who asked for advice on potential staff officers, because Haig 'had come to the end of those he knew personally'. Teck apparently told Haldane that Haig 'prefers to provide for his friends first'. Haig would probably have defended himself by arguing that his favourites were also officers of real ability and sterling character, but it is well to remember that he was never an astute judge of men.[72]

Where favouritism had less influence (because it would have been more conspicuous) was in the most senior appointments, and in this area Haig promoted officers who were in no sense cronies. He suggested that Rawlinson, a man whom he respected but did not particularly like, should be given command of the 1st Army. Likewise, Murray, though 'rather lacking in decision and judgement' as CIGS, was 'quite fit to command a Corps on a defensive front'. The difficulty arose with Wilson, whom Haig despised, particularly because of his capacity for intrigue, his connections with French, and the fact that he was an acknowledged Francophile. Wilson, probably aware of Haig's dislike, decided that it might be best for him to go on half-pay. In response Haig told Rawlinson that 'on no account was it possible for an officer of his standing to do that. I was willing to help him in every possible way to find a suitable appointment . . . this war [is] so gigantic in its proportions, that there [is] room for everyone of us.' Robertson wisely advised that Wilson 'would probably do less harm in France than in England'. Haig agreed, but could not see his way to giving him a corps, deciding instead to insult him with a division.[73]

One other controversial appointment remained. Winston Churchill, who had escaped to France after the Dardanelles débâcle, had been promised an infantry brigade by French. Haig vetoed this idea because he thought Churchill, though keen, still had a good deal to learn about modern warfare. The matter was left in abeyance until Haig saw French on 18 December, preparatory to assuming command. Haig dreaded this meeting because, as he told his wife, French 'has been so deceitful for a long time and all the time made the most of me as a friend' (Needless to say, French could have said the same of Haig.) In fact, the meeting did not turn out to be as unpleasant as Haig had feared. After exchanging pleasantries, French (who 'did not look very well and seemed short of breath at times') told Haig that he 'wish[ed] to help me and the Army in France to the best of his power at home'. Reference was then made to Haig's refusal to give Churchill a brigade. Would he, as a favour, give him a battalion instead? Haig agreed, and then hastily said goodbye to his one-time friend and patron.[74]

Haig took over command the next day. His diaries and letters reveal little apparent anxiety about his fitness for command of the largest army in Britain's history. He confidently believed that he had risen to his rightful place. 'I can honestly say that no one in this army has been so highly tested as I have been in this war,' he told his wife. As he indicated to Rothschild, he was mainly relieved that the past was the past:

> These are terrible times that we have been passing through, and our difficulties and anxieties have been greatly added to by having at the head of the Army in France a general who is not only very ignorant of the principles of the higher leading of a large Army but is also lacking in the necessary temperament! He is so hot tempered and excitable – like a bottle of soda water in suddenness of explosion – that he is quite incapable of thinking over a serious situation and coming to a reasoned decision.

> Now that the whole matter is settled, I can write this to you my old friend, without feeling that I am disloyal to my commanding general.

The implication is clear. Where French had been hot tempered and excitable, Haig would be cool, measured, methodical and patient. Where French had failed, he would succeed.[75]

10

'Patience, Self-Sacrifice and Confidence'

A few weeks after Haig assumed command on the Western Front, Henrietta forwarded him another message from their deceased brother George:

> I am so anxious to send a few lines to Douglas because I have been beside him and seen his earnest and good work for his army. Almighty God is his helper and guide and by the blessing of God a great soldier is allowed to be always near Douglas to advise him in his task. Napoleon is that soldier . . . And all the prayers of a great nation are united in asking God to guide His armies to victory . . . Our Douglas is the instrument he uses to crush the German invaders in France and Belgium. So tell Douglas with my love and blessing to go on as he is doing trusting to the mighty power above to shew him the way. And tell him he will not ask in vain.

Since Haig never referred to this letter in diaries or correspondence it is impossible to say whether he actually felt that the spirit of Napoleon was by his side. There is no doubt that he was sympathetic to the rest of George's message, specifically the reference to the influence which God had over him. A week after assuming command, Haig commented that his colleagues at GHQ 'all seem to expect success as the result of my arrival, and somehow give me the idea that they think I am "meant to win" by some Superior Power'. He admitted that 'while doing my utmost, I feel that one's best can go but a short way without help from above'.[1]

217

The ramifications of Haig's belief in divine inspiration will be discussed later. It is, however, important to mention a related incident which occurred at this time and profoundly influenced Haig's attitude towards himself and his command. On Sunday, 2 January 1916, he

> attended the Scotch Church at 9.35 a.m. . . . A most earnest young Scotch man, George Duncan, conducted the service. He told us that in our prayers we should be as natural as possible and tell the Almighty exactly what we feel we want. The nation is now learning to pray and that nothing can withstand the prayers of a great united people. The congregation was greatly impressed, and one could have heard a pin drop during the service.

Thereafter, Haig attended the Presbyterian service almost every Sunday. 'The half hour of worship', wrote Duncan, 'was not merely something he valued; it was apparently something which must not be missed.' Whilst religion had played an important part in Haig's life ever since he was a very young boy, his commitment to it was never as strong as during his period of supreme command. According to Duncan, 'by this time his religion had become a vital element in his life . . . he had come to view in a more definitely religious light both the issues at stake in the war and the part which he himself was being called to play in it'.[2]

This sudden thirst for religious inspiration is only partially explained by the need for the solace at a time of enormous strain. Equally important, and indeed complementary, was the almost mesmerising power which the young Reverend George Duncan had. Haig admitted to Duncan that he 'had a hard trial before I came across you at St. Omer'. Before then, he attended church regularly, but seldom recorded the subject of a sermon. After 2 January 1916, hardly a Sunday passed without Haig writing his reflections upon what had been preached. He was especially anxious that the effect which Duncan had upon him should be enjoyed by the rest of the Army. Thus at one of his first conferences with his Army commanders, Haig

> called attention to the large number of clergyman who are being sent out to join the Army. Army commanders must look to the efficiency of these as well as to any part of their commands. We must have large minded, sympathetic men as Parsons, who realise *the great cause* for which we are fighting. Men who can imbue their

218

hearers with enthusiasm. Any clergyman who is not fit for his work must be sent home.

The most important subject about which clergymen could preach was 'the great object of the war, viz, the freeing of mankind from German tyranny'.[3]

Haig's religion was essentially practical; it fuelled his optimism, gave him a purpose, and provided life with a plan.

His faith was not the product of some fanciful theory; it sprang from a calm recognition of the challenges and needs of everyday life. That being so, it was not a cloak to be put on or off as occasion arose; it was an essential part of the man himself, vitally alert no doubt in times of crisis, but never wholly unrelated to his normal habits of thought and action.

Duncan stressed that 'Haig did not wear his religion on his sleeve. Never once during the war . . . did he appeal in any public utterance to the Divine Name.' That was Duncan's job, not Haig's. It was nevertheless clear to Haig that God was on the side of Britain and the Empire, and that he was God's appointed agent for winning the war. But this belief, Duncan correctly argued, did not 'reliev[e] him for a moment of his responsibilities, it rather impelled him to take them the more seriously'. Haig saw himself as God's industrious servant. The sermons he found most uplifting were the ones in which Duncan reminded his congregation that 'your lives are not your own but purchased at a price . . . The Empire is living thanks to the gallant lives which have and are being expended in this war.'[4]

Shortly after assuming command, Haig learned that Kitchener had rejected his advice and appointed Monro instead of Rawlinson to command the First Army. Kitchener also refused to allow Haig to retain Butler as his chief of staff, on the grounds that he was too junior for the post. Haig argued, to no avail, that though Butler was indeed young, no one 'had such experience in practical Staff work in the Field . . . or had done so well'. On Kitchener's recommendation, Kiggell was made CGS, and Butler became Deputy CGS. Haig, when informed of Kiggell's appointment, commented that he had 'the greatest confidence in him as a soldier also as a gentleman'.[5]

219

The confidence was not justified. Kitchener's emphasis upon the sanctity of seniority resulted in Kiggell – an able but weak and obsequious officer – replacing Butler – at least as talented and, more importantly, temperamentally better equipped to withstand the strains of life at GHQ. Nor was Kiggell's insufficient mettle compensated by the other men Haig brought with him from the First Army. Brigadier-General J. H. Davidson, who assumed control of Operations, was notable for his lack of spine. Charteris, who took over Intelligence, had 'a good fifty per cent more brains, imagination, decision and initiative than the average of his fellow regulars on the staff',[6] but, as has been shown, was tied in too sycophantic a fashion to his chief. Haig's personal staff, which included Fletcher and Sir Philip Sassoon (Rothschild's nephew), completed the circle of simpering, awestruck admirers.

It took Kitchener until 28 December to supply Haig with his formal instructions as Commander-in-Chief. Certain portions of this lengthy document deserve discussion as they shed light on the problems Haig would encounter in the subsequent three years. Kitchener confirmed that the 'mission of the British Expeditionary Force . . . is to support and cooperate with the French and Belgian Armies against our common enemies'. Expanding on this subject further on, he wrote that the 'closest cooperation' between the French and British armies must be 'the governing policy', but Haig was *distinctly to understand that your command is an independent one, and that you will in no case come under the orders of any allied General*. Reference was also made to the conflicting necessities of defending the Channel ports and maintaining contact with the French. If a full-scale retreat became imperative, Haig was to make the latter his priority. Hints of future controversy came with the statement that Haig would be periodically informed of the number of troops available to him, but 'owing to the number of different theatres in which we are employed, it may not always be possible to give the information definitely a long time in advance'. There was likewise a warning that risks of serious losses had to be 'authoritatively considered to be commensurate with the object in view'. Finally, Kitchener assured Haig that he could rely on the 'whole-hearted and unswerving support of the Government, of myself and of your compatriots'.[7]

Evident in Kitchener's letter is a desire to make a fresh start, though it would of course remain to be seen whether his specific instructions to Haig would result in a system of military administration less chaotic than that existing during French's tenure. Another attempt at a fresh start was made by J. St Loe Strachey, editor of the *Spectator*, who courted Haig with the following letter of 31 December:

> When I look back upon the record of my profession during the war I am bound to say it is a very sorry one. We have far too frequently given criticism where it was useless and refrained from giving it where it might have been of advantage. The thing in which we could have been of most use we have practically not done at all, that is, to try to make the public realise that the conduct and direction of armies is the most difficult job in the whole world and that as a general rule nothing is more futile than to judge by bare successes – the way in which the public generally does judge.[8]

Though Haig undoubtedly agreed with Strachey, it would be some time before he would accept the olive branch extended to him. In the meantime, he would fail to benefit from the enormous advantage of having the Press on his side.

A fresh start was virtually impossible in the area of Anglo-French relations. When Haig's promotion was first discussed, Kitchener warned him of the importance of keeping

> on friendly terms with the French. General Joffre should be looked upon as the C. in C. in France, where he knew the country and the situation well . . . we must do all we can to meet the French C. in C.'s wishes whatever may be our personal feelings about the French Army and its Commanders.

Haig would have found this advice very hard to swallow. It was difficult for him to rid himself of past prejudices, since French actions seemed repeatedly to confirm and reinforce those prejudices. Even before Haig assumed command, he was bombarded with strident demands from Joffre that the British should take over 9,000 yards of French trenches. Haig dealt with this extremely undiplomatic request as patiently as he could manage, politely pointing out that he saw 'considerable difficulties'. Eager to help, Robertson reminded Haig that they are Frenchmen and not Englishmen, and do not and never will look at things in the way we look at them. I suppose that they think we are queer people. It is a big business having to deal with the Allied Commanders, and one has to keep oneself very much in check and exercise great tolerance.

Unfortunately tolerance was not one of Haig's more conspicuous virtues.[9]

Another problem which the change of command did not alter was that of the uncertain supply of men. On 13 January, Robertson told Haig that within the Cabinet

there is a great deal of wobbling, and it is bound up with the question of the size of our army, a matter which is not yet settled . . . The fact is they are not showing the necessary grit and determination to see the thing through, now that the shoe is beginning to pinch a little. As a matter of fact, it pinches exceedingly little in this country yet. It is scarcely noticeable.

On the following day, Kitchener warned Haig that Reginald McKenna (Chancellor of the Exchequer) and Walter Runciman (President of the Board of Trade) were 'making a determined attack on the number of divisions I have found for the field because they say we cannot afford them either in men, withdrawn from trade, or money'. Kitchener was extremely sceptical. 'When one looks at the streets full of loafers, and see the extravagance going on in all departments of government and in the country, their statements are given the lie.' Similar feelings of disgust came over Haig when he reflected upon the conscription debates going on at this time:

It is sad to read of the selfishness of many people at home over the Universal Service Bill. The French have shed their blood lavishly, all married men have been fighting for their country since the very beginning and have suffered very heavily . . . and now in England only the unmarried are to be sent out to fight! How very different the British Public would feel if they had Germans on their soil, and how anxious they would be to leave nothing undone to secure that the enemy is driven out![10]

As with men, so with munitions. After nearly a year and a half of war, the supply of guns and ammunition still did not satisfy Haig. Though Lloyd George, as Minister of Munitions, had brought about significant improvements, Haig was more interested in the shortages which still existed. These were automatically the fault of the dreaded Welshman:

> Mr. Lloyd George will not be able to produce all the ammunition promised until late in the year, i.e. July instead of March, and in order to cover up his own shortcomings [he] would like our demands to be so excessive that he would be provided with some excuse to put forward for failing to produce what he had promised.

Haig was inclined to believe any rumour about Lloyd George which came his way, including one particularly malicious allegation that 'much of the money now spent on munitions is sticking to the hands of someone', in other words, 'Lloyd George's friends are drawing large salaries and doing very little in the way of turning out ammunition'. Since the supply of arms was controlled by politicians and since politicians could not, as a rule, be trusted, Haig saw little prospect of improved supplies.[11]

Robertson believed that the shortage of men and munitions resulted from the politicians' inability to agree on a general strategy. 'It is deplorable the way these politicians fight and intrigue against each other,' he told Haig on 5 January. 'They have no idea how war must be conducted in order to be given a reasonable chance of success, and they will not allow professionals a free hand.' It all sounded depressingly familiar to Haig. Equally so were Robertson's subsequent elaborations:

> There is a fairly strong party in the Cabinet opposed to offensive operations on your front in the Spring or indeed at any other time. One wants to go to the Balkans, another to Baghdad, and another to allow the Germans 'to attack us' . . . some of the above people are trying to get their way by urging us to wait for an offensive until we are at full strength, which they say will not be until well on in the summer.

Among the latter, apparently, was Mr Lloyd George.[12]

Kitchener, who shared Robertson's frustrations, thought that the government was reluctant to send men and arms to Haig because of the previous string of failures on the Western Front. This reluctance had to be overcome, otherwise 'we shall run a terrible risk of an unsatisfactory stalemate peace' which would in turn mean 'hostilities again in about 5 years when we shall have few allies and be unprepared'. Both Kitchener and Robertson agreed that 'what we really want is a big success somewhere' (in the West) in order to silence the Cabinet. 'I need not tell you', Robertson wrote, 'why it should be as early as possible, though I am sure we both agree it should not be premature.' Kitchener was certain that if the attack was launched in March, the Germans could be defeated by August, and then 'you must allow three months after that to make them accept terms of peace'.[13]

Haig was at least as eager for immediate results. 'I quite understand', he replied to Kitchener, 'the importance of beginning early, and will see to it that operations in proportion to the ammunition available are arranged for.'[14] Without specifically mentioning it, Haig revealed a dilemma which would plague him for the rest of the war. In order to convince the government to supply him with sufficient men and *matériel*, he needed to prove that he was capable of achieving victory on the Western Front. But, as he saw it, impressive results were impossible without adequate raw materials.

In January 1916, this dilemma was less acute than it would later become. At that time, Haig was still flush with enthusiasm for his new command and eagerly anticipating the change in British fortunes which he expected inevitably to result. His thoughts on the future course of the war are revealed in one of the first reports compiled by his GHQ staff. The report predicted that the Germans would launch a heavy blow against the Russians in spring 1916, which would perhaps necessitate a withdrawal to a shorter front in France. The enemy's aim was for a negotiated peace – something to which the Russians would be amenable, but the British and French would not. Haig nevertheless thought that 'the French manpower situation is serious' which meant that 'they are not likely to stand another winter's war'. It was therefore concluded that 'the war must be won by the forces of the British Empire'.[15]

Having accepted the British responsibility, Haig began to plan how victory would be achieved. The classical objective was to defeat the enemy army in the field, basically by effecting a breach in its defences. Unfortunately, in this war, whilst it had been relatively easy to overrun the first (and sometimes second) lines of defence, it had so far been impossible to capture the third line, which was well beyond the range of the infantry in its first rush. Consequently, after the attack lost its momentum the enemy brought up reserves and stalemate ensued. Though this was a new problem, Haig proposed an old solution. His prescription for victory came straight out of Camberley and the ancient tomes he delighted in reading. There would be a three-phase offensive: (1) a wearing out fight would prepare the way for (2) the drawing-in of enemy reserves, which would be followed closely by (3) the decisive battle. As to the preliminary phase, Haig argued that it 'should be carried on simultaneously (or nearly so) from the right of the Russians on the Baltic, right round via Italy to our left on the North Sea'. It was furthermore imperative that the French, despite their weaknesses, 'take their share with us in the wearing out fight, otherwise it is possible that the Allies get worn out in detail!' Haig had already discussed his ideas with Joffre, who 'quite agreed with the principle'.[16]

More explicit plans were presented to General Plumer on 14 January. For the time being, the British would carry out 'winter sports' – raids on enemy trenches. In the spring, the 'wearing out fight' would begin, the aim being to 'draw in the enemy reserves'. This would take 'about three weeks'. Afterwards would come the 'decisive attacks' at weak parts of the line. Breakthroughs would result, and the cavalry would be released. What is abundantly clear is that Haig did not believe that a long campaign of attrition would be necessary. Indeed, his timetable for victory did not extend past 1916. The stalemate of the previous fifteen months had not, in other words, shaken his faith in classical military patterns. He was certain that he could restore movement to the war. A breakthrough and a decisive defeat of the German Army in the field was, he felt, not only possible, it was also the most sensible goal to pursue. It was this belief which prompted him to urge Robertson, on 9 January, to re-open recruiting for the cavalry.[17]

Haig's faith in the eventual re-emergence of mobile warfare is evident in his revived enthusiasm for the plan to clear the Belgian coast. On 26 December 1915, he discussed this operation with Admiral Bacon who 'said that the front from Zeebrugge to Ostend was of vital importance to England because the Germans command the East end of the Channel from there and threaten England'. It was agreed that they would work out details, 'but the time of execution must depend on General Joffre's plan for the general offensive in the Spring'. It is not immediately clear where or how this idea fits into the strategy outlined above. But, if the plans for the 1917 Flanders offensive can be taken as a guide to what Haig was thinking in 1916, it appears that he intended the coastal operation to fulfil all three phases of his general strategy. In other words, the Germans would defend their right flank desperately, pouring in reserves. Eventually, however, they would be worn out and the decisive battle would follow. The flank would be turned, the cavalry released and a brilliant (and, most importantly, British) victory would result.[18]

Though Haig thought that victory could be achieved quickly, he never claimed that it could be won without great loss of life. The spectre of massive losses did not deter him. His faith in the resilience of his men was absolute. This faith arose from the assumption that his men shared his religious convictions and his patriotic acceptance of the need for supreme sacrifice. His occasional reflection on the nature of heroic death is revealing:

> The following extract from a speech by the Emperor Baber to his troops on March 16th 1527 when fighting the Lord of Mewar, the great Rana Sanga, is curiously appropriate now! 'The most High God has been propitious to us in such a crisis that if we fall in the field, we die the death of martyrs; if we survive, we rise victorious the avengers of the cause of God.' This is the root matter of the present war.

After the Battle of Loos, Haig complained that 'it is impossible to adequately reward those who have done their share of the fighting in this great war'. Their 'chief reward was their own feeling of satisfaction at having done their duty'. To Haig, sacrifice provided its own reward and death, the ultimate sacrifice, the ultimate reward.[19]

Studies conducted since the war have generally indicated that the men in the trenches were inspired by very different emotions from those of Haig. An image of glorious martyrdom did not, contrary to his thinking, propel them from the trenches into the storm of fire. In this sense, Haig was seriously out of touch with the emotions of his men. Contact with them was at best sporadic and usually so contrived as to be virtually meaningless and probably misleading for both sides. Haig's confidence in his ability to command meant that he failed to notice the wide gulf between himself and his men. To him, the good commander had an intuitive knowledge of his men; he did not have to share their conditions to understand their emotions. Since he was a good commander, that was that. But what is ironic is that, for reasons which Haig did not understand, the Tommy in the trenches was extremely resilient. He did, almost without fail, march forth into the storm of fire. The explanations as to why he did so are too complicated to discuss here. What is important for this study is that, quite coincidentally, Haig's men were equal to the pressures he imposed and the sacrifices he expected.[20]

In the New Year, a swarm of politicians, eager to poke their noses into Haig's business, passed through GHQ. They were as thick as midges on a summer day – and just as annoying. One visitor, the Attorney-General F. E. Smith, got the surprise of his life when he was arrested for entering Boulogne without a pass. The sentry was apologetic but explained that General Haig had ordered that the pass system was to be enforced without exception. Haig, though unrepentant, later managed to soothe Smith's ruffled feathers with liberal applications of old brandy. 'We all parted friends', Haig wrote, while admitting that 'I was only too glad to be rid of [him] and be free to get on with my work.'[21]

In late January Lloyd George arrived, eager to be ingratiating on his first meeting with Haig. Charm flowed in sickeningly sweet abundance. The silver-tongued Welshman wrote afterwards:

> If you will permit me to say so the visit . . . left on my mind a great impression of things being *gripped* in that sphere of operations; and whether we win through or whether we fail, I have a feeling that everything which the assiduity, the care, and the trained thought of a great soldier can accomplish, is being done.

Honeyed words had little effect upon the phlegmatic Haig. Lloyd George was 'most anxious to be agreeable and pleasant', but unable to promise what was most needed: men and munitions. Haig judged him as 'shifty and unreliable'. In contrast, Bonar Law, who visited at the same time, was 'a straightforward honourable man, indeed, so honest that he is too much so for the crowd he is with'. The greatest praise was, however, reserved for Curzon who arrived in early February. Haig found that 'his old pompous ways have disappeared, and he is much simpler and more natural in his manner'. It was regrettable that he was 'not at the head of the government in these troublous [sic] times. He has all the brains, and also the ability to decide on large issues.'[22]

Unfortunately – as Haig saw it – good men like Curzon were thin on the ground. He sympathised with Kitchener who, according to Haig, had complained that

> the politicians are constantly intriguing against one another and have come to him to join them against Asquith. He has always declined because he feels that A. is the best man for Prime Minister, and he has found that Asquith can be trusted but he (K) did not trust the others.

Kitchener added that 'rightly or wrongly' the people trusted him. Consequently, 'it is not me the politicians are afraid of, but what the people would say to them if I were to go'. Aware that this was indeed the case, Haig appreciated that Kitchener, in spite of his faults, remained valuable as a restraint upon the politicians. It was therefore with genuine concern that Haig noted how he 'looked pinched and rather tired' and had aged considerably over the past few months. 'I felt pained that his mind should be losing its power of comprehension and decision at this time of crisis in our country's history.'[23]

The New Year seemed at least to promise better relations with the French. On 29 December, at Haig's first meeting with French politicians since assuming command, the Prime Minister, Aristide Briand, opined that 'if the present good feeling had existed between us from the commencement the situation would now be very different'. These good feelings were sustained when Haig and Kiggell met Joffre and de Castlenau at Chantilly on 14 February. Since assuming command, it had become clear to Haig that he and Joffre disagreed over the nature and duration of the wearing out fight. Joffre, who was less than enthusiastic about the idea, wanted a series of sharp attacks at various parts of the line, mainly carried out by the British. Though Haig had himself begun to worry that politicians and the public might misunderstand a costly *bataille d'usure* (even if it was intended to lead

228

to a breakthrough), he was still keen on a sustained, coordinated, but relatively short offensive from the Baltic to the North Sea. Prepared for a heated argument with the French on this subject, he was pleasantly surprised when

> General Joffre began the discussion by giving way on the question of the wearing out fight. He admitted (no doubt on Castlenau's advice) that attacks to prepare the way for a decisive attack and to attract the enemy's reserves were necessary, but only some 10 to 15 days before the main battle, certainly not in April for a July attack.

Though the wearing out fight had suddenly shrunk to less than a fortnight, Haig concluded that the agreement 'seemed quite a victory for me'.[24]

Strengthened by this, Haig was better prepared to answer Joffre's demand that the British should relieve the French Tenth Army. Haig stood his ground, pointing out that since the British forces were seriously below strength and in need of essential training, any relief was impossible at present. In response, Joffre 'asked if I would accept the principle of relieving the 10th Army. I said "Certainly" and he asked "When?" I replied "Next Winter". The old man laughed and I remarked we could not do impossibilities . . . General Joffre argued no more.' Haig had won on the two issues most important to him. 'The whole position of the British Army in the operations of this year depended on my not giving way.' Proud of his achievements, he explained that the 'anxious and difficult struggle' had been won because he had been 'firm without being rude'. Reflecting upon his success, he later confided to his diary that he 'had been given some power not always in me'.[25]

Haig could not long savour his success at Chantilly. By the 18th, de Castlenau was again pushing for the relief of the 10th Army. The French change of heart had resulted from fears that the Germans would soon attack near Verdun. Haig ridiculed these fears; in his opinion, the enemy had not moved enough divisions into the Verdun area to accomplish anything decisive. In fact, he told Robertson, *'the main German attack is likely to fall against the British front fairly soon'*. This conclusion arose from a rather dubious interpretation of intelligence reports. On 10 February, Charteris relayed rumours of a planned German attack upon the British in Flanders, but stressed that they were unreliable. He placed a great deal more faith in evidence which suggested sizeable German troop movements around Verdun. Nine days later, he was able to conclude that 'without doubt a big concentration has taken place opposite the Verdun salient'. Haig ignored Charteris's solid evidence and trusted instead his own intuition. From his knowledge of the German mind, he concluded that the effort around Verdun was an attempt to disguise an offensive against the British which 'might eventually turn out to be their main attack'.[26]

Certain that it was the British who were in the greatest danger, Haig was scathing of the renewed French request for relief. Though he confessed to being unable to understand their attitude, he nevertheless indulged in an explanation:

> the fear of ceasing to be the strongest military power on the land . . . may have something to do with the present air of despair assumed by some of the French General Staff. Some Frenchmen too find it hard to conceal their jealousy of Great Britain. They hate to think that the British Army is on French soil saving France.

No explanation was given as to why these jealous Frenchmen were so eager to place even more of their soil under the control of the British. The good feelings of the week before had evaporated. 'The French are really very tiresome, but one has to keep on friendly terms,' Haig told his wife. 'The truth is, we are too much of gentlemen for them.' It was obvious, as it had always been, that the French 'mean to get all they can out of us'.[27]

On 21 February, the Germans attacked Verdun with incredible ferocity. Contrary to Haig's predictions, the move was no diversion – a massive assault on the British did not follow. It was a somewhat chastened and concerned Haig who discussed the situation with Kitchener in London a few days later. Haig announced that the relief of the French 10th Army would now go ahead, and all available reserves from the British 3rd Army were to be moved to the rear of Joffre's 6th Army, south of the Somme. He also told Kitchener that he saw three possibilities arising from the fighting near Verdun, each necessitating a different British response. If the French were able to hold back and counter-attack the Germans, the British would respond by attacking the depleted enemy forces opposite the 3rd Army astride the Somme.

If, on the other hand, the Germans were successful in breaking through, it would be necessary for the British to counter-attack in the area where the French line had broken, mainly in order to restore French morale. Finally, in the event of a stalemate, the British should consider an attack on the front from Ypres to Armentières, north of the river Lys. The French might even be persuaded in such an instance to relieve British troops elsewhere so as to enable them to take part in this attack. Thus Haig had once again returned to his pet project of an all-British offensive in Belgium. Central to the plan, as always, was the capture of Ostend and Zeebrugge, with the cooperation of the Royal Navy. During his brief visit to London, Haig again discussed the idea with Admiral Bacon. Though both agreed that the project would not be feasible until the Germans had drawn off their reserves in the area, Haig felt confident enough to order that 'the whole scheme should be worked out in the most complete detail'.[28]

Upon his return to France, Haig was given the grim news of the fighting near Verdun by Colonel des Vallières. 'The German artillery fire is said to have been terrific, the French lost very heavily and their front trenches were flattened.' On the following day, Joffre tried to counter Haig's alarm by assuring him that Verdun would be held and that his army was 'suitably placed for every eventuality'. Though pleased with the news, Haig was more concerned about the effect Verdun would have upon the resilience of the French government. Joffre brushed his fears aside, claiming that relations between the government and the military had 'quite changed and he now had quite a free hand'. He did not, however, inspire much confidence when he asked Haig to put in a good word on his behalf to the British Ambassador in Paris, Lord Bertie; the idea being that the favourable report would then make its way to Briand and Poincaré through the back door. Eager to do whatever was necessary to keep France in the war, Haig complied with Joffre's wishes, and was pleased when Bertie assured him that 'the French Government was quite stable and they would not agree to a premature peace'.[29]

Haig would have preferred a situation in which no such reassurance (by Joffre or Bertie) was necessary. Verdun had done nothing to allay his doubts about the French. In fact, those doubts were encouraged when Robertson (another great Francophobe) opined that Joffre 'has no idea of ever taking the offensive if he can get other people to take it for him. So far as I can make out he has no longer any confidence in himself.' Contemptuous of the 'class of work done by the French round Verdun', Robertson was

> more convinced than ever that it is we who will have to finish this war, and therefore in every way we possibly can we must take the lead or at any rate refuse to be led against our own judgement. I am preaching this every day to all the powers that be. I hope I am getting a little more manliness and courage into some of those in higher places.

Commenting upon this letter in his diary, Haig recorded that 'this rather agrees with my opinion too'.[30]

Though Haig suspected that the frightfulness of the Verdun attack had been exaggerated by the French, he was nevertheless intrigued by the innovations immediately apparent. In a report of 3 March these innovations were examined and responses were proposed. The German effort was different from earlier attacks in two important ways. First, the bombardment had been of very high intensity but very short duration, with little registration of enemy targets. Secondly, the Germans did not dig starting trenches close to the enemy lines, but instead advanced directly from their own front trenches, 'even when these were 500 or 600 yards distant'. These tactics facilitated an extremely effective artillery bombardment, without the sacrifice of surprise. As a result, 'The infantry appear to have had little more to do than to take possession of ground already practically won by the artillery.'[31]

Haig saw a pressing need for changes in British offensive and defensive tactics in response to these innovations. On the subject of defence, he made the rather radical (for him) suggestion that the British might occasionally have to abandon voluntarily an unimportant section of their line in order to absorb and cushion the German blow with minimum loss of life. Such a retreat was advisable because 'The possession of a few acres of ground of no importance for tactical or other reasons can have no influence on the course of the war, which must be decided by the defeat of the enemy's forces.' In true Haig style it was emphasised that the best defence was still the offence; especially since the British were superior in men and munitions. 'With such odds in our favour, hostile attacks should offer the least costly means of reducing the enemy's numbers and hastening his downfall.' This was also a direct dig at the French, whom Haig suspected of being content to allow the enemy to attack.[32]

Haig nevertheless felt that Verdun provided some lessons from which the British could profit. The German bombardment, he thought, resembled 'the system adopted by us a year ago in the attack on Neuve Chapelle rather than anything we have done since. On that occasion, in spite of a small number of heavy guns and a very restricted supply of ammunition, we succeeded in effecting a complete surprise.' Therefore, Haig concluded:

> The increase in our artillery and munition supply . . . have opened up for us great possibilities of surprising the enemy, and of exploiting the results gained thereby, provided pains are taken to think out and prepare sound plans, suited to the particular circumstances of each operation.

Unfortunately, the path from premise to conclusion was not as smooth as Haig supposed. Surprise at Neuve Chapelle had been achieved precisely because ammunition was limited and the attack itself was small. Any attempt to expand upon the Neuve Chapelle model would automatically make the task of maintaining secrecy much more difficult. The extra guns would have to be hidden; the roads would be clogged with ammunition trains; more men would mean a greater risk of leaks.[33]

Haig sometimes had difficulty grasping the need for tactical flexibility at a time when the mechanics of war were ever changing. This difficulty was especially evident when it came to new weaponry. Though Haig heartily welcomed new inventions, he did not always understand that, in order to gain the best advantage from them, it was necessary to rethink one's tactics. His failure to do so is all the more significant in view of the fact that quite often his attention was specifically directed to this need. For example, in mid-March he received a War Office report dealing with the employment of tanks, still in their developmental stage at this time. The report outlined possible uses for the new weapon and emphasised the need for a readjustment of infantry and artillery tactics in order to accommodate it. But, from the evidence of Haig's papers, it appears that this call to action was largely ignored.[34]

In contrast, far more attention was paid at this time to a more traditional weapon of war. On 18 March, Haig convened a conference

233

of army commanders at which he discussed the future role of cavalry in the war. He stressed:

> The action of mounted troops under existing trench warfare conditions follows on the actions of infantry and artillery, who must first effect a breach in the enemy's outer system of defence. This breach will at first be narrow in comparison to the great extent of the enemy's front, and in making it we attain only to a local success. But having attained that success we must at once endeavour to exploit it without a moment's delay and to the utmost of our resources.

Thus eighteen months of trench warfare had not altered Haig's basic tactical principles. Cavalry was still, in his view, the only arm of exploitation. In a subsequent memorandum, he insisted, 'When a break in the enemy's line is made, cavalry and mobile troops must be at hand to advance at once.' These troops, he warned, would very likely encounter enemy cavalry, which would have to be 'attacked without a moment's hesitation and routed'. By closing his eyes and dreaming of the past, Haig could still hear the ring of slashing swords. Acting upon these dreams, he ordered Gough to carry out rigorous inspections of cavalry divisions, the aim being to prepare them for the role set forth in the memorandum. Gough was told to 'spread the "doctrine" and get Cavalry Officers to believe in the power of their arm when acting in cooperation with guns and Infantry'. This was necessary because, to Haig's bewilderment, there were 'some officers who think that Cavalry are no longer required!!!'[35]

At the end of March, Haig moved his headquarters from St Omer to Montreuil, a change dictated as much for reasons of comfort as for practicality. As Sassoon, Haig's private secretary, described, the chateau at Montreuil was a vast improvement on French's old headquarters: 'It is such a relief to get into the country and to leave the cobbles and smells of St. Omer. We have got a very nice little house on a hill with jolly rolling country all round and the sea breezes.' Sassoon's cousin, Leopold Rothschild, kept GHQ well supplied with gourmet foods. Haig could have whatever he desired; his wishes being relayed by Sassoon:

As you are kind enough to say that you would like to know what would please him – might I make a suggestion – namely that occasionally instead of mixed fruits and Foie Gras – a chicken or shoulder of Lamb (which the King's Messenger could bring out) would be most gladly and greedily welcomed. He loves good meat and is rather hard put to get it out here.

Within a week, the meat was delivered. A case of turtle soup arrived a few days later. Haig asked for fresh fish (the war meant that 'there is not much fishing done at this end of the channel') and it was dutifully sent. Rothschild's 'good English mutton' was 'so delicious after the frozen beef which is the normal rations'. As Sassoon told his cousin: 'The King's Messenger is continually arriving bowed down under delicacies from you who convert our humdrum meals into veritable festivals.'[36]

While Haig slept in a cosy bed in a quiet country chateau, and dined on the best food Rothschild could provide, his men lived in muddy, noisy trenches, sharing their bully beef and biscuit with big, bloated rats. It apparently did not bother Haig that his war was so much more comfortable than that of the men he commanded. Nor did he see any injustice in using the Army transport system to send meat and dairy products from the Army's store to his wife so that she would not have to suffer the shortages at home. The luxuries were the privilege of his class and his high rank. The idea of denying himself simply because there was a war on was unthinkable. Britain had not gone to war to destroy the Edwardian social system and the privileges it implied, but to defend it.

The Edwardian social system was grossly unequal but inherently stable, and, being so, provided Haig with a stable Army. The men in the trenches by and large did not know about the privileges Haig enjoyed, but had they known, the great majority would have fatalistically accepted them as the natural order of things. The 'natural order' was so natural that it was hardly noticed. When he looked at his army Haig did not see millions of impoverished and deferential working-class men, but a band of brothers fighting side by side and thrilled by the privilege of serving their country. He told Rothschild: 'All the troops here are very fit and cheery. Indeed . . . it is the troops in the field who write home to cheer their friends and not the other way!' He seldom received any evidence to contradict this rosy picture. The censors combed the soldiers' letters home for the most optimistic statements, and periodically compiled these in reports to the Commander-in-Chief. When Haig visited his troops, he inspected the most impressive units which the local commander could find, because it would obviously reflect upon that officer if he took Haig to see men of poor condition or low morale. Other 'evidence' that all was well with Tommy sometimes came from unlikely sources. Ben Tillet, the dockers' leader (who was apparently 'quite converted from his anarchist views'), visited the front in June 1915 and announced that ' "his friends" have unbounded confidence in their officers, and could not get on without them'. When the 'late revolutionist' saw Haig again on 27 December, 'He said that the men were all in splendid spirits – much better even than on his last visit.' The papers repeatedly referred to the sense of well-being at the front; the troops, it was reported, 'trust [Haig] absolutely. They have the most supreme confidence in him.'[37]

Whilst it is difficult to know what the men did feel (since adequate sources simply do not exist), it is possible that the newspapers were not far wrong. There is certainly no evidence of widespread contempt for Haig; the claim that ordinary soldiers universally thought him a butcher does not accord with their continued willingness to fight. But if the men did trust Haig, their trust was nothing special. In one sense, it was reactive: disasters had occurred under French, therefore (since hope springs eternal) success would come with Haig. Confidence was fuelled by ignorance. The supreme command seemed too far removed to affect the everyday life of the ordinary soldier. If mistakes occurred on his part of the front, they were assumed to be the fault of the commander on the spot, or perhaps the man above him, but not of Haig. As one soldier put it: 'I remember being asked on leave what the men thought of Haig. You might as well have asked the private soldier what he thinks of God. He knows about the same amount on each.' If Tommy saw Haig at all, he saw a man in the distance, a man who cut a fine figure on a horse. After one of his tours of inspection, Haig wrote, 'My visit had evidently been looked forward to with some pleasure . . . The men like to see their C. in C. . . . and it shows all ranks that they are being considered and their needs thought about.' It was all so false, but because it was false the system worked. Image was all important and confidence was based upon faith rather than reason. Haig looked a leader, therefore he was trusted. As one junior staff officer wrote:

I don't think I shall ever forget the impression that the Chief made upon me . . . I fell immediately under the spell of his personal magnetism . . . with Haig I felt immediately such a longing to gain a word of praise from him that I would have liked him to ask me to do some impossible exploit that I might prove my devotion to him . . . he exhales such an atmosphere of honour, virtue, courage, and sympathy that one feels uplifted like as when one enters the Cathedral of Beauvais for the first time.

This was from a man who saw Haig on a daily basis. The image was probably intensified the farther removed one was from the actuality.[38]

On 21 March, Charteris reported that a German attack other than in the Verdun area was 'very improbable in the immediate future'. Unable to pretend any longer that an attack upon the British was imminent, Haig was confronted with an urgent need to relieve the pressure on the French. But, since relations with the Allies had grown even icier, he was less than sympathetic to their predicament. A fresh supply of grist for Haig's anti-French mill was supplied by Kitchener on 29 March. He related how, at a recent meeting in Paris, Briand had expressed a desire to show 'to neutral countries and the world generally that the Allies were united'. But, when pressed to transfer troops from Salonika to the Western Front, Briand curtly replied that his country 'had lost severely in men and it was now time for the British to play their part'. Kitchener interpreted this as an indication that the French 'are aiming at a development of the dominions in the Eastern Mediterranean, and will not now fight actively to beat the Germans in France'. He therefore advised Haig to 'beware of the French and . . . husband the strength of the British Army in France'. Haig replied that he 'had never had any intention of attacking with all the available troops except in an emergency to save the French from disaster, and Paris perhaps from capture'. Verdun apparently did not qualify as a disaster from which the French required saving. Haig, who had worried about the French bleeding the British white, was now content to let the Allies absorb the brunt of the German attack. His main worry was that the French desire to 'economise men', meant that it was 'possible that the war will not end this year'.[39]

Haig was reluctant to help the French immediately because he did not feel that his new troops were ready for an attack, and, more importantly, because those troops were already committed to a massive offensive scheduled for the summer. He and Joffre had, earlier in the year, agreed upon a combined action in the area where their two armies joined on the Somme. It was understood from the beginning that the aim was a breakthrough. On 1 April, Rawlinson noted in his diary, 'D.H. is for breaking the line and gambling on rushing the third line on top of a panic.' It was also understood that the French would make the larger contribution to this offensive. Of late, Haig had begun to worry whether, in view of Verdun, they were still committed to their end of the bargain. An additional worry was the fact that Joffre 'did not seem capable of seeing beyond the left of the French army'. After the two met on 7 April, Haig concluded:

> Joffre was talking about a tactical operation which he did not understand . . . it was a waste of my time to continue with him . . . I gather that he signs anything which is put in front of him now and is really past his work, if indeed he ever knew anything practical about tactics as distinct from strategy. Joffre was an Engineer.

After complaining to Commandant E. A. Gemeau, a French liaison officer at GHQ, about the 'foggy state of the Generalissimo's mind', Haig was assured that the French would cooperate fully with the plan. He therefore felt confident enough to tell Joffre on 10 April that, since the Verdun action had served the purpose of wearing down the German Army, the Somme offensive would be a 'decisive attack'. In other words, Acts 1 and 2 having already been completed, the stage was set for Act 3 – the breakthrough.[40]

Kitchener was feeling less confident. The government was pressing him to restrain Haig at the same time that Haig was pressing him to persuade the government to approve the offensive. Within the War Committee there was a feeling (significant but not unanimous) that the British did not have the superiority in men and munitions to justify a massive offensive. (Lloyd George, true to form, preferred a plan of 'smashing the Turks'.) There was considerable alarm at the prospect of losses in the hundreds of thousands, especially since the men Haig proposed to use were those of Kitchener's New Armies, the majority of whom had never participated in an attack. Ministers understandably questioned whether these men were ready for the strains they would have to endure. (Haig himself had admitted, on 29 March, 'I have not got an Army in France really, but a collection of divisions untrained for the Field.') Under pressure from the government, Kitchener repeatedly warned Haig (during meetings at the end of March) about the need to husband resources. Like Rawlinson, he preferred a series of small attacks aimed only at killing Germans. But when Kitchener returned to London, he switched to arguing Haig's case. With help from Robertson, he persuaded the War Committee that Haig 'would not make a fool of himself', and that the French could be trusted to do their bit. The offensive was subsequently approved, mainly because, despite significant misgivings, no solid and coherent case could be marshalled against it. Haig, the new commander, was to be given his chance to prove that he could succeed where others had failed.[41]

Haig learned of the War Committee's approval when he saw Kitchener in London on 14 April. The visit occurred against the backdrop of the political crisis over conscription. A real possibility existed that the government would fall. On the 15th, Kitchener informed Haig that he had come to the reluctant conclusion that conscription was essential, and asked for his support at the Cabinet meeting scheduled for that afternoon. The meeting convinced Haig that 'the real issue of the war in the "Civilians" minds was votes, and not the destruction of the German military power'. Asquith, to Haig's astonishment and dismay, 'was dressed for golf and evidently anxious to get away for his weekend'. Austen Chamberlain, the Secretary for India, argued that since Britain was having to bear the burden of the war's expense for all the Allies, British trade should not be impaired by withdrawing men to fight in Europe. The argument struck no chord with Haig. In his view, the manpower problem was wholly 'due to the government at home being afraid to tackle the labour question. There are numbers of available men at home but they won't work, and the Government is afraid to compel them.' After the meeting adjourned without agreement, he remarked, 'I felt sad that the inner Cabinet of this great Empire should be so wanting in decision and public spirit. Real War, and the basic principles of success seemed hardly to have entered their mind.'[42]

Disgusted, Haig returned to his headquarters. His concern at the lack of mettle evident among British politicians was soon extended to their French counterparts. On 4 May, Clemenceau urged him 'to exercise a restraining hand on General Joffre', because, if Joffre attacked and failed, 'then there will be a number of people in France who will say that the time has arrived to make terms'. Two weeks later Sassoon relayed rumours that the French were opposed to any offensive until the Allies were as strong as possible, and that Briand in fact had 'no intention of making an attack this year!' 'The truth is that there is no strong man in France to guide its policy', Haig concluded. With the French contribution to the proposed Somme offensive growing ever more uncertain, he decided to delay his attack until his army was 'as strong as possible'. When that would be was anyone's guess.[43]

Though anguished by the French attitude, Haig did not abandon plans for a breakthrough. His refusal to do so was due in part to a rather curious intelligence report he received around this time. On 8 May, Charteris announced that the Germans had lost the initiative and would probably fall back on the defensive for the rest of the year. He was, however, careful to point out that the Allied superiority in men and arms was still 'not . . . sufficient to render certain the success of any attempt by the Allies to break the German line'. Intent upon hedging his bets, Charteris continued by writing that there had been a large number of 'local disturbances' in Germany, but these were 'not generally of sufficient importance to justify the name of riots'. The German people were definitely weary of war but 'not to such an extent as to offer hope of a coherent attempt to force the Government to peace'. Nevertheless:

> The effect of success by the allies at the present moment would undoubtedly have a very great effect on opinion in Germany and might well lead to such an outcry as would result in peace. But such a success must be positive. It would not be sufficient merely to beat off German attacks. It would require the actual capture of important ground or the defeat . . . of a large proportion of German troops.

Thus Charteris had in essence told Haig that a breakthrough, though virtually impossible, would so demoralise the Germans that they would probably seek peace. The problem with the report, as with many others, was that it gave too much scope to the dangerously sanguine Haig to interpret it as he wished. On this occasion, he had received the justification for the Somme operation which he sought. 'I don't suppose', he told Rothschild on 14 May, 'that the Germans will give the terms the allies want for some time yet, indeed not until they have suffered a military check.'[44]

Charteris's report and uncertainties over the future French effort combined to encourage a degree of circumspection in Haig. He had begun to accept that the war might last into 1917. In addition, it was possible that the British would henceforward have to shoulder the greater share of the burden. But these possibilities did not dampen Haig's spirit. That they did not do so can be attributed in large part to the timely encouragement of Duncan. On 7 May, the padre

> alluded to the number of brave patriots who had come to France 'by Faith'; they had 'a call'. They knew not whither they went, but whether they returned home again or not, the end would be satisfactory. They had done their duty and all was in the hands of the Lord. He alone could guide and direct us.

'We lament too much over death,' Duncan stressed in another sermon. 'We should regard it as a welcome change to another room.' The message on 4 June was particularly appropriate:

> Mr. Duncan took as his text a letter from St. John to the Christians at Smyrna. 'Be ye faithful unto the end. To you shall be given a crown of everlasting life.' The contents of the letter might have been addressed to the British Army in France today. We must look forward to still harder times, to the necessity for redoubled efforts, but in the end all will be well. How different are our feelings today to those with which the British people and the men in the Army began the War. Then, many people prophesied a race to Berlin, with the Russian steam roller etc. Now we were beginning to learn our lesson, and to be sobered by hard experience and to be patient.

Duncan's messages were a powerful stimulant to Haig's spirit. Eager that his troops should be similarly energised, he urged a party of clerics on 21 May to 'preach . . . about the objects of Great Britain in carrying on this war. We have no selfish motive but are fighting for the good of humanity.'[45]

It was also necessary to instruct the public about the noble cause for which Britain was fighting. The people had to be prepared for the sacrifices ahead. Along these lines, Haig compiled a 'Memorandum on Policy for Press' in which he argued:

A danger which the country has to face at the present is that of unreasoning impatience. Military history teems with instances where sound military principles have had to be abandoned owing to the pressure of ill-informed public opinion. The press is the best means to hand to prevent the danger in the present war.

In addition to signalling a significant shift in attitude towards the Press, the memorandum reveals how Haig's thoughts on the course of the war had changed. 'It would be optimistic to anticipate that lack of men alone will force the Germans to make peace during the next twelve months.' The enemy would have to be beaten, therefore a great deal of fighting and a great deal of dying remained.

Together with patience, the nation must be taught to bear losses. No amount of skill on the part of the higher commanders, no training, however good, on the part of officers and men, no superiority, however great, of arms and ammunition, will enable victories to be won without the sacrifice of men's lives.

On the subject of losses, he concluded that

the nation must be prepared to see heavy casualty lists for what may appear to the uninitiated to be insufficient object and . . . unimportant results . . . the lessons which the people of England have to learn are patience, self-sacrifice, and confidence in our ability to win in the long run. The aim for which the war is being waged is the destruction of German militarism. Three years of war and the loss of one-tenth of the manhood of the nation is not too great a price to pay in so great a cause.

Thus, the price of victory had been set. Though still confident that he could achieve a breakthrough on the Somme, Haig was careful to make sure that the public was prepared for much less.[46]

Having accepted that the war could last at least another year, Haig was in no hurry to begin the Somme offensive. In early May, he persuaded Joffre that it was wise to delay until British troops were fully trained and amply supplied. Joffre, however, insisted that, because of the urgent need to relieve the pressure on the French at Verdun, the attack would have to begin by 1 July. Haig, influenced more by the prospect of a British success than that of a French disaster, was non-committal. On 24 May, Charteris reported that 'as regards resources in men and material in Germany, it makes no great difference whether we attack in June, July or August'. Haig was therefore inclined to delay as long as possible – perhaps until 15 August. When Joffre heard of this possibility two days later, he

> at once got very excited and shouted that 'The French Army would cease to exist if we did nothing till then' . . . I pointed out that, in spite of the 15th August being the most favourable date for the British Army to take action, yet, in view of what he had said of the unfortunate condition of the French Army, I was prepared to commence operations on the 1st of July or thereabouts. This calmed the old man, but I saw that he had come to the meeting prepared . . . to be very nasty.

Apparently unsympathetic to Joffre in his precarious position, Haig once again concluded, 'They are, indeed, difficult Allies to deal with!' He found, however, that liberal doses of 1840 brandy 'had a surprisingly soothing effect'.[47]

Inebriation did not an agreement make. During the first weeks of June discussions between Allied military and political representatives regarding the date of the offensive proceeded on both sides of the Channel. The matter was complicated by the larger issue of the French desire to launch a joint offensive in Salonika. The British were not prepared to commit themselves on the Somme offensive as long as the French persisted in pressing this hare-brained scheme. Therefore, though many a temper was lost, the only agreement reached was a negative one: the British made it clear that they would have nothing to do with French plans in Salonika.

Haig was mainly a passive observer at these proceedings, though he did point out, at regular intervals and with increasing stridency, that the Western Front 'was the decisive point and that we ought to have every available Division here ready to strike at the *decisive* moment'. Though annoyed at the French obstinacy, he was at least able to draw the reassuring conclusion that the Allies were still committed to the war. 'I don't think what you say about "France being inclined to make a separate peace" is quite right,' he told his wife. 'The Army and the Government are determined to go on for another year, but there are some weaklings about Paris and the south away from the war who would of course welcome peace.' Within a fortnight, however, came disturbing evidence to the contrary. On 16 June, Gemeau revealed that

> after the last German attack some of the French troops became disheartened and said that 'they had had enough of it'. Several commanders and staff officers were also disheartened and felt worn out with continuous fighting. Had the enemy continued his pressure, the capture of Verdun seemed certain. The French Higher Command however at once took prompt action. A certain number of the disaffected were at once shot. This number included several officers who were shot in front of their troops.

This was apparently enough to shake Haig out of his complacency. On the 17th, much to the surprise of Joffre, he agreed to launch the attack by the 29th, with the option of a short delay in the event of inclement weather. A week later, Haig's decision was given grim justification when a frantic Briand revealed that 'Gen. Petain . . . at a recent Council meeting had stated that "the game was up. The French Army could not go on", etc. unless the British attacked at once.'[48]

Meanwhile, tragic and disturbing news was arriving from all directions. On 3 June, word of the Battle of Jutland reached Haig. 'General opinion . . . is that we have not won a great victory at sea, so we are a little disappointed.' Three days later, he was shocked to learn, upon his arrival in England, that Kitchener had gone down with the *Hampshire*, which had struck a mine on its way to Russia. Haig was remarkably silent about the death of the man who had had such a profound influence upon his career. The war went on.[49]

During his stay in London, Haig was considerably annoyed to find that the King was in favour of reducing the number of cavalry divisions. This proposal had of late become popular within the War Committee. The politicians, worried about the shortage of shipping, had been astonished to discover how much cargo space was taken up with feed for apparently redundant horses. (What they did not entirely grasp was that most horses – not to mention donkeys – on the Western Front were used for transport; the feed for cavalry horses was a drop in the bucket.) The War Committee proposal raised two issues, both of which prompted a heated response from Haig. The first was the question of reducing the mounted arm. On this point, Haig told the King that 'in order to shorten the war and reap the fruits of any success, we must make use of the mobility of the cavalry'. The same point had been expressed in an earlier letter to Robertson:

I have an inward feeling that events will make us regret a reduction in mounted troops. It seems to me that troops and material are so imbedded in the ground in trench warfare that a general retreat will be most difficult. We ought therefore to be prepared to exploit a success on the lines of 1806. [Murat's cavalry chase after the Battle of Jena.]

The second issue concerned government meddling in what was perceived to be Army affairs. As Haig wrote to Robertson: 'It appears that the War Committee have overlooked the fact that I am responsible for the efficiency of the Armies in France.' When Robertson conveyed Haig's message to the Cabinet, Lloyd George

said that he considered it a perfectly insolent letter . . . Sir D. Haig . . . talked about his responsibility – to whom was he responsible? He was responsible to them, to the Government, and through the Government to Parliament, and through Parliament to the people. The effect of this letter was to tell the War Committee 'to mind their own business' and not to interfere with his . . . They had the perfect right to investigate any matter connected with the war that they pleased.

The issue was one which would be returned to, with ever increasing rancour, in the months to come.[50]

During their meeting, the King told Haig that he thought the war would end in October 1917. In response, Haig revealed that 'signs are not wanting to show that the Germans might bargain for peace before the coming winter'.[51] No indication was given as to what these 'signs' were. As Haig had repeatedly insisted over the previous few months that the country needed to prepare itself for a long and costly war, his stance on this occasion seems curious. The inconsistency is puzzling, but not unique; Haig had a peculiar habit of contradicting himself. These contradictions usually arose because Haig's role as Commander-in-Chief in a static war and his background as a cavalry officer were fundamentally anomalous. Thus it is probably no coincidence that Haig predicted an early victory at the same time that he was arguing with the King about the need to maintain the cavalry at full strength. When Haig was in a rational frame of mind, he could patiently accept the reality of a long, slow and static conflict. When he donned his cavalryman's hat, he was prone to ridiculous flights of fancy. A cavalryman had to believe that the enemy lines could be breached and the Germans defeated in a single battle, for if he did not, there remained no justification for the cavalry. When the dull repetition of cavalry dogma echoed in Haig's ears, victory seemed but a short distance away.

11

'Drive on, Illustrious General'

The cavalry fantasies apparent during Haig's conversation with the King (discussed at the end of the last chapter) are evident in his plans for the Somme offensive. It is perhaps best to backtrack somewhat and investigate the process by which the operation unfolded. On 1 March, the Fourth Army was created and assigned to the command of Rawlinson. Shortly afterwards, he was ordered by Haig to prepare for the offensive. The conflict of opinion evident at Neuve Chapelle was thus revived. After studying the problem, Rawlinson

> came to the conclusion that two courses were open to me . . . The first, and most alluring one, was to attempt to capture the whole of the enemy's lines of defence . . . in one attack. The second, less ambitious, but in my opinion more certain: to divide the attack into two phases, the first of which would give us possession of the enemy's front system, and all the important tactical points between the front system and the second line.

The second option was a purely tactical operation; Rawlinson was not interested in strategic objectives because

> It does not appear to me that the gain of two or three more kilometres of ground is of much consequence . . . Our object rather seems to be to kill as many Germans as possible with the least loss to ourselves, and the best way to do this appears to me to be to seize points of tactical importance which will provide us with good

observation and which we may feel quite certain the Germans will counter attack.

In Haig's mind, it was not enough to 'kill Germans'. Contemptuous of Rawly's pessimism, he aimed at 'getting as large a combined force of French and British across the Somme and fighting the enemy in the open!' Simply stated, one commander was talking about a campaign of attrition, the other was dreaming about mobility.[1]

Haig was certain he could win the war in 1916. Rawlinson had no such illusions. On 31 March, after discussing the merits of 'limited as opposed to . . . unlimited objective[s]' with a staff officer, Rawly recorded:

> All my Corps Commanders are opposed to the unlimited. After what K[itchener] said yesterday I think we should be wiser to adopt the limited one and to look to winning the war in 1917. If K cannot replace our losses it would be foolish to incur them without a certainty of success which I cannot guarantee. I shall have to have it out with D.H. tomorrow.

There is no evidence that Rawlinson ever properly 'had it out' with Haig. Differences of opinion were probably never adequately aired because of the basic problems of communication between the two men. Haig, according to Marshall-Cornwall, 'was slow of speech and frigid of manner. One felt that it would be difficult to alter his pre-conceived ideas.' He was never comfortable with the quick-witted, gregarious and articulate Rawlinson, his polar opposite. Rawly, in turn, still feared Haig because of the Davies incident, and was consequently reluctant to question him. Plans were therefore announced but not discussed; one could have caught a chill in the icy atmosphere of their meetings. Differences were still evident on 27 June, when Haig, rejecting Rawlinson's plans for a slow, methodical assault, ordered him

> to prepare for a rapid advance, and as soon as the last line had been gained to push on advance guards of all arms . . . I told him to impress on his Corps Commanders the use of their Corps Cavalry and mounted troops . . . In my opinion it is better to prepare to advance beyond the enemy's last line of trenches, because . . . if no

preparations for an advance are made till next morning, we might lose a golden opportunity.

On the 30th, Rawlinson claimed that he had bowed to the dictates of his senior commander. 'The attack is to go for the big thing. I still think we could do better to proceed by shorter steps; but I have told D.H. that I will carry out his plan with as much enthusiasm as if it were my own.' This was an overstatement. The plan was in truth an amalgam of Rawlinson's 'bite and hold' ideas and Haig's unlimited objectives. The British Army went into action wrapped in contradictions.[2]

The internal contradictions aside, the strategic plan was Haig's. Simply stated, he foresaw a suitably destructive artillery bombardment preparing the way for the infantry who would overrun dilapidated defences and breach the enemy line. A reserve army consisting of three cavalry and two infantry divisions under General Gough would rush into this gap and sweep the Germans from the open country around Bapaume, rolling back the defences as far as Arras. Apologists for Haig have argued that the Somme offensive was a virtual *fait accompli* when he assumed command. This is a gross overstatement. It is true that Haig was committed to a joint offensive with the French on the Somme. But aside from the location and the units involved, the real shape of the offensive was determined mainly by Haig – especially after it became apparent that the French contribution would be much smaller than anticipated. In April, Haig boasted that French commanders had agreed to do everything in their power 'to assist me in the execution of my plan. They were all agreed that my plan of attack was the best one.' Foch, during meetings in May and June, tried to steer Haig's thinking along lines similar to Rawlinson's, but Haig would not budge, mainly because he was convinced that the Frenchman had sinister motives. 'Foch seems anxious that the British should do all the fighting required to get the French on open ground.'[3]

The glaring contradictions in the plan were not confined to those between Haig and Rawlinson. It had originally been intended that France would play the lead in this drama. In the end, she was but a minor supporting actor. The script had therefore to be rewritten; the southerly advance was suddenly changed to a northerly one, and the objective of crossing the Somme altered to that of capturing the high ground around Pozières. Haig wanted tanks, but these were not available.[4] Contradictions in tactical plans were evident at every rung of the chain of command. Haig, reflecting his predilection for decentralised leadership, left it to 'the various subordinate commanders . . . to gradually work out their parts of the business'.[5] Uniformity was naturally absent. Finally, in a mistake which is inexplicable in the light of Loos, no special reserves were positioned at the point on the left at Thiepval where the breakthrough was intended.

There were serious problems with the area upon which the offensive was to be launched. It had been chosen not because it suited the attackers but because it was where the French and British Armies joined. Unfortunately, it did not suit the attackers. The transport and supply facilities behind the lines fell short of the requirements of a massive offensive. Worse still, the German position was extremely strong. As the area had been relatively quiet since 1914, there had been plenty of time to fortify the defences. The enemy was on the high ground, with the first line on the forward slope of the Combles–Thiepval ridge. This was supported by an intermediate line of deep dug-outs which provided front-line defenders with shelter during heavy bombardment. Three kilometres further back was the second or main line of defence, built around a series of fortified villages providing German machine-gunners with concealment virtually secure from even the heaviest artillery barrage. This second line was also protected by dense wire entanglements. A third German line, situated another four kilometres to the rear, completed a system of defence unlike any the British had so far encountered.

It was up to the artillery to break this defensive stronghold, but the artillery plan was also riddled with contradictions. Haig wanted a hurricane bombardment, Rawlinson a prolonged systematic effort designed to destroy the front defensive zone. The resultant compromise satisfied neither man. A breakthrough necessitated a heavy concentration of the guns at the point of the main thrust. They were instead spread over the entire front and directed at all lines of the German defence. Consequently, the shelling was everywhere ineffective. The bombardment had two general objectives: to annihilate German machine-gunners in the front line trenches and to cut the wire. The machine-gunners in dug-outs twenty to thirty feet deep, were, however, secure from everything but a direct hit from a very heavy high-explosive shell. Of these, the British had relatively few. Twelve-thousand tons of shells were fired in the preliminary bombardment. Only 900 tons were high-explosive. Unfortunately, high-explosive shells were also best at destroying wire. The British tried to improvise by sweeping the wire with shrapnel shells from 18-pounder guns, an extremely difficult manoeuvre beyond the skills of the recently trained artillery batteries of the Territorial and New Army divisions. To make matters worse, the expansion of the munitions factories in 1915 had resulted in a decline in the quality of the shells used. Duds littered the field.

The wire was not cut and the dug-outs not destroyed. Towards the end of June, information to this effect was coming into Corps and Army headquarters, but no one, apparently, dared tell the emperor that he had no clothes. Haig carried on, blissfully ignorant and supremely confident. On 20 June, he told his wife that 'the situation is becoming more favourable for us – and it almost seems as if the crisis of the war were approaching'. Two days later he was more explicit about the source of his confidence:

> Now you must know that *I feel* that every step in my plan has been taken with the Divine help and I ask daily for aid, not merely in making the plan, but in carrying it out, and this I hope I shall continue to do until the end of all things which concern me on earth.

On 25 June, Duncan stressed that '[God's] plans rule the Universe . . . We are merely tools in His hands, used for a special purpose.' Haig admitted that this knowledge gave him a 'tranquillity of mind' and enabled him 'to carry on without feeling the strain of responsibility to be too excessive'. Eager that this feeling of tranquillity should continue during the offensive, he arranged for Duncan to accompany him to his advanced headquarters at Beauquesne.[6]

On the eve of the battle, Haig assured his wife that 'everything possible for us to do to achieve success has been done. But whether or not we are successful lies in the Power above.' Since that Power was benevolently inclined towards the British cause, Haig could feel 'hopeful':

> The men are in splendid spirits. Several have said that they have never before been so instructed and informed of the nature of the operation before them. The wire has never been so well cut, nor the Artillery preparation so thorough. I have seen personally all the Corps Commanders and one and all are full of confidence.

On the next day, thousands of British martyrs – considerably less tranquil than Haig – met their Maker.[7]

The 57,000 casualties of the first day of the Somme were overwhelming proof that the wire had not been adequately cut nor the German machine-guns sufficiently silenced. Unaware of the extent of the losses, Haig sent a telegram to his wife at 11 a.m., describing the 'Very successful attack this morning – captured portion of enemy second line on a front of 8,000 yards – we hold the hills about Longueval and hope to get the cavalry through – All went like clockwork.' He admitted that in places the British had been held up, particularly on the front of VIII Corps, but put this down to a lack of resolve, not to the impossibility of the situation. 'I am inclined to believe that few of the 8th Corps left their trenches.' This was explained by the fact that 'Hunter Weston [the commander] and the majority of his officers are amateurs in hard fighting and some think that they know much more than they really do of this kind of warfare, simply, because they had been at Gallipoli.' (To have been at Gallipoli was an inexcusable fault.) In fact, VIII Corps suffered 14,000 casualties on 1 July.[8]

On the 2nd, the Adjutant General set the first day's losses at 40,000. The figure did not shake Haig's belief that he had succeeded. 'This cannot be considered severe in view of the numbers engaged, and the length of front attacked.' A cheery report was sent to Rothschild:

> The Battle is going very well for us and already the Germans in our front are surrendering more freely. The enemy too is so pushed for men that he is collecting them from all parts of his line, with the result that we are being opposed by a collection of units of all kinds. Our troops are in wonderful spirits and full of confidence.

Though Haig's confidence did not diminish as the days passed, a subtle change of emphasis in his diary and letters is noticeable. He referred less to the imminence of a breakthrough, more to the effect which the British attacks were having upon the enemy. The Germans were being worn down; they would eventually collapse. The wearing out fight which had not been necessary and not intended was nevertheless proceeding well. On 7 July, he told his wife that he was 'hopeful that before long the enemy's resistance will break down'. The need for 'patience and determination' was repeatedly stressed. 'I . . . feel confident and believe that strength is being given to me that will enable us to win . . . But it will be a hard struggle.'[9]

As the days wore on, he became increasingly vague about what he expected to achieve on the Somme. On 8 July, he wrote, 'In another fortnight, with Divine help, I hope some decisive results may be obtained,' but he did not elaborate upon what the 'decisive results' would be. This refrain was echoed on the 13th:

> I think we have a good chance of success. If we don't succeed this time, we'll do so the next! The enemy is, I think, feeling the strain of continuous fighting, and is not fighting so well. My troops on the other hand are in the best of spirits! and feel they are going to win.

Four days later, Haig took care to emphasise that there was 'no question of *discussing* peace conditions, we must *dictate* peace terms to the Germans'.[10]

Statements such as these have been cited, justifiably, as evidence of an intentional blindness to the facts – the intelligence reports, casualty figures, etc. As if to pre-empt such criticism, Haig recorded some advice from Duncan which he found particularly cogent: 'the difficulties of any problem depends very much on the way the individual regards it. But we must not be optimistic . . . simply by shutting our eyes to the truth, but, through confidence in God's help, believe that we can and will overcome what opposes us.'[11] In other words, faith was at least as important as facts. Confident of God's blessing, Haig was certain the British would eventually emerge victorious. With the end predetermined, the events along the way became less significant. In this sense, it is perhaps correct to claim that Haig occasionally ignored adverse intelligence, but he did so only because he believed that the goodness of God was a more reliable indicator of the way the war would be resolved.

The fighting continued according to a pattern not remarkably different from earlier battles. Some isolated gains were made, but these were minute compared to the original objectives. During the second week, Rawlinson, convinced that it was impossible to break the highly fortified German second line in a frontal assault by day, suggested a night attack on the front between Mametz and Trones. Attacking in the dark would, he hoped, lessen the effectiveness of the deadly German machine-guns. Haig was sceptical: 'The experience of war, as well of the teachings of peace are against the use of *large masses* in night operations, especially with inexperienced staff officers and young troops.' He suggested a more conventional attack. 'It was', according to one of Rawlinson's staff officers, 'an academic plan that would have been given good marks at the Staff College.' On this occasion, however, Rawlinson persevered, and Haig surprisingly relented. The result was one of the most successful battles of the entire campaign. On 14 July, on a frontage of over five kilometres the British advanced nearly 1,500 metres, in the process capturing three important fortified towns (Longueval, Bazentin-le-Petit, Bazentin-le-Grand) in the German second line. All this was achieved at the relatively small cost of 9,200 lives.[12]

Prior to Rawlinson's night attack, on 11 July, Falkenhayn terminated offensive operations at Verdun. The Somme offensive had thus achieved one of its primary objectives – the relief of the pressure on the French. But Haig had been aiming for much more. According to his criteria, the offensive had so far been nothing less than a tragic disaster.

When previous battles failed to achieve their original objectives and deteriorated into stalemate, they were terminated. The Somme offensive continued for another four months. The decision to carry on was Haig's. Had he felt the need to, he would have justified this decision by arguing that the war could not be won by standing idle. He also feared, with some justification, that as soon as he relaxed the pressure the Germans would resume their attack on Verdun or send troops to other fronts.

These reasons aside, it is impossible to ignore aspects of Haig's personality which contributed to the decision to prolong the offensive. He was a very stubborn man. Despite his apparent optimism, he must have been aware that the Germans had proved him wrong on 1 July. Somewhat chastened, he reacted not by crawling away and licking his wounds, but rather by pushing forward with teeth bared, intent upon proving himself right. His attitude was similar to that assumed after Neuve Chapelle. In other words, failure motivated him not to change his plan, but to magnify its elements. Whilst he may have realised (though he did not admit) that a breakthrough was not as easy as he had anticipated, he did not conclude that it was impossible. What was required was more energy, more time, more guns, more men and, therefore, more casualties. As another Sunday sermon promised, it would all be worthwhile in the end:

Mr. Duncan took as his text 'The Kingdom of Heaven is likened under treasure hidden in a field' which in order to buy 'a man sells all he possesses with joy'. Anything worth having has always to be paid for fully. In this war, our object is something very great. The future of the world depends on our success. So we must fully spend all we have, energy, life, money, everything, in fact, without counting the cost. Our objects cannot be attained without the greatest sacrifice from each one of us.[13]

Haig was essentially right. More of everything would have broken the German Army. But what he did not realise at this time was quite how much more.

The task ahead seemed quite simple and straightforward. Haig did not doubt that he could withstand the pressure, and expected that his Army could do likewise. Proof of the resiliency of his men was provided by Sir Berkeley Moynihan, a Leeds surgeon, who revealed on 25 July that 'the spirit of the wounded was beyond all praise . . . all were now very confident, very cheery and full of pluck. Truly the British race is the finest on Earth!' Haig thought that the same spirit characterised the people at home. As with every battle during his command, letters poured in congratulating him on his great victory. But these, though encouraging, had less effect upon him than those written in the following strain:

Illustrious General,

The expectation of mankind is upon you – the 'Hungry Haig' as we call you here at home. You shall report 500,000 casualties, but the Soul of the empire will afford them. And you shall break through with the cavalry of England and France for the greatest victory that history has ever known. And Scotland shall be forever; and Kitchener shall smile from the depths of the ocean . . .

Drive on, Illustrious General!

The anonymous note was probably preserved because it echoed Haig's own feelings. It, and similar messages, reinforced his belief that there existed a great mass of people who shared his willingness and determination to pursue victory at all costs.[14]

A sense of unease was, however, apparent in other quarters, particularly the War Committee. On 7 July, Robertson appealed to Haig for some evidence that his attacks were having the desired effect. 'If you would send me a short letter which I could read to the War Committee I am sure it would be to their general interest, and to *your* interest in particular.' Haig forwarded some regurgitated pap from Charteris's intelligence reports, but the politicians apparently found it hard to swallow, as Robertson indicated on the 29th:

> The powers that be are beginning to get a little uneasy in regard to the situation. The casualties are mounting up and they are wondering whether we are likely to get a proper return for them. I do my best to keep the general situation to the front, and to explain what may be the effect of our efforts . . . But they will persist in asking whether I think a loss of say 300,000 men will lead to really great results, because if not we ought to be content with something less than we are now doing, and they constantly enquire why we are fighting and the French are not.

Robertson warned Haig that he might be summoned to London to justify his actions. Haig, in response, pencilled angrily in the margins that this was 'Not exactly the letter of a CIGS! He ought to take responsibility also! I have no intention of going before the War Committee while this battle is going on!'[15]

Haig was not being entirely fair. Robertson was having to carry the can for the questionable achievements on the Somme, with little solid information from Haig to support his case. He had been placed in a difficult position because he had originally sold the plan to the War Committee, by (according to Hankey) promising that 'there was no idea of an attempt to break through the German lines. It would be only a move to *degager* the French.' Since the pressure upon Verdun had been relieved, Robertson was left with no further justification for continuing the offensive. To make matters worse, he had genuine misgivings about Haig's methods, feeling that he was too extravagant with men's lives. Preferring the more methodical technique favoured by Rawlinson, he wrote to the latter and to Kiggell (behind Haig's back) in an effort to counsel caution. Wilson feels that Robertson was at this time trying to undermine Haig in order to step into his position, a suggestion which seems far-fetched and is probably another example of Wilson's taste for conspiracy. Robertson was probably instead only trying to make things easier for himself while at the same time saving a few lives.[16]

It just so happened that two days after Robertson's letter Charteris reported on the state of the German Army. He claimed that, if the British attack was maintained for another six weeks, the German reserves would be virtually exhausted, 'and the enemy's power of resistance will have been weakened accordingly'. Armed with this information, Haig sent an official reply to Robertson, which outlined his reasons for continuing. The letter, though little more than a restatement of Charteris's report, did significantly diverge on the question of relieving the pressure upon Verdun. Charteris had stated that the Verdun offensive had been indefinitely postponed, and probably cancelled. Haig, undoubtedly aware of the use the War Committee would make of this information, instead wrote that only 'six enemy Divisions besides heavy guns have been withdrawn', thus implying that it was premature to conclude that the pressure on the French had been relieved. On the other hand, he argued, the recent Russian success (the Brusilov offensive) would have been impossible had the Germans not been kept occupied on the Somme. But probably the most important effect of the British attack was described by Haig in the following rather garbled way:

> Proof given to the world that the Allies are capable of making and maintaining a vigorous offensive and of driving enemy's best troops from the strongest positions has shaken faith of the Germans, of their friends, of doubting neutrals in the invincibility of Germany. Also impressed on the world, England's strength and determination, and the fighting power of the British race.

In other words, 'the maintenance of a steady offensive pressure will result eventually in [the] complete overthrow' of the German Army.[17]

Continuing his case, Haig drew attention to the fact that the losses during July were only '120,000 more than they would have been had we not attacked'. This was to become a favourite rebuttal to those advocating a passive defence. Attacks were not as expensive as they seemed. The losses 'cannot be regarded as sufficient to justify any anxiety as to our ability to continue the offensive'. Haig was referring to an arithmetic problem – the ability of the Army to maintain full strength – not to the effect the losses might be having on soldiers or the people at home. As has been shown, he had few worries about the resilience of the English – a great martial race. He ended, significantly, not with recommendations, but 'intentions'. These were:

(a) To maintain a steady pressure on Somme battle.
(b) To push my attack strongly whenever and wherever the state of my preparations and the general situation make success sufficiently probable to justify me in doing so, but not otherwise.
(c) To secure against counter-attack each advantage gained and prepare thoroughly for each fresh advance.

Unrepentant, Haig concluded, 'Proceeding thus, I expect to be able to maintain the offensive well into the autumn.' There was no mention of an imminent breakthrough, nor was an attempt made to define 'success'. He was, quite clearly, firmly entrenched in one of his *bataille d'usure* phases, so much so that he specifically emphasised that the process of attrition would take a very long time. 'It would not be justifiable to calculate on the enemy's resistance being completely broken without another campaign next year.'[18]

The politicians (including, significantly, Mr Lloyd George, the new War Minister) were prepared to swallow Haig's bitter medicine. Robertson was instructed to 'send a message to General Sir D. Haig that he might count on full support from home'. Most importantly, the memo completely negated the effects of a Cabinet paper by Churchill which scorned Haig's methods. This paper was first brought to Haig's attention when Robertson revealed, on 6 August, that there was considerable disquiet at home, but that this was confined to 'Winston, French, Fitzgerald and various "degommed people" [who] are trying to make mischief' and who, fortunately, 'have not a friend in the War Committee'. After hearing a similar story from the King, Haig commented that 'these were trifles and we must not allow them to divert our thoughts from our main objective namely "beating the Germans". I also expect that Winston's judgement is impaired from taking drugs.'[19]

The fact that the support of the government had to be confirmed indicates that Haig's position was not as secure as it once was. Perhaps realising this, he came to the reluctant conclusion that it was to his advantage to be friendly to newspapermen. Esher had for some time been urging Haig to use the Press as a means of communicating directly with the people and thus of counteracting the doubts and mischief of politicians. But it took the pressures of a major offensive to demonstrate the soundness of Esher's advice. On 6 July, Haig took the extraordinary step of consenting to a meeting with the despicable Repington, explaining: 'I hated seeing such a dishonest individual, but I felt it was my duty to the Army to do so. Otherwise he would have been an unfriendly critic of its actions.'[20] Had Haig been more honest, he would have admitted that Repington was potentially an unfriendly critic of *his* actions, and that meeting him was in truth an act of self-preservation.

Haig soon found that newspaper men were not the monsters he had imagined them to be. Even the terrible Lord Northcliffe, who visited in late July, impressed Haig by his

desire to do his best to help win the war. He was most anxious not to make a mistake in anything he advocated in his newspapers and for this he was desirous of seeing what was taking place. I am therefore letting him see *everything* and talk to anyone he pleases.

Two days later, Northcliffe asked Haig 'to let Sassoon send him a line should anything appear in *The Times* which was not altogether to my liking'. He also promised to keep Repington under control. Satisfied, Haig assured Northcliffe that in future his correspondents would be welcome as long as they behaved.[21]

Lady Haig was uncomfortable about the newspaper reports which followed: 'It gave me no pleasure to hear of this pandering to public and press.' 'You must think I am an Advertiser!' Haig explained sheepishly. 'That is not so . . . I see these people for the good of the Army.' Not convinced, she demanded, from Fletcher, an explanation as to why her husband was suddenly 'pandering to the public and press' – especially (worst of all) the Northcliffe Press. Fletcher replied with a summary of what was obviously Haig's own attitude:

the British public badly require educating as to the conduct of the war and the conditions out here. People at home measure the success achieved solely on *the casualties* and as these appear high and *should* this great battle finish in a deadlock there will be a lot of stupid talk at home let alone criticism. It is for this reason that Derby as Under Secretary for War advised Lord Northcliffe to see all he could and . . . if necessary, explain for the *very first time* in the Press . . . the difficulties . . . that the C. in C. . . . ha[s] to contend with in carrying out this offensive. Lord Derby and Esher did it as they knew the feeling of the Cabinet at home as being so *very ignorant* of the colossal affairs out here . . . it is only intended to educate the country as a whole to what we are in for and to let them know that the losses are all well earned.

Lady Haig was still not happy. 'D's greatness', she replied, 'has entirely been because . . . he is so straight and has never mixed up with intrigues, putting his personal advantage aside.' Fletcher apparently had 'no idea . . . how Douglas really is looked up to by the general public'. In other words, his reputation was so secure that it should not have been necessary for him to sully his hands by mixing with men like Northcliffe. Leaving aside the questionable accuracy of Lady Haig's opinion of her husband, it is clear that by this time he had become more pragmatic than she.[22]

Meanwhile, Haig's Army continued to hurl itself headlong into the German defences. It is not surprising that there was a tendency to judge the Somme offensive by the number of casualties, since there was no other readily apparent way to judge it. The advances looked miniscule even on a large-scale map. And, since even Haig admitted that he was now fighting a battle of attrition, was it not the British body count, in relation to the German, that was most important? Unfortunately, the respective casualty figures were not significantly different to justify an assumption that the British were winning the numbers game. Nor was the German morale rapidly draining away, as Haig was forced to admit on 2 August:

the enemy has brought up considerable reinforcements of men and guns, and can continue for some time still to replace tired troops. He has also strengthened, and continues to strengthen his positions; and he has recovered to a great extent from the disorganisation caused by the success of the Allied attacks last month. In consequence, although most of his troops in our front have been severely handled and must be somewhat tired, they are still too formidable to be rushed without careful and methodical preparation; and may even be capable of developing strong and well-organised counter-attacks.

This was the closest Haig came to admitting that he had underestimated his enemy. It is also significant that this document was considerably less sanguine than the one sent to the Cabinet. Nevertheless, Haig still felt confident enough to predict that the 'wearing out' battle would eventually be brought to a 'successful termination' whereupon the 'crisis of the fight' would ensue. The meaning of these terms was left intentionally vague. It was revealed that the 'crisis' would come 'not . . . sooner than the last half of September'.[23]

Because Haig was certain that the Germans were being pushed towards a 'crisis', he eagerly looked for evidence that the crisis was imminent. He consequently gave too much weight to rather spurious rumours and intelligence reports. For instance, on 15 August, he enthusiastically recorded 'news' that the Germans were planning an evacuation of Belgium and proposing peace through the King of Spain. Likewise, on 1 September, he gave great weight to reports of the 'imminent' collapse of the Austrians and the German preparations for their 'last stand'. What is clear is that Haig had difficulty sifting facts from rumours. It was probably the latter which inspired a message to Lady Haig on 17 August: 'Reports from Germany all point to a serious situation there and the potato seems to have certainly failed. All this must induce the enemy to give away, and will at any rate cause much unrest and possibly revolt before many months are over.' The quotidian reports of a German crisis, usually the product of Charteris's fertile imagination, reveal a fundamental flaw in Haig's intelligence-gathering network. The purpose of intelligence is to provide information on how the enemy can be beaten. Charteris too often looked for evidence that the Germans were beaten – or at least nearly so. When this intelligence reached Haig's desk, he assumed that victory was around the corner, and planned accordingly. For instance, he ended the 17 August letter by telling his wife, 'Mean time we must all do our utmost to inflict a military defeat on his army in the field without delay.' In fact, the time was not right for the sort of knockout blow which he intended: the Germans were not weak enough, nor the British sufficiently strong.[24]

Haig, bolstered by Charteris's intelligence reports, was in fine fettle when he, Poincaré, Joffre, Foch and others met to discuss the future of the offensive on 12 August at Beauquesne. The French President was eager for the Allies to 'make some decisive advance in order to keep the people from England and France from grumbling'. Haig reassured his Allies by stating that 'we had yet at least 10 weeks of good weather before winter set in, probably more, and . . . much will be done by us in that time'.[25]

As if to demonstrate his sincerity, Haig launched an attack on the 19th which resulted in the capture of the ridge overlooking Thiepval. Beside himself with pride at this success, he penned another glowing report on the progress of the Somme offensive. The report, sent to the CIGS, was obviously designed for the consumption of the War Committee. In the three weeks which had passed since his 1 August memo, Haig had become ever more convinced that his 'method of procedure . . . is well-suited to the situation . . . a steady offensive pressure has been maintained with very satisfactory results and at small costs, in proportion to the results gained'. A bit of magic with the figures led to the conclusion that the casualties were 'not . . . more than some 28,000 greater than would ordinarily have occurred during three weeks of normal trench warfare'. German losses, on the other hand, 'cannot have been less than our own' – a devious way of saying that they were hardly more. Maintaining the pressure would 'eventually enable us to obtain a definite mastery'. What this meant, and what would lead from it, Haig did not divulge. The masterpiece of semantics continued:

> That such a mastery will be gained by the means adopted I am confident, though how long it may be before it is so complete as to yield great results it is as yet too soon to say. There is satisfactory evidence that we are making steady progress towards gaining it, and there is no room for doubt that when it has been gained considerable results will be within our reach.

Matters were under control. Brighter days lay ahead. 'Trust me,' Haig was saying. Turning the politician's tactics upon themselves, he had promised a great deal but guaranteed nothing.[26]

The 'definite mastery' was to follow from an enormous attack in the latter part of September in which the British would drive through suitably softened German lines. Having planned this action for some time, Haig was rather dismayed to find, during a conference at Saleux, on 27 August, that the French were demanding British cooperation in another action earlier in the month. He reluctantly agreed to the Allies'. wishes, on the understanding that he would then be free to carry out his major attack some two weeks later. Joffre and Poincaré protested that the second attack should follow immediately after the first, but to no avail. The French were apparently eager for Haig to apply continuous pressure because they feared that Germany was aiming for a separate peace with Russia, and the latter had therefore to be shown that her Allies remained determined. Haig discounted this possibility; in his opinion matters had gone too far for the Russians to quit the war at this stage.[27]

On 29 August, Robertson advised Haig to 'do as you think best and do not be influenced by Joffre and Co'. He explained that the French were unduly worried that the approach of winter would soon force a halt to the offensive, whereas, in his opinion, the British should and would continue fighting 'winter or no winter'. On this point the Cabinet allegedly agreed, including Lloyd George who (the CIGS assured Haig) 'thinks you are playing absolutely the right game, and doing your job absolutely the right way'. Robertson had either been deceived by Lloyd George or was himself benignly deceiving Haig, for the truth was that the War Secretary's always tenuous support for the Somme offensive was rapidly draining away. A leak had sprung when the Germans called off their action around Verdun. Then, in late August, Rumania entered the war on the side of the Entente. Lloyd George feared that, unless the Allies shifted their attention eastward, Rumania would suffer the fate of Serbia, and be crushed by the combined weight of Germany, Austria-Hungary and Bulgaria. In a dramatic shift from his 29 August statement, Robertson warned Haig on 7 September that 'L.G. has got the Servian fit again' and was making trouble.[28]

On 11 September, Lloyd George arrived at GHQ, no doubt intent upon digging up material to use against Haig's Western Front strategy. His arrival, coming soon after a visit by Asquith, caused Haig to reflect upon

> how much superior in many ways Mr. Asquith is to L.G. I have got on with the latter very well indeed, and he is anxious to help

263

in every way he can. But he seems to me so flightly – makes plans and is always changing them and his mind. . . . On the other hand Mr. Asquith has such a clear and evenly balanced mind.

'You will gather', Haig told his wife, 'that I have no great opinion of L.G. *as a man or leader*.' The visit was nothing but a 'joy ride': 'Breakfast with newspaper men, and posings for the Cinema Shows, pleased him more than anything else. No doubt with the ulterior object of catching votes.' Reflecting upon the media circus, Sassoon wrote that he 'was sorry we hadn't an elephant for them to ride'.[29]

Lloyd George was under the impression that, due to hidebound artillery tactics, the British had suffered proportionately higher losses than the French, who were intent upon conquering ground with guns rather than men. Though this was a somewhat simplistic assumption, it had some basis in fact. Eager to know what the French were doing differently, he asked Foch some very frank questions during a supposedly 'private' interview. Foch, however, could not keep a secret. He subsequently told Haig about the interview, specifically how Lloyd George had enquired whether higher British losses were an indication of lower quality generalship. According to Foch, 'L.G. was sufficiently patriotic not to criticise the British Commander-in-Chief', though the standard of generals below Haig was questioned. Haig was livid: 'Unless I had been told of this conversation personally by Gen. Foch, I would not have believed that a British Minister could have been so ungentlemanly as to go to a foreigner and put such questions regarding his own subordinates.' When Robertson heard of the interview, he offered to confront Lloyd George, but did not do so after Haig advised that 'the wisest course is to let the matter drop'. In fact, Haig did nothing of the sort, deciding instead to utilise his new weapon, Northcliffe. A letter of protest was quickly sent by Sassoon to the Press baron, and shortly afterwards leading articles extremely critical of Lloyd George appeared in various papers. The War Minister then complained about Press bias, but it was his own fault. Both sides had hit below the belt, but it was Lloyd George who had thrown the first illegal punch with his disreputable questioning of Foch. Whilst he was correct in arguing that it was his 'right to be told the truth', there were more direct and honourable paths he could have taken. If a higher ideal, such as the more efficient prosecution of the war, had been his object, he had only endangered that efficiency by antagonising Haig in this way.[30]

The combined Anglo-French attack, agreed upon during the meeting of 27 August, was launched on 3 September in the vicinity of Delville Wood. It quickly went the way of previous ventures. The first line was breached in places but the ground gained could not be held, and enemy counter-attacks drove the British back near to their original position. During a post-mortem, Gough and Haig agreed that the failure was due to the fact that some units 'did not really attack, and some men did not follow their officers'. Haig was, for instance, angry that 'the total losses of [the 49th] Division are under a thousand!' Recalling a 'lack of smartness and slackness of one of its Battns. in the matter of saluting when I was motoring through the village where it was billeted', Haig surmised 'that such men were too sleepy to fight well'.[31] He did not speculate whether the failure of the 49th Division might have indicated the same weariness of the war which he was so quick and eager to find evidence of in the German Army.

The French contribution to the battle of 3 September did not materialise, due, Haig thought, to the fact that their infantry 'is of very poor quality now, and lacks the offensive spirit'. The allies had of late only made progress when they faced 'a much smaller concentration of Artillery than the enemy has collected against the British'.[32] Though annoyed with the French, Haig had never been fully committed to the battle of 3 September, and was not overly bothered by its failure. His attention had for long been focused on the massive assault on the front Flers–Courcelette, scheduled for two weeks later. It was certain to lead to 'decisive results'.

The long-awaited breakthrough was to be achieved with the help of tanks, which were slowly arriving from Britain. Haig's attention had been alerted to this new weapon in mid-March when he received a memorandum by Lieutenant-Colonel E. D. Swinton, who was principally responsible for developing the tank. It is clear that Haig read the report, for in his copy he underlined the following paragraph:

Since the chance of success of an attack by tanks lies almost entirely in its novelty and in the element of surprise, it is obvious that no repetition of it will have the same opportunity of succeeding as the first unexpected effort. It follows, therefore, that these machines *should not be used in driblets* (for instance as they may be produced), but that the fact of their existence should be kept as secret as possible until the whole are ready to be launched, together with the infantry assault, in one great combined operation.

The memo also emphasised that infantry and artillery tactics would have to be adjusted to accommodate the tank's unique potential. But, aside from underlining the above paragraph, Haig seems to have paid very little attention to the development of the weapon or its potential use. On 5 April, he suggested to Rawlinson that tanks might be used in the offensive on the Somme, but he did not pursue this matter with any vigour. Much more time, significantly, was spent in preparing the cavalry for its role in the offensive.[33]

Haig had asked for 150 tanks by 31 July. In the event, these were not delivered, though a significant number were promised for 1 September. By mid-August, Haig had decided to ignore Swinton's advice about using the machines in driblets, as he indicated to Robertson:

I am counting on having at least 50 tanks available for [the offensive]. If I get them, I hope and think they will add very greatly to the prospects of success and to the extent of it. Even if I do not get so many as I hope I shall use what I have got, as I cannot wait longer for them and it would be folly not to use every means at my disposal in what is likely to be our crowning effort for this year.

The same urgency influenced Haig's attitude towards the tactical handling of tanks. After attending a demonstration on 26 August, he recorded the following in his diary:

The tanks crossed ditches and parapets representing the several lines of a defensive position with the greatest ease, and one entered a wood, which was made to represent a 'strong-point' and easily 'walked over' fair sized trees of six inches diameter! Altogether the demonstration was quite encouraging, but we require to clear our ideas as to the tactical handling of these machines.

A fitting end to this paragraph would have been: 'Unfortunately we do not have the time.' The tanks were to be used within three weeks – hardly enough time to formulate a suitable tactical plan. In fact, ten days *before* this demonstration – the first time Haig had set eyes on a tank – instructions on their use were given to the commanders of the 4th and Reserve Armies.[34]

In Haig's view, the war would soon be over and the post-war period would provide time enough for the proper consideration of tank tactics. In the meantime, they might hasten victory, if only by destroying German morale. The belief that a turning point was imminent is evident from Haig's criticism of Rawlinson's plans on 29 August: 'In my opinion he is not making enough of the situation with the deterioration and all round loss of morale of the enemy's troops. I think we should make our attack as strong and as violent as possible, and plan to go as far as possible.' Once again, Rawlinson was sceptical. On 31 August, in a memo obviously directed at the Fourth Army commander, Kiggell emphasised that, 'The slow methods of trench warfare are unsuited to the style of operations [we] will be called upon to undertake after the enemy has been driven from his prepared lines of defence.' Five days before the battle the penny had yet to drop: Kiggell was again told to impress upon Rawlinson 'the need for bold action, and no unnecessary delay'.[35]

On 13 September, two days before the launch of the attack, Haig issued the following stirring words to his commanders:

> On the front of attack, besides a superiority of at least four to one in infantry, we have a more numerous artillery, practical supremacy in the air, and a large mass of cavalry immediately available to exploit to the full a successful assault by the other arms. In addition we have a new weapon of war which may well produce great moral and material effects . . . the assault must be pushed home with the greatest vigour, boldness and resolution, and success must be followed up without hesitation or delay to the utmost limits of . . . endurance of the troops.[36]

In a by now familiar pattern, the battle did not live up to Haig's grandiose expectations. The British attacked on a front of twelve kilometres, but nowhere gained more than two. More lamentable than the paltry advance was the way in which the tank's potential for surprise had been so carelessly squandered. On the fateful morning, only forty-nine tanks were available, of which only thirty-four were able to reach the front line. These were foolishly scattered in twos and threes over the entire frontage. Few of the infantry attacking alongside the tanks had ever before seen the new machines. But the biggest mistake was to employ the tanks on ground which had been heavily shelled over the previous three days. Many of them became stranded in deep shell craters, there to be methodically picked off by German gunners like fish in a barrel. What is significant is that despite these mistakes, a few of the tanks were spectacularly successful – a testimony to what might have been achieved had Haig waited until more were available and until ample consideration had been given to their tactical handling.

Despite the limited success of the tanks, Haig was sufficiently impressed with their performance to request another 1,000 from the War Office on 17 September. There is no doubt that he saw immense possibilities for the machines. It was, however, another new development which fired his imagination even more. On 28 September, he noted:

> Sergeant Scheerer who has been working at a hospital at Corbey has made some very remarkable discoveries with electrical rays such as are used in radio telegraphy. He photographs the internals so that the surgeon can see before he operates exactly what the trouble is. The photo is produced in 45 seconds. Similar photos of any object can be taken at any distance, through any intervening obstacle! . . . Besides that, and *this is most secret*, he can with his rays kill rats (or other small animals) at 20 yards distance. The discovery is so important that I am moving Scheerer to Beauval where the hospital will be organised as a 'Radio Therapeutic Institute'. The future possibilities of this discovery seem enormous . . . [it] will possibly be of greater effect ultimately than this World War!

The exploits of Sergeant Scheerer were followed enthusiastically over the subsequent months. On 1 November, Haig observed a test in which a ray gun was used to kill a rabbit at a distance of fifteen metres. 'Everyone connected with Scheerer with whom I spoke believe that he is genuine, and they have been unable to detect any fraud.' Two weeks later, however, Charteris discovered that Scheerer had been exposed as a fake, and that he had earlier posed as a parson. Acutely embarrassed, Haig demoted him to private and sent him to a particularly active part of the front.[37]

On 19 September, Rawlinson recorded that 'Kig[gell] says D.H. means to go on until we cannot possibly continue further either from the weather or want of troops. I'm not sure that he is right.' If indeed they were voiced, Rawlinson's reservations made no impression on Haig; the attacks continued through September, October and into November. The best explanation for Haig's stubborn persistence is also the simplest: he had always believed that victory went to the commander who refused to relent. As the days grew shorter and colder, Haig grew ever more insistent that he was achieving success, even if his success could not be measured in ground gained. On 7 October, he sent another piece of propaganda to the CIGS, in which he maintained, 'The troops are fully confident of their power to win and there is strong evidence that a very large number, if not yet all, of the German forces in our front feel that the task of stopping our advance is beyond their ability.' There was consequently only one course: 'Our offensive must be continued without intermission as long as possible.' Optimistic forecasts were again expressed in the vaguest of terms. 'There are fair grounds for hope that very far-reaching success – affording full compensation for all that has been done to attain it – may be gained in the near future.'[38]

The argument for continuing the offensive was based, as always, on the certainty that the German Army was near collapse. Apparently unaware that this argument was losing credibility through over-repetition, Haig insisted, in the 7 October report:

It is not possible to say how near to the breaking point the enemy may be, but he has undoubtedly gone a long way towards it. Many of his troops have reached, and even passed, it at times during the last few weeks, and though the great difficulties of our advance, and the severity of the German discipline, have enabled the enemy's leaders to reorganise resistance afresh after every defeat, this cannot go on indefinitely if constant pressure is maintained.

Though the tone was more circumspect than in earlier memos, too much should not be made of this. Haig did, after all, feel confident enough to tell Poincaré, on 2 October, that 'the enemy showed signs of demoralisation . . . and if this spreads it might be possible for us to be in Cambrai by the end of October!'[39]

269

In a very basic sense, Haig was right: if constant pressure was maintained the enemy *would* eventually break. But what he seldom seems to have considered was whether his own army was capable of unrelenting attacks. In the equation leading to victory, the condition of the enemy was the variable, that of the British Army the constant. He therefore ignored the latter and paid unhealthy attention to the former. As usual, it was Charteris who provided the fodder for Haig's bloated optimism. On 20 October, came another prediction of the imminent collapse of the German economy. Four weeks later, an intelligence report set German casualties on the Somme at 680,000 – a figure significantly higher than even the most generous post-war estimates.[40]

Whilst it is true that incessant British attacks did seriously damage the morale of the German Army, this damage was never as extensive as Haig imagined, because it never produced the breakdown which he predicted. Since his tactical plans were based on an assumption that collapse was imminent, it is natural to question the wisdom of those plans. Haig, of course, did not do so. As far as he was concerned, the German collapse had not materialised because the French had reneged on their commitment. Again, Haig was basically right: a more concerted French effort might have led to the defeat of the Germans in 1916. But their massive losses in the first two years of the war, especially at Verdun, precluded anything but a half-hearted approach on the Somme. The important point is that Haig had every indication (and indeed every suspicion) that they would not be capable of the role he intended for them. In other words, failure had resulted because the goals he had set were foolishly unrealistic.

The French became scapegoats for Haig's frustrated ambitions. The sacrifices the Allies had so far made in the war were conveniently ignored. French failures were easily explained by deficiencies in their character: 'the French are too busy talking and criticising one another. They are very conceited, and because the British have been getting along well and quietly, they compare what they have gained with our results and are dissatisfied . . . [They] are very like children.' He continued in this vein on 1 October in a letter to Doris: 'It is not to my interest to belittle the French. We must work together. I could, however, if I judged it necessary, compile a very full record of facts showing that there are very few points in which our Army is not *a good deal* in front of the French!' It was indeed not in Haig's interest to belittle the French. Nevertheless, he repeatedly did so. On 13 October, he sent Rothschild a chart purporting to show that German divisions became exhausted much more quickly under British attack than under French. What benefit could possibly have been derived from this information? This was certainly not the stuff out of which an effective alliance could be forged. The cooperative spirit was, admittedly, absent on both sides. The French made unreasonable demands. But Haig's suspicions of them became at times paranoiac. He made no effort to understand the unique pressures they faced in fighting a static and demoralising war on their own soil.[41]

It was particularly galling when a Frenchman questioned (however mildly) Haig's tactics. On 6 October, Clemenceau praised British accomplishments but then had the cheek to add: 'but your losses are said to have been very heavy'. Haig 'at once took him up and asked him who had said so, and what the losses were supposed to amount to etc.'. Besides, French reports of dead and wounded varied 'to suit the impression the Government wished to produce on the people'. Haig was obviously becoming extremely sensitive to criticism of the ever-lengthening casualty lists. He had no difficulty withstanding the losses but those of weaker spirit apparently did not. How then to stiffen their resolve? One favourite method of Haig's was to stress, again and again, that attacks were hardly more costly than normal trench warfare. Likewise, great weight was given to evidence of a proportional reduction in casualties compared with earlier in the offensive – proof positive that 'the Germans are not fighting anything like so well as they did when the battle began on 1st July'.[42]

With the clouds of doubt growing thicker and more oppressive, encouragement from St Loe Strachey had the effect of cool morning breeze. In a letter to Haig, on 27 October, the editor of the *Spectator* attacked politicians and newspapermen who practised 'casualistry' – defined as a 'most dangerous . . . attempt to work on people's feelings in regard to casualties and to ask whether they are really worthwhile'. According to Strachey:

That, of course, is *ruin*, and therefore I thought the best thing was to stamp upon it at once, especially as in reality people are wonderfully good and if they are not maliciously incited to take the wrong attitude, they will take the right one. I have seen this in many parents and wives who have to mourn personal losses.

271

Other journalists also began at this time to align themselves with Haig in the campaign against casualistry. In mid-September, Lord Northcliffe again visited the front, bringing with him Wickham Steed, Foreign Editor of *The Times*. Both men were 'most anxious to help the Army in every possible way'. Likewise, J. A. Spender of the *Westminster Gazette*, a visitor on 9 October, seemed an 'honest patriot' – in other words, he supported Haig's policies. Though doubts about journalists died hard, Haig was nevertheless appreciative of their support. H. A. Gwynne, the editor of the *Morning Post*, was, for instance, 'like most newspaper men . . . very self-satisfied and talks as if he rules the universe'. But, to his credit, he was 'anxious to do the right thing' and had 'a commendable dislike of politicians'.[43]

Like Strachey, Haig believed that if the British people were to continue to make the sacrifices necessary for victory, politicians with the courage to lead were required. Unfortunately, the existing lot, in his view, too often put politics and personal ambition before the safety of the Empire. As the Somme battle wore on, reports of the mischief of men like Churchill and Lloyd George became more frequent. On 25 August, Haig was alerted to the danger of the former, who was 'openly very hostile'. Two months later, he recorded a warning from Leo Maxse that F. E. Smith and others 'have banded themselves together with the object of having me removed from the Command of the Armies in France'.[44]

Most of these warnings were treated with the contempt they deserved. The threat posed by Lloyd George was real – though Haig was at first slow to perceive its implications for himself. As he indicated in response to his wife's desire to 'wring the necks' of 'those intriguers at the War Office':

> The fact is that both L.G. and Robertson *both* wish to be in the lime light and to direct the War Office and War policy. Hence the trouble at home. The intrigue is not against me, but by Lloyd George against Robertson. The latter is cunning but clumsy and no match for the politician's subtlety.

Haig was referring to the continuing argument over the Rumanian question and its implications for British strategy. Though he agreed with Robertson that the best way to help Rumania was to attack unrelentingly on the Western Front, he did not otherwise want to become involved in what was, in his view, an internal and somewhat personal squabble. As far as he was concerned, Lloyd George and Robertson deserved each other. The latter, like Kitchener before him, was 'most necessary to the Country', but by no means a friend. As to his own position, Haig was certain that it was 'quite secure as long as the Army here continues to be successful. The danger is, if there was to be a check, which with God's help, I hope we may avoid.'[45]

Haig's opinion of both Robertson and Lloyd George declined even further as a result of a visit by Field Marshal French to the Western Front. Lloyd George had come up with the idea of sending Sir John to Joffre's headquarters to uncover the secrets of French artillery expertise. Haig reacted angrily: 'French's visit to Joffre at this time can do no good to anyone, but only tend to make discord.' Whilst he claimed that he had 'no intention of allowing the tactlessness of the War Office Authorities to interfere with my peace of mind', it is clear that the visit had precisely that effect:

How unnecessarily difficult these Authorities of ours at home seem to make things for me, struggling to do one's best against the enemy! If Lloyd George wishes to know about French guns and their tactics, he should ask me. But he has already got my reasoned opinion on the matter of guns, and doubtless wants another opinion different from mine.

Haig was angry not only because Lloyd George was again skulking behind his back, but also because he had chosen the vile Sir John as his weasel. Haig instructed Fletcher to tell French that if he 'desired to see the work of the British Army, arrangements would be made for him to do so'. But, 'I would not receive Viscount French in my house. I despise him too much personally for that.' Haig's feelings received another bruising when he discovered that Robertson had known about the visit well before it occurred. 'R. never said a word to me . . . on the subject. And yet he tells me that he is "wholeheartedly anxious to help" me in my difficult task.'[46]

On 20 October, Lloyd George saw Haig briefly before a conference with French politicians at Boulogne. Haig derived a great deal of sinister delight out of the Welshman's fumbling attempt to explain the notorious conversation with Foch. Lloyd George went on to complain that 'some people' were trying to 'drive a wedge in between him and the soldiers' and that 'the General Staff at the War Office don't let him know *everything*, but only feed him what *they think* is suitable for him to know'. Haig, rather surprisingly, sympathised and promised to raise the matter with Robertson. He was obviously still susceptible to the Welshman's silver tongue. 'I get on very well with Lloyd George,' he subsequently told his wife.[47]

Haig's confidence was unwarranted. Lloyd George was at that very moment conducting a determined campaign to shift strategy to the East. Not long after his return to London, he launched a blistering attack upon the Somme offensive at a War Committee meeting, arguing that, while it had relieved the pressure on Verdun, it had not (as promised) enabled the Russian offensive to succeed, protected Rumania, or – most significantly – broken through the German lines. The War Committee, according to Hankey,

> generally agreed that the offensive on the Somme, if continued next year, was not likely to lead to decisive results and that the losses might make too heavy a drain on our resources having regard to the results to be anticipated. It was therefore generally agreed that we should examine whether a decision might not be reached in another theatre.[48]

All this was in preparation for Lloyd George's attempt to secure general agreement for an offensive in the Balkans during the conference in Paris scheduled for 15 November. It was also an attempt to wrest control of strategy from those in the Haig camp.

When wind of Lloyd George's intentions reached GHQ, a mild panic ensued. The folly of sending more troops to the Balkans had somehow to be brought home to the ministers at the Paris conference. What better way than to demonstrate (once again) the effectiveness of the Somme offensive? Thus, on 13 November, the last great attack on the Somme was launched. According to Kiggell, rumours had circulated 'that Lloyd George meant to make trouble for D.H.', therefore 'the value of a good and "cheap" success . . . just before the Conference, came to me'. Haig did not need much persuading. Other factors obviously influenced his decision in favour of one last effort, and there is no doubt that Haig, being Haig, would have attacked even if the political considerations had not applied. It is nevertheless significant that after the war Kiggell confessed that, in a purely military sense, 'the latter stages of the fight were hardly justified'.[49]

On 13 November, a prodigious concentration of firepower was directed on the spurs around Beaumont-Hamel. As a result, when the British went forward, 'the enemy surrendered much more readily than on any previous occasion'.[50] The important positions of Beaucourt and Beaumont-Hamel (among the original objectives for 1 July) were finally captured. But the German line, though extended, did not break. Five days later the Somme offensive ended.

Was it worthwhile? Did it achieve anything? The questions continue to this day. The argument has been needlessly complicated by futile disagreements over the body count – how many died and which side lost the most. Exact figures will not provide the solid foundation upon which a vindication or condemnation of Haig can be based. It seems safe to say that British casualties exceeded 600,000, with German losses perhaps slightly higher. The figures have varied but the variations are insignificant to the analysis. The inescapable fact is that the Somme offensive was nothing more than a campaign of attrition. In this sense, the British won, because the Germans were less able to afford the losses. It is perhaps also to their credit that by forming a large salient, the British forced the Germans to defend a longer line. Thus the demands upon the German Army were increased at the same time that its power of resistance was diminishing. 'The strain on the physical and moral strength', Ludendorff admitted in 1919, 'was tremendous.'[51]

If the British won, does it follow that Haig was successful? He had shown that he had the courage to incur massive losses without being detracted from his overall purpose. He had proved to the French, to the Germans and to the rest of the world that the British were capable of sustaining a long and costly offensive. He had also learned a great deal about tactics. The use of the artillery, for instance, was far more effective on 15 November than it had been on 1 July. But his 'victory' was in a sense fortuitous; the offensive did not follow his original plan. He did not intend to fight a campaign of attrition. When the breakthrough which he anticipated did not materialise, he began to talk about a 'wearing out process' but this always had, in his mind, a fixed duration – the 'decisive result' was always just around the corner. In fact, it was light years away. When it began to dawn on him that he would not achieve his objectives, Haig blamed the French for failing to pull their weight rather than himself for being unrealistic. Important questions, therefore, arise: Is excessive optimism inherently dangerous? Is a sense of realism an important attribute in a commander? The answer, in both cases, is yes. Haig may have proved that he was capable of fighting a *bataille d'usure*, but it seems clear that he could have fought it better had he accepted that that was what it was – in other words, that cavalry charges would not come tomorrow.

None of these issues seemed ever to have bothered Haig. He did not doubt that he had been successful. In his final report on the battle, submitted to the CIGS, he wrote:

> The . . . picture is full of encouragement and promise. The enemy's losses have undoubtedly been very heavy – far heavier than those of the Allies – and there is convincing evidence of a sensible depreciation in his moral. From this evidence it is safe to conclude that an appreciable proportion of the German soldiers are now practically beaten men ready to surrender if they could find the opportunity, thoroughly tired of the war, and hopeless of eventual success . . . even German discipline, obedience to authority and love of country will not suffice to enable the German commanders to enforce their will if the majority of their men lose courage and confidence, as we know beyond doubt that many of them have done.[52]

The message was clear. If the Germans had not been beaten this year, they soon would be, simply by applying the same tactics which had been successful on the Somme. But two points niggle the reader of the above passage. First, the dilapidated Army which Haig described does not suggest a force which would be able to fight on for another two years. Secondly, his description of the German Army echoes his reports of early 1916, in which the 'practically beaten' state of the enemy was used as justification for the proposed Somme offensive.

On 31 March 1917, after a visit to the Somme battlefield, Haig recorded his personal reflections upon the offensive:

> No one can visit the Somme battlefield without being impressed with the magnitude of the effort made by the British Army . . . credit must be paid, not only to the private soldier in the ranks, but also to those

splendid young officers who commanded platoons, companies and battalions. Although new to this terrible 'game of war' they were able, time and again, to form up their commands in the darkness of night, and in spite of shell holes, wire and other obstacles, lead them forward in the grey of the morning to the attack of these tremendous positions. To many it meant certain death, and all must have known that before they started. Surely it was the knowledge of the great stake at issue, the existence of England as a free nation, that nerved them for such heroic deeds. I have not the time to put down all the thoughts which rush into my mind when I think of all those fine fellows, who either have given their lives for their country, or have been maimed in its service. Later on I hope we may have a Prime Minister and a Government who will do them justice.

The offensive, Haig thought, would be a watershed in the history of the British Empire. As Duncan promised on 24 September, the goodness of God and the experience of sacrifice would lead to a glorious rebirth: 'this Great War was accomplishing the preparation of the world for better living. It was ruthlessly sweeping away all shams, and in a larger sphere, was performing what was done by John the Baptist centuries ago for the Jews and the coming of the Lord.' More specifically, Haig was 'greatly struck' by the predictions of an American newspaper proprietor who visited him on 5 October:

England would be the greatest gainer, the whole Empire would be welded together into one great whole, and imbued with a higher spirit. On the other hand the United States, though more money had been amassed, would decline because of the spirit of luxury and extravagance which was being developed.

In other words, the losses, tragic though they were, would indeed prove worthwhile.[53]

Haig was not too humble to consider the effect that victory would have upon his own life. 'I think you may take it', he told his wife during the Somme offensive, 'that a grateful nation will not allow me to have a smaller income than what I am receiving now! So we will be quite well enough off to make ourselves comfortable.' When F. S. Oliver suggested that the country should buy him Bemersyde as reward for services, Haig commented:

It was nice of him to think of the country presenting me with Bemersyde, that old place on the Tweed that has never belonged to anyone but Haig. We must finish the war first before we think of such things. Besides, it is sufficient reward for me to have taken part in this great struggle, and to have occupied no inconsiderable position amongst those who have helped our country weather this storm.

All would be wonderful when the storm had passed. But, in the meantime, a task remained to be done. Haig entered a new year of war as determined and as confident as he had been in December 1915. The hardships of the past and those to come were endurable because of the inner peace which he derived from the glory and grace of God. 'The war has educated many of us', he reflected, 'so that we have found that peace of mind.'[54]

12

Two Wars

War is too important a business to be left to generals – or so it is said. Politicians are adept at politics; soldiers seldom are. Therefore, war, an extension of politics by other means, is too complex for the ordinary general fully to comprehend. Decisions can seldom be made purely on the basis of military expediency. 'First win the war, then worry about the peace' is advice formed in a dreamworld. That being so, some sort of political control over the military machine is expedient and inevitable. But the organs for control, formed in peacetime, are seldom equal to the test of war. New institutions are quickly improvised and they, too, crash in flames. Soldiers and statesmen, by nature suspicious of each other, do not readily form effective partnerships. The success rate is extremely low because the people involved are prone, even in wartime, to human frailties. The path to the 'right' decision is often blocked by jealousy, spite, prejudice and vindictiveness.

Nineteen-sixteen was Haig's year. The minor interference and petty irritations aside, he had been left virtually to do things his way. But because things did not work out as he planned and promised, doubts increasingly arose. Left to himself, Haig would have simply carried on as he had done into 1917. It was thus obvious to men like Lloyd George that he could not be left to himself. Consequently, for the next two years, Haig fought two wars: one against the Germans, the other against the politicians. It is not immediately clear which was the more difficult enemy.

On 16 November 1916, French and British leaders gathered in Paris to discuss future plans. Haig and Joffre had the day before met in Chantilly and agreed upon a continuation of the Western Front strategy and a resumption of the offensive on the Somme as soon as possible in the New Year. Though Lloyd George again pressed for sending more troops to Salonika, the political leaders could do little but ratify what had already been decided at Chantilly. Haig could hardly conceal his delight at the War Minister's defeat. Lloyd George, his tail between his legs, went home to plot new schemes to control Haig.

More specific plans for the offensive were left for Joffre and Haig to arrange at a later date. The first such meeting took place on 29 November at the French GQG. Differing perspectives regarding the prospects for the coming year were quickly revealed:

> General Foch stated that he did not think it possible to . . . force the passage of the Somme. General Castlenau retorted that we would not only cross the Somme but the Rhine as well! In his opinion, with the English attacking North of the River and the French on the South, the enemy would be so beaten in the battle that he would have no fit troops to fall back and hold the line of the river! General Joffre also emphasised the demoralised state of the enemy, and the effect of attacking him vigorously on a very wide front.

Haig naturally agreed with Joffre and Castlenau. As far as he was concerned, the 'wearing out' phase of the war was nearly over. This belief caused him to be extremely scathing of the practice of drafting trained cavalrymen into the infantry, describing it as 'a serious mistake, because . . . a rapid termination of the war may depend on keeping our Cavalry Divisions up to strength'. Referring to the question again on 16 December, he remarked that 'the enemy is no longer the same as he was six months ago. He is much more ready to surrender.' It was, therefore, 'a short-sighted policy to abolish Reserve Cavalry Regiments now'.[1]

There was no doubt in Haig's mind that a turning point had been reached. He was, however, concerned that the politicians, unaware of this fact, would let the Germans off the hook, either by not providing his army with sufficient men and munitions or by pursuing hare-brained schemes in the Balkans. Determined that the policies agreed upon at Chantilly and Paris (specifically those pertaining to the Western Front as the decisive theatre) be pursued wholeheartedly, he travelled to London on 22 November. Upon his arrival, he was shocked to find that ministers were distracted by other affairs. As Lloyd George revealed three days later: 'the political situation [was] serious. Lord Lansdowne had written a terrible paper urging that we should make peace now, if the Naval, Military, Financial and other heads of Departments could "not be certain of victory by next autumn".' Haig was not overly concerned, mainly because the demoralised state of the German Army made it virtually certain that the war would be over by autumn anyway. Thus, when Derby told him on 26 November that 'a large section of the government is determined that things cannot go on as they are, but more energetic action must be taken' (a reference to the rather lackadaisical habits of Asquith), Haig interpreted this favourably, since it was energetic action which he had been urging all along. As he told his wife on 4 December, 'The Government crisis at home seems likely to do good, in that the arrangements for winning the war will be controlled with more determination and thoroughness.'[2]

As the result of machinations too complex to describe here, Asquith resigned two days later. As Bonar Law was unable (not to mention unwilling) to form a government, Lloyd George, on 7 December, established a new coalition. The new Prime Minister was put into power on the sufferance of his old opponents in the Unionist party: Bonar Law, Curzon, Chamberlain *et al*. Lloyd George had gained their support by promising, among other things, that Haig would remain in his position – undoubtedly a difficult promise for the Welshman to make. Another part of the deal called for Lord Derby to become Secretary of State for War. In any argument between soldiers and statesmen, Derby was almost certain to take the side of the former.

Haig's immediate reactions to the change of government were mixed. 'I am personally very sorry for poor old Squiff,' he told his wife. 'He has had a hard time and ... seems to have had more capacity and brain power than any of the others.' He nevertheless admitted that 'more action and less talk is needed now' – something which Lloyd George seemed to promise. The new Prime Minister, perhaps in contrast to the old, was 'really in earnest to win the war'.[3]

Haig was wary of the Welshman's potential for mischief. The imprint of Lloyd George's kiss had hardly left the King's hand when a doom-laden letter arrived from Haig, via Wigram. 'I am afraid honestly that [Lloyd George] may squander our resources on side shows i.e. Salonika,' Haig confessed. 'On no account should he be allowed to send more units there. I could write to you on this as strongly as I used to over the Dardanelles adventure. *You* must prevent another

281

such failure.' On 15 December, Robertson fuelled Haig's fears when he gave it as his impression that Lloyd George, though 'in real earnest to leave nothing undone to win the war', wanted 'to pose as the prime instrument and mainspring of the Allies. With this object, he was now anxious to help Italy with guns, and also Russia, so as to get hold over these countries.'[4]

Robertson's fears were confirmed by none other than Lloyd George himself when he met Haig later that afternoon. The Prime Minister spoke of his desire for an early success, and announced that he hoped to get it through an attack in Egypt towards Jerusalem. He hoped Haig would release two divisions for this purpose. In addition, he wanted 200 heavy guns to be sent to Italy, on the promise that they would be returned in the spring. To Haig's considerable alarm, he confessed that though he agreed the Western Front was the principal theatre, he 'could not believe that it was possible to beat the German Armies there – at any rate, not next year'.[5]

Haig responded by bombarding Lloyd George wth reasons why it was impossible to send troops to Egypt. His men were in no fit state to fight after the long offensive on the Somme. They were already overextended, having recently taken over a portion of the line from the French. Finally, they needed time to train for next year's attacks. Haig thought that, as a result of his argument, the Prime Minister 'seemed less determined to withdraw troops from France to go elsewhere'. In fact neither man had made much of an impression on the other.[6]

The upheaval within the British government coincided with similar tumultuous events in the French Army. Joffre was replaced by General Robert Nivelle, who had had a brilliant but brief success at Verdun. The choice of Nivelle was a mystery to Haig, until he learned on 13 December that

Foch was objected to . . . because he has a Jesuit brother and is a churchgoer. Also his handling of . . . the Somme battle was much criticised. Petain, because he was brought up by the Dominicans and is also a churchgoer. Castlenau is still more objected to because he goes to mass and is very Catholic.

Haig, despite all the anxiety Joffre had caused, at first objected to the promotion of Nivelle, of whom he had little knowledge. The change, he decided, was part of a devious effort by Briand to keep himself in power. But Haig's reservations soon evaporated when he met Nivelle, who was immediately judged 'a most straightforward and soldierly man'. 'Altogether I was pleased with my first meeting . . . He is . . . alert in mind, and has had much practical experience in this war.'[7]

Nivelle's stated intentions go a long way towards explaining Haig's positive impression:

> he is unable to accept the plans which have been worked out for the French Armies under Joffre's directions. He is confident of breaking through the enemy's Front now that the enemy's morale is weakened, but the blow must be struck by surprise and go through in 24 hours. This necessity for surprise after all is our own conclusion.

When Haig later heard that Joffre had been shelved completely, he remarked, 'I am sorry for poor old Joffre but from what I have seen of Nivelle up to date, I think he is the more energetic man.' It was obvious that he was 'better qualified than dear old Joffre to bring this war to a successful end'. These positive feelings inspired Haig to instruct Rawlinson to work out plans for relieving the French Army as far as the Somme. This relief, initially scheduled for February, was 'desirable . . . earlier in order to help the French to carry out their plans as far as we possibly can'.[8]

As far as Haig was concerned, the turbulent events of December had greatly improved the prospect of an early victory. Thus the year ended with him basking in golden rays of good hope. All about him seemed perfect. On a visit to the Second Army, on 22 December, he found the troops 'in the best of spirits'. Impressed by their 'quiet, determined gaze', he reflected upon how privileged he was to command 'such splendid fellows'. 'People at home have no idea what a splendid army we have, and of what *men* the nation is really composed.' The sense of contentment was increased when the King wrote:

> It gives me great pleasure and satisfaction to tell you that I have decided to appoint you a Field Marshal in my Army. By your conspicuous services you have fully merited this great position. I know this will be welcomed by the whole Army in France, whose confidence you have won. I hope you will look upon it as a New Year's gift from myself and the country.[9]

Good feelings were prolonged as a result of a harmonious meeting with Nivelle at Chantilly on the last day of the year. Haig conveyed his agreement with French plans, but sought similar accord with regard to his renewed ambitions in Flanders. Whilst assuring Nivelle that he was confident of a French success, Haig nevertheless pointed out:

> In the event of being held up, a rapid decision was required and every effort must be made to pierce the enemy's front in the North. In this case could I rely on the French Army to take over sufficient of the British front to set free the necessary number of British Divisions to ensure success?

Nivelle immediately replied that there need be no worry about the French giving their support to the Flanders operation. Haig, pleased with this answer, repeated that he 'was quite favourably impressed' with the new French commander.[10]

The sense of well-being did not last long. On 4 January, Haig received Nivelle's formal proposals for the French offensive, which omitted any reference to his intended response in the event of failure. Since Haig considered this point vital (bearing as it did upon his own plans in Flanders), he wrote a long and angry letter to the French commander on 6 January. 'It is essential that there should be no misunderstanding between us on this question,' Haig stressed. He went on to outline four possible phases to the combined offensive. The first was to be a short 'wearing out' fight, composed of 'strong attacks . . . by our respective armies with the object, not only of drawing in and using up the enemy's reserves, but of gaining such tactical success as will open the way for decisive action on the fronts of attack'. With regard to this phase of the battle, Haig emphasised:

> I have already agreed to launch such an attack . . . but not to an indefinite continuation of the battle to use up the enemy's reserves. Such continuation might result in a prolonged struggle, like that on the Somme this year, and would be contrary to our agreement that we must seek a definite and rapid decision.

Both commanders agreed that in the second phase Haig would continue attacking, while Nivelle shifted to another front for what was intended to be a decisive action. Haig nevertheless stressed that his consent was contingent upon Nivelle beginning this assault within two weeks of the commencement of the first phase. He also demanded that Nivelle agree to call off this attack if he was not immediately successful. 'You will remember', Haig wrote, 'that you estimated a period of 24 to 48 hours as sufficient to enable you to decide whether your decisive attack had succeeded or should be abandoned'.[11]

Assuming that the first two phases were successful, the third phase would follow. This would 'consist in the exploitation by the French and British Armies of the successes previously gained', or, in simpler terms, the Allies would drive the Germans out of France and Belgium. Haig made one careful qualification: 'This is, of course, on the assumption that the previous successes have been of such magnitude as will make it reasonably certain that by following them up at once we gain a complete victory and, at least, force the enemy to abandon the Belgian coast.' The last point was Haig's main reason for writing the letter. If events went according to plan, the Germans would be so severely beaten that they would be forced to abandon the Belgian coast in order to protect their troops further south. Thus the dream which Haig had retained since the beginning of the war would be achieved indirectly.[12]

But, if the French attack did not force a voluntary abandonment of the coast, a fourth phase was, Haig insisted, in order. A British offensive in Flanders would immediately commence, with the aim of capturing the Channel ports. The French role would come in relieving British troops in order to free them for the attack. Haig reassured Nivelle by mentioning that the need for carrying out this phase 'may not, and I hope will not, arise'. But he stressed that 'The clearance of the Belgian coast is of such importance to the British Government that it must be fully provided for before I can finally agree to your proposals.' This was an exaggeration. In October 1916, the War Committee gave encouragement to the idea, but since then there had been a change of government. The politicians had never been as enthusiastic about Haig's plan as he was.[13]

The agreement which Haig wanted from Nivelle reached GHQ on 13 January. Thus, after a minor hiccup, it appeared that an amicable settlement had been reached. But at this time a new threat to the offensive arose. On 1 January, Northcliffe told Haig that Briand was pressing the British government to send two divisions to Salonika. After hearing of Haig's vehement opposition to the transfer of any troops eastward, Northcliffe decided to consult Clemenceau, promising Haig that he would 'not hesitate to urge the downfall of Briand's government in order to check this fatal policy'. While in Paris, Northcliffe discussed Briand's request with Lloyd George and warned him 'that it would be impossible to continue to support his Government, if they continued to scatter their forces in the Balkans, when all sound military opinion urged concentration on the Western Front'. Up to this point, it appears that Northcliffe's actions were taken on his own volition, not on Haig's direction. There is nevertheless no doubt that the 'sound military opinion' was Haig's and that Northcliffe's interventions had Haig's blessing. The rule about steering clear of intrigue appears to have been permanently cast aside.[14]

Over the next few days, the Press baron and the Field Marshal continued to discuss the dangers of Lloyd George. Haig believed that since the Prime Minister 'is quite under the thumb of M. Albert Thomas [the French Minister of Munitions] . . . the Salonika blunder will continue'. After again emphasising the need to prevent the transfer of any men or material from the Western Front, Haig was delighted to find that Northcliffe was 'fully alive to his responsibility for putting Lloyd George into power' and was 'determined to keep him in the right lines or force him to resign the Premiership'. Northcliffe also told Haig how he had little admiration for Robertson: 'You call him Wully. I think "Wooly" would suit him better because he is not firm enough.' Haig, displaying a remarkable insensitivity to the pressures under which Robertson had to operate, responded, 'There seems to be some truth in this opinion because the British forces are not yet being concentrated at the decisive front, i.e., in France.'[15]

Haig was due to meet Lloyd George and Nivelle on the 15th to discuss future operations. Prior to this meeting, Kiggell, who had seen the Prime Minister on the 10th, conveyed some disturbing news:

Lloyd George began talking about the merits of the relative fronts – taking the line that we only thought of our own side; that we had not really effected much there and did not believe we could; that we must strike against a soft front and could not find it on the Western Front; that much of the Somme loss was useless and the country would not stand more of that sort of thing and so on. In fact he poured out a lot of heretical, amateur strategy of the most dangerous and misleading kind and was far from complimentary to what had been done by our armies here . . . I told him that he had better make peace at once if England was going to take the line that heavy losses could not be allowed, and that everything he sent to other theatres before we had all we wanted would reduce our chance of winning the war.

During a private meeting with Haig on the 15th, Lloyd George repeated almost word for word what he had said to Kiggell. Much to Haig's disgust, he compared the achievements of the British and the French during 1916 and concluded that the latter 'were better all around and [were] able to gain success at less cost of life'. Haig responded with some of his best stories about the lack of discipline of French troops and the idiocy of their commanders, but the Prime Minister was not impressed.[16]

Nivelle arrived later and proceeded to give a lucid and impressive explanation of how he would break through the German lines within twenty-four hours of attacking. Discussion then centred on his request for British relief as far as the Amiens–Roye road, which would free French troops for the proposed attack. Though previously amenable to this request, Haig was now reluctant because, as he argued, his troops were already overstretched and any transfer would weaken his own attack planned for later in the year. When the War Cabinet met again on the following day, Lloyd George summarily announced that Haig should comply with Nivelle's wishes. Explaining his decision, the Prime Minister maintained that, since the French were the larger force, their wishes were paramount. Furthermore, it was only right that the British should do their utmost to help the Allies achieve success and, since they had already refused to send troops to Salonika, they could hardly refuse again. Lloyd George also directed Haig to agree to Nivelle's wishes regarding the date of the attack. Thus, when Nivelle arrived later in the morning, the date was set for no later than 1 April.[17]

Haig was baffled at the way his reservations had been swept aside. His confusion was shared by Robertson who commented:

Until Nivelle arrived in London, the P.M. in particular and the Cabinet in general were frightfully anxious that you should not go off until you were fully ready and all the Allies ready too . . . Nivelle's appearance has caused an entire change and on several occasions since you attended the conference the P.M. and Lord Curzon have emphasised the importance of your going off as soon as possible . . . I cannot follow what the Prime Minister has now got on his mind but he seems to have an idea that you and Nivelle are going to do something very effective in the course of three weeks, although he has always hitherto told me that he doubted if we would ever be able to do anything useful on the Western Front.

The articulate and charismatic Nivelle had charmed Lloyd George in a way that Haig, who had none of these qualities, had never been able to do. Lloyd George explained the drastic about face in very simple terms to his mistress Frances Stevenson: 'Nivelle', he told her, 'has proved himself to be a Man at Verdun; and when you get a Man against one who has not proved himself, why, you back the Man!' An equally valid explanation (but one more in keeping with the Welshman's devious ways) is that, as Hankey admitted, 'Nivelle promised a smashing blow or nothing.' It would be clear within forty-eight hours whether he had failed, whereupon Lloyd George could, if appropriate, shift his attentions eastward.[18]

Robertson was alarmed at the way the Prime Minister had been led astray by the effervescent Frenchman. He feared that the plan for clearing the Belgian coast had been put at risk and proposed sending a stern memo to the War Cabinet outlining the dangers of the Prime Minister's reckless decision. Haig did not at this stage share Robertson's alarm, and was therefore willing to comply with Lloyd George's directives. As he explained:

we must do our utmost to help the French to make their effort a success. If they succeed, we also benefit. If they fail we will be helped in our turn, and we then have a right to expect their full support to enable us to launch our decisive attack, in the same way as we are now helping them.

The important point in Haig's mind was that the French seemed eager to attack – a welcome change from the previous year. He also found it reassuring that the offensive would be launched early in the year, thus leaving plenty of time for the British to proceed with their plans, if need be. Nevertheless, as he confessed to General Maurice on 7 February, complying with French requests would deprive the British Army of its chance of attacking in force and reaping a decisive success. We willingly played a second role to French, that is, we are to make a holding attack to draw in the enemy's reserves so as to make the task of the French easier. We shall at any rate have heavy losses with the possibility of no showy successes, whereas the French are to make the decisive attack with every prospect of gaining the fruits of victory. I think it is for the general good that we play this role in support of the French, but let the future critics realise that we have adopted it with our eyes open to the probable consequences.

At Chantilly, Joffre had made it clear that the British would play the major role in the 1917 offensive. The prospect of supremacy delighted Haig. Its sudden sacrifice stuck in his gullet. He was therefore eager that future historians should be aware that he had unselfishly stood aside so that the French could pass first up the pathway to glory.[19]

The London meeting caused Haig to alter his opinion of the new Prime Minister. It was not so much that Lloyd George had supported Nivelle (Haig, after all, did not oppose the Frenchman's plans) but that he had so ruthlessly intervened in strategy – in a way that Asquith had never done. Prior to the meeting in London Haig had assumed a very pragmatic attitude, as indicated by a conversation with Esher:

he thinks Lloyd George is a 'dangerous experiment'. 'Would you trust him', he said, 'to bring up your daughter or to do any business for you?' I pointed out that I would not have chosen either Asquith or many of his predecessors, Disraeli for instance, to bring up the children. None the less they made satisfactory Prime Ministers.

After the meeting, Haig tended to sympathise with Maurice, who

From being an admirer of Mr. Lloyd George . . . has got to distrust him, since he has got to know him better. He says that L.G. is so sketchy and goes into nothing thoroughly. He only presses forward the measures which he thinks will meet with popular favour. Further, M. does not think he really cares for the country or is patriotic – in fact, he does not trust him.

289

In Haig's opinion, it was 'a calamity for the country to have such a man at the head of affairs in this time of great crisis'. It was essential, though, to 'try and make the best of him'.[20]

Events during February did nothing to restore Haig's confidence in Lloyd George. On the 7th, Robertson warned: 'We are still in trouble with regard to the supply of men, and what the result will be I do not yet know.' Some time before, Haig had alerted the government to the fact that he would require 1,500,000 men for the 1917 campaigns. He assumed that the change of government, and the more 'energetic' prosecution of the war which was promised, would result in a much more steady flow of men into his armies. Robertson corrected this misconception when he warned Haig that Lloyd George, as a remedy to the manpower shortage, planned to reduce divisions from twelve to nine battalions. The idea was based on the assumption that war had become more mechanical, and that if a division's manpower was reduced whilst its armament was increased, its actual strength would stay the same. Though the idea had some merit, Haig and Robertson saw it as the lunatic ravings of a mad politician.[21]

By the 13th, prospects seemed even bleaker; Robertson told Haig that 'we may not be able to supply you with drafts after April next'. This was a foretaste of the ludicrous manner in which the manpower situation would be handled over the next two years. It was probably inevitable that Haig had to make do with fewer men than he requested. But the manner in which he was continually kept in the dark about actual numbers was unnecessary and counter- productive. Information changed from one day to the next and too often Haig had to rely on rumours and hearsay. On this particular occasion, he was informed only because the General Staff had, according to Robertson, 'at last insisted that we shall tell you what your prospects are'. Determined that the War Cabinet's mismanagement should be exposed, Wully advised Haig to tell Nivelle about the problem, the idea being that he would 'no doubt tell his own government, and then the fat will be in the fire'.[22]

On 11 February, Derby warned Haig that other problems loomed on the horizon: 'The submarine danger is very acute, and as someone put it very tersely – it is a question of whether the Army can win the war before the Navy loses it! Rather cruel on the Navy because they are really at their wits end as to how to deal with these submarines.' Haig was inclined to believe that the Navy had only itself to blame. Admiral

Bacon aside, senior naval officers seemed of suspect quality. Haig liked Jellicoe, but confessed that he was 'not . . . a man of great power of decision or character'. As far as Haig was concerned, the solution to the submarine threat was quite simple: the government should allow him to capture the U-boat bases on the Belgian coast. While he was at it, he would deliver the German Army a blow from which it could not recover. But, while teeth were gnashed at the shipping losses, Haig's advice continued to be ignored. The unqualified commitment to Nivelle's plan seemed, to him, dafter by the day.[23]

While disaster loomed on the seas, Haig saw nothing but bright prospects on land – if only sufficient men were made available to realise them. As usual, his confidence was strengthened by Duncan and Charteris. Duncan's 'fine manly Christianity' inspired Haig to ask the Lord 'for further "strength which is not our own" to enable us to win through, and to look beyond the present into the far distance of a life to come!' Haig did not need to be told that God was supreme or that He had a divine plan for British victory. What he needed, and what Duncan provided, was 'nourishment for the spiritual side of life', in other words, the feeling that God was communicating directly with him, and that he had been allotted an important part in the divine plan. With this need satisfied, Haig was serene in the knowledge that 'this life leads naturally on to the next . . . so we are safe whatever happens'.[24]

In a very different way, Charteris also strengthened Haig's spirit. By definition Intelligence Officer, he was in fact much more than that, being in charge of 'censorship, Press correspondents, ciphers, all communication with foreign Government's Secret Service . . . contre-espionage, all map work and distinguished visitors'. As the war progressed, official despatches, meteorological surveys, and propaganda were added to this list. But more important than the specific tasks Charteris performed was the peculiar relationship he had with Haig. A junior member of the staff, Sir James Marshall-Cornwall, claimed that Charteris 'always felt that his main object in life was to maintain the morale of his Commander-in-Chief who trusted him implicitly'. Charteris 'had an almost mesmeric influence on Haig who . . . gradually became a slave to [his] influence'. Marshall-Cornwall, like many other staff members, distrusted Charteris, a feeling which is probably reflected in his appraisal of him. Though Charteris did perceive of himself as a bulwark to Haig's morale, it is doubtful that he had the sinister effect described above. Nor is it even likely that

Haig actually needed the moral encouragement which Charteris was so keen to provide.[25]

An examination of Haig's attitude towards his personal staff sheds light on this subject. As will be recalled, before the war Haig campaigned energetically for the professionalisation of staff officers. But the standards he sought for the Army were not applied very stringently when he chose his own staff. Sycophancy seems to have been more important than skill. Haig had, according to Charteris, an 'aversion for the hard-bitten man and [a] fondness for Caesar's "fat counsellors"'. The staff was 'a brotherhood of officers, all united in common admiration and trust in . . . the Commander in Chief'. There was, according to a junior officer, 'no more loyal band of brothers than the Grand Staff of the British Army'. Loyalty is an important attribute for a staff officer, but the extent to which it was stressed at Montreuil meant that it often became blind. Rather than complementing the talents of their superior, Haig's loyal disciples exacerbated his weaknesses. Certain as he was that he knew the way to victory, Haig tended not to seek guidance from subordinates. 'In many ways D.H. is his own Chief of Staff,' Charteris wrote in 1915; 'his Chief of Staff has little to do except to see that things go smoothly'. Esher, likewise, commented that Haig's 'general staff seems to be an excellent machine, formed to carry out his ideas and intentions. They initiate nothing. All initiative remains with him.'[26]

It is inaccurate to claim that Haig was plagued with mediocre subordinates. His staff was his creation. Though he did not always get the men he wanted, an officer to whom he objected was never forced upon him. Nor is it accurate to absolve Haig by claiming that he was 'perhaps a poor judge of character'. Rather, it seems that mediocrity was often the standard he sought. Whilst it is true that the staff was 'too much in awe of papa'; it is doubtful that papa would have had it any other way.[27]

Charteris was the black sheep in Haig's family – the antithesis of the 'gentlemen' on the staff. He was, Haig admitted, 'dirty and fat'; he enjoyed brandies before breakfast and was always ready with a bawdy joke. Despite all these faults, Haig found him 'good value'. Charteris's eloquent explanations of the way intelligence was collected, or what could be concluded from it, captivated Haig. He was impressed by Charteris's considerable administrative talents, and therefore repeatedly gave him additional tasks upon which to work his magic. Charteris was consulted every morning and often at other times during the day regarding the state of the fighting and the course of the war.[28]

Haig's confidence in Charteris's abilities was not shared by the man himself. He did not want to be Intelligence Officer, preferring instead Operations. Nor did he find the job particularly easy, being acutely aware of the peculiar pressures which Haig placed upon him. As he indicated before Haig became Commander in Chief:

> Intelligence work teaches scepticism if it teaches nothing else . . . The Head Intelligence Officer at GHQ [MacDonogh] has this scepticism developed to the highest point. His strongest affirmation is that 'Something or other appears not improbable', that means it is practically certain. D.H. demands more than this. Everything that goes to him has to be sharply divided into Fact, Probability, Possibility, Improbability . . . and he holds me responsible that everything is in its proper category.

In part because of its sordid and ungentlemanly nature, the British paid little attention to intelligence before the war. Charteris had therefore to start virtually from scratch; not only did he have little idea how to collect information, he was uncertain how to interpret that which he collected. His task was complicated by the lumping together of propaganda and intelligence, a problem which Esher recognised: 'The cardinal principle . . . is the separation of propaganda and intelligence. The one is mainly a system of falsehood, while the other aims at the exact truth. It is corrupting for the furnishers of truth that they should be engaged in manufacturing lies.' Haig was apparently unaware of this contradiction. Charteris was given both tasks simply because Haig had unlimited faith in his abilities.[29]

A more serious problem arose over the kind of information Charteris was directed to collect. Haig, as has been shown, put too much emphasis on the state of enemy morale. Charteris explained why:

> The Battle of the Aisne, which had enabled [Haig] to gauge the fighting qualities of the German troops, confirmed his belief that man-power would ultimately decide the war and he directed his staff to begin the study of the man-power which the German nation

could effectively employ in the field . . . the studies of the man-power of the German army . . . were developed at each successive stage of Haig's progress in the war, and he rarely allowed more than a day or two to pass without himself inquiring into the developments of this investigation.[30]

In other words, instead of concentrating on enemy intentions, Haig directed Charteris to collect data on the durability of the German nation. Rather than showing how the enemy could be beaten, the intelligence showed that he was being beaten. Whilst evidence of the emotional state of the enemy can be of value, it is never as valuable as indications of his movements, his intentions, the distribution of his men and guns, etc. This information (which Charteris incidentally was adept at providing) unfortunately had less effect upon Haig than the more emotive material pertaining to German moral deterioration.

Greatest weight was ironically given to the information Charteris was least able to provide. Strategy and tactics was therefore based upon grossly inaccurate estimations of German durability. Charteris never quite came to terms with the complex nature of morale and the myriad emotional factors which determine it. For instance, he placed great store in the testimony of captured soldiers, without apparently realising that prisoners seldom mirror the feelings of those who are not captured. For understandable reasons, those captured have a tendency to say exactly what the captor wishes. Charteris also mistakenly based his conclusions on the evidence given by prisoners captured in the active parts of the front. This explains why the War Office intelligence reports, which were derived from a much wider sample, usually presented less encouraging estimates of the deterioration of enemy morale. Furthermore, Charteris wrongly assumed a direct correlation between physical privation and emotional deterioration. In other words, as far as he was concerned, massive casualties and dwindling rations was evidence enough to conclude, as early as January 1916, that the Germans were on the brink of collapse. By concentrating on these factors, he ignored the best indicator of German morale: that being the impossibility of breaking the German line.

Charteris has been widely accused of misleading Haig. It is true that his estimations of German moral decline were inaccurate. But it is wrong to speak of a guilty and an injured party; Charteris was not a devious deceiver, nor was Haig innocently led astray. It was Haig's misguided concentration upon morale factors which forced Charteris into an area of intelligence gathering which was prone to miscalculation. Also, whilst Charteris provided the information, it was Haig who usually interpreted it. Thus, if Charteris said that strikes were breaking out in Germany, Haig predicted an imminent revolution. Finally, it is worth stressing that Haig's optimism was not merely 'a sentiment but a policy'. As Duff Cooper rightly argued, it was his 'deliberate intention to give pre-eminence to the more favourable aspects of any situation'. Desmond Morton, an ADC in the latter stages of the war, confessed that Haig 'hated being told any information, however irrefutable, which militated against his preconceived ideas or beliefs'. Devoted staff officers might therefore have occasionally equated loyalty with the manufacturing of good news (not to mention the quashing of bad). Thus, to argue that Charteris misled Haig is to assume that Haig would have tolerated an intelligence officer who consistently supplied him with depressing (albeit accurate) intelligence – a very large assumption indeed.[31]

It was usually Charteris's intelligence reports which got him into trouble. But in February 1917, he caused a stir in his function as a press officer. His role as liaison to newspaper correspondents had expanded with Haig's sudden change of heart regarding the Press. Esher, who had been behind this change, had also urged Haig to cultivate a better relationship with French journalists so that the French people could be made aware of British sacrifices. On 1 February, Haig met three such journalists and gave them what they interpreted as an interview, but what he interpreted quite differently. Articles were subsequently written and then submitted to Charteris, who censored them from a military point of view. He assumed that they would then be approved by Haig for publication, but they somehow escaped his notice. A crisis had materialised out of thin air.

Haig claimed that the French articles (subsequently translated in *The Times*) were no more than 'general recollections of a conversation . . . and were in no case quotations'. He did not, and could not, deny that they accurately reflected his opinions on the war. Haig, it was reported, had poured scorn upon 'sham' German peace feelers which were, he felt, solely aimed at gaining time. In his view, there could be no peace without victory, and this victory must not be gained merely by economic pressure, but by the infliction of defeat, palpable and unquestioned, in the field. Anything less – an incomplete victory, a premature or halting victory – would enable German 'militarism' to make ready its revenge.

Reference was made to Haig's belief that victory could only be won on the Western Front, and he was quoted as saying: 'This war of trenches must make way for a war of movement which will secure for us the great advantages upon which we reckon.' The 'decisive event' would most likely come in 1917.

But if we cannot beat him so entirely this year that he will crave for [peace] on our terms, we shall not shrink from carrying on the war until he does. That, we are confident, is the settled purpose of France, as it is ours . . . Her people, like ours, know in their hearts that [their] sacred heritage, handed down to them through long ages of effort and glory, now stands in jeopardy. But in France, as in England, public men have seemed at times to forget the advantage of keeping this truth vivid and ever present to the mind of the masses.

Politicians from all parties objected to the way the article questioned their patriotism and resolve. Lloyd George in particular was angered at the references to shortages of shells and guns, which he interpreted as a direct attack upon his record as Minister of Munitions. More generally, there was widespread concern at the way Haig had expounded on the sort of peace the Allies would be prepared to accept, something which was not strictly his business. Philip Snowden, the pacifist Labour MP for Blackburn, claimed that Haig's 'blazing indiscretion . . . has shaken the confidence of many people in his judgement'. Snowden was worried that the door to a negotiated peace had been slammed shut.[32]

Bonar Law skilfully quashed debate on the subject in the House. The embarrassed government was nevertheless determined that someone should pay, and therefore summoned Major Neville Lytton, the officer in charge of foreign press correspondents, to London for questioning. An indignant Haig recorded how 'Lloyd George and Lord Curzon were most hostile, and cross examined him as if he were trying to tell what was untrue!' Haig had heard that the French 'were delighted with what was published and have never been so friendly towards the British as they are now. They cannot understand why so much fuss is being made in England over it.' Neither could he understand, but this did not stop him from attempting an explanation:

Lloyd George seem[s] to resent my bulking large in the public eyes at all. He wishes to shine alone. As for Curzon, it seems that he still has a grudge against the soldier and would like to re-introduce a new system with a Military Member as at Simla . . . The attacks seem to have been made by discredited socialists and 'peace at any price' people.

In a letter to his wife, Haig suggested that Lloyd George was 'slipping down the hill in popular favour, and is looking about to find something to increase his reputation as the man of the hour and the saviour of England!' The Prime Minister was trying to 'rouse public opinion against me', so as to 'order my recall'. In response to this threat, he maintained:

I am doing my best and have a clear conscience. If they have some-one else who can command this great army better than I am doing, I shall be glad to hand over to him and will be *so happy* to come back to my darling wife and play golf and bring up the children.

Haig had exaggerated the threat to him; on this occasion, neither the War Cabinet nor Lloyd George wanted his scalp.[33]

The politicians were, however, intent upon retribution. Government guns were eventually trained upon Charteris, whose actions, according to Derby, had been 'absolutely unjustifiable'.

He has let you down very badly, and let you down in a respect which you in France can hardly realise at the present moment. He has destroyed in this country all confidence in his judgement, and everything which passes through his hands as having been approved by him will be a subject of suspicion.

Derby stopped short of advising Haig to sack Charteris, but did suggest that it was in his interest to give the censorship duties to someone else. He also advised that Haig would be 'amply justified if, in the future, you definitely refuse to give any further interviews to anybody'. The War Minister concluded by emphasising, 'I am not in any way exaggerating the effect the interview has had not only on the Cabinet, but on the people of this country.'[34]

Responding to the last sentence, Haig scribbled in the margins: 'Possibly correct as to the Cabinet, but absolute rubbish as regards the people.' The comment reveals how extensive was Haig's ignorance of public opinion. In his mind the British were united in their unqualified support for the war. He thought, therefore, that his 'interview' could have nothing other than a positive, stirring effect. Unlike the politicians, he did not understand that while support for the war was widespread, it was nevertheless fragile. Since he could not accept this, he naturally interpreted the attitude of the government as cowardly and devious. Whilst it is perhaps true that Lloyd George and others who were not well disposed towards Haig made political capital out of the incident, there is no denying that the fears expressed by Derby (a staunch supporter of Haig) were genuine. This was not the time, Derby feared, to tell the public that the war might continue for years and that German peace feelers would be summarily rejected – however true such statements might be.

Comfortably isolated from public opinion, Haig was unable to see the affair as anything other than an attempt to undermine him. As he commented to Derby:

> What however interests me most is for whose advantage it has been to misrepresent what appeared in the French papers! If L.G. has a man in his eye who will run this great Army better than I am doing, let him appoint him without more ado. You will find that I am sufficient of a patriot to withdraw as a man, and I trust gracefully!

As it happened, Lloyd George did not have 'a man in his eye' to replace Haig. On 24 February, the War Cabinet, according to Hankey, had come to the conclusion that 'Haig is the best man we have, but that is not saying much'. He added, rather ominously, that 'as between Haig and Nivelle, L.G. [intends] to support the latter'.[35]

The argument over Haig's interview ran its course by 25 February. Acting upon Derby's advice, Haig transferred the press duties to another officer, but stressed to his wife, 'There is no question of

Charteris going . . . [he] is invaluable as Intelligence Officer and very clever at that work.' *The Times* called the affair a 'storm in a teacup' – a description which, though accurate as far as the event itself is concerned, does not do justice to its wider significance. The little storm was a precursor of the typhoons which loomed on the horizon. Though the controversy was forgotten by the beginning of March, the mutual suspicion between Lloyd George and Haig which it engendered would not disappear.[36]

It was inevitable that these two men should have disagreed on the conduct of the war. The origins of their disagreement can be traced to their personalities: two more different individuals would be difficult to find. Lloyd George was the quintessential politician. Haig loathed politicians. The Prime Minister was a fiery, ebullient, quick-witted, and devious Welshman who saw himself as the friend of the common man. Haig was a dour, inarticulate and laconic Scotsman from the upper echelons of society for whom gentlemanly values were sacrosanct. As regards the war, Haig believed in victory at any price. Victory would cleanse and purify Britain, preparing her for a post-war world in which she would remain transcendent. Lloyd George, to his credit, was more sensitive to the long-term costs of the war. This greater sensitivity inspired his search for a strategy which would ease the burden of the war on the British people. Though he may have been deluded in believing that such a strategy existed, he should not be criticised for wanting to find one.

Lloyd George and Haig were not just different, they were antagonistic. It was unfortunate that their only common characteristic was their stubborn determination. Each wanted desperately to win the war; each had different ideas about how to win. Each thought his way was the only way; each saw the other as an obstacle. It must also be remembered that Lloyd George had earlier been brilliantly successful in bringing the munitions industry under control. He wrongly assumed that he would be as successful in taming the Army. But, as Hankey warned him in November 1916:

> he was not dealing with munitions workers, to whom he had been able to appeal with marvellous success, and to secure, as it was, individual support from them, but with armies led by the most conservative class in the world, forming the most powerful trades union in the world.[37]

Any attack upon Haig caused the rest of the Army to circle the wagons. Lloyd George ignored Hankey's warning and was as a result consistently frustrated in his efforts to bring the Army under control. But just as he underestimated the support Haig could command, so Haig underestimated him. Each man met his match in the other. Therefore, neither was sufficiently dominant to impose his will on the other. Consequently, conduct of the war suffered. Ascendancy shifted back and forth, and with it policy. Consistency was absent. Worse still, the relations between the two men became frustrated, paranoid and petty as personal antagonisms clouded common sense. Policies were sometimes chosen not because they were militarily justifiable but because they undermined the opposite number.

The Calais conference of 26–27 February was one such instance of personal antagonisms run amok. During the four weeks since the London meeting, Haig's cooperation with Nivelle had been less enthusiastic than the Frenchman and Lloyd George wanted. Haig was supposed to be preparing for an attack in Arras which would pave the way for the decisive French action further south. This time the shoe was on the other foot: it was Haig's delays which were threatening to postpone an offensive. Haig pleaded, with justification, that preparations could proceed only as quickly as the dilapidated French railways would allow. The British required 200 trains per day in order to collect stores for their attack. During February, due to the heavy winter, only seventy per day had been available. With Nivelle increasingly impatient and unsympathetic, Haig was in favour of another Anglo-French conference to sort out the railway difficulties and to set a new date for the offensive. This suggestion alarmed Robertson. 'So long as Ministers take part in the discussion of plans of operations, we shall always have trouble of the worst kind I am sure,' he told Haig on 14 February. 'Whereas if you and Nivelle can come to some sort of settlement the two Governments will have to agree.' Heeding this advice, Haig saw Nivelle two days later and was pleased to find that the Frenchman 'agreed with me that *no attack should start until all our requirements had been provided*'. He also promised to press his government to give assistance with the railway problem.[38]

Nivelle and Haig agreed to meet again to finalise the date for the attack. Up to this point, events seemed to be proceeding smoothly. Then, on 22 February, Robertson announced that Lloyd George wanted to hold a meeting at Calais or Boulogne in order to discuss the railway problem with Briand, Lyautey (the new War Minister). Robertson did not let on that two days earlier he had been present at a War Cabinet meeting at which it had been decided that the terms of reference of the approaching conference would include not only the railways 'but also . . . the operations of 1917'. Haig had no reason to suspect that devious plans were afoot. Indeed, on the 18th, he recorded how a boastful Robertson had told him that 'he had been fortunate lately in putting L. George and the Government in their place, and so he had been having his own way more'.[39]

In fact, while Robertson was telling white lies to Haig, he was having the wool pulled over his eyes by Lloyd George. On the 19th, the Prime Minister met the Assistant French Military Attaché, Commandant Bertier de Sauvigny, and announced that in his opinion Nivelle 'is the only man who is capable of bringing the operations to a successful conclusion this year. But, for this to be possible, it is necessary in the last resort that he should be able to make use of all the forces on the French front, ours as well as the French Armies.' Lloyd George pointed out

> that the prestige which Field-Marshal Haig enjoys with the public and the British Army will make it impossible to subordinate him purely and simply to the French Command, but if the War Cabinet realises that this measure is indispensable, they will not hesitate to give Field-Marshal Haig secret instructions to this effect, and, if need be, to replace him.

It was up to the French to make the subordination of Haig to Nivelle seem 'indispensable' by demanding its implementation. De Sauvigny subsequently told Lyautey and Nivelle that Lloyd George wanted them to submit a scheme to this effect at the upcoming conference in Calais.[40]

Lloyd George realised that the plot had to be kept absolutely secret until the last moment, so that Haig and Robertson would not be able to mobilise their supporters. On the 24th, the War Cabinet met to discuss the Prime Minister's proposals. Not by chance, Robertson and Derby were not able to attend. According to Curzon, support was given to the idea of subordinating Haig to Nivelle because:

1. The French had practically twice the number of troops in the field that we had.
2. We were fighting on French soil to drive the enemy off French soil.
3. Independent opinion shows that without question the French Generals and Staffs are immeasurably superior to British Generals and Staffs, not from the point of view of fighting but from that of generalship, and of the knowledge of the science and art of war.
4. The War Cabinet did not consider Haig a clever man. Nivelle made a much greater impression on the members of the War Cabinet.[41]

Meanwhile, Nivelle, on de Sauvigny's urging, had prepared his *Projet d'Organisation* which reduced Haig to the equivalent of an adjutant general, with control over personnel and discipline only. The commanders of the various British armies would receive their orders from Nivelle, through a British chief of staff, a post which had been set aside for Henry Wilson.

The stage was set for the Calais conference. Still completely ignorant of the plot, Haig was surprised when, after a short discussion of the railway problem, Lloyd George directed the technical experts to continue their negotiations elsewhere, so that the more important question of 'Plans' could be addressed. 'This was a quite new and unexpected development. But doubtless this had all been planned by L.G. with Briand beforehand.' Even bigger surprises were in store. Haig's description of subsequent events reads like the script of a play – an indication of how well Lloyd George had coached the principal actors (except Haig and Robertson) on their lines. After Nivelle explained his plan for the offensive (which had been heard many times before) he

> concluded by saying that he would answer any questions which L.G. cared to put to him. But L.G. said, 'that is not all – I want to hear everything', and to Briand he said, 'Tell him to keep nothing back' and so forth 'as to his disagreements with Marshal Haig'.

Haig recorded that, 'This was quite a surprise to me, and apparently to Nivelle to some extent.' Actually Nivelle was just a good actor.

Though Lloyd George's behaviour seemed curious, Haig still did not smell a rat.[42]

When it was his turn to speak, Haig explained the points upon which he disagreed with the French plan. Nivelle did not accept the need to attack the Vimy Ridge, whereas he thought it essential. Furthermore,

> I was doing my utmost to comply with the strategical requirements of N.'s plan, but in the matter of tactics I alone could decide. That is to say, N. having stated that his plan required the British to break the enemy's front N. of the Somme and march on Cambrai, I decided where and how I would dispose of my troops for that purpose.[43]

Haig had walked blindly into Lloyd George's trap by providing the Prime Minister with the sort of disagreement which he needed to justify the subordination of the British command to the French.

The discussion continued according to Lloyd George's script. After hearing Haig, he disingenuously remarked that 'he did not understand about strategy and tactics', but wanted it 'clearly stated what the respective responsibilities were'. The French were then asked to draw up proposals for a 'system of command' which the British could discuss after dinner. The proposals submitted were, of course, the *Projet d'Organisation* which had been prepared a week before.[44]

Upon reading the French proposals, Robertson 'showed every sign of having a fit'. Haig, in contrast, retained a passive exterior while the fuses blew inside. Both men rushed to Lloyd George, who must have been squiggling with glee when he announced that the War Cabinet was on his side. Astonished at this revelation, Haig replied that 'it would be madness to place the British Forces under the French'. He 'did not believe that our troops would fight under French leadership'. Enraged, Lloyd George retorted: 'Well, Field-Marshal, I know the private soldier very well, and there are people he criticises a good deal more strongly than General Nivelle!' Haig's outburst had nevertheless dented Lloyd George's resolve. He realised that he was on shaky ground, since the War Cabinet approval pertained only to the duration of the offensive, not to the more permanent change which the French plan implied. Agreeing that the proposals were 'excessive', he 'insisted on R. and myself considering a "scheme for giving effect to the War Cabinet's decision"'. Haig and Robertson then retired to the latter's room, where they concurred 'that we would rather be tried by Court Martial than betray the Army by agreeing to its being placed under the French . . . we must resign rather than be partners in this transaction'. The soldiers went dejectedly off to bed, 'thoroughly disgusted with our Government and the Politicians'.[45]

Early the next morning, Haig was called to Lyautey's room, where he also found Nivelle:

> They both spoke of the 'insult offered to me and the British Army by the paper which Briand had produced'. They assured me that they had not seen the document until quite recently. Indeed, as regards Lyautey, he had not seen or heard of it until he entered the train at Paris to come to Calais today. I understand that the paper was drawn up in Paris with Lloyd George's approval and, of course, of Briand.[46]

Nivelle claimed that he thought Robertson and Haig had known of the plan before the conference began. All of this was untrue, and only proved that he and Lyautey were as devious as Lloyd George. Haig, however, remained ignorant of the complicity of the two Frenchmen for the rest of the war. This was probably all for the best, since it would have been impossible for Haig to work with Nivelle had he known the truth.

During the night, Hankey devised a compromise plan which made a distinction between the period of preparation and the battle itself. In the first period, Haig would conform to Nivelle's instructions, but would be able to depart from them if, in his view, 'the safety of the Army is endangered, or success prejudiced'. During the battle, he was 'to act entirely as Nivelle orders'. Objecting to this, Haig negotiated a clause giving him 'a free hand to choose the means and methods of utilising the British troops' in the relevant sector. After Nivelle agreed to the new plan, a formal document was drawn up and signed. Eager to see things in the best light, Haig concluded:

> As it stands, the way in which I have worked with the French is not changed. I have always acted on General Joffre's 'General Instructions' as if they had been Orders, but retained absolute freedom of action as to how I carried them out. This power must, however, remain to me. In Nivelle's present proposals,

I am relieved of responsibility, both for the plan of the battle now being prepared, as well as for the details of execution of the plan.

Haig took comfort in the fact that 'the battle is expected to last a fortnight, and after that the normal state of arrangements will be reverted to'. He left Calais reasonably satisfied. The affair was given new light when, upon his return to Beaurepaire, Haig was told by General Michelet that 'it does not matter what the politicians may decide, the French soldier is not going to fight after the autumn'.[47]

On 28 February, Haig assured his wife that 'the decisions regarding "Command" arrived at at the Calais Conference should work without difficulty provided that there is nothing further behind'. But, 'one can never be sure that these Politicians are not scheming with some ulterior object'. There was a limit to his patience: 'if my position is made impossible, I know that you at any rate will be ready to give me a loving welcome when I return home!' Thanking his wife for 'contributing in no small degree to my peace of mind', he assured her that he was 'quite happy and ready to confront the present difficulties . . . with a manly heart'.[48]

He did not, however, have to confront the difficulties alone; the King, as always, was ready to lend support. On the 28th, Haig wrote that though he did not foresee any problems with the agreement as it stood, he felt it necessary to write, 'in order that Your Majesty may be watchful, and prevent any steps being taken which will result in our Army being broken up and incorporated in French Corps'. The letter ended with an offer of resignation:

> I have never suggested that I would like to resign my Command . . . as any change of Command at this time might be a disadvantage to the Army in the field. It is possible, however, that the present War Cabinet may think otherwise, and deem it best to replace me by someone else more in their confidence. If this is so, I recommend that the change be made as soon as possible.

The King responded with a telegram confirming the sort of support which Haig had undoubtedly been soliciting. Stamfordham followed this with a lengthy letter in which he wrote that the King had been greatly dismayed by Lloyd George's actions, which he would have blocked had he been aware of them beforehand. The letter concluded: 'You have the absolute confidence, of [the] Army from the highest to the lowest ranks: a confidence which is shared to the full by the King.' Curzon, meanwhile, had assured Haig of the 'thorough confidence in you and appreciation of your services by the War Cabinet'. Ruffled feathers were smoothed. 'You were right', Haig told his wife on 2 March, 'when you wrote "things would turn out all right" . . . most people, and all who really matter, are anxious to help and support me.'[49]

The ramifications of Calais were less reassuring. The conference had barely broken up when Haig received a letter from Nivelle demanding details of British preparations and expressing a desire for Wilson to be appointed to head the British Mission at Beauvais. Though always extremely suspicious of the 'arch-intriguer' Wilson, Haig was on this occasion more upset by the 'very *commanding* tones' in which Nivelle had expressed his requests. 'It is a type of letter which no gentleman could have drafted, and it is also one which certainly no C. in C. of this great British Army should receive without protest.' A stern letter was quickly sent to the War Cabinet 'with a request to be told whether it is their wishes that the C. in C. in command of this British Army should be subjected to such treatment by a junior *foreign* Commander'. Haig reflected, 'It is too sad at this critical time to have to fight with one's Allies and the Home Government, in addition to the enemy in the Field.'[50]

On 3 March, Haig predicted: 'the Germans will help me . . . by doing something which will quite upset the Agreement . . . so carefully prepared for a situation which even now no longer exists'. He was referring to the German withdrawal to the *Siegfried Stellung* or Hindenburg Line, a brilliant manoeuvre which shortened the line between Arras and the river Aisne by forty kilometres, thus freeing fourteen divisions. These divisions were earmarked for an offensive in the east designed to knock the Russians out of the war. The new line, which took nearly six months to construct, was an attacker's nightmare. Haig did not immediately appreciate its significance. 'The question to decide is whether the enemy has begun a big movement in retreat, or whether he has merely evacuated the ground . . . for local reasons.' Haig initially favoured the former (wrong) explanation. 'On the whole, such a withdrawal seems to have greater disadvantages than advantages for the enemy.'[51]

Eventually, Haig came to terms with the brilliance of the enemy manoeuvre. In a report to the War Cabinet of 2 March, he postulated that the Germans were trying to pre-empt another costly Allied offensive like the Somme. The withdrawal was designed to demoralise and disorganise the Allies whilst at the same time freeing troops for action on other fronts. 'We must expect a gigantic hostile attack somewhere.' The most likely place, Haig thought, was near Ypres: 'An attack against Ypres and the coast ports, would fit in well with his submarine war; and the capture of our communications with England must mean the end of the war for both England and France. Such a blow if successful would mean decisive victory for Germany.' Haig was intentionally exaggerating the threat. He was too optimistic ever to believe that any move by Germany could mean a defeat of the Allies. What he was trying to do was to alarm the War Cabinet so that the Calais decisions would be reversed. As he wrote: 'With such uncertainties and possibilities confronting us [around Ypres] . . . the folly of definitely placing the British C. in C. under the orders of the French . . . becomes more marked than it seemed at the Calais Conference.' In other words, the reserves committed to Nivelle were urgently required for the protection of the coastal sector. Haig's real attitude towards the withdrawal is evident in a letter to his wife in which he referred to it as a 'great sign of weakness' which had been brought on by 'their defeat in the Somme Battle last year'.[52]

Nivelle, upon studying this memo, penned an angry reply to Haig on the 7th, in which he insisted that the British contribution to the offensive 'must not be reduced by a single man, or gun'. This was all too much for Haig:

> It is difficult to receive these communications with patience. He . . . has gone beyond the letter and also the spirit of the Calais agreement. I suppose in time, if I give him enough rope he will hang himself! Meantime the process is annoying for me, and a waste of time which ought to be devoted to thinking out plans for beating the enemy, instead of replies to Nivelle.

Nivelle in fact thought it might be as easy to hang Haig. In a secret communication with Lloyd George, he emphasised that 'the situation cannot improve as long as Sir Douglas Haig remains in command'. Gough was suggested as a replacement.[53]

During the second week of March, the air was thick with talk of Haig's possible resignation. Lloyd George considered forcing Haig to resign (or, alternatively, sacking him) but could not muster the necessary support. When Hankey canvassed the War Cabinet, he found only Bonar Law even remotely in favour of the idea. Hankey cautioned Lloyd George that if Haig was forced out

> the result would be to cause elements to coalesce which would never otherwise do so. The late Prime Minister would, I believe, on this issue rally to him his old followers, and many waverers; they would be joined, from sheer mischief, by the disunited Irish, by the pacifists, and possibly by some Tories. Court and society influence, and all elements within reach of the General Staff would be thrown into the scale against the Government, and, whether the Government were defeated or not, they would be very seriously weakened.

A better summary of Haig's support was never written. Hankey went on to advise Lloyd George that if he insisted upon getting rid of Haig, 'it is of first importance that he should not resign, but should be recalled, and should, if possible, be given a high military command e.g. at Salonika'. It was like suggesting that a Rangers supporter should take a job as ball boy for Celtic.[54]

Ironically, Haig's friends were equally frightened at the prospect of his resignation. On 9 March, Wigram visited GHQ and related how such an eventuality was 'apparently the last thing the War Cabinet would like ... [since] Lloyd George ... would then appeal to the country, and might possibly come back as a Dictator'. Wigram, who thought that the Prime Minister wanted to destroy the monarchy, believed that the Calais plot had been aimed at weakening the royalist Army 'by breaking it up and distributing it amongst the French Armies'. Similarly irrational fears were expressed by the King himself when, on 11 March, he advised Haig to

> be careful not to resign, because Lloyd George would then appeal to the country for support and would probably come back with a great majority, as L.G. was at present very popular it seems. The King's position would then be very difficult. He would be blamed

for causing a General Election which would cost the country a million, and stop munition work etc.

Haig reassured the King (through Wigram): 'I would not resign unless the Government wished me to do so. Indeed, I felt it a cowardly thing to shirk going through a difficult situation by sending in one's resignation.'[55]

From 11 to 14 March, French and British representatives met in London to try to solve the problems which had arisen because of Calais. Haig saw himself as a helpless, but still magnanimous, victim: 'I felt that I had been very forgiving, and only the need of working with the French Army in order to win had dragged me there.' Lloyd George, crushed by the weight of support for Haig and the growing impatience with French demands, found himself having to tell Nivelle that 'Haig possessed the full confidence of the War Cabinet, and was regarded with admiration in England'. With Lloyd George on his side, proceedings generally went Haig's way. After much bickering, an agreement was reached, which he signed with the following proviso:

> I agree . . . on the understanding that, while I am fully determined to carry out the Calais Agreement in spirit and letter, the British Army and its C. in C. will be regarded by General Nivelle as allies and not subordinates, except during the particular operations which he explained at the Calais Conference.

After weeks of bickering matters had returned essentially to where they were after the conference at Downing Street on 15 January.[56]

Calais was little more than a very tall Tower of Babel. As far as Haig's position *vis à vis* the French was concerned, little had changed. The most important (and unfortunate) effect of the conference was the way in which the relationship between the government and the Army deteriorated still further. This was unnecessary. Lloyd George had recklessly gambled away whatever remaining trust Haig may have felt for him. If Haig was henceforth suspicious to the point of paranoia, Lloyd George had only himself to blame. Whilst unity of command was perhaps a noble goal, the cavalier fashion in which it was pursued precluded any noble results. As Haig realised, the real goal was unity of effort, which he had subscribed to all along. It was to Lloyd George's advantage, and Haig's credit, that the Calais scandal was kept largely secret from the public.

On 16 March, Haig told his wife that 'the Higher Power has been good to me in so many ways, especially in giving me health and strength to carry on'. This strength had enabled him to overcome the deviousness of Lloyd George, an achievement of which he was very proud. During the difficult weeks, he had drawn comfort from visits to his troops; their 'honest determination and confidence' had made it possible to forget 'those wretched intrigues'. He had, on 6 March, been

> greatly struck with the fine bearing and proud appearance of the troops. Each man looks directly at one, and catches my eye as he passes with an absolutely confident air, as much as to say, 'I feel I can do my duty.' And I notice too how seasoned the men look now – so different in their expressions this year as to what they were last . . . And I felt sad at times too at the thought of how much suffering is in store for many of these brave fellows before the war can end.

Haig concluded, 'It is beyond the power of any Frenchman to ever command such troops! They [would] not submit to the Frenchman's underhand ways.' He delighted in speculating upon what his 'splendid Army will do to the politicians after the war!'[57]

Though Haig had initially failed to appreciate the wisdom of the German withdrawal to the *Siegfried Stellung*, he correctly surmised that it meant 'the advisability of launching Nivelle's battle at all, grows daily less'.[58] Leaving aside the fact that they possessed more reserves than previously, the Germans were obviously no longer in the vulnerable strategic position upon which Nivelle's plans had originally been founded. The intended strike in the Oise valley, for instance, had to be jettisoned because the Germans were no longer there. This meant that what had been a combined offensive was reduced to two separate attacks – one by the British against the Vimy Ridge and environs, the other by the French in the Aisne valley – each with little strategic relation to the other. Nivelle, quite unperturbed, remained determined that the attack should go ahead as planned, and continued to boast that it would break through the enemy lines in twenty-four hours. His subordinates, on the other hand, had their doubts, which were voiced with increasing frequency and resonance. In the midst of this tumult, Lyautey resigned on 16 March, pulling

Briand, Nivelle's chief supporter, down with him. Alexandre Ribot took over as Prime Minister. The new War Minister, Paul Painlevé, had little faith in the offensive and was ready to strangle it if it was not immediately successful.

Haig, who still believed that Lyautey was a 'straightforward and honest gentleman', was agonised by his resignation. Painlevé, a 'revolutionary Socialist', was by definition untrustworthy. Haig was therefore canny in his replies to Painlevé's inquiries (during a meeting on 24 March) about Nivelle, being 'careful to say that he struck me as a capable General'. His relations with Nivelle had 'always been excellent'. The assurances given to Painlevé were not inspired merely by politeness or even political posturing. Haig still sincerely believed that 'the Calais Conference was a mistake, but it was not Nivelle's fault'. Relations between the two commanders remained cordial, as a meeting of 23 March demonstrates:

> Nivelle was most pleasant, and I think is a straightforward man. He is in complete agreement with me regarding the general plan namely to launch our attacks as arranged and if enemy does not await our attack, to follow him up, and at the same time to organise attacks as soon as possible elsewhere.

This seems to contradict Haig's earlier statement that the German withdrawal reduced the advisability of launching Nivelle's attack. He had obviously not abandoned all hope in it, even if French politicians had. Nevertheless, the possibility of failure did cross Haig's mind:

> the difficult question for me to decide would be whether the present operations are going to free the Belgian ports by late summer! If (say) we are still West of the line Lille–Valenciennes–Hirson–Verdun by the end of May, it would be desirable to attack elsewhere as proposed by us!

In other words, an eager eye remained focused in the direction of Flanders.[59]

The British offensive in the Arras sector was to consist of three main thrusts. While the First Army, north of Arras, pushed towards the Vimy Ridge, the Third would aim to capture the spur of Monchy-le-Preux, and the Fifth would attack on the right near Bullecourt. As he was reasonably certain that his forces would break the German lines, Haig allotted two cavalry divisions to the Third Army, one to the Fifth, and kept another in reserve. About sixty tanks were also assigned to the attack, though the mistake of dispersing them across the entire frontage was repeated. Haig, significantly, also rejected the Third Army commander Allenby's suggestion to confine the preliminary bombardment to an intensive forty-eight hours, instead insisting that it be spread over five days.

On the first day of the battle, 9 April, the British were reasonably successful, though less so than Haig had expected. The German first lines were overrun almost everywhere, and the important Vimy Ridge was captured. Soon, however, the battle assumed a by now familiar pattern, with each new thrust yielding diminishing returns. Gough's Fifth Army stalled, due to a lack of cooperation between the tanks and the infantry. At Monchy, a terrible and avoidable disaster occurred when the cavalry was foolishly pushed forward before the German line had actually been broken. The mounted troops were annihilated by a determined German counter-attack. Haig, considerably anguished, wrote dejectedly of the 'numbers of cavalrymen marching back on foot having had their horses killed'.[60]

The cavalry's failure was quickly forgotten. Haig was in no doubt that a victory had been won, the effects of which would be profound. 'It would', he thought, 'put a stopper on all the disgraceful intrigues which [have] been going on at home against me.' The War Cabinet had been forced to realise 'the right not only of the British Army but of the British peoples to consider themselves a "martial race" no matter what rubbish the present P.M. . . . may have said'. He took care to assure his wife that:

> As to the battle of Arras, I know quite well that I am being used as a tool in the hands of the Divine Power, and that my strength is not my own, so I am not at all conceited, and you may rest assured that I am not likely to forget to whom belongs the honour and glory for *all* our good work and success.[61]

In comparison to earlier efforts, Arras was a success. The British penetration (to a maximum depth of six kilometres on a front of twenty-five) was the most impressive since trench warfare had begun. But it was still a long way from a breakthrough. Discussing the battle with Haig, General Horne commented on how, 'owing to the amount of Artillery and Ammunition now available, the frontal assault on a position had become . . . the easiest task'. But what the British had not yet discovered was how 'to advance later on when the enemy had organised a defence with machine guns'. Haig did not entirely accept this pessimistic appraisal, preferring instead to blame the limited results on the War Cabinet, which had forced him to take over a large section of the French line in January. 'But for that ill-timed decision I should now have at my disposal a large Reserve of well-trained divisions with which to exploit our recent successes.' He wondered whether history would 'ever forgive the members of the War Cabinet for declining . . . to have any confidence in the power of the British Army to play its part with credit on the Western Front'.[62]

The offensive should have been called off after the initial success. The Germans, by this time fully aware of British intentions, had rushed forward massive reinforcements. But Haig insisted on continuing, partially because he felt an obligation to Nivelle, who had yet to launch his attack on the Aisne. After postponing on three successive days, Nivelle finally attacked on the 16th. It was clear by the end of the first day that the French commander's grandiose expectations would go unrealised. 'It is a pity', Haig commented, 'that Nivelle was so very optimistic as regards breaking the enemy's line.'[63] The irony of this statement apparently escaped him.

On 18 April, the Prime Minister, through General Maurice, requested Haig's opinion on what 'would be the effect of the French War Cabinet ordering General Nivelle to cease offensive operations at an early date'. Both the French, and, to a certain extent, Lloyd George, were considering going on the defensive until the Americans (who had declared war on 6 April) arrived in force. Haig was alarmed at this prospect, as he indicated to Robertson the next day: 'The struggle is following a normal course. Great results are never achieved in war until the enemy's resisting power has been broken, and against a powerful and determined enemy, operating with great numbers on wide fronts, this is a matter of time and hard fighting.' In other words, Nivelle's only error was to assume that he could effect a breach within twenty-four hours. This mistaken assumption aside, his efforts had been successful. 'The present battle is proceeding satisfactorily, and to abandon the good prospects of success now would be most discouraging to our Armies, and encouraging to the enemy.' Ceasing to attack, Haig argued, would increase the effect of the submarine threat by prolonging the war, and might even put Britain herself in danger of attack. It was therefore necessary for 'all the allies to do their utmost . . . to keep the enemy fully occupied everywhere'. Lloyd George, embarrassed by the failures of his French messiah (and Haig's comparative success) could do nothing but pinch his nose and swallow Haig's horrible medicine.[64]

It was clear to Haig that the battle was 'following a normal course'. His confidence was a magnifying glass which made microscopic gains appear significant. He found it easy enough to readjust objectives according to what the Army actually achieved. Though the enemy lines remained intact, the German morale was clearly cracking. Charteris, as usual, provided the bricks for these mythical constructs. During the Arras offensive, 'evidence' of the deterioration of German morale flowed steadily in. On the 13th, a prisoner revealed that 'the moral [sic] in his unit was very bad'. A few days later Haig heard that the enemy was short of food, and that boys of 17 had appeared in the line. Meanwhile, the internal state of Germany was 'reported to be very bad, and a serious shortage all round exists'. The country was riddled with strikes. On the 30th, great weight was given to 'reports from several sources that there is to be a general strike in order to insist on food being provided and peace made!' Had a complete German collapse indeed been so close, Haig's advice on maintaining the pressure would have been wise. Unfortunately, the intelligence was wrong, and so was Haig.[65]

The French government was not privy to Charteris's fantasy machine. On 24 April, Esher told Haig of the 'strong determination on the part of Minister of War to make radical changes in the [French] High Command'. Wilson likewise described the 'difficulties under which Nivelle had to carry out his operations on account of gossip and lack of confidence'. It was in this atmosphere that Haig met Nivelle in order to discuss the future course of the offensive. He reminded the French commander of the original agreements and the unalterable need to clear the Belgian coast. This objective, Haig thought, could still be achieved indirectly by attacking as they had been doing, 'but for this to be successful, the continued action of the French Army is essential'. He feared that 'after the British Army had exhausted itself in trying to make Nivelle's plan a success, the French Govt. might stop the operations'. The British would then be unable to capture the Belgian ports.[66]

Nivelle promised that the French would continue to attack, an assurance reiterated by Painlevé when he met Haig secretly on 26 April. The War Minister also pledged to do his utmost to help with any Flanders operations. The real object of the meeting, however, seems to have been to encourage Haig to speak out against Nivelle – something which he refused to do. Painlevé wanted to replace Nivelle with Pétain, but Ribot told Haig later in the afternoon, that 'this was no time for making a change in the Higher Command' – a point upon which Haig entirely agreed. Though he welcomed the assurances given by Nivelle, Painlevé and Ribot, Haig was not impressed with the courage they had shown. 'It seems to me that there is not a *real man* among either the soldiers or the Civilians.' He was nevertheless certain that his visit had strengthened their resolve: 'I feel that my arrival today has done good and that I have given the French Government confidence. They have "imagined" so much that they have made themselves believe that the French Army, if not already defeated, will very soon be so.' On the following day Haig was pleased to find Painlevé 'much quieter and steadier'. Though the War Minister hinted that Nivelle was on his way out, he again guaranteed that the French would continue fighting. He was, according to Haig, 'much more confident of ultimate victory than when I saw him yesterday'.[67]

Either the French had been lying or Haig had heard what he wanted to hear. On the 28th and 29th, news broke that Nivelle was to be replaced by Pétain, and that the French intended to pursue an 'aggressive defence', the object being to 'avoid losses and to await American reinforcements'. Haig, feeling that he had been swindled, told Robertson that Pétain 'doubtless . . . figures the British Army doing the aggressive work, while the French Army "squats" on the Defensive!' Disgusted, Haig turned his eyes northward.[68]

The ructions in the French command distracted attention from the operations around Arras. Haig had long ago given up on the original aim of capturing Cambrai, but was determined to continue the attacks in order to establish a secure defensive line and maintain pressure on the enemy. The fighting therefore dragged on until 23 May, with prodigious casualties buying minute gains. Arras was in almost every sense a failure. It had been designed to draw off German reserves as an aid to the French attack further south. Some reserves were perhaps drawn off but the French efforts nevertheless failed. The British inflicted heavy casualties on the Germans, but lost 160,000 men themselves. As was the case on the Somme, Haig had begun with bold objectives and had ended by opportunistically justifying the action with the claim that the process of attrition had at least been advanced.

13

High Hopes, Deep Mud

Nivelle's failure and his subsequent demise caused the pendulum of political favour to swing back towards Haig. Though he would never again command the support which he had enjoyed in early 1916, it is true to say that his cool, methodical nature suddenly seemed a better bet than Nivelle's impetuosity. At the same time, the French assumption of a defensive posture shifted responsibility for winning the war towards the British Army and thus further strengthened Haig's hand.

Though Haig was annoyed with the French reluctance to attack he was delighted at being able to put into effect what he termed 'our plan'. It was immediately clear to him what the British response to this new situation should be. Robertson had earlier revealed that the shipping situation was 'very serious indeed . . . There may soon be a serious shortage of food in this country, and this has to be taken into consideration in regard to all theatres of war.' Haig saw no choice but to put the 'alternative plan' of clearing the Belgian coast into effect. The fact that his plan had always included a very large French contribution in the manner of drawing off enemy reserves was conveniently forgotten.[1]

Haig's disappointment about the French was overshadowed by his delight at being able to put into effect what he called '*our* plan'. No time was wasted setting the machine in motion. On 30 April, Gough was told that he would be commanding the northern half of the proposed operations including the seaborne force. He was instructed to consult Bacon about using tanks with landing craft. On the following day, Haig sent the War Cabinet a memo entitled 'Present Situation and Future Plans', designed to sell the Flanders idea to the politicians. He reminded them that, 'The guiding principles are those which have proved successful in war from time immemorial, viz., that the first

317

step must be to wear down the enemy's power of resistance and to continue to do so until he is so weakened that he will be unable to withstand a decisive blow.' The 'fruits of victory' would afterwards be reaped. Haig admitted that the Germans were not yet worn out, as Nivelle had discovered to his cost. Though he could not say how long the wearing out process would have to continue, he was certain that once it was completed, the British would be able to deliver the decisive blow in Flanders. Aware that he had promised a breakthrough before, and that his credibility was not high, Haig carefully hedged his bets:

> Success seems reasonably possible. It will give valuable results on land and sea. If full measure of success is not gained, we shall be attacking the enemy on a front where he cannot refuse to fight, and our purpose of wearing him down will be given effect to. We shall be directly covering our own most important communications, and even a partial success will considerably improve our defensive positions in the Ypres salient.

Haig even spoke, uncharacteristically, of the British ending up in a better position 'next winter'. But all this was intended for the weak stomachs of the War Cabinet. In his own mind, the Flanders offensive would be the decisive blow; by next winter the troops would be safe in their homes. The operation was never meant to be another Somme offensive.[2]

The rise of Pétain did not bring with it any clear indications of future French intentions. Though Lloyd George had been forced, as a result of the Nivelle fiasco, to be more supportive of his own generals, he was not about to approve Haig's Flanders plan unless the French promised to pull their weight. He therefore demanded a conference with the Allies in Paris, on 4 May. Haig, by now extremely wary of the Prime Minister's tactics, arrived a day early in order to see Pétain and gain 'time to think over what the French can and will do before putting my proposals to Lloyd George'.[3]

Haig's immediate impression of Pétain was of a man easy to manipulate. No doubt in preparation for the following day's meeting with Lloyd George, he lectured the Frenchman on the need for the wearing out process to continue unabated. He nevertheless stressed that 'a moment will come when our advanced guards and Cavalry will be able to progress for much longer distances until a real decision is reached'. Haig was perfectly willing to continue his attacks upon the *Siegfried Stellung*, but only if the French were ready to do the same in the Aisne valley. If not, a new plan was necessary. Pétain told Haig that French reserves were so dangerously low that each month one division would disappear unless the Americans sent men to enlist in his Army. This was ironically exactly what Haig wanted to hear, for it allowed him to propose a shift of emphasis towards Flanders. The French, he suggested, could assist this effort by relieving six British divisions and by continuing to press the enemy on their own front. After Pétain conveyed his agreement, Haig concluded that the Frenchman was 'most clear-headed and easy to discuss things with'. Experience had, however, taught him that, 'There is always the difficulty . . . to know to what extent we can depend on the French to carry out these attacks.' Unbeknown to him, at that very moment mutinies were erupting in the French Army near Soissons.[4]

When Lloyd George arrived he announced, to a stunned Haig, that he would 'press whatever plan Robertson and [you] decide on'. Unfortunately, common ground was not easily found; the course of the war had caused the two men to develop in different strategic directions. On 20 April, Robertson told Haig that

> no war has ever differed so much from previous wars as does the present one, and it is futile, to put it mildly, hanging on to other theories when facts show them to be wrong. At one time, audacity and determination to push on regardless of loss were the predominating factors, but that was before the days of machine guns and modern armament.

Strategic advances, Robertson thought, were pies in the sky; there was no escaping the fact that this was a war of attrition. Haig, of course, did not agree; he had, after all, only recently assured the War Cabinet that the 'guiding principles are those which have proved successful in war from time immemorial'.[5]

These differences were bound to surface at the Paris conference. They did, but what is interesting is that they apparently went unnoticed. In a statement to ministers following a meeting with Haig and Pétain, Robertson announced that it had been 'unanimously agreed' that the ideas behind the Nivelle offensive were 'no longer operative'. 'It is no longer a question of breaking through the enemy's front and aiming at distant objectives. It is now a question of wearing down and exhausting the enemy's resistance, and if and when this is achieved to exploit it to the fullest extent possible.' According to Robertson, it had also been agreed that 'it is absolutely necessary to fight with all our available forces' and that the idea of fighting defensively was 'tantamount to acknowledging defeat'. Furthermore, future offensives would have 'limited objectives' gained by the 'fullest use of our artillery' and 'with the minimum loss possible'.[6]

What is extraordinary is that four men of decidedly different opinions agreed with this statement. For Robertson, it was simply a reiteration of what he had written to Haig on 20 April. Pétain, in contrast, interpreted it as a commitment to 'an offensive by limited action with definite objectives' – the emphasis no doubt being on the word 'limited'. Lloyd George, on the other hand, could live with the statement because it apparently guaranteed that the British would not be attacking alone. Satisfied, he told the conference that he made no pretence to be a strategist and was therefore leaving the British Army free to attack where and when Haig thought best. The French, he argued, should treat their commanders in the same way. Haig was delighted with the reformed Prime Minister: 'In fact I have quite forgiven him his misdeed up to date in return for the very generous words he said yesterday about the British Forces in France and the way in which he went for the French Government and insisted on *vigorous action*. He did well.' Finally, Haig interpreted the agreement as an approval of the Flanders plans. In his mind, the opportunity to 'exploit . . . to the fullest extent possible' would come sooner rather than later. He left the conference with high hopes, pleased with the way the British and French 'were united in the determination to act vigorously, and carry on the war "jusqu' au bout"'.[7]

Lloyd George followed Haig back to GHQ, there to apply more soft soap. 'He seemed quite converted in his views of the British Army, was loud in its praises, and heartily congratulated me on the success of my operations,' Haig told his wife. 'We have been getting on very well indeed . . . he is a reformed character.' Though Haig was to a certain extent drawn in by the Welshman's charm, he was wise enough to realise that Lloyd George 'has changed solely because the Army has been successful, and he must keep in with successful people'.[8]

There was, however, an important qualifier to Lloyd George's support. On 14 May, Robertson told Haig that the

Prime Minister desires me to remind you of War Cabinet's intentions to support your policy . . . but on the express condition that the French also play their full part . . . He is anxious that you should clearly realise this . . . because Cabinet could never agree to our incurring heavy losses with comparatively small gains, which would obviously be the result unless French co-operate wholeheartedly.

Given Lloyd George's capacity for deviousness, it is possible that his support for Haig was just a front. In other words, he may have felt safe giving his approval to the Flanders operation, feeling as he did that it would never come off because the required French contribution would never materialise. (He had, after all, told Pétain that he was 'certain that for some reason or other you won't fight'.) That possibility aside, the letter from Robertson left Haig in a dilemma. No one (not even Pétain) had any idea what the French would do. It was therefore a rather desperate Haig who assured Robertson on 16 May that, in his opinion, 'the French Armies will not fail to maintain the degree of offensive activity promised by the French Government at the recent Paris Conference'. Despite repeatedly complaining that the French could not be trusted, Haig was now asking the War Cabinet to have complete faith in the flimsiest of promises.[9]

In other respects also, Haig painted a roseate picture. In the letter to Robertson, he explained that the offensive would be divided into two phases. The first would aim at capturing Messines–Wytschaete Ridge in 'a few days' in order to gain the high ground and protect the right flank. The second phase, in which the objective was to clear the coast, would 'not be carried out unless the situation is sufficiently favourable'. In response to War Cabinet fears that a possible Russian collapse would allow the Germans to transfer troops westward and thus thwart Haig's plan, he wrote:

It is very unlikely that the Russian situation will develop with sufficient rapidity to enable the enemy to mass forces large enough to render it useless to enter on the execution of the first phase, but if he should succeed in doing so, it will be within my power up to the last moment to abandon the intended attack.

The optimism conveyed to the War Cabinet was not insincere. As he indicated to his wife, Haig did actually believe that 'even if Russia

. . . [makes] a separate peace, that would not make a really serious difference to the rest of the Allies, because the situation of Germany seems already very desperate'. Charteris had again told him, on 10 May, that Germany was racked by food riots and mutinies among the troops. All of this demonstrated that Haig's step-by-step approach was the only sensible option. 'My arrangements commit me to no undue risks, and can be modified to meet any developments in the situation.' In the meantime, it was important to maintain the pressure, in order to 'prevent the initiative passing to the enemy'.[10]

On 18 May, Pétain visited GHQ in order to discuss the offensive. Haig went straight to the point: 'Did the French intend to play their full part as promised at the Paris Conference? Could I rely on his wholehearted cooperation?' Since Haig was desperately eager for an affirmative answer, Pétain had no difficulty convincing him that 'the French Army would fight and would support the British in every possible way'. He revealed plans for four attacks of considerable scale which would draw off German reserves. All doubts about French sincerity quickly dissolved; Pétain was 'businesslike, knowledgeable and brief of speech. The latter is, I find, a rare quality in Frenchmen!' Two days later, Pétain revealed to Wilson that he considered Haig's plan 'impossible' given the limited assistance the French could provide.[11]

Events (as far as Haig was concerned) seemed to be proceeding smoothly when dark clouds suddenly formed. On 26 May, Robertson informed Haig that the 'Prime Minister told us that the time has now arrived when we must face the fact that we could not expect to get any large number of men in the future but only scraps'. More details were supplied by Derby on 27 May. Lloyd George had told the War Cabinet that 'as far as men were concerned we were down to bedrock'. He again put forward the idea of reducing divisions from twelve battalions to nine, and

> further added that we must very much limit our attacks and wait till the Americans came in. In other words we are to do exactly what he hoped me to tell the French they were *not* to do . . . the Government is really scared at the last strike – and with the general condition of the country – and really I sympathize with them. The state of affairs is very bad and there is no doubt the Russian revolution has created an unrest which is revolutionary and dangerous.

Derby concluded by warning Haig that 'it is more than probable your shortage of men may be very large by the end of July'.[12]

Haig, replying to Robertson, suggested that the Prime Minister needed to be reminded of the opportunities which had been squandered in the past because the British Army had not been kept up to strength. None of those opportunities, he emphasised, had been as promising as present ones. Responding to Lloyd George's renewed enthusiasm for 'knocking out the props' by attacking Germany's allies, Haig stressed that, 'Victory on the Western Front means victory everywhere and a lasting peace.' Nor was he in any doubt that the British could win on their own. 'Indeed our Army is the only one with the heart and stamina to do so!' It was, however, 'sad to see the British government failing at the XII hour'.[13]

Meanwhile, depressing news trickled in from another source. On 2 June, Major Lytton told Haig about 'a feeling of despondency' in France:

> people say their losses have been very great, and that the last French attack was very badly managed, and, in fact, a certain number of Frenchmen are wondering whether the war has lasted long enough. There have been strikes recently, and some of the soldiers on leave sided with the women strikers.

On the same day, General Debeney told Haig that the French Army was 'in a bad state of discipline'. French soldiers were angry about long-delayed furloughs. In order to stem the discontent, many soldiers had been granted leave, which meant that the attack scheduled for 10 June would have to be postponed for four weeks. On 7 June, Pétain was more explicit: 'two French Divisions had refused to go and relieve two Divisions in the front line . . . Some were tried and were shot . . . The situation in the French Army was serious but is now more satisfactory.' The situation, Haig admitted, 'causes Pétain grave concern'. Little did Haig know how grave. French morale, severely tested by the enormous losses of 1915 and 1916, was shattered by the Nivelle offensive, which promised much but delivered nothing new. After 19 May, strikes – usually taking the form of a refusal to enter the battle zone – were occurring on a daily basis. The influence of the Russian Revolution was readily apparent and extremely worrying. By mid-June more than half the French divisions were affected, with few of the remaining being anything near reliable. Though Haig, on various occasions, heard rumours of the French troubles, he was never given the true picture.[14]

Had he been able to take a reasoned view, Haig would have realised that the logic of his offensive had disappeared. His plans had always depended upon significant French support *and* adequate numbers of drafts from Britain. It was now clear that neither of these prerequisites would be satisfied. Haig, however, remained unaffected; he had no doubts that the war could be won by the British before the end of the year. When Churchill, visiting GHQ on 2 June, 'spoke about aiming at reaching a decision in August, 1918', Haig dismissed this as preposterous. 'Churchill no doubt has great brainpower, but his mind is quite unbalanced.'[15]

Further evidence of Haig's extraordinary sanguinity can be found in the memo to his Army commanders issued on the eve of the Messines attack. 'I feel justified in stating', he wrote, 'that the power of endurance of the German people is being strained to such a degree as to make it possible that the breaking point may be reached this year.' Furthermore, 'we are now justified in believing that one great victory, equal to those already gained, may turn the scales finally'. The Army commanders were urged to make their men aware 'how far on the road to victory the splendid efforts already made have brought us and how hopeful a careful and unbiased examination of the evidence shows the present situation to be'. The memo was a virtual carbon copy of those issued before and during the Somme offensive. It had as little justification in June 1917 as a year earlier. This was not optimism, it was delusion.[16]

The first phase of the Flanders operation, the attack on the Messines –Wytschaete Ridge, was assigned to Plumer's Second Army. Though Haig was not particularly fond of Plumer (animosities dated back to the War Office period), he did recognise that his controlled, careful and methodical style was well suited to the task at Messines, which was basically a siege operation. As it turned out, the first day of the battle (7 June) went exactly according to Plumer's plans. An extensive bombardment first softened the enemy's resistance. Then, a crushing blow was delivered when nineteen mines (containing nearly a million pounds of explosive) were detonated under the German trenches. The infantry were able to reach the first objective within thirty-five minutes, and the final by nightfall. In the week that followed, however, the fighting disintegrated into the pattern of previous battles, with British casualties nearly equalling German. The enemy (whose morale was supposed to have been destroyed) was still able to mount fearsomely effective counter-attacks. It was to Haig's advantage that the success of the first day obliterated this unpleasant evidence.

The Messines success was convenient ammunition to use against those who questioned the wisdom of Haig's grand plan. First to do so was, significantly, Robertson. While visiting on 9 June, Wully mentioned in the nicest possible way that

> He wished me to realise the difficult situation in which the country would be if I carried out large and costly attacks without full cooperation by the French. When autumn came round, Britain would then be without an Army! On the other hand it is possible that Austria would make peace, if harassed enough. Would it not be a good plan, therefore, to support Italy with guns?

Haig sensed the influence of Lloyd George. 'Altogether, I thought Robertson's views unsound. I told him that I thought the German was now nearly at his last resources' which indicated 'only *one sound* plan to follow, viz., *without delay*' to

1. Send to France every possible man.
2. "   "   "   "   " aeroplane.
3. "   "   "   "   " gun.

On the following morning, Haig noted how 'A night's reflection and Duncan's words of thanksgiving for our recent victory seemed to have had a good effect' on Robertson, who appeared 'less pessimistic and seemed to realise that the German Army was in reduced circumstances'. Pressing home the advantage, Haig 'again urged the need for increased activity by the Allies *all round*. There must be no thought of staying our hand until America puts an Army in the field next year.'[17]

Robertson was troubled by the rampant optimism of GHQ, which only made his job more difficult. On 12 June, Haig submitted his 'Appreciation of the Military Situation, Present Situation and Future Plans' which repeated the standard arguments in favour of the Flanders offensive. Though Robertson agreed with the basic premises, he objected to the appendix, wherein 'evidence' purported to show that German reserves were nearly depleted. The CIGS, whose support for the Flanders operation was at best tenuous, certainly never believed that the Germans were ripe for a knockout blow, and felt that it was suicidal to justify the operation on this basis. This was especially true since MacDonogh, the director of Military Intelligence at the War Office, had recently come to decidedly less optimistic conclusions on the condition of the German Army than those included in the 12 June report. Wully wisely suggested to Haig that, 'It would be very regrettable at this juncture if different estimates of enemy resources were presented to the War Cabinet.'[18]

Robertson, being on the spot, was heedful of the growing opposition to the Flanders offensive within the War Cabinet. Haig, buoyed by the success of the Messines operation and the daily diet of pap from Charteris, could not understand how anyone could question his wisdom. Aware of the effect which preposterous predictions of dramatic successes would have upon the politicians, Robertson tried to counsel circumspection on the eve of Haig's trip to London in mid-June. Haig was to attend a meeting at which a proposal by Lloyd George to send twelve divisions and 300 heavy guns to Italy was to be discussed. Robertson, adamantly opposed to the plan ('They will never go while I am CIGS'), gave the following astute advice: 'don't argue that you can finish the war this year, or that the German is already beaten. Argue that your plan is the best plan – as it is – that no other would even be *safe* let alone decisive, and then leave them to reject your advice and mine. They dare not do that.' Referring to political subtleties for which Haig had little understanding, Robertson concluded: 'We have got to remember . . . that the government carry the chief responsibility, and that in a war of this kind many things besides the actual Army must be considered.'[19]

Haig crossed to England on 17 June, seeing on the way Admiral Bacon who was 'wholeheartedly with us'. The first meeting with ministers occurred two days later. Haig recorded how 'The members of the War Cabinet asked me numerous questions, all tending to show that each of them was more pessimistic than the other.' Lloyd George 'seemed to believe the decisive moment of the war would be 1918' and therefore argued that it was necessary to 'husband our forces and do little or nothing, except support Italy with guns and gunners'. Annoyed, Haig quickly forgot Robertson's advice:

I strongly asserted that Germany was nearer her end than they seemed to think, that *now* was the favourable moment for pressing her and that everything possible should be done to take advantage of it by concentrating on the Western Front *all* available resources. I stated that Germany was within six months of total exhaustion of her available manpower, *if the fighting continues at its present intensity*. To do this more men and guns were necessary.

Lloyd George could not help being impressed at Haig's 'dramatic use of both his hands to demonstrate how he proposed to sweep up the enemy – first the right hand brushing along the surface irresistibly, and then . . . the left, his outer finger ultimately touching the German frontier'. Charteris, on the other hand, was astounded at the way Haig had gone 'rather further than the paper I wrote'. On the following day, the arguments continued and 'a most serious and startling situation was disclosed':

Admiral Jellicoe . . . stated that owing to the great shortage of shipping due to German submarines, it would be impossible for Great Britain to continue the war in 1918. This was a bombshell for the Cabinet and all present . . . Jellicoe's words were 'there is no good discussing plans for next Spring – We cannot go on'.

Haig admitted that 'No one present shared Jellicoe's view.' He obviously sensed, however, that his own case had received an unexpected boost.[20]

The battles in the War Cabinet continued over the next few days. On the 21st, Lloyd George, in what Haig called 'a regular lawyer's effort to make black appear white!', expressed doubts about the relative strengths of the British and German forces as contained in the GHQ report. Haig answered 'that war could not be won by arithmetic and that the British Army being in touch with the enemy was able to realise how much the latter's moral [sic] had decreased'. He agreed 'that we ought not to push in attacks that had not a reasonable chance of success' and assured ministers that he 'had no intention of entering into a tremendous offensive involving heavy losses'. Robertson, wishing to present a united front, added that he did 'not advocate spending our last man and last round of ammunition in an attempt to reach the coast if the opposition we encounter shows that the attempt will entail disproportionate loss'. When Lloyd George countered by stating that he had 'grave misgivings' about the advice given by the GHQ staff, Haig agreed to spend the weekend reviewing the material he had submitted to the War Cabinet.[21]

A second look did not yield a second opinion. 'Further investigation of the problem', Haig argued on the 25th, 'has confirmed me as strongly as ever' that 'there is a marked and unmistakeable fall in the moral [sic] of the German troops.' When pressed, an uneasy Robertson supported Haig. Lloyd George, lacking the strength to over-ride both men, tried to be as non-committal as possible, concluding that Haig's plan 'was the only thing to do'. Haig was instructed to proceed with his preparations for another two weeks, at which time a meeting with the French would take place in order to determine what they could contribute, Haig had received the Prime Minister's acquiescence, but by no means his support.[22]

July was spent anxiously preparing for the offensive which Haig expected to be the crowning achievement of his career. His work was repeatedly interrupted by visitors eager to feel themselves in the thick of the action, among them the King and Queen. The latter was the 'first lady to have a meal at my H.Qrs. since the war began'. (Whether this was an expression of disappointment or satisfaction is not clear.) Though generally pleased with the visit, Haig was disappointed when, during a discussion of the manpower shortage, the King 'spoke about the need for building ships and submarines, agriculture, etc., etc.' Haig concluded that 'he really did not grasp the problem of *beating the enemy*'.[23]

Later in the month Haig was 'quite delighted' when Lady Haig announced that she was expecting a third child. 'How proud you must feel that you are *doing your duty* at this time by having a baby and thereby setting a good example to all other females!.' He assured her that, 'Whether a boy or a girl I shall be so proud that *you* have done your duty like a dear good wife as you have always been to me. In any case I hope you will not worry your dear little head over having "a boy".' The subject of duty was a frequent topic in his letters. 'Your *first duty* is to your husband,' he wrote in January 1917. 'Be a good wife, and bring up the children, and make our home happy and bright.' During the course of their marriage, she became unreasonably obsessed about matrimonial obligations, worrying, for instance, that she had failed him because she had not already given him a son. As the devoted wife of a great man, she perceived her function as being to serve him, an arrangement which virtually ruled out any consideration of her own needs. Thus, she often apologised when she complained about the war, because she did not feel it was right that he should have to concern himself with her petty anxieties.[24]

Because she lived through her husband, she found being away from him for long periods of time intolerable. 'I often feel so forgotten and left out,' she confided, significantly, to Fletcher. 'I have since the outbreak of the war lived this beastly lonely life because I realised for Douglas's sake I should avoid any talk, also it is necessary too for me to keep clear of any intrigue!!!!!!!!' In response to her fears that she was a failure, he would reassure her that she was a perfect wife, at the same time defining his conception of perfection:

I am proud to think that you are not one of those *platform* females who lecture and advertise themselves! My darling, believe me, that you do your duty far more effectively, and more to my liking, by going about your daily life in an unassuming way, doing a kind act here, and speaking a friendly word there.

For Haig, his wife's most important function was to listen sympathetically to his complaints and confidentialities as Henrietta had earlier done. His letters to her were a way of releasing the tensions of war; the more stress he felt, the longer and more detailed were his letters. There is no doubt that she performed her role to perfection, but there is also no doubt that this role, and the restraints it imposed, caused her a great deal of strain.[25]

As the date for the great offensive approached, uncertainties regarding French intentions remained. On 28 June, the normally Francophile Wilson warned of the serious 'state of indiscipline' in the French ranks, news confirmed a few days later by General Anthoine who refused to make any promises regarding when the French would attack. Though Haig found Anthoine 'most anxious to help . . . he seemed terribly afraid of the lack of determination to fight on the part of his men'.[26]

Wilson thought that 'the only way to save France' was for the British to remain constantly on the offensive. Though it was not intended to be such, Haig took this as support for his plans. Thus, in contrast to Lloyd George, his determination to fight increased in proportion to the worsening news from the French camp. There is no doubt that he accepted this news at face value. When Poincaré promised that the French Army would 'continue to press the enemy to the utmost extent possible', Haig commented: 'this does not mean very much really'. He was more impressed with Pétain who was 'able to look at the situation in the face, and does not . . . see it as he would like it to be!' Pétain obviously sensed that depressing news would only increase Haig's determination to fight. But his awareness of the condition of the French Army placed Haig in a difficult position. Lloyd George had repeatedly stated that approval of the offensive was contingent upon French participation, it was therefore essential that Haig withhold the information from Poincaré and Pétain. Deception, though inexcusable, was in this case understandable, especially in light of the distrust which had arisen since Calais.[27]

As the weeks passed, British ministers continued to prevaricate. On 18 July, Robertson revealed that 'no official approval of your plans have been given'. Lloyd George was still pushing the Italian venture. Though the rest of the War Cabinet favoured going ahead with Haig's plan, all expressed 'the fear that you might endeavour to push on further than you were justified' and wanted prior agreement on 'how many losses we ought to incur before stopping'. On the 21st, Lloyd George told Robertson that he wanted Haig to promise, as Nivelle had done, to terminate the attack if success was not apparent within 'one or two days'. Finally, on the 25th, Robertson informed Haig that the

> War Cabinet authorises me to inform you that having approved your plans being executed you may depend on their whole-hearted support and that if and when they decide again to reconsider the situation they will obtain your views before arriving at any decision as to cessation of operations.

It was not a document calculated to inspire confidence.[28]

Haig found the lack of support intolerable. 'This is not the time to have dishonest men at the head of affairs,' he complained to his wife. 'Lloyd George is not to be trusted, the sooner he goes and we get another better man, the better it will be for the country.' In a letter to Derby, Haig protested about the lack of 'some practical indications on the part of the War Cabinet that they have confidence in my plan and mean to do their utmost to help me to achieve success'. What bothered him most was how different this was 'to the whole-hearted, almost unthinking support given by our Government to the Frenchman (Nivelle) last January'. He wondered whether 'the Government is really *determined* to concentrate all possible resources at this the decisive point, at this the decisive moment!' Derby sympathised, but Haig felt hardly more secure. The War Minister, he remarked, 'seems quite unable to act up to his appearance! He looks so strong and thoroughly British, yet is really feeble.'[29]

As the War Cabinet grew more uneasy about the offensive, Haig grew more certain of its success. As usual, Charteris aided the cause with ever more impressive data on the enemy's demoralised state. To bolster Haig's confidence, he concluded, from evidence of troop movements, that 'the enemy is in ignorance of our preparations'. In contrast, a junior staff officer was of the opinion that, after Messines, 'the Germans can have had little difficulty in sizing up the intentions of D.H.'. The latter, and not Charteris, was in fact correct; during June and July the Germans were busily preparing pill-boxes in the Passchendaele sector, from which they would eventually be able to gun down Tommies in their thousands. But by this time Haig's ears were open only to what he wanted to hear. Charteris's pronouncements enabled him to conclude that 'the German faith in the submarine must soon be abandoned entirely. Confidence in the invincibility of the German armies has already been so severely shaken that it cannot survive many fresh defeats. Any hope of Russian inaction has now been dispelled.' Charteris's reports and a visit to the fighting front would, Haig decided, convince 'even the most doubting that the German is on the down grade and well-nigh beaten'. This was probably true, but not in the sense that Haig meant. GHQ had become Cloud Cuckooland; in this environment delusions grew like weeds.[30]

Unlike Haig, Lloyd George had to live in the real world. He had to base his decision upon past performances and political factors which Haig conveniently ignored. Though his doubts were justified, he could do little about them – hence the vacillation. His difficulties in arguing against the Flanders offensive are similar to those experienced by Haig's critics even today. He had always to contend with the very obvious fact that he was an 'amateur strategist' and Haig an expert. His problems were compounded by the lack of obvious alternatives to Haig's way. The 'indirect approach' – the idea of 'knocking the props' from under Germany – was weakened by the failures at Gallipoli and

Salonika, and the very real evidence that it was not Turkey, Austria and Bulgaria who were propping up Germany, but vice versa. It was therefore almost impossible to refute Haig's contention that victory could only be gained by defeating the Germans on the Western Front.

The next question was: did the British have to fight in Flanders? Probably not, but it was difficult to counter the myriad justifications which Haig had marshalled in favour of doing so. His plan was a castle fortified by concentric walls of reasoning. His critics (then and now) might clamber over, or destroy, one wall, only to come up against another of greater height and breadth. The offensive, Haig argued, might possibly win the war. If it did not, it might clear the Belgian coast and thus relieve the threat of German submarines. Both these walls are relatively easy to surmount. Such bold objectives were far-fetched even with French help; without it, they were incredible.

The next wall is massive. Haig argued that if his offensive achieved nothing else, it would at least wear down the enemy and prepare the way for a decisive blow the following year, in the process giving the French time to recover. The latter justification was his favourite after the war. He had, he stressed, been forced to attack and keep attacking in order to prevent the Germans from finishing off the weakened French. This wall of reasoning might be surmounted by arguing that the mud of Flanders was not the place to wear down the Germans or relieve the French. But one can predict Haig's reaction: with a condescending smile he would have replied, 'Perhaps, but if the plan also offers a reasonable prospect of clearing the coast and defeating the Germans, is it not sensible regardless?' Thus the critic would once again find himself confronted by the outer walls. The entire fortress was further strengthened by Haig's repeated assurances that he would call off the offensive if it was too costly or achieved too little. This was a clever tactic. Though he spoke repeatedly of glorious advances, unlike Nivelle, he only *promised* a wearing out fight. Such a campaign merely required that the British maintain parity with the Germans in casualties. It would also take months before a proper judgement on whether the Germans were indeed being worn down could be reached.

According to Major-General John Davidson, the DMO at GHQ, in preparing for the Flanders offensive, 'Haig had repeated many times that our intention was to wear down the enemy, but at the same time have an objective'. These two aims could be (and were) contradictory.

In a memo of 14 February, Rawlinson and Plumer proposed that the first day's advance be limited to the German second line one mile distant. The memo also underlined the absolute necessity of capturing the Gheluvelt Plateau before any further advance could proceed. In other words, the push towards the coastal ports would be delayed until the high ground was properly secured and enemy reserves sufficiently depleted. It had originally been intended that these plans would be implemented by Rawlinson and Plumer, both of whom favoured a slow step-by-step approach. Haig, always contemptuous of such an approach, was even less favourably inclined towards it at this stage of the war than at any time in the past. He therefore decided to replace Rawlinson's Fourth Army with Gough's Fifth Army. Gough – by no coincidence a cavalryman and a 'thruster' – was assigned the leading part in the operation, i.e. the push to the coast. (Rawlinson, meanwhile, took over the sector from Nieuport to the sea, previously held by the French XXXVI Corps.) Gough took over his new front on 10 June and almost immediately revised the plans mentioned above, expanding the first day's objectives to include the fourth line and, 'if possible . . . the main ridge at Broodseinde, with a view to exploitation'. Gough also objected to the preliminary operation to capture Gheluvelt, on the grounds that 'it would only throw the troops employed into a very pronounced salient, and expose them to the concentrated fury of all the German artillery'. Haig, receptive to the views of a fellow cavalryman, approved the change.[31]

Davidson, however, felt 'that there was ambiguity as to what was meant by step-by-step attacks with limited objectives, and . . . that the time was not yet ripe for an "all-out" assault'. He was worried that Gough's plans for a rapid penetration would result in some units advancing much further than others, giving rise to a 'ragged, irregular front' difficult to defend against counter attack. A much better idea would be to 'recognize that we were undertaking siege operations, that our first task was to blast a breach in the defences; when that had been satisfactorily achieved and the enemy sufficiently shaken, then we could exploit, but not before'. Gough, of course, disagreed with Davidson's objections. But what is surprising is that Plumer sided with Gough. 'Do you think', Plumer told Davidson, 'that after making the vast preparation for attack on this position over a long period of months, and after sitting in the salient all this time, I am going to agree to limiting the progress of my troops at the outset on the first day? I say definitely *no*.' Thus, 'two Army commanders very different in temperament, Plumer cautious and deliberate, Gough bold and quick-witted . . . took more or less the same view'. Since Haig was himself partial to that view, he did not overrule the two men.[32]

But ambiguity remained, partially because, as Gough described: 'there were not enough discussions, between the H.Q. staff and the Army Commanders concerned, – when we could sit around a table with all the maps before one, and really thrash out the problems. Haig's conferences were too big and too formal.' Gough's statement is an indicator of serious faults in Haig's method of command. At Camberley, and over a thirty-year career, he learned that the authority of the senior commander was supposed to be supreme. Subordinates were not to question his wisdom, nor was he to seek advice from them. But it must be remembered that he also favoured decentralised leadership. In other words, he provided the general strategical outline and left it to subordinate commanders to formulate the tactics suitable to their sector. The system, though perhaps wise in theory, could only work in an atmosphere of free and open discussion. This, as Gough admitted, did not exist. As a result, consistency was sadly absent; division and battalion commanders sometimes pursued tactics which worked at cross purposes to those of their colleagues in the vicinity. Worse still, local conditions occasionally did not suit the general strategy dictated by Haig. Since subordinates were not encouraged to express reservations, these anomalies were not corrected. This 'command vacuum' was exacerbated by the ineffective manner in which Haig's orders were communicated. According to Morton:

> what [Haig] was thinking about [concerning] the war as it stood on any particular day, no one, not even his Chief of Staff, could fully make out. He gave his orders quick enough, but never explained them. Moreover, men say he was tongue-tied. If it came to public speaking that was abundantly true. He was anyway a 'silent' man. But such silence was babbling compared with what he said when he gave an oral . . . order. You had to learn a sort of verbal shorthand, made up of a series of grunts and gestures.

Elaborating, Morton recalled one particular briefing which

> consisted of D.H. with a pointer in front of a large scale map . . . pointing at various spots and making grunting noises with a few

334

words interspersed. 'Never believed' . . . 'Petrol' . . . 'Bridge gone' . . . 'When Cavalry?' and so on. . . . I am sure that D.H. felt he had given me a long and lucid lecture on the whole affair.

The ramifications of the 'command vacuum' in the case of Passchendaele were disastrous. According to Davidson, the British 'entered the battle . . . with two objectives, or rather a double objective, to wear out and to penetrate, with the emphasis on the latter'. 'In this mixture of motives lay grave disadvantages.'[33]

The attack, after repeated delays, finally began on 31 July. By the end of the day, Davidson had been proved right. Gough's objectives were not reached; 'the line occupied was ragged'. 'The artillery did not know the exact line which had been gained', and could not therefore pour in accurate protective fire. Heavy German counter-attacks began at midday. Davidson admitted that the resultant 'physical hardship and mental strain on the troops was severe'. Haig saw a different picture. He told his wife that 'on the whole it was a *most successful* day's work and such a good beginning promises well for the future'.[34]

The future in fact promised very little. The most significant feature of that first day was the heavy rain, the effects of which Haig described:

The low-lying clayey soil, torn by shells and sodden by rain, turned to a succession of vast muddy pools. The valleys of the choked and overflowing streams were speedily transformed into long stretches of bog, impassable except for a few well-defined tracks, which became marks for the enemy's artillery. To leave these tracks was to risk death by drowning.

Thirty-three of the fifty-two tanks employed had to be ditched in the mud. The rain did not abate in the days that followed. By the 4th, Haig had to write dejectedly that 'In view of the bad weather and wet ground, General Gough has cancelled orders which he issued for the continuance of the attack.' The offensive that was supposed to clear the Belgian coast and end the war became a failure as soon as the first drops began to fall. The rain, wrote Charteris, 'has killed the attack. Every day's delay tells against us. We lose, hour by hour, the advantage of attack. The Germans can reorganise and reinforce. We can do nothing but wait.'[35]

The decision to fight what was intended to be a mobile offensive in Flanders predetermined its failure. Movement in this war was strictly limited by the advantage of firepower over mobility. Haig limited it even further by choosing to attack in a duck's paradise, where the only device which could have increased his mobility – the tank – was useless. Admirers of Haig have defended him by arguing that the rain in the summer of 1917 was heavier than normal. Whilst this may have been the case, any rain would have been disastrous. In other words, Haig's plans required a drought of Ethiopian proportions to ensure success. Nor was it the rain alone which washed out this offensive. Haig aided the process by employing a bombardment ill-suited to terrain in which the water table was just below the surface. To ignore the effect which four weeks of heavy shelling would have on this low-lying land required a capacity for self-delusion which is beyond comprehension.

Despite the rain, the offensive continued and the casualties mounted. The attacks in August were even less successful than that of the first day. The great decisive blow had become a gruesome and clumsy wrestle in the mud. Attrition was now its only justification. Haig as much as admitted this when he reported to the War Cabinet, on 4 August, that 'the total of [enemy] casualties exceeds ours by as much as 100%'. But, in the same report, he also boasted of the ability of his army 'to drive the enemy from any position . . . without undue loss'. Though his letters increasingly emphasised the battle's effect upon German morale, he had by no means abandoned hope of a breakthrough. On 19 August, army commanders were assured that '*if we can keep up our effort*, the final victory may be won by December'. A few days later Haig told his wife, 'I *think* the Germans mean to put forward *definite* peace proposals soon.'[36]

Haig had no difficulty interpreting the news from the front opti-mistically. Early in the campaign, he remarked that though the rain 'will delay things very much . . . it may be all for the best as the enemy must be in almost worst conditions than our men who have had a great success'. Referring to the case of a cavalry officer who 'got into trouble through writing a very desponding letter to his wife which the censor opened', Haig confessed that he found this attitude perplexing, since 'cavalry commanders above all . . . should be hopeful!' The incident demonstrated 'how difficult it is even in the Army to make people realise how we are beating the Enemy, unless one is actually in the front where the battle is going on, and one can see the ground gained, state of enemy prisoners, etc.'. The unfortunate cavalry officer had been much closer to the front than Haig.[37]

Lady Haig was apparently not as sanguine as her husband. He found her worries perplexing: 'Why should *we* not have time left this year in which to beat the Germans before Winter? If our Government would only stir themselves it is to be done.' What he meant was: more men, more guns, and more ammunition. In fact, as Haig's friends at home warned, the government was unlikely to stir itself in this way. On 9 August, General Sir Robert Whigham (the Deputy CIGS) related how Lloyd George 'said openly . . . that he had known all along that this latest offensive was doomed to failure'. In a conference with Allied representatives, the Prime Minister had again suggested sending troops and guns to Italy. A few weeks later, Esher alerted Haig to the 'simple, almost childish ignorance of the facts' prevalent among the War Cabinet, and referred specifically to questions which Hankey had raised regarding Haig's optimistic reports. 'One does not hear quite such confident accounts from those nearer the front,' Hankey had written. Esher explained this attitude as 'hostility (based upon jealousy) to Charteris', and suggested that Haig should promote his Intelligence Officer to Major-General – 'just as a smack in the eye for those people at home'.[38]

In the letter quoted above, Whigham implored Haig to come to the aid of Robertson, who was having a 'real bad time' with Lloyd George. Confirming this, Wully explained that the problem was compounded by the ineffectual characters on the War Cabinet: 'Milner is a tired, dyspeptic old man. Curzon a gas-bag. Bonar Law equals Bonar Law. Smuts has good instinct but lacks knowledge.' All were 'afraid' of Lloyd George, and unlikely to mount a determined opposition to his Italian scheme. An alarmed Haig responded by urging Robertson to impress upon the War Cabinet that 'The only *sound* policy is . . . to support me *wholeheartedly* and concentrate all possible resources here. . . . In my opinion the war can only be won here in Flanders.' As usual, Haig based his certainty on intelligence reports which 'would convince even the most sceptical of the truth of what I write'. The despondency in London was caused by the 'pessimistic estimates' produced by MacDonogh. 'They do, I feel sure, much harm and cause many in authority to take a pessimistic outlook, when a contrary view, based on equally good information, would go far to help the nation on to victory.'[39]

Haig was becoming extremely suspicious of those who doubted him. 'I have been in the field for three years and know what I write about.' There was, he thought, something sinister behind the pessimism:

> Personally I feel we have every reason to be optimistic; and if the war were to end tomorrow, Great Britain would find herself not merely the greatest power in Europe, but in the World. The chief people to suffer would be the Socialists, who are trying to rule us all, at a time when the right minded of the Nation are so engaged in the country's battles that they (the Socialists) are left free to work their mischief.

Events in Russia had caused Haig to be especially concerned about the socialist menace. This unparalleled threat required, he felt, extraordinary vigilance. On 27 April, he remarked upon the case of the Prince of Wales who had been travelling around Paris 'under another name'. The Prince was 'quite right to move about and see people in a natural way . . . he should study human beings and move with the times. This was all the more necessary in view of the wave of revolutionary feelings which were now so noticeable in Europe against ruling dynasties.' According to Haig, the Church had an important role to play in this battle against revolutionary socialism. In a conversation with the Archbishop of York, Cosmo Gordon Lang, he suggested 'organising a great Imperial Church to which all honest citizens of the Empire could belong. In my opinion, Church and State must advance together, and hold together against those forces of revolution which threatened to destroy the state.' The war was being fought to protect the established order. Haig even advocated maintaining the Hohenzollerns in power after the Germans were defeated. Their removal would 'result in anarchy just as was the case in Russia'. 'It is impossible to foresee to what extent it might spread. Certainly to France, possibly to England!'[40]

Though Haig's fear of social and political change is understandable in a man of his background, what is interesting is the way in which he automatically equated opposition to himself with 'socialism'. The path of his reasoning is easy to trace. Socialists objected to the established order. He defended it. Therefore, socialists were *ipso facto* his enemies, and his enemies socialists. Early in the war, this suspicion pertained only to those obviously susceptible to 'revolutionary feelings': trade union leaders, lazy workers, etc. Later, a 'socialist' was defined as anyone who questioned him, including, significantly, Lloyd George.

Throughout August, Lloyd George searched for a way to kill the Flanders offensive but, lacking the necessary political support, was unable directly to overrule Haig. When promising news of Cadorna's latest venture against Austria reached him, the Prime Minister hit upon a way of controlling Haig indirectly. If, he speculated, the British were to send 300 guns (and possibly some divisions) to the Italians, Cadorna's efforts might achieve real success, and, as a valuable side-effect, Haig's offensive might be strangled. But, by the time the matter came to a head in early September, the Italian advance had stalled, and the gift of guns had been reduced to a token number from the French First Army. Nevertheless, when Haig heard of the plan, he rushed to London, protesting that since the French guns were on his front, any transfer would be deleterious to his efforts. (It was the principle rather than the actual issue which concerned him.) At a meeting on the 4th, Foch argued that the transfer was justified 'because the *political* effect of a success [in Italy] would be greater . . . than one in Flanders'. Haig of course did not agree. Lloyd George then took him aside and explained that 'We must not give the French the power of saying that *they wanted* to send 100 guns, but the British would not let them go.' Accepting this logic, Haig told the Prime Minister that, 'if we could possibly liberate 50 guns, it would be done'. He no doubt sensed an excellent opportunity to score points against Lloyd George by appearing reasonable. Three days later nearly 100 guns were miraculously found and Lloyd George landed in the awkward position of having to thank Haig for his flexibility and generosity toward the allies.[41]

Meanwhile, arguments concerning British strategy continued to rage. In a conversation with Kiggell on 13 September Winston Churchill (Minister of Munitions) had openly admitted that he and Lloyd George were 'doubtful about being able to beat the Germans on the Western Front'. Haig, though not surprised, was worried at the way in which Churchill 'can hardly help meddling in the larger questions of strategy and tactics'. He was dangerous 'because he can persuade Lloyd George to adopt and carry out the most idiotic policy'. Churchill, he suspected, had come over simply to spy for the Prime Minister.[42]

Robertson was usually Haig's first line of defence against the meddling of Lloyd George. But the relationship with Robertson, never comfortable, had of late become strained. Haig had never completely trusted Wully, whose humble background (he thought) made him susceptible to the crudest sort of ambition. When Robertson innocently asked permission to visit GHQ during the Battle of Messines, Haig considered the request 'tactless'. 'It is all for his own advertisement. No doubt he tells the War Cabinet that we here in France cannot get on without him!!!' Nor was Haig very pleased when, on 15 September, Robertson deigned to discuss tactics. The CIGS, worried about the meagre advances, suggested that 'the difficulty is the ground in Flanders'. Specifically,

> We would seem to be confronted with the problem that unless we use a great deal of artillery fire we cannot get on, and if we do use it the ground is destroyed . . . Therefore the problem to be solved is how to get forward without too much destruction of the ground.

This was the Passchendaele problem in a nutshell – a problem to which Haig, in order to continue the offensive, had to turn a blind eye. He, significantly, did not reply to the letter.[43]

The logic of Robertson's letter was demonstrated when the Second Army attacked the Gheluvelt Plateau on 20 September. Some weeks earlier, Haig had transferred the main effort from Gough to Plumer and had returned to the original idea of a step-by-step campaign aimed at securing the plateau. Plumer, the master of the set piece, assembled nearly 750 guns, a third of them heavy, and pulverised the area for three weeks. The attack was technically a success since its modest objectives (advances limited to one kilometre) were secured. But perhaps the most significant feature of the battle was the way in which all but one of thirty-four tanks were immobilised in the heavily blasted ground before they reached their first objective. The apparent impossibility of movement on the Flanders battle-front did not bother Haig, who was certain that the difficulties were temporary. Fresh evidence from Charteris convinced him that, due to the rapid demoralisation of the enemy, 'we shall be able to accomplish things *after* the next offensive, which we could not dare even to attempt now'.

Therefore, after a discussion with Admiral Bacon on 23 September, Haig decided that there was no reason to abandon plans for the naval action on the Belgian coast.[44]

Encouraged by the Gheluvelt 'success', Haig ordered Plumer to carry out a virtual carbon copy on 26 September. Similar results were achieved. In preparing for the next attack, scheduled for 4 October, Haig told his army commanders that 'the Enemy is tottering and . . . a good vigorous blow might lead to decisive results'. Another limited advance was achieved, but decisive results were not. Afterwards, Charteris noted in his diary, 'We are far enough on now to stop for the winter, and there is much to be said for that. Unless we get fine weather for all this month, there is now no chance of clearing the coast.' Senior commanders, he noted, 'though willing to go on, would welcome a stop'. Haig, of sterner stuff, told Gough and Plumer to keep pressing 'in order not to miss any chance of following up our success if the enemy were really demoralised'.[45]

While the battle raged in Flanders, news arrived of a German peace feeler made through the Spanish government. As it turned out, this was only a bit of mischief-making designed to split the Entente. Lloyd George nevertheless took the German 'offer' seriously. Alarmed at the recent inactivity of the Russians, Italians and French, he asked Haig on 26 September whether it was sensible for the British to continue fighting alone. Buoyed by his recent success, Haig had a confident and quick answer: 'We should go on striking as hard as possible with the object of clearing the Belgian coast.' Troops should not therefore be sent to any other theatre, nor should the British accede to French requests to take over more line. Though the Prime Minister declined to indicate his preferences, Haig remained suspicious, since 'one never knows what rascality he may not be plotting'.[46]

On the following day, Robertson speculated, in a letter to Haig, on what would happen if a Russian collapse freed German troops to fight elsewhere. 'Certain people here think it would be exceedingly difficult to bring about a decision on the Western Front.' They were thus 'frequently looking about for means of detaching some of the hostile powers'. 'It is not an easy business to see through the problem,' Robertson confessed.

My views are known to you. They have always been 'defensive' in all theatres but the West. But the difficulty is to *prove* the wisdom of this now that Russia is out. I confess I stick to it more because I see nothing better, and because my instinct prompts me to stick to it, than to any convincing argument by which I can support it. Germany may be much nearer to her staying power than available evidence shows, but on the other hand France and Italy are not much to depend upon and America will require a long time. Further it is argued that stagnation will destroy the Nation's determination.

To Haig, Robertson's doubts were nothing short of heresy. In a stern reply, he reminded him that 'Our troops are elated and confident; those on the enemy's side cannot but be depressed.' The ground already gained 'gives us considerable advantages and renders us less dependent on weather in following up our successes further'. It was patience, not another strategy, that was needed. As Duncan had promised a few days before: '*At the right time* the Lord [will] bring about a great victory . . . we must be able to endure and not be impatient.'[47]

Further evidence of Robertson's unreliability came on 3 October when 'a great bombshell arrived . . . from the CIGS stating that the British Government had "approved in principle" the British Army in France taking over more line from the French'. Haig was by this stage even less inclined to assist the Allies than he had been in the past. Their recent postponements and cancellations of attacks had prompted him to remark, on 29 September, 'What a wretched lot the majority of the French are!' According to Gemeau, French morale was 'now excellent'; but still they did not fight. Haig predicted that 'History will doubtless conclude that the French are not playing the game!' But what really annoyed him was the way in which the relief of the French had been settled on 25 September without consulting him, and neither Lloyd George nor Robertson had told him of the decision when they visited GHQ on the following day. Though he had come to expect this sort of behaviour from the Prime Minister, he was accustomed to better treatment from Robertson. The latter, Haig thought, 'comes very badly out of this'.[48]

The continually perplexing questions regarding French intentions and their effect upon British strategy prompted a memo from Haig to Robertson. He began by stating that

neither the French Government nor the military authorities will venture to call on their troops for any further great and sustained offensive effort, at any rate before it becomes evident that the enemy's strength has become definitely and finally broken. Though they are staunch in defence and will carry out useful local offensives against limited objectives, the French Armies would not respond to a call for more than that.

This statement conflicts with a March 1927 letter to Charteris in which Haig argued that he continued the Passchendaele offensive because

the possibility of the French Army breaking up in 1917 *compelled me to go on attacking*. It was impossible to change sooner from the Ypres front to Cambrai without Pétain coming to press me not to leave the Germans alone for a week, on account of the *awful* state of the French troops!

Leaving aside the fact that the diary mentions no such discussions with Pétain, the memo to Robertson proves conclusively that Haig was not overly worried about the state of French troops. They were after all, able to remain 'staunch in defence'. It is also unlikely that Pétain would have asked the British to relieve part of his line if at the same time he wanted Haig to keep attacking. Gemeau had likewise indicated that there was nothing seriously wrong with French morale. Whether or not this was actually true is less important than the fact that Haig believed it to be true. It is difficult to see the 1927 letter as anything other than an attempt by Haig to justify an action which, nine years later, seemed to many extremely ill-conceived.[49]

Haig did not continue the Flanders offensive because he was afraid for the safety of the French. He continued it because, as Charteris admitted, 'his studies had led him to the definite view that premature abandonment of a plan had been a most fruitful cause of failure'. Haig believed, even as late as 8 October, that it was still possible to end the war in 1917. Reiterating this point in the memo to Robertson, he argued that 'since the British Armies alone can be made capable of a great offensive effort it is beyond argument that everything should be done . . . to enable that effort to be made as strong as possible'. In other words, the War Cabinet should 'refuse to take over more line and . . . adhere resolutely to that refusal, even to the point of answering threats by threats if necessary'. Furthermore, Haig stressed, 'we must

. . . cut down our commitments in all other theatres to the minimum necessary to protect really vital interests'.[50]

Replying on 9 October, Robertson described Haig's memo as 'splendid', but added that

> I gather . . . that you are perhaps a little disappointed with me in the way I have stood up for correct principles, but you must let me do my job in my own way. I have never yet given in on important matters and never shall. In any case, you and I must stand solid together. I know we are both trying to do so.

It was a plaintive plea for understanding from a man who was 'sick of this d—d life'. Haig's memo in fact increased Robertson's troubles since the War Cabinet did not agree that it was 'splendid'. Ministers felt that it 'did not provide a convincing argument that we could inflict a decisive military defeat on Germany on the West front next year'. Lloyd George used this disapproval to push through a proposal calling for French and Wilson to study the strategic situation with a view to deciding on three alternatives. These were to continue the offensive on the Western Front, to go on the defensive until the Americans were organised or to 'knock out the German props'. Robertson, incensed at being side-stepped in this way, asked Haig if he should resign. Haig told him to withhold his resignation 'until your advice has been rejected'.[51]

Lloyd George hoped that French and Wilson would give their blessing to his latest scheme for a push against Turkey. In this sense, the plan backfired. Both men roundly rejected efforts other than on the Western Front, though French did recommend waiting for the Americans. Otherwise, the Prime Minister was provided with little more than anti-Haig propaganda. French exploited to the full the opportunity to release some of his pent-up hatred for Haig. Wilson's memo, though not as vitriolic, nevertheless included a particularly pithy criticism of Haig's strategy. 'It is no use', he wrote, 'throwing "decisive numbers at the decisive time at the decisive place" . . . if the decisive numbers do not exist, if the decisive hour has not struck or if the decisive place is ill-chosen.' Wilson also took the opportunity to blow his own trumpet when he recommended the creation of an 'Inter-allied Council' – a body which he probably wanted to head.[52]

Meanwhile, Haig continued to press the Germans in the vicinity of the Gheluvelt Plateau. The three earlier successes were not, however, repeated. Plumer's troops, pushed forth on 9 October, made almost no progress across impossibly muddy ground. It was, Charteris noted in his diary,

> the saddest day of the year. We did fairly well but only fairly well. It was not the enemy but mud that prevented us doing better. But there is now no chance of complete success this year . . . [Haig] was still trying to find some grounds for hope that we might still win through here this year, but there is none.

While Charteris's spirits sunk, Haig's remained buoyant. Oblivious to the failure, he concluded that 'we ought to have only the one thought now in our minds, namely *to attack*'. Thus, Plumer pushed forward again, with similarly depressing results. On the 13th, Haig adjusted his plans slightly, telling Gough and Plumer that 'our attack would only be launched when there is a fair prospect of fine weather. *When the ground is dry* no opposition which the enemy has put up has been able to stop our men.' The mindless bashing would continue.[53]

Haig's proponents have argued that he prolonged the offensive after 10 October because he did not want his troops to spend the winter on low-lying, muddy ground, dominated by German artillery on the Passchendaele Ridge. Leaving aside the fact that it was his gross miscalculation of tactical factors which landed his men in this unenviable position in the first place, it is plainly inaccurate to suggest that, after 10 October, his sole objective was to gain the high ground. Haig continued the offensive because he still believed that the Germans were on the brink of collapse, and that one great push would lead to that elusive breakthrough. His attitude is revealed by his violent objection to a statement made by MacDonogh around this time. In 'The Manpower and Internal Conditions of the Central Powers', MacDonogh argued:

> The moral [sic] of the troops in the field, though naturally shaken in sectors of great hostile activity, is on the whole good and gives no cause for anxiety to the German High Command. Any feeling of depression caused by Allied successes in the west is counterbalanced by the full certitude of superiority in the east.

On his copy, Haig surrounded this paragraph with large question marks. In his diary, he wrote:

> I cannot think why the War Office Intelligence Department gives such a wrong picture of the situation except that General McDonogh [sic] (D.M.I.) is a Roman Catholic and is (perhaps unconsciously) influenced by information which reaches him from tainted (i.e. Catholic) sources.

In a rejoinder submitted to Robertson, Haig cited 'reliable and accurate' information from Charteris which indicated not only that the Germans were down to their last reserves, but that those reserves were suffering from malnutrition and a significant depletion of morale. To the unbiased, it must have sounded like a broken record.[54]

On 24 October, six divisions of the 'demoralised' German Army blasted through the Italian lines at Caporetto, captured 250,000 prisoners and 3,000 guns, and drove the enemy back over sixty kilometres. Three days later, Robertson advised Haig that the 'Government have decided to despatch two Divisions to Italy as quickly as possible'. Haig, convinced that 'If the Italian Army is demoralised we can not spare enough troops to fight their battles for them', replied as follows: 'by going to Italy we lose the initiative which we have here – in fact we are playing the Germans game. The best way to help the Italians is to put all our strength into attacks against the German on the Western front.' The protests fell on deaf ears.[55]

The depletion of his force did not stop Haig from pressing on with the offensive. The Second and Fifth Armies slowly slithered their way towards Passchendaele village, capturing it on 6 November. This, Haig thought, was a 'very important success'.[56] In the course of fourteen weeks, the ridge had been miraculously transformed from a first objective to a glittering final prize. But it was certainly not a prize worthy of the 300,000 casualties required to secure it. Though German losses were admittedly at least as high, they lost only one-third as many officers. Nor does the popular claim that the offensive destroyed the morale of the German soldier hold much water. Such a claim ignores the effect which the battle had on the morale of the British. It could not have done much for Tommy's spirit to watch his comrades drowning in mud. Those who lived had to live with failure. Those who died, died in hell.

Before the final attack on Passchendaele, Haig attended a meeting in Paris convened to discuss Lloyd George's latest brainstorm, an 'Inter-Allied Supreme War Council'. Underneath the wrapping of 'allied unity' was another devious plan to undermine the authority of Haig and Robertson – a bedraggled but still formidable duo. Haig immediately condemned the council as a French ploy 'to retain control of operations, notwithstanding that their army has ceased to be the main factor'. In common with Pétain, he thought that such a scheme could only work if one Army was dominant, as in the case of the Central Powers. Haig conveyed his objections to Lloyd George on 4 November, but was told that the council was virtually a *fait accompli*. Foch had already been appointed chairman, with Wilson the British military representative.[57]

Haig was certain that the supreme council would 'prove very difficult to work satisfactorily'. In other words, he opposed the plan not because he divined Lloyd George's mischievous intent, but rather because of very real misgivings about what it would bring into being. He feared that the composition of the council would vary with inevitable changes in Allied governments and this would lead to inconsistencies, dangerous in wartime. Even more important, 'the conflicting interests of States and . . . the failure of some Governments to realise that in the conduct of war the common good is the highest interest' would mean that 'if agreement is reached at all . . . it will be reached only by compromise – and the danger of action in war based on compromise is evident'. These were all legitimate complaints. But the existing system (if that state of anarchy can be so called) was surely no better, if not much worse. Haig had himself repeatedly complained about the lack of cooperation between the Allies. It is therefore curious (and hardly praiseworthy) that he automatically opposed any scheme to promote Allied unity.[58]

During their meeting in Paris, Lloyd George complained to Haig about Press attacks on him, which were, he thought, 'inspired by the military'. He threatened to 'make a speech and tell the public what courses he had proposed and how, if he had his way, the military situation would have been much better to-day, but that the Military

Advisers had prevented him from carrying out his intentions!' Haig thought that Lloyd George was

> like our German enemy who, whenever he proposes to do something extra frightful, first of all complains that the British or French have committed the enormity which he is meditating. L.G. is feeling that his position as P.M. is shaky and means to try and vindicate his conduct of the war in the eye of the public and try and put the people against the soldiers. In fact, to pose as the saviour of his country, who has been hampered by bad advice given by the General Staff!

According to Haig, the Prime Minister had in fact 'never taken the soldier's advice, namely, to *concentrate all our resources* on the Western Front'. Ironically, at about the same time that Lloyd George was complaining about pro-Haig newspapers, Haig was protesting about 'the criticism of the military by Lloyd George's slavish press'. Both the pot and the kettle were black.[59]

Lloyd George in fact carried out his threat to 'make a speech' on 11 November at the launching of the Supreme War Council. The speech was mainly intended to educate the British public about the need for Allied unity. Comparisons were made between the massive achievements of the unified Central Powers and the disappointments of the fragmented Entente. 'Personally I had made up my mind that, unless some change were effected, I could no longer remain responsible for a war direction doomed to disaster for lack of unity.' Lloyd George did not waste the chance to make a more direct dig at Haig. Referring to the so-called 'victories' on the Western Front, he reflected how 'the appalling casualty list' sometimes made him wish 'it had not been necessary to win so many'.[60]

The speech was deeply embarrassing to Cabinet ministers. Carson publicly repudiated it while Derby quickly assured Haig of 'my entire confidence in you'. Haig was, however, unaffected. 'Whatever happens [it] won't make me modify the way in which I carry out my duties here.' The reaction of Derby and Carson was proof that 'L.G. has put the bulk of right thinking people against him'. His government would therefore not last another six weeks – 'the country will never forgive him'. Haig was nevertheless concerned that the speech would 'go a long way towards encouraging the Germans to continue the war realising as they must do . . . that our Government is despondent and doubtful about winning'.[61]

It was impossible for Haig to accept that the opposition of Lloyd George was inspired by anything other than gross political opportunism. 'The fellow's own position is very shaky', he explained to his wife, 'and so he would like to make the soldiers the scapegoat in the hope of remaining on in power for a little time longer.' It would be impossible for Britain to win 'this great struggle of right against wrong with such a dishonest fellow as Prime Minister'. What Haig could not understand was how a man of such 'rascality' could be popular. His confusion arose from the fact that both he and Lloyd George – two very different individuals – commanded widespread public support. Unable to solve this conundrum, Haig assumed that one day the country would come to its collective senses and cast out the rascal. Though Haig was of course wrong on this count, his political analysis was not always faulty. He did, for instance, realise that Lloyd George 'is afraid of me with the Army at my back, and he would like to discredit me first of all and then little by little break the Army into factions'. He was able to take this threat in his stride: 'Personally I have a tranquil mind. I am doing my best and if there is anyone else whom the Government think will do this work better, let them appoint him in my place. For I have done my duty and have an easy conscience.'[62]

The furore over Lloyd George's speech was followed closely by news of Plumer's transfer to the Italian front, along with five more divisions and heavy artillery. On 15 November, Haig warned Robertson of the effect this move would have. 'Any further offensive on the Flanders front must be at once discontinued,' he wrote – a clear indication that he had not intended the offensive to end with the capture of Passchendaele. Furthermore, the Germans, let off the hook in Flanders, would immediately attack one of the Allies, though how they would do so if they were 'morally exhausted' was not explained. Looking further into the future, Haig warned that the movement of troops would deprive the rest of his Army of essential relief and training, while at the same time giving the Germans the 'time and opportunity to recuperate'. This would 'render impossible any serious offensive on this front next Spring'. In contrast, it was 'not unlikely' that the Germans would attack, at a time when 'the power of British and French Armies to resist will be comparatively low'.[63]

349

Thus, the transfer of a few divisions to Italy had magically trans-formed the strategic situation. The British Army, on the brink of victory a few weeks before, was suddenly under serious threat. With the future so bleak, Haig would have been excused for postponing any further attacks in order to prepare his depleted and exhausted force for a desperate defence. Instead, in the memo above, he referred to plans for a 'surprise operation' in the vicinity of Cambrai which he hoped still to carry out. 'The nature of this operation', he emphasised, 'is such that it can be stopped at once if it appears likely to entail greater losses than I can afford.'[64]

Whilst Haig claimed that the operation was designed to maintain pressure on the Germans, it goes without saying that he was also attracted to the idea of ending the year with an impressive victory – a difficult pill for Lloyd George to swallow. The Cambrai scheme seemed to promise such a success. Charteris had indicated that the eighteen-kilometre front upon which Byng's Third Army was to attack was defended by three weak German divisions in 'absolute ignorance' of the fate that was to befall them. Moreover, he was certain the enemy would be unable to push forward significant numbers of reserves, because it would not be possible to transfer divisions from Russia before winter.[65]

Against this easy target, the British planned an unprecedented attack. It was novel in a number of important respects. First, the enemy wire and machine-gun emplacements were to be neutralised not by the preliminary bombardment but by tanks. The plan had been conceived by Brigadier-General Hugh Elles, the Tank Corps commandant, who was eager to demonstrate what the new weapons could accomplish, given the right terrain and appropriate tactics. Secondly, the artillery was to be registered without preliminary firing. In other words, firing would begin with the release of the tanks, thus allowing them and the infantry to advance over virtually unbroken ground. Finally, Cambrai was novel in its coordination of all arms and in the use of air power in ground attack. Because of these changes, Cambrai has been called 'the first truly modern battle'. Haig, however, did not see it as anything unique. Whilst accepting the new ideas, he stressed that the overriding objective was still 'to break through the enemy's defences *by surprise* and so to permit the Cavalry Corps to pass through and operate in open country'. He was concerned that 'This was not . . . fully realised in all the units I saw.'[66]

Seven divisions, 1,000 guns and 325 tanks went into action against the heavily fortified defences of the *Siegfried Stellung* on 20 November. The Germans were completely surprised by the ferocity of the assault. By noon, the British had overrun the forward defences on a front of ten kilometres. The cavalry was then pushed forward but, as should have been expected, men and horses were annihilated by machine-gunners in the second defensive system. By late afternoon, the momentum of the attack had dissipated. Nevertheless, the British had advanced almost as far in one day as they had during the three months in Flanders. All this had been achieved at the comparatively low cost of 4,000 casualties.

As had been demonstrated many times, the difficulty in this war lay in following up an initial success. The British, having overrun an important position, should have consolidated their gains and then waited for the Germans to waste their resources in costly counter-attacks. But, aside from the useless cavalry divisions, Haig had no reserves available for consolidation, much less exploitation. Nor were the Germans as weak as Charteris had indicated. On the eve of the battle, he told Haig that the enemy would not be able to reinforce for forty-eight hours. In fact, fresh divisions were taking their place in the trenches at that very moment. Charteris, who had been informed of the arrival of German reserves by junior intelligence officers, 'refused to have [them] shown on the location map . . . saying that he did not accept the evidence, and in any case he did not wish to weaken the C-in-C's resolution to carry on with the attack'. Thus, as late as the 28th, Haig still believed that 'the enemy is at present suffering from the blows we have dealt him this year, and is very short of men . . . therefore the best plan is to continue to attack him to the utmost of our power'. In fact, Cambrai should never have been fought.[67]

Rather than quitting while he was ahead, Haig pushed forward fresh attacks. He did so for three reasons – none of which was militarily sound. First, he assumed that the ease of the initial assault had been due to the German front being 'soft' – not to the novel tactics. Therefore, since the Germans would supposedly be slow to reinforce, the possibility of a breakthrough remained. Secondly, Haig thought that this breakthrough would open the way for a glorious cavalry charge such as had so far been impossible in this war. The ring of cold steel had a siren-like effect. Finally, he realised that the initial success was deeply embarrassing to Lloyd George, who had of

351

late been so critical of British generals. The possibility of increasing the Prime Minister's embarrassment proved intoxicating.

In the end, it was Haig who was embarrassed. Over the succeeding days, he recklessly gambled his Army in a desperate attempt to extend his success. Some small gains were made, such as the capture of Bourlon Wood on the 23rd, but nothing of strategic value was won. Meanwhile, fresh German divisions poured into the sector. On the 30th, a massive counter-attack began. The British were pushed back, in places beyond their original line. As the Germans pushed relentlessly forward, the mood at GHQ approached panic. On 3 December, Byng was ordered to withdraw from what had become a dangerous salient. 'The abandonment of ground recently won', Haig admitted, had become 'quite secondary' to the need to establish a line 'gaining security of defence with economy of troops'.[68]

The British suffered nearly 50,000 casualties in fifteen days at Cambrai. German losses were about equal. Nothing of strategic value was gained. In the end, this was just another battle of attrition. Whilst the British could not afford such a battle, the Germans, for the moment at least, could. The moral victory was theirs. The British did learn some techniques relating to the handling of tanks and artillery. But the enduring lesson of Cambrai pertained to what might have been: an impressive (and morally inspiring) victory could have been achieved, had Haig not wasted his reserves in mindless assaults in the Flanders mud.

As he indicated to his wife, Haig was unperturbed by the massive German counter-attack on the 30th: 'You will think I am a terrible optimist! Even when we suffer a check! The truth is that I know and feel that our troops, man for man, are better than the Germans and that given a fair chance our fellows will come out "on top".' Four days later, after the enormity of the situation had sunk in, Haig confessed that he had had 'an anxious time'. Whilst admitting that 'whatever happens, the responsibility is mine', he repeatedly alluded to what might have been possible had troops not been transferred to Italy. (He did not explain why, if he knew about the transfer beforehand, he still went ahead with the attack.) But by far the most revealing comment on the débâcle came in a 12 December letter to Lady Haig:

As regards the disappointment . . . of not taking Cambrai, as you know I have had many similar disappointments before. But one must expect these in war! As a matter of fact our main objective was not Cambrai but Bourlon Wood . . . But for the mishap on the 30th we would have succeeded I think. As a matter of fact, however, the mishap has been a good lesson for many of our officers were getting careless by reason of our uninterrupted successes all this year.

This astonishing ability to turn black into white was Haig's secret weapon in his battles with the Germans and with Lloyd George.[69]

Unlike Haig, the Prime Minister did not see Cambrai as a valuable and timely lesson. On 6 December Robertson warned that

L.G. was in one of his abominable moods . . . His great argument is that you have for long said that the Germans are well on the down-grade in morale and numbers and that you advised attacking them though some 30 Divisions should come from Russia; and yet only a few Divisions have come and you are hard put to it to hold your own!

In reply, Haig reminded Robertson (and thus the War Cabinet) that his plans and predictions had always been made 'with the proviso that our Divisions were kept to war establishment'. The politicians, of course, answered that Haig's optimistic reports led them to believe that manpower was not a problem. It was not an argument for which there could possibly be an amicable solution. Haig ended his letter by writing

I gather that the P.M. is dissatisfied. If that means that I have lost his confidence, then in the interests of the cause let him replace me at once. But if he still wishes me to remain, then all carping criticism should cease, and I should be both supported and trusted.

Lloyd George would dearly have loved to sack Haig, but he could not risk the resultant uproar among the Army, the civilian population and the government. He suggested instead making Haig generalissimo of British forces (a position with status but no power) but this was unacceptable to Derby who intimated that he would resign.[70]

The Prime Minister was nevertheless determined that changes be made. On 7 December, Derby signalled that the first target was Charteris:

For a long time past he has appeared to me and many others to take a quite unjustifiable view of the fighting value of the enemy. I can believe that you realise he may exaggerate and give unduly optimistic opinions, and that you endeavour to make allowance for this failing, but at the same time it is hardly possible for you to avoid being influenced to some extent by his opinions, though probably unconsciously so.

Replying on 10 December, Haig objected to Charteris being made 'the whipping boy for the charge of undue optimism brought against myself'. This was not simply a case of loyalty to a trusted subordinate. Rather, Haig realised that Derby's complaints were as damaging to himself as to Charteris. Unwilling to admit that he had been naively misled, Haig emphasised:

His duty is to collect, collate, and place before me all evidence in respect to the enemy . . . The responsibility for the judgement formed on the evidence obtained and for the reviews put forward to the War Cabinet rest on me and not on him, and if the War Cabinet are not satisfied with the views put forward by me it is I, and not Charteris who should answer for those views.

In other words, Charteris was not the well from which Haig's optimism flowed. This was an entirely accurate admission and certainly a courageous one to make. Haig also suspected that the issue had very little to do with intelligence – work which 'certainly no one could do . . . better than C'. Rather, it was probably a case of Lloyd George wanting 'to remove him because he (Charteris) has influence with the correspondents and so the Press, and consequently is in L.G.'s way'. But it was Charteris himself who provided the best explanation when, according to Haig, he said that 'the Government . . . was striking at me through him'. Haig, who concurred with this view, realised that if he agreed to Charteris's removal he would only weaken his own position.[71]

On 11 December, Derby denied that Charteris was being made the 'whipping boy' and insisted in stronger terms that he had to go. On the following day, Northcliffe, who had changed sides after Cambrai, wrote of 'blundering' at GHQ and the need for the 'prompt removal of every blunderer'. 'Sir Douglas Haig's position cannot but depend in large measure on his choice of subordinates,' *The Times* commented. 'His weakness is his inveterate devotion to those who have served him longest – some of them perhaps too long.'[72]

Neither the article (which Haig suspected was 'written to Lloyd George's order') nor Derby's letter had any effect, since Haig had already made up his mind to remove Charteris. As he claimed in his diary on 9 December, he had made this decision without being influenced by outside pressure:

> Kiggell . . . spoke to me about Charteris. That although he did his work well at H.Qrs. he was much disliked in Corps and Armies . . . if what he (K) said was based on good evidence, we ought to give Charteris another appointment, but there was no question of moving C. because of supposed inefficiency in his work. No one had done or could do the Intelligence work better than C. But I realised C.'s faults towards his equals and his own subordinates.

As he told his wife, 'it would be wrong of me to keep an Officer who seems really to have upset so many people and to have put those who ought to work in friendliness with him against him'. Though it was perhaps an exaggeration to claim that 'the change has nothing to do with the Cambrai battle' it is clear that Charteris was removed mainly to preserve the all-important harmony of Haig's staff.[73]

Haig never accepted that he had been misled by his Intelligence Officer. As a snub to the War Cabinet, Charteris was found a comfortable sinecure at GHQ, there to be available for frequent consultation. On 20 December, he submitted his last formal intelligence report. His study of the German Army and the movement of troops from the Eastern Front had led him to conclude that 'the enemy's big blow' would fall in March.[74]

14

But for the Grace
of God . . .

On 9 January, Haig had lunch with Derby and Lloyd George at Downing Street. It was, surprisingly, 'a very cheery party. Conversation turned on the length of the war and some betting took place. Derby bet the P.M. 100 cigars to 100 cigarettes that war would be over by next New Year.' Haig agreed with Derby. The war would be over by the end of the year 'because of the *internal* state of Germany'. As Herbert Lawrence (then the Intelligence Officer but shortly to become CGS) indicated a few days later, 'there was no cause for anxiety' since 'even after the Germans had brought over all their reserves from Russia they would still have too small a superiority over the French and British to ensure a decisive victory'.[1]

Though certain of ultimate victory, Haig expected the coming four months to be 'the critical period' of the war. He anticipated that the Germans would move approximately thirty-two divisions from the Eastern Front, at the rate of about ten per month. Thus, as Charteris had predicted, they were likely to attack in March. But there was uncertainty about the nature of this attack. On 7 January, Bonar Law asked Haig: 'If you were a German Commander, would you think there was sufficient chance of a smashing offensive to justify incurring the losses which would be entailed?' Haig answered that limited attacks were the most likely eventuality because 'an offensive on a large scale made with the object of piercing the front and reaching Paris or Calais . . . would be very costly . . . If he attacked and failed his position would become critical in view of the increasing forces of the allies in August.' Suspicious as Haig was of the politicians, his statement seems incredible. As Robertson predicted, mischief-making ministers were bound in future to use it against Haig – either to blame him for not warning of a massive German attack or to argue that his demands for drafts were exaggerated. Haig tried to repair the damage during the conversation with Derby and Lloyd George, but only muddied the waters further:

> Germany having only one million men as Reserves for this year's fighting, I doubted whether they would risk them in an attempt to 'break through'. If the Germans did attack it would be a gambler's throw. All seemed to depend on the struggle now going on between the Military and Civilian parties. If the Military party won, they would certainly attack and try and deliver a knock-out blow against the Western Front. We must be prepared for this.

The best way to meet this threat 'would be to continue our offensive in Flanders, because we would then retain the initiative and attract the German reserves against us'. By this time, however, the politicians were hardly likely to sanction more escapades in the Flanders mud.[2]

It was not just the German threat that made these months critical. Myriad problems, most of them agonisingly familiar, plagued Haig at this time. Lloyd George was again pushing alternative theatres – Palestine being the latest flavour of the month. The supply of drafts remained shrouded in mystery, the Prime Minister again insisting on reducing the number of battalions in British divisions. And, as usual, the French caused anxiety. In December came another request for the British to take over more of the line. Haig thought this 'most ungenerous of them, after the way we have been fighting all year to save their Army and their Country'. He was, however, delighted when he and Pétain were able to reach a quick and amicable solution to the problem on 17 December. Struck by 'the different bearing and attitude of the present officers at GQG', he thought relations with the French 'better than I have ever known them'. He was nevertheless still 'doubtful whether the French Army can now withstand for long a resolute and continued offensive on the part of the enemy.'[3]

Such good relations with the French could always be upset by outside interference. On 14 January, the Supreme War Council decided to extend the British line further than Haig and Pétain had agreed. Haig justifiably pointed out that 'this raises the whole question as to the status of the "War Council" . . . The Government now have two advisers!

Will they accept the advice of the Versailles gentlemen or will they take my advice?'[4] It was not likely that Haig would receive an answer which he considered satisfactory. Lloyd George had originally been attracted to the idea of an inter-allied council specifically because he wanted advice different from that of Haig and Robertson.

Relations with the new ally, the United States, were also proving problematic. At first, Haig was impressed by the Americans. General Pershing, the Commander-in-Chief, was 'most anxious to learn' and had a 'quiet, gentlemanly bearing – so unusual for an American'. Haig was equally impressed with the junior officers, as he told his wife:

I must say our idea of what American men are like was quite wrong! Those we are working with are quiet, unassuming, practical fellows. Entirely unlike the fashionable Yankees we used to see in London following in the wake of some loud-mouthed American beauty! Personally, I am finding the American men connected with the USA Forces very much like our own officers. I need give them no higher recommendation.

First impressions proved deceptive. The Americans may have looked impressive, but they did not seem very willing to fight. Haig was worried that the Germans would attack before America could contribute significantly to the defence. His concern was increased by the American insistence that divisions were not to be broken up in order to supply drafts for beleaguered British units. After some home truths from Haig, Pershing agreed to the idea on 28 December but only 'if the situation became critical'. The definition of what was 'critical' remained unresolved.[5]

In the past, Haig derived solace from external problems by immersing himself in his wonderful Army. By late 1917, however, British morale seemed less resilient than it had once perhaps been. Robertson warned that 'There are gradually accumulating in the country a great many wounded and crippled men who are not of a cheery disposition.' These 'grousers' were combining with 'mere wasters . . . without patriotism' and with the 'various Trade Unions' to sap the will of good honest soldiers. Haig, though attentive to these warnings, was more worried about the effect of recent articles in the 'Lloyd George press'. The soldiers had in effect been 'told that the attacks in Flanders were a useless loss of life, and that all the suffering and hardship which they had endured was unnecessary'. The Prime Minister was 'undermining the confidence which the troops now feel in their leaders' and would 'eventually destroy the efficiency of the Army as a fighting force'. Haig was also concerned that his Army might be wrongly influenced by the apparent willingness of Germany to accept a peace based on no annexations. It was, he thought,

> very desirable to tell the Army in a few unambiguous sentences, what we were fighting for. The army is now composed of repre- sentatives of all classes in the Nation, and many are most intelligent and think things out. They don't care whether France has Alsace and Italy Trieste; they realise that Britain entered the war to free Belgium and save France. Germany is now ready, we have been told, to give all we want in these respects. So it is essential that some statement should be made which the soldier can understand and approve of. Few of us feel that the 'democratising of Germany' is worth the loss of a single Englishman!

No mention was made of what sort of statement would satisfy the soldiers, but Haig was quite clear as to what they should not be told. On 23 December, he complained to the Adjutant General about 'the discussions which sometimes take place on "reconstruction after the war"'. He was alarmed to find that 'Sometimes advanced socialistic and even anarchical views are expressed.' Though he did not want to 'stop free discussion', it did seem advisable to 'guide it by having really capable men to lecture and control any subversive talk'.[6]

Haig's anxieties were meanwhile compounded by the fact that the attacks upon his staff continued apace. The removal of Charteris was followed in quick succession by that of Maxwell (the QMG) and Kiggell. Neither change caused much stir; Maxwell's departure, in fact, went almost unremarked. Haig was at first ready to resist efforts to remove Kiggell, but then had to bow to irrefutable evidence of his lack of fitness. On his first inspection of the Passchendaele front – *after* the battle – the CGS reportedly burst into tears and cried, 'Good God have we been asking men to go through this! If I had only known!' A subsequent medical examination revealed that Kiggell was suffering from 'nervous exhaustion'. As a result, when Derby advised that he be replaced, Haig did not object, though he admitted that he was 'very sad to make this decision, especially when I reflect over all I and the whole Army owe to Kiggell'.[7]

It is tempting to see the changes in the GHQ staff as Lloyd George's attempt to 'knock the props' from under Haig, a similar strategy to the one he wanted to pursue against Germany. If the praetorian guard were removed, it would, presumably, be easier to get at the Emperor. It seems unlikely that such a grand plan existed. Though he still occasionally dreamt of sacking Haig, the pro-Haig forces were ever ready with cold water to jolt him from these dreams. It is even possible that the changes in Haig's staff, far from being inspired by Lloyd George, were part of an attempt by those forces, particularly Derby, to frustrate the Prime Minister. Charteris, Kiggell and Maxwell may have been removed as part of an effort to sanitise Haig and render him safe from Lloyd George's assaults. This would explain Derby's advice to Haig that his choice of Butler as a replacement for Kiggell was unwise because Butler 'was not liked by any of the Authorities at home'. Some quite fancy footwork by Derby ensured that Lloyd George was never given an issue over which to force Haig's resignation, and Haig, in turn, was never made so angry as to resign. It is regrettable that Haig never really appreciated Derby's contribution. Though he was pleased with his support, Haig did not derive a great deal of security from it, since he did not believe that the War Secretary had sufficient mettle to stand up to Lloyd George. Oblivious to the severe strains under which Derby had to operate, the insensitive Haig remarked, 'D. is a very weak-minded fellow I am afraid, and like the feather pillow, bears the marks of the last person who has sat on him.'[8]

On 19 January, Robertson informed Haig that Smuts, a member of the War Cabinet, was to visit GHQ and the Western Front, accompanied by Hankey. 'The more he sees of your difficulties, the greater help he will give.' According to Robertson:

> the proposal emanated from the Prime Minister from what I can hear. He was remarking that he did not know many of the various Generals at the front, and therefore he suggested that it would be a good thing for Smuts to go round and see as many as he could and so be able to tell him his opinion about them.

Robertson's apparent naiveté is astounding. In fact, as the Prime Minister himself later admitted, Smuts and Hankey had been sent to 'look and see for themselves whether among the Generals they met, there was one whom they considered might with advantage attain and fill the first place'. Lloyd George even considered making Hankey CGS at GHQ to keep an eye on Haig if a suitable replacement for the latter could not be found. It is not entirely clear whether Smuts and Hankey were aware of the Prime Minister's devious intent. According to Haig, they 'went out of their way to assure me that Lloyd George has no wish to replace me. On the contrary, although he and I discuss matters with some energy, his object they say is to get my views in order to support me!' In other words, either Smuts and Hankey were lying through their teeth or Haig was as naive as Robertson.[9]

Hankey found that 'the atmosphere of complaisant optimism that formerly pervaded GHQ was conspicuous by its absence'. Neither he nor Smuts could find a Messiah among British senior officers. The only benefit to be derived from the tour, as far as Lloyd George was concerned, was Hankey's claim that those in the know on the Western Front doubted that the Germans would attack in force. This information would be useful in subsequent arguments over manpower. As for Haig, his visitors' assurances that the Prime Minister's only desire was to be supportive were given the lie when he learned that his command had been harshly criticised in a recent Commons debate. 'I am astounded at the Government allowing this sort of thing to continue,' he told his wife. Believing the attacks to have been inspired by Lloyd George, Haig again speculated that 'L.G. hopes to make England a Republic and to achieve this end the Army must be got rid of and rendered powerless. This can only be done by discrediting the Army leaders and getting some of his civilian friends into the chief appointments.' What is astounding is that Haig had repeatedly to be reminded that Lloyd George was basically a twister. 'He is always so pleasant to me when we meet, it is difficult to believe that he is such a knave behind my back!'[10]

Haig's persistent (and misguided) belief that Lloyd George could be brought around to the 'correct' line was revealed when the Supreme War Council met at Versailles on 29 January. The important issue, in his mind, was the shortage of reserves which threatened a massive reduction of British strength, a reduction which American replacements could only partially offset. Haig saw his task at Versailles as being 'to bring home to our Prime Minister's mind the seriousness of our present position and to cause him to call up more men while there is yet time to train them'. In an address intended to galvanise both Lloyd George and the dilatory Americans into action, Haig presented the blackest possible picture of the situation: 'estimating for a loss of 1/2 million if the enemy (as was possible) attacked, I showed that the British should be prepared for a reduction of 30 Divisions by the Autumn unless action were taken at once to get men.' Pétain, in support, estimated that his Army would be reduced by twenty-five divisions simply because of normal wastage. The histrionics of the Haig–Pétain double act did not impress the rest of the conference. Hankey felt that the two commanders 'made asses of themselves by absurd, panicky statements'. Lloyd George, to Haig's considerable dismay, remained 'anxious to prove by *figures* that we had ample men on the Western Front'.[11]

Leaving the manpower problems unsettled, the representatives moved on to the 'plans for 1918'. A defensive strategy was agreed upon for the short term, though the various Commanders-in-Chief were allowed to 'prepare for offensive projects suitable for the forces at their disposal'. Approval was given to Lloyd George's proposal for an offensive against the Turks, much to Haig's chagrin. He did, however, derive considerable enjoyment from watching Clemenceau (who had succeeded Painlevé as Prime Minister in November) haul Lloyd George over the coals in the Turkish debate. 'He is a grand old man, full of go and determination,' Haig wrote of the Frenchman, 'L.G. cannot touch him in practical sound sense.' Haig was also pleased when the proposed extension of the British front (by fourteen miles), whilst accepted in principle, was left to Pétain and himself to implement. In other words, he was confident that he could convince Pétain of the wisdom of delaying the extension indefinitely.[12]

The most significant, and ominous, decision reached at Versailles pertained to the formation of a General Reserve. Haig had always been lukewarm about this idea. It was not necessary on the Western Front, because 'Pétain and I get on very well'. It would, on the other hand, be a beneficial way of controlling the Italians who were always ready 'to beg for something they want, but . . . never have the slightest intention of parting with anything for the general good'. Haig's deepest misgivings pertained to the question of command; he did not want a Frenchman to have authority over British soldiers. He was therefore considerably alarmed when agreement was reached on a proposal calling for the military representatives to the Supreme War Council (in other words Wilson and Foch) to direct the reserve, with Foch being the senior partner. Haig, ever mindful of Calais, inquired, 'By what channel am I to receive orders from this new body?' Lloyd George, who had backed the proposal, answered that orders would come directly from the military representatives. Haig concluded that 'To some extent it makes Foch a "Generalissimo".' Though the change threatened to diminish the power and influence of himself and Robertson, Haig was not vehement in his opposition to it. He doubted that he would be able to spare any men for the reserve and so did not expect it would affect his plans. The troops might in fact have to come from the Italy, Salonika or other secondary theatres, in the process starving those operations. For Haig, the Versailles settlement was a case of swings and roundabouts. In comparison to other notorious conferences, this one 'went off quite well'. Besides, Haig assured his wife, 'The machinery . . . is so big and clumsy it will take some time before it can work fast enough to trouble me.' Rather prophetically, he concluded, 'I expect the Germans will help us get out of this mess which is due to too much talking!!'[13]

Robertson, unlike Haig, was prepared to make an issue of his opposition to the Versailles agreement. He made his acceptance of it contingent upon the post of military representative and that of CIGS being amalgamated. Lloyd George, who had been eager to rid himself of Robertson for some time, welcomed the showdown. Haig was warned of an impending crisis in a letter from Derby: 'there is a certain gang who want to get rid of Robertson, . . . and they think that I stand in the way of their doing so, which is quite true. I do stand in the way and I mean to as long as I have the confidence in him that I now have.' Derby expected that he and Haig would march together in support of Robertson. He was, however, bewildered to learn (from Lloyd George) that Haig had agreed to the main points of the Versailles agreement, and requested confirmation:

> If it is really so that you agree with the principles . . . then I should be justified in remaining in office, because it would then only be a question of Robertson opposing a scheme to which you had given your assent. If, on the other hand, you are in agreement with Robertson, and Robertson is got rid of because he won't agree to it, then, naturally, I should have to go too.

Haig replied, 'I consider General Reserve desirable but do not concur in system set up for commanding it.' The ambiguity was probably intentional.[14]

On Derby's urging, Haig rushed to London in order to monitor the situation more closely. Upon his arrival, he learned from Derby that the War Cabinet was determined to replace Robertson. A number of other changes had been proposed. The responsibilities of the Secretary of State for War and those of CIGS would return to the status quo pre-Robertson. The military representative at Versailles was to become Deputy CIGS and would sit on the Army Council. Orders concerning the handling of the General Reserve would come to Haig directly from this Deputy CIGS, who would therefore in effect have more power over the handling of troops than the actual CIGS.

Haig objected to the idea of Foch and Wilson – both of whom he did not trust – having so much power. When he met Lloyd George, he explained his objections in less personal terms:

> I pointed out the tremendous powers now being given to Versailles, that the Military Representatives there had full powers to commit the Government *possibly against my opinion* and take decisions which the British Government ought alone to take . . . I suggested that Robertson's original proposal, by which he (as CIGS) after consultation with Foch, should send me orders re Reserves was probably the best solution of the difficulty.

Lloyd George handled Haig's objections with the usual dexterity. He was, he claimed, 'anxious to get into more direct touch with me as C. in C. in France . . . under the present system he always felt that in seeing me he was going behind the back of the CIGS'.[15]

Having lured Haig in, Lloyd George sprang the trap: he suggested that Wilson and Robertson could switch places, and that the latter, as Versailles military representative, would be 'absolutely free and unfettered in the advice which he gives'. In making such a proposal Lloyd George cleverly drove a wedge between Haig and Robertson. With the latter instead of Wilson at Versailles the scheme became palatable to Haig. As military representative, Wully might even 'save us from defeat by opposing Lloyd George's desire to send troops to the East against the Turks'. Furthermore, Haig's reservations concerning the channel by which he received orders from Versailles were quashed when Lloyd George proposed to make the military representative automatically a member of the Army Council – which 'rendered any instructions I received from him lawful commands'. Haig still thought it was a 'bad scheme' but decided to 'do my best to work under it'. Robertson was advised to do the same. 'This was no time for anyone to question where his services were to be given. It was his *duty* to go to Versailles or anywhere else if the Government wished it.'[16]

After clearly stating his position, Haig returned to the front on the 11th. The arguments between Robertson and Lloyd George continued for another tension-packed week. Tired of Wully's obstinacy, the Prime Minister presented three options. He could either go to Versailles, remain as CIGS under the new system, or resign completely. In truth, Lloyd George realised that the first two were out of the question. In a letter to Haig, Robertson explained, 'I could not possibly accept a position as CIGS which I had already condemned as dangerous.' On the other hand, he 'would have been a useless fool at Versailles, with Wilson here as CIGS, who could always have scotched me'. He correctly surmised, 'The whole thing is, in fact, a plot to get me out of here.'[17]

On the 17th, Haig was back in London to lend a calming influence in the crisis which had been developing because of the threatened resignations of Robertson and Derby. When presented with a second opportunity to state which side he was on, Haig, according to Lloyd George, 'put up no fight for Robertson' and 'sniffed . . . aside with an expression of contempt' the possibility of Derby's resignation. Haig reiterated his opposition to the Versailles scheme, but emphasised that since 'the Cabinet had given its decision' he intended loyally to do 'my best to make the system run. I had only one object, viz. to beat the Germans.' Shortly afterwards, Wilson became CIGS, and Rawlinson went to Versailles.[18]

How was it that Haig could, with such apparent ease, abandon a man who had sweated blood for him for over two years? There is no easy answer. He confessed that Robertson 'comes out of the controversy as a "mullish irreconcilable" individual' – but this hardly seems sufficient reason to ditch him so precipitously. It is possible that in truth no issue could have prompted Haig to resign. Resigning meant depriving the country of his talents, which were, he thought, unique and godgiven. Likewise, he was probably quite sincere in his belief that it was his duty to obey the orders of his government. But there were also problems with Robertson himself. Haig had never been comfortable with the CIGS, considering him power-crazed, meddlesome, egotistical, common and coarse. But perhaps the most important reason for the estrangement was revealed to Lady Haig:

> I, like you, am sorry for Robertson, but then it seems to me . . . that he has not resolutely adhered to the policy of 'concentration on the Western Front' – He has *said* that this is his policy, but has allowed all kinds of resources to be diverted to distant theatres at the bidding of his political masters.

This was an extremely uncharitable and insensitive (not to mention inaccurate) judgement. Haig, however, obviously did not think so. In his mind, Robertson had committed a crime which was unforgivable.[19]

Lady Haig, more sympathetic to Robertson, commented that the best idea would have been to make him Prime Minister. (This may have been a reference to a suggestion which Gwynne made to Margot Asquith, among – perhaps – others.) Haig confessed that the prospect of Wully in Downing Street made him 'smile'. 'To be a successful politician', he wrote, 'requires practice and training like every other profession. There are depths of insincerity and almost dishonesty in politics to which no soldier could stoop.' As to his own possible political career, Haig wrote:

> I quite agree with you that I would cut a sorry figure talking to the existing House of Commons, but let me get a chance of having a go with the Army in reorganising the House, then, with my own audience, and the Northcliffe Press well in hand, you would be surprised at how popular I would be!!! But that moment has not yet arrived.

For the meantime, Haig preferred a more subtle political role. During the second visit to London, he was able to convince Derby, who was bent on resigning, that 'in the interests of the Army there should be no change'. Haig was convinced that 'as a result of my visit to London . . . a saner view is now taken of the so-called military crisis, and the risk of a quarrel between "civilian and soldier" . . . has been avoided'. It was almost as if Robertson had never existed.[20]

Pleased with himself, Haig turned his attention to his Army. At a conference on 16 February, Cox, the new Intelligence Officer, '*indicated that we must be prepared to meet a very severe attack at any moment now.*' Haig was nevertheless confident that on Gough's front, where the attack was expected, 'Everything seemed carefully thought out . . . if we only have another month in which to work, this sector *ought* to be very strong.' He reminded Gough that 'whenever we had attacked we had always been able to break the enemy's front, and to advance well into the German system of defence', therefore 'we must expect the Germans to do the same'. Gough was specifically told to put extra effort into the preparation of his 'Reserve Lines'.[21]

In a letter to Doris, Haig confided that he found Gough 'a great asset'. 'Although in his 4th year of war, he looks young and fit, and might well just be starting the war! He is always so cheery too, it is quite a tonic to meet him. Yet, as you know, certain critics have been speaking evil of him at home.' One such critic was Derby. 'It has been borne in on me from all sides', he wrote on 5 March, 'that [Gough] does not have the confidence of the troops he commands, and that is a very serious feeling to exist with respect to a Commander at such a critical time as the present.' Lloyd George, according to Derby, also felt that Gough was 'rather out of his depth in so large and important a Command as that of an Army'. Though Haig was not instructed to sack Gough, it was made clear that he would have the full backing of the government if he chose to do so. Derby should have realised that any advice from Lloyd George or himself was likely to have the opposite effect intended. Haig became ever more determined to support Gough.[22]

During the first weeks of March, Haig received numerous indications 'that an offensive on a big scale will take place during the present month'. This threat did not worry him. 'I must say that I feel quite confident, and so do my troops,' he told his wife 'Personally, I feel in the words of 2nd Chronicles, XX Chap., that it is "God's battle" and I am not dismayed by the numbers of the enemy.' In fact, as he told his Army commanders, he 'was only afraid that the enemy would find our front so very strong that he will hesitate to commit his Army to the attack with the almost certainty of losing very heavily'.[23]

Haig's confidence was based on his belief that his Army remained basically sound. On 25 February, he learned that some soldiers, when questioned by Labour MPs had 'expatiated on the horrors of the war, and said that they wanted to know for what they were fighting;

and hoped that the horrors of the war would be made to cease!' Unconcerned, Haig thought that

> the best remedy was to let the M.P.s see the best and most thoughtful of our soldiers. There is no doubt that we have, in this very large Army, men of all opinions – ultra socialists, principalists and conscientious objectors, as well as very real hard fighting men of the Bull-dog breed! The latter are in the majority.

Whilst confident about the quality of his men, Haig was deeply concerned about their quantity, as he indicated on 10 March:

> *The manpower situation is most unsatisfactory* ... with heavy fighting in prospect, and very few men coming in, the prospects are bad. We are told that we can only expect 18,000 drafts in April! We are all right under normal conditions for men for the next three months, but I fear for the *autumn! And still more do I fear for the situation after the enemy has started the attack.*

Discussing the problem with Derby on 13 March, Haig predicted a shortage of 100,000 men by June. Derby announced that the Army Council had arrived at a similar figure. Haig did not at this stage accuse the government of intentionally starving his Army of men. Rather, the politicians were only to blame in the sense that they were being duped by the workers at home who 'are now so well paid that they have no incentive to work full hours. Certainly in my opinion, more men should be withdrawn to fight in the field.'[24]

Haig's worries over manpower were compounded by pressures placed upon him to contribute to the General Reserve. On 25 February, Rawlinson, the new Military Representative arrived with the new CIGS, Wilson, in tow. The latter asked Haig to earmark divisions for the reserve, but Haig, eager for a showdown on this subject, refused. His mistrust of these two men, and of Foch, convinced Haig that any divisions contributed to the reserve would never be seen on his front again. He therefore put his faith in the system of defence which had been agreed upon with Pétain, who was equally suspicious of the General Reserve and especially of Foch. Haig claimed that he would 'prefer to be relieved of my command', rather than jeopardise that defence. Wilson later reminded Haig that the reserve was designed to assist him, and warned that if ever he had 'to live on Pétain's charity . . . he would find that very cold charity'. Haig remained suspicious, fearing that Wilson 'means to help Lloyd George to detach troops from my Command to fight against the Turks'. Even Rawlinson, who was prepared to back Haig's refusal to contribute to the reserve, did not, in the process, earn Haig's trust. Like Wilson, he was deemed a 'humbug' – it was 'difficult to decide what is at the bottom of the mind of each of them'.[25]

The manpower situation and the problem of the General Reserve was discussed at the Allied conference which convened in London, on 14 March. Before this meeting, Lloyd George and Bonar Law, according to Haig,

> did their best to get me to say that the Germans would not attack. The P.M. remarked that I had 'given my opinion that the Germans would only attack against small portions of our front'. I said that I had never said that. The question put to me was: if I were a German General and confronted by the present situation, *would I attack*? I now said that the German Army and its leaders seem drunk with their success in Russia and the Middle East, so that it is impossible to foretell what they may not attempt. In any case we must be prepared to meet *a very strong attack indeed on a 50 mile front, and for this drafts are urgently required.*

Argument then shifted to the General Reserve. Haig recorded how Lloyd George first tried to frighten and then to cajole him into releasing the divisions which Foch and Wilson wanted. Standing firm, Haig insisted that 'this was a military question of which I was the best judge'. Foch and Wilson were 'too distant and not in touch with the actual military situation'. Lloyd George, unwilling to risk another fight with the military, reluctantly relented. It was subsequently decided that the General Reserve would be shelved until the arrival of the Americans again made raising the necessary troops a realistic possibility. The security of the Anglo-French defence now rested solely on the personal agreement between Haig and Pétain.[26]

Though he had won his point, Haig remained sceptical of the government's commitment to the manpower problem. He was, for instance, alarmed when on 19 March he learned that Churchill (the Minister of Munitions) was advocating the 'reorganisation of the Army so as to employ mechanical applicances to take the place of men'. The War Cabinet had approved the manufacture of 4,000 tanks. Despite having seen what massed tanks could achieve, Haig scorned this decision which, he felt, was made 'without any consideration of the manpower situation and the crews likely to be available to put into them'. He was especially angry because, on the same day, the War Office suggested abolishing the cavalry as a way to raise extra troops.[27]

While Haig was in London, on 15 March, his wife gave birth to a son. The birth went very smoothly, thanks to the help of the GHQ medical officer, Colonel Ryan, who was present during the final days of confinement. Haig also sent half a sheep and some butter from the Army stores, fearful as he was that British rations (which were 'much more strict than in France') would not provide his wife with enough nourishment. A few days after the birth, he wrote that he was struck by the 'mass of letters of congratulations from all parts – many from poor people quite unknown to me. How happy it makes one feel that so many kindly thoughts and prayers are being lavished *on us three* at this time.' Among the letters was an interesting one from Esher:

> Many congratulations. You are really wonderful. *Now*, how about Bemersyde and a Peerage, and all sorts of things! Mind you give this Bairn a good Scots name – if not Douglas then Angus!
>
> I wish he could be given Bemersyde in a christening cup by a grateful nation.

The question of a peerage had been raised earlier. On 24 June 1917, Haig replied to an offer from Derby by writing: 'I and my wife [are] thoroughly happy in our present position. If I were made a Peer, I would at once have to live beyond my means and so get into debt. Again I did not wish to found a dynasty.' Haig saw little sense in worrying over the issue of rewards at this time. He was confident that 'At the end of the war . . . the country will give me a grant to keep me independent for the remaining days of my life!'[28]

When Haig returned to France he learned that rumours were current 'to the effect that the enemy is prepared to offer peace terms giving France all she wants on the West Front, and will guarantee the debt owed by Russia'. His interpretation of the news was that 'it almost looks as if the Germans are shaking the mailed fist at us from the other side of "no man's land" and are about to offer peace terms. If we don't accept, they are ready to attack in order to compel us to negotiate.' In the past, Haig had consistently rejected the idea of a negotiated peace. A different stance was taken in a conversation he had with Churchill on 19 March:

I stated that from the point of view of British interests alone, if the enemy will give the terms Lloyd George recently laid down, we ought to accept them at once; even some modification of our demands for Alsace Lorraine might be given way on. At the present moment, England is in a stronger position than she has ever been and by continuing the war she will get weaker financially and in manpower. On the other hand, America will get stronger, and finally will dictate *her* peace which may not suit Great Britain.

Two days later, the Germans made the question a purely academic one by attacking.[29]

Early on 21 March, seventy-six German divisions pressed forward on the front from Arras to Laon, in an attempt to drive a wedge between the British and the French. The British defence consisted of twenty-six infantry and three cavalry divisions, with another eight divisions in GHQ reserve. Haig, mirroring the confidence which he had displayed over the previous few months, was not alarmed when the blow fell:

I am glad that the attack has begun at last because our men are eager for it . . . I was beginning to be afraid if the attack did not come till later, that our men might have become stale from expecting and preparing for so long. But they are in the best spirits now, and I have every confidence that the enemy will get more than he anticipates.

By the end of the first day, the British were forced to withdraw along a significant portion of Gough's line. Haig remained unabashed: 'Having regard to the great strength . . . and the determined manner in which the attack was everywhere pressed, I consider that the result of the day is highly creditable to the British troops.'[30]

The next day brought further retreat. Still optimistic, Haig was pleased to learn that 'All reports show that our men are in great spirits.'

By the 23rd, however, after Gough's Army had in places been pushed back twenty kilometres, Haig admitted that the 'situation is serious'. What, he wondered, had gone wrong? 'I was surprised to learn that his troops are *now behind* the Somme and the R. Tortville. Men were very tired after two days fighting and long march back . . . but I cannot make out why the Fifth Army has gone so far back without making some kind of a stand.' Ludendorff had originally planned to establish a defensive left flank on the upper Somme, while his Second and Seventeenth Armies swung right against Byng's Third Army. The attack had revealed that Gough's front was softer than Byng's. Ludendorff therefore decided to continue to push in a southwesterly direction against Gough, in order to exploit the success so far gained.[31]

Haig was alarmed at the prospect of the British and French becoming separated, with the consequent possibility that his Army would be 'rounded up and driven into the sea!' He alerted Pétain to this danger on the 23rd, and found him 'most anxious to do all he can to support me'. But, when Haig suggested that twenty French divisions be moved to the critical area, Pétain, worried that he was about to be attacked in Champagne, released only two. As Wilson had warned, Pétain's charity was very cold indeed. Whistling in the dark, Haig tried to reassure himself that the Frenchman would still 'do his utmost to keep the two Armies in touch'. On the next day, Pétain seemed 'very much upset, almost unbalanced and most anxious'. Certain that the main German blow had not yet fallen, he ignored another request for French reserves to be moved toward Amiens. To Haig's astonishment, he also announced that, if the German advance continued, the French Reserve Army Group on the British right, would retreat south-westwards in order to cover Beauvais.

> It was at once clear to me that the effect of this order must be to separate the French from the British right flank and so allow the enemy to penetrate between the two Armies. I at once asked Pétain if he meant to abandon my right flank. He nodded assent and added 'it is the only thing possible if the enemy compelled the Allies to fall back still further'.

Haig could hardly believe his ears. 'In my opinion, our Army's existence . . . depends on keeping the French and British armies united.'[32]

In response, Haig implored Milner and Wilson to come to France immediately, 'to arrange that General Foch or some other determined General who would fight, should be given the supreme control of the operations in France'. His misgivings about Foch had dissipated as quickly as his admiration of Pétain. At Doullens on the 26th, French and British representatives decided that the Amiens railway junction, the loss of which would be disastrous for the British, had to be covered 'AT ALL COSTS'. Clemenceau proposed that Foch should command an Anglo-French force for this specific purpose and to ensure that the two fronts remained united. Haig, sensing that the time had come to jettison nationalistic pride, objected, because

> In my opinion, it was essential to success that Foch should control Pétain; so I at once recommended that Foch should *co-ordinate the action of all the Allied Armies on the Western front*. Both Governments agreed to this . . . Foch seemed sound and sensible but Pétain had . . . the appearance of a Commander who was in a funk and has lost his nerve.

Within days, Haig was able to conclude that 'Foch has brought great energy to bear on the present situation . . . He and I are quite in agreement as to the general plan of operations.' Probably coincidentally, the German advance began to slow, and eventually ground to a halt on 5 April. In just two weeks, the British had lost 175,000 men. Even more frightening, was the apparent ease with which the enemy had advanced, covering distances unknown since the beginning of trench warfare.[33]

The slowing of the German advance brought time for recriminations. Since Haig could not admit German brilliance, he naturally concluded that 'fewer men, [an] extended front, and increased hostile forces' were to blame for the retreat. In other words, it was all the government's fault. The accusation remains popular to this day; Lloyd George, so it is said, starved Haig of troops. Unfortunately, history provides few clear-cut cases of guilt and innocence, and this is not one of them – as a recent book by David Woodward demonstrates. Whilst it is impossible to go into the detail which this controversy deserves, it is worth mentioning that it was the War Office – not Lloyd George – which was responsible for the decision to hold a general reserve of 120,000 men at home instead of in France. The decision was made for three reasons: (1) it would be easier to conceal the men from enemy intelligence; (2) it would be better for British morale to keep the men at home as long as possible; and (3) it would be better for the domestic economy if the soldiers spent their money in Britain instead of France. But the clincher was Haig's assurance that he could withstand any German attack for at least eighteen days with the forces at his disposal. Finally, Haig's claim that he had been starved of troops loses credibility when it is considered that he sanctioned leave for 88,000 men on the eve of the March attacks.[34]

Lloyd George was not entirely free of guilt. He had gone out of his way to cast doubt on Haig's demands for men, and could have been more assertive by insisting that an Allied general reserve be brought into being. And, as Woodward admits, prior to the German attack, 'Lloyd George and his colleagues in the War Cabinet had hoped to preserve Britain's staying power and limit British losses by not providing the War Office with all the fresh recruits it wanted.' Haig demanded 334,000 men, and received 174,000. 'Hence, if Haig lost because he did not have enough men to defend his longer line, Lloyd George must bear part of the responsibility.'[35]

But so must Haig. It must be remembered that it was his faith in Pétain which destroyed the idea of the General Reserve. Whilst such a reserve may not have been sufficient to avert disaster, Haig could not have received less help than he got from Pétain. Furthermore, with regard to the need for reinforcements from home, Haig did not present his case very convincingly. In his effort to justify his 1917 operations, he painted himself into a corner. At one and the same time, he had to argue that his Flanders offensive had seriously weakened the Germans and that those same Germans now posed a very serious threat. The inarticulate Haig found no way of talking himself out of this contradiction. It was a contradiction which Lloyd George exploited to the full. Thus, Haig's Army suffered because he could not convince the authorities that it was in danger.

It also suffered because he did not believe that there was a danger. His Army was, he thought, fully prepared. He eagerly awaited the attack and welcomed it when it came. He could not bring himself to believe that the Germans would be able to achieve what he had failed to do in 1916 and 1917 – in other words, advance. This confidence probably explains why it took a full three days before the seriousness of the crisis dawned upon Haig, and why he expressed incredulity at the extent of the damage. He was obviously not as prepared as he had imagined. After being on the offensive for two years, Haig did not adapt well to a defensive stance. Though the British tried to imitate the German 'defence in depth', far too many men were concentrated in the first line. And, though Haig claimed to his wife that 'The Enemy's attack seems to be coming exactly against the points on our front which we expected and where we are prepared to meet him',[36] this was not in fact the case. Haig thought that the Germans would attack in the direction of Calais and Boulogne – in other words, that the northern sector would hold the same attraction for them as it had for him. This area was therefore heavily reinforced – at the expense of areas further south. Along the entire front, the Germans had a six to four advantage over the British. In Gough's crucial sector the advantage was five to one. Gough had to defend the longest part of the line with the fewest number of divisions.

Gough and his staff had many times in the weeks prior to the attack alerted GHQ about the danger on the 5th Army front, but these warnings were ignored. When, on 19 March, Gough requested that two reserve divisions be moved to his front, Lawrence replied that 'it was not sound to move reserves before the situation was clear'. In patronising tones, Lawrence, according to Gough,

> spoke in general terms and gave me . . . a little lecture on the conduct of military operations in accordance with the teachings of the great Masters. I was quite well aware of these principles, but they did not apply to the situation in which the Fifth Army was placed at that moment.

Though hesitant to commit himself on the question of culpability, Gough admitted that 'both GHQ and Byng are deserving of criticism in their handling of affairs previous to and during [the] . . . battle'. He remained strangely hesitant about criticising Haig, at one time remarking that, though stones could perhaps be thrown, 'I don't think I am the right person to throw them'.[37]

Haig, on the other hand, could never accept that he had been at fault and, to his dying day, stuck to his story of government incompetence and deceit. He did not, at first, blame Gough for the disaster. On the 26th, he told Milner and Wilson that 'whatever the opinion at home might be . . . he (Gough) had dealt with a most difficult situation very

well. He had never lost his head, was always cheery and fought hard.'
This was not enough to silence Gough's critics, among whom Lloyd
George was the most vehement. On 3 April, Haig reminded the Prime
Minister that

> '[Gough] had very few reserves, a very big front entirely without
> defensive works, recently taken over from the French, and the
> weight of the enemy's attack fell on him' . . . Also that in spite of a
> most difficult situation, he had never really lost his head. L.G. said
> that he had lost the Somme bridges, not destroyed them, and that
> G. must not be employed. To this I said that I could not condemn
> an officer unheard, and that if L.G. wishes him suspended he must
> send me an order to that effect.

Haig concluded (quite correctly) that the 'cur' Lloyd George 'expects
to be attacked in the House of Commons for not tackling the
manpower problem'. He was therefore 'looking out for a scapegoat'.[38]

Derby ordered Haig to dismiss Gough on 4 April. After carrying
out the order, Haig wrote that Gough 'quite understands that I have
supported him to the utmost of his power, and that it is the Cabinet
which has now taken action'. In a rather defensive tone, Haig
commented that he had done 'all I can to stick up for him, but the
Cabinet want to divert criticism from themselves onto someone else!'
This was not entirely honest; Haig did not go to great lengths to defend
Gough. In a candid conversation with Brigadier- General Sir Edward
Beddington (a close friend of Gough's) in 1919, he explained why:

> [Gough's] treatment was harsh and undeserved: but after consid-
> erable thought I decided that the public at home, whether right
> or wrong, demanded a scapegoat, and that the only possible ones
> were Hubert or me. I was conceited enough to think that the Army
> could not spare me.

Haig's position had indeed been under threat; according to Wilson,
the War Cabinet was 'unanimously agst. Haig and the whole GHQ'. But
it was probably the stalwart support of Derby, rather than the sacrifice
of Gough, which caused this threat to be averted. Haig, sensing that
his stock had plummeted even further, defended himself by telling
Derby (during the 4 April meeting) that he had done his best with the

limited means at his disposal. He had a 'clear conscience' but, if the government so desired, he would resign. Derby, always ready with a white lie, assured Haig that there was no lack of confidence in him.[39]

Meanwhile, the Doullens agreement had run into difficulties. Clemenceau wanted Foch to be given authority to issue orders, something which Wilson, among others, resisted. On 3 April at Beauvais, it was decided that Foch would be given 'the strategic direction of military operations', with tactical decisions being left to the local Commanders-in-Chief. Each commander could also appeal to his government, 'if in his opinion his Army is endangered by reason of any order received from General Foch'. Haig, satisfied with this agreement, nevertheless demanded that the French commit themselves to launching an attack as soon as possible in order to relieve pressure on the British. Despite receiving such a commitment, he doubted 'whether the French Army, as a whole, is now fit for an offensive'. He was also sceptical of an American promise that 500,000 men would arrive over the next four months: 'I hope the Yankees will not disappoint us in this. They have seldom done anything yet which they have promised.'[40]

It was clear to Haig that the second stage of the German offensive would be directed against the 1st and 2nd British Armies north of the La Bassée Canal, an area which had been weakened somewhat in order to supply men to reinforce Gough. Aware of this weakness, Haig asked Foch for French reinforcements. A subsequent refusal prompted him to comment, 'How difficult these "Latins" are to deal with! They mean to bleed the British to the utmost.' Foch was, he speculated, 'afraid to trust French Divisions to the battlefront'.[41]

While Haig and Foch argued, the Germans attacked. A numerical advantage of two to one enabled them to duplicate the success achieved in March, advancing more than five kilometres on 9 April. On the following day, Foch admitted that the situation was serious and agreed to move a large French force into the area. In spite of this assistance, Haig remained worried. The Germans had attacked a particularly sensitive part of the British line; the Channel ports seemed at risk, as was contact with the French Army. In response to this dual threat, Haig issued his famous dispatch on 11 April:

Words fail me to express the admiration which I feel for the splendid resistance offered by all ranks of our Army under the most trying circumstances . . . Many amongst us are now tired. To those I would say that victory belongs to those who hold out the longest . . . There is no other course open to us but to fight it out! Every position must be held to the last man: there must be no retirement. With our backs to the wall, and believing in the justice of our cause, each one of us must fight on to the end. The safety of our homes and the freedom of mankind alike depend on the conduct of each one of us at this critical moment.[42]

Though the words were certainly stirring, the men for whom they were intended were too preoccupied to be affected by them. By this stage, they were simply fighting for their lives.

This was the most honest despatch issued from GHQ during the war. Gone were the confident predictions of an imminent breakthrough. In their place was a resigned acceptance that victory would go 'to the side which holds out the longest'. Haig had finally accepted the reality of attrition both in his head and his heart. Further evidence of his changed state of mind can be found in an 11 April letter to Doris:

If one has full confidence that everything is being directed from above *on the best lines*, then there is no reason for fussing. Do the best we can, and I am confident that everything will come out right in time. But we must be patient, fully realising that *our* ways may not always be the ways chosen by the Divine Power for achieving the wished for end.

Haig's confidence remained steadfast, but its nature had changed. The man who had seen himself as *the* instrument of God's will had begun to wonder if he was instead only a bit player in a divine drama – the plot of which he did not understand.[43]

Crisis followed upon crisis. The Germans continued to push forward; the British continued their desperate resistance; and the French, in Haig's mind, continued to prevaricate. On 14 April, Haig asked Foch about the promised, but undelivered, French assistance. The latter 'spoke a lot of nonsense' and seemed to Haig 'very disinclined to engage *French* troops in the battle'.[44] What Haig did not appreciate was that Foch, despite his senior position, was still finding it difficult to persuade Pétain to release reserves. In response to this difficulty, Foch asked to be appointed Commander-in-Chief of the Allied Armies, with unlimited power to move troops as he wished. The War Cabinet baulked at this idea, but agreed that he could be called 'General-in-Chief' – a distinction without a difference.

Relations with the French remained precarious. A French attack near Hangard on the 18th was not as energetic as Haig wished. On the following day, Foch offered Haig fifteen French divisions as a reserve, on the understanding that tired British troops take up the vacated French positions. A suspicious Haig reluctantly agreed, but made it clear 'that any idea of a permanent "Amalgam" must be dismissed from his mind at once, because that would never work'. Meanwhile, the Germans ploughed forward. On the 24th, the British were driven from Villers-Bretonneux, in spite of assistance provided by the First French Army. The resistance around the strategically important Mount Kemmel crumbled on the following day. 'The place was abandoned by French troops after two hours' fighting,' Haig commented. 'What Allies we have to fight with!' He was not as dismayed as he might have been by these setbacks, and by the end of the month a change in the situation became apparent. 'The enemy was not fighting with the same determination he showed at the beginning of the battle.' Counter-attacks seemed to meet with less resistance. 'The prisoners too seem now to be careless as to who wins so long as the war ends!' Could it be that the worst was over?[45]

In May, the British front grew temporarily quiet. Politics, in turn, reached a crescendo. In the Commons debate on the March disaster Bonar Law claimed, on 23 April, that the extension of the British line had been arranged between Haig and Pétain without interference by the British government. Though this was technically correct, Haig objected to the way in which the government appeared to be minimising its role in the decision. He protested to Milner, who had replaced Derby (with surprisingly little fuss) in mid-April. 'I [do] not wish to embarrass the Government at this time, but I must ask that a true statement of the facts be filed in the War Office.'[46]

Before this issue could be properly settled a bombshell exploded with the publication of General Maurice's letter on 7 May, objecting (among other things) to an earlier claim by Lloyd George that the British Army had been stronger on 1 January 1918 than it had been a year before. Maurice, until recently DMO, was in essence accusing Lloyd George of starving Haig of troops. Though no doubt agreeing with Maurice's accusation, Haig thought the letter a 'grave mistake', remarking, rather too sanctimoniously, 'No one can be both a soldier and a politician at the same time. We soldiers have to do our duty and keep silent, trusting to Ministers to protect us.' On the basic issue of ration strength in January 1918 compared to the year before, Lloyd George was correct. But to be correct is not necessarily to be honest. The Prime Minister 'neglected' to make a distinction between ration strength and fighting strength; in the latter category the Army *was* substantially weaker. (Whether this weakness was Lloyd George's fault is another matter entirely, and is too complicated to discuss here.) In the Commons debate on the Maurice letter, Lloyd George withheld recent War Office statistics which showed a drop of 110,000 *fighting* men. He cleverly turned the debate to his own advantage by pleading that 'for our common country, the fate of which is in the balance . . . there should be an end of this sniping'. A motion for a select committee was easily defeated. 'How terrible to see the House of Commons so easily taken in by a clap-trap speech by Lloyd George,' Haig subsequently reflected. 'The House is really losing its reputation as an assembly of common-sense Britishers.' Displaying rather more wishful thinking than political prescience, he concluded, 'I don't suppose . . . Maurice has done with L.G. yet.'[47]

The political wrangle was followed by fresh attempts to sack Haig – this time originating from Wilson. When Haig heard of these, he commented that he was 'ready to serve wherever the Government thinks fit to send me . . . I don't want to stay here a day longer than the Government have confidence in me.' With doubtful sincerity, he claimed that if he was removed he would 'come home with the greatest satisfaction and delight!' The blustering tone was possible because, as in the past, Haig knew that 'they will find it difficult to find a successor *at this moment*. As long as the situation is critical here, Lloyd George would not risk moving me!'[48]

The relative calm on the battle-front during May ended abruptly when the enemy attacked on the Chemin des Dames on the 27th. For Haig, the shoe was suddenly on the other foot. The area was held mainly by French troops; thus it was Foch who immediately demanded British reinforcements, and it was Haig who replied that the main German attack was certain to fall elsewhere, most likely on the Arras–Albert front. He could not imagine why the Germans would waste their time attacking the French; after all, according to a prisoner, the enemy was certain 'that the French would give satisfactory peace terms once the British Army had been defeated'.[49]

The Germans soon proved Haig wrong. Their penetration – to a depth of forty kilometres at some points – proved that this was not merely a feint. Alarm bordering on panic gripped Allied politicians gathering at Versailles on 1 June. Discussion centred on the delicate question of manpower. Though the statesmen unanimously agreed that 100 American divisions should be fighting by the following May, no one really believed that this could actually be accomplished. When Foch requested that all American troops presently under training with the British be sent to the French sector, so as to release French divisions for battle, Haig protested. An American commander had recently told him that 'it would be little short of murder to send his men into the trenches in their present ignorant state'. The real issue was 'whether the French Army was fighting or not'. From what Haig could tell, they were not. It was therefore 'a waste of good troops to relieve French Divisions by Americans'. Confiding to his diary, he wrote: 'In three weeks time these Americans will be fit for battle. I doubt if the French Divisions they relieve will ever really fight in this war.'[50]

As it turned out, Foch was as annoyed with the British as Haig was with the French. The former accused Lloyd George of withholding men, an accusation which he vehemently denied. Haig, though reluctant to come to Foch's defence, did claim that his Army would be reduced to twenty-eight first line divisions by the autumn, a figure which Milner rejected as being far too pessimistic. It was difficult to tell who was on whose side; all that was achieved was the nurturing of ill-will. Considerably disillusioned, Haig left the conference convinced that 'a Democratic form of government is a bad one, as compared with the German's, for controlling a war'.[51]

Haig's contempt for the French increased daily. He delayed releasing the American divisions, but in the end had to bow to Foch's superior authority. When ordered to place three British divisions astride the Somme, Haig complied, but only under protest, complaining that 'Our troops are being used up to the last man in order to give the French courage and induce them to hold their ground and fight!' He reflected upon how the inferior quality of French troops had been obvious at the beginning of the war and how

The Somme battle confirmed my view that much of the French good name as efficient fighters was the result of newspaper puffs. Then came Nivelle's fiasco in the spring of 1917, and for the rest of that year the French Armies 'rested'. And now, when the result of the war depends on their 'fighting spirit' many of their divisions won't face the enemy.

In a conversation with Gemeau on 13 June, Haig opined:

Pétain ought to have shot 2,000 instead of only 30 when so many mutinied this time last year. The situation of the French Army was very grave then, and required severe measures to remove the canker. Instead of training, the men were given 'leave' and 'repos'.

However appropriate Haig's remedy may, or may not, have been, he consistently ignored the fact that French casualties in the war were nearly twice the British.[52]

Foch's handling of British troops also alarmed Milner and Lloyd George. Like Haig, they doubted that the attack on the French would turn out to be the main German effort. At yet another conference, this time in Paris on 7 June, Haig, citing the Beauvais agreement, protested that Foch's intentions imperilled the British Army. Foch, citing the same agreement, asserted his authority to move troops where he saw fit. The conference ended with a typically weak recommendation that Haig and Foch should meet more frequently to discuss the movement of troops. Though Haig did not question the authority Foch had been given, he was worried about its implications: 'The responsibility for the safety of the British Army in France could no longer rest with me because the "Generalissimo" can do what *he* thinks right with *my* troops.' He therefore demanded 'that the British Government should in a document modify my responsibility for the safety of the British Army'.[53]

Contrary to British expectations, attacks against the French continued. On 9 June, the *Gneisenau* offensive was launched in the vicinity of the river Matz, in the direction of Compiègne. Though the attack stalled after an advance of fifteen kilometres, it encouraged a more sympathetic attitude towards French requests for assistance. On 17 June, Milner and Lloyd George announced their intention 'to support Foch to the utmost of their power . . . by allowing him to move British

Divisions as he deems right'. Haig was informed that the subordinate British position, though regrettable, was 'a temporary arrangement . . . necessary because it is the only means of holding our own diplomatically at present'. The government, he was assured, would assert itself and 'put the British army on a sound footing' when the crisis passed. Though Haig was not entirely satisfied with this solution, he accepted its rationale. He drew some consolation from the fact that Milner and Lloyd George were angry with the Allies 'because they were taking too large a share in the direction of the war, and gave little credit to Great Britain for what she was doing'. The French had 'acted in this style since the beginning of the war' – it was therefore about time that they were seen for the rascals they were. Haig was also relieved to receive the requested clarification of his responsibility and equally pleased with an assurance (not entirely honest) that the government was no longer interested in replacing him.[54]

A desire to preserve the apparently serene relations with the government was perhaps behind Haig's attitude towards the deposed Gough, who was making trouble. At the time of the sacking, Haig had emphasised that Gough 'has many fine qualities as a commander' and that 'Lloyd George . . . has made a mistake in removing [him] against my advice'. But, when Gough looked to Haig for support in his attempt, in early June, to clear his name, he was given the cold shoulder. Haig had apparently decided that Gough's removal (like Robertson's) was not an issue which warranted a firm stand. Attempting to back out of the matter as gently as he could, he explained to Doris that

> Gough . . . is talking stupidly . . . Some of his friends are advising him to keep quiet. I am doing all I can to help him, but, as a matter of fact, some orders he issued and things he did were stupid – and anything of the nature of an inquiry would not do him any good.

Nor, obviously, would it have done Haig any good. Realising this, he advised Gough on 6 July 'to remain quiet until more history is made and the events of the 21st of March and following days have faded somewhat from the memory of people at home'.[55]

The attacks upon the French continued through June and into July. Though casualties were high and much ground was lost, it was clear that the Germans were not attacking with the same vigour as in March. Meanwhile, the Americans had begun to arrive in earnest;

by mid-June, Foch had fourteen divisions under him, Haig another five. Both were pleased with the fighting qualities of the new troops. With the pressure somewhat eased and reserves relatively abundant, better relations between Haig and Foch resulted. When the two met on 28 June, 'Foch seemed in the best of spirits.' Both agreed that the Germans could no longer hope to end the war by military means alone and that the Allies should consider mounting an offensive in August. Haig announced that in the meantime he would launch a series of minor attacks – the aim being to secure strategic points essential to the subsequent general offensive. One such attack followed on 4 July. Ten battalions of Australians (reinforced by four American companies), commanded by General Sir John Monash, captured the village of Le Hamel with relatively few casualties. When Haig met Milner a week later in London, it was agreed that though the Germans still had sufficient reserves to mount a significant attack, the state of British and French defences 'justify us in regarding the future with less anxiety than [we] did in the first weeks of March this year'.[56]

The optimistic mood was shaken slightly when the Germans again attacked, with limited success, on the Marne on 15 July. When Foch moved four British divisions southward, the War Cabinet, still certain that an attack upon the British was imminent, went into a minor panic. On 15 July, Haig was instructed to 'rely on the exercise of your judgement, under the Beauvais Agreement, as to the security of the British front after the removal of these troops'. Angered by the difficult position in which he had been placed, Haig concluded that it was 'a case of "heads you win and tails I lose". If things go well, the Government take credit to themselves and the Generalissimo; if badly, the Field Marshal will be blamed!' In the end, he and Foch were able to resolve their differences with a minimum of strife, largely because both sensed that the danger had passed.[57]

The large reserves held by Kronprinz Rupprecht in the north, which had not been committed to the offensive against the French, nevertheless continued to cause concern. On 19 July, Haig told his wife that he still expected to be attacked on the Hazebroucke–Ypres front. This expectation was justified – the Germans were planning an offensive north of the river Lys. The German strength also made Haig hesitant to assume the offensive himself. Rupprecht's reserves were finally drawn off when the French Tenth and Sixth Armies counter-attacked with considerable success on the Aisne, on 18 July.

By 5 August, the enemy had been pushed out of the salient south of the river. The tide had turned.

A new mood was immediately evident. When the success of the French counter-attack became obvious, Haig and Foch, meeting on 24 July, decided that the time had come for 'regaining the initiative and passing to the offensive'. It was agreed that the British would launch a surprise attack east of Amiens, in the sector held by Rawlinson, as soon as possible. Haig was flattered when Foch gave him command of the First French Army in order to expand his operations. At a subsequent meeting on 3 August, Foch postulated that 'the Germans are breaking up'. Haig, who agreed, predicted that the attack on Amiens would be enormously successful. As in the preparation for the Somme, he ridiculed Rawlinson's 'final' objectives, advising him simply 'to advance as rapidly as possible'. The cavalry, he was certain, would finally have its day.[58]

On the eve of the attack, the King visited GHQ. 'H.M. looked well and very cheery. So different to his frame of mind on the occasion of his last visit in March.' Haig was told that Lloyd George was determined to support him against the French. 'L.G. wishes me to insist strongly on having our front reduced before the autumn comes, so that men can be given leave and troops be rested and trained.' What the King did not reveal (and probably did not know) was that the Prime Minister was again plotting to remove Haig and to put in his place General Cavan. A consequent shift of British strategy eastwards was also being discussed. Haig, blissfully unaware of these plots, by this stage cared little for what Lloyd George was thinking. With characteristic singularity of purpose, he was concerned only with the coming offensive. Ironically, for the first time in the war, he did not predict that the fighting would be over by the end of the year, expressing, instead, 'the belief that the British front would be much further forward before winter arrived'.[59]

On the following day, Rawlinson pushed forward on the Amiens front with three corps, 300 Mark V and ninety-six Whippet tanks and, of course, the cavalry. The attack, like those for the remainder of the war, followed the Cambrai model – the emphasis being upon predicted firing and massed tanks. Strategic objectives no longer impinged upon tactical possibilities; the point was to kill Germans and destroy defences. The mounted arm aside, the attack was a resounding success. Along the entire line, almost all the final objectives were reached by noon of the first day. Haig admitted that 'the situation . . . developed more favourably for us than I, optimist though I am, had dared even to hope!' 'Who would have believed this possible even two months ago?' he commented to his wife, adding: 'I am only the instrument of that Divine Power who watches over each one of us, so all the Honours must be his!' Haig's confidence – and his belief in God's grace – had returned to normal.[60]

Due perhaps to the influence of Haig's circumspect staff, confidence did not stray to dizzying heights. He was, in fact, ironically more cautious than the French. When, on 10 August, Foch pressed for the British attack to continue, Haig 'pointed out the difficulty of the undertaking unless the enemy is quite demoralised and we can cross the Somme on his heels'. He thought that '*some* German Divisions are demoralised but not *all* yet'. Haig sang a by now familiar lament: the French were intent upon bleeding the British white. Concerned about the enemy reserves still in the area, he decided that Rawlinson should halt, whereupon Byng could perhaps take over in the Arras sector. The issue was not resolved until 15 August, when Haig, refusing to budge, 'spoke to Foch quite straightly and let him understand that *I was responsible to my Government and fellow citizens for the handling of the British Forces*'. A startled Foch allowed Haig to do as he thought best.[61]

Haig subsequently shifted his attention to Arras. On 19 August, he criticised Byng's plans as 'too limited in scope', stressing that the objective was to 'break the enemy's front and *gain Bapaume as soon as possible*'. He especially disagreed with the limited role given to the cavalry:

> I told [Byng] that the cavalry was now 100% better than it was at Cambrai. *He must use the Cavalry to the fullest extent possible*. Now is the time to act with boldness, and in full confidence that if we only hit the enemy hard enough . . . his troops will give way on a very wide front and acknowledge that he is beaten.

Whilst Haig was perhaps right about the state of the German Army, he was wrong about the role the cavalry could play. At Amiens, on 8 August, the tactic of combining the mounted arm with the Whippet tanks had been a disaster. According to Liddell Hart, 'When there was no fire, the cavalry outstripped the tanks, and as soon as fire was opened the cavalry were unable to follow the tanks.' Haig, however, saw things differently: 'without the rapid advance of the Cavalry the effect of the surprise attack on the 8th would have been much less and very probably the Amiens outer defence line would not have been gained either so soon or so cheaply.' Four years of modern warfare had not roused Haig from his cavalry dreams. On 1 September, he complained to Wilson about the shortage of cavalry which was 'daily becoming noticeable'. He reminded the CIGS that, when the 'decisive moment' arrived, it was essential to have 'an efficient Cavalry Corps ready to act vigorously . . . [to] reap the fruits of victory'.[62]

On 21 August, five divisions of Byng's Army, attacking on a front of twenty-two kilometres, pushed the Germans from their positions with relative ease. On the same day, Churchill arrived at GHQ to discuss munitions programmes. To Haig's astonishment, these were 'all timed for "completion . . . *next June!*"' Flush with success, Haig argued that 'we ought to do our utmost to get a decision this autumn'. His troops were 'engaged in a "wearing out battle" and are outlasting and beating the enemy. If we allow the enemy a period of quiet, he will recover and the "wearing out" process must be recommenced.' Churchill, no doubt reflecting that this all sounded painfully familiar, remained unconvinced. The General Staff, he announced, thought that the decisive period of the war would not arrive until July 1919. Lloyd George, in fact, was making plans for 1920.[63]

Haig ignored Churchill. When Byng suggested a rest after the first day's fighting, he was ordered to keep pushing. 'The enemy's troops must be suffering more than ours, because we are elated by success, while the enemy is feeling that this is the beginning of the end for him, viz., DEFEAT.' In a memorandum to his Army Commanders, he referred to the need

for all ranks to act with the utmost boldness and resolution in order to get full advantage from the present favourable situation. The effect of the two severe defeats, and the continuous attacks to which the enemy has been subjected during the past month, has been to wear out his troops and disorganize his plans . . . The enemy has not the means to deliver counter-attacks on an extended scale, nor has he the numbers to hold a continuous position against the very extended advance which is now being directed upon him. To turn the present situation to account . . . let each one of us act energetically, and without hesitation push forward to our objective.

The memorandum was a virtual carbon copy of those issued in 1916 and 1917 – the only difference being that this time Haig was right. Byng continued to push, advancing six kilometres and capturing 5,000 prisoners by the 23rd. On the next day, Rawlinson resumed the attack, followed shortly afterwards by Horne, whose First Army advanced on a ten-kilometre front astride the river Scarpe. The strategically important high ground at Monchy-le-Preux was recaptured on the 26th. It was, Haig thought, 'the greatest victory which a British Army has ever achieved'. The situation demanded unrelenting pressure. Haig was, without doubt, the man best able to deliver it.[64]

The news was not, however, unreservedly bright. On 12 August, Pershing announced that he wanted to withdraw the five American divisions training with the British. Haig politely pointed out that a great deal of effort had been put into their training, therefore the British deserved something in return. Pershing refused to relent. Making no attempt to hide his bitterness, Haig remarked that 'the arrival in this battle of a few strong, vigorous American divisions, when the enemy's units are thoroughly worn out [could] lead to the most decisive results'. He privately wondered: 'What will history say regarding this action of the Americans leaving the British zone of operations when *the decisive battle* of the war is at its height, and the decision is still in doubt!' He subsequently urged Foch to 'put the Americans into battle *at once*'.[65]

Haig was certain that the momentum of the previous three weeks could be sustained, even though the formidable Siegfried, Wotan and Flandern defensive lines remained intact. On 30 August, he promised his Army commanders that 'the enemy would be engaged by the Allied Armies on a very wide front from now on'. In truth, as Haig was aware, the British would do most of the attacking. The Americans seemed to have cold feet, and 'very few French Divisions are said to be in good heart now . . . most are "war-weary"'. Ignoring these factors, Haig announced that since 'there was no risk of *heavy attack* by the enemy' the Army commanders were 'justified in taking very great risks in our forthcoming operations'.[66]

Away from the scene, the War Cabinet was less sanguine. Though they accepted that there was little risk of the Germans attacking, ministers feared that the enemy was still capable of an agressive defence. Relaying their fears, Wilson cautioned Haig on 31 August about 'incurring heavy losses in attacks on Hindenburg Line . . . I do not mean to say that you have incurred such losses, but I know the War Cabinet would become anxious if we received heavy punishment in attacking the Hindenburg Line, without success'. Haig saw Wilson's telegram as a cowardly attempt 'to save the Prime Minister in case of any failure'. Whilst allowing him to proceed with his offensive, the War Cabinet was divorcing itself from responsibility for it. 'If my attack is successful, I will remain on as C. in C. If we fail, or our losses are excessive, I can hope for no mercy!' In his reply, Haig argued that he had no intention of carelessly wasting men's lives; he had, after all, rejected Foch's plans for continuing the Amiens battle two weeks earlier because of the risk of heavy casualties. 'What a wretched lot!' he wrote. 'And how well they mean to support me! What confidence!' He could not of course accept that he had severely tried that confidence in the past. Wilson, in turn, tried to wriggle his way back into Haig's good favour:

> it isn't really want of confidence in you, it is much more the constant – and growing – embarrassments about Manpower that makes the Cabinet uneasy . . . No, it isn't want of confidence in you so much as the feeling that, when the end comes, we must still possess a formidable Army. My wire therefore was only intended to convey a sort of distant warning and nothing more.

Haig was neither pacified nor convinced. The telegram merely showed 'How ignorant our present statesmen are of the principles of war.' He emphasised, as he had in the past, that 'it is much less costly in lives to keep on pressing the enemy . . . than to give him time to recover and organize a fresh line of defence'.[67]

Haig, of his own volition, decided to go to London in order to impress upon the War Cabinet the need to 'provide the means to exploit our recent great successes to the full'. In a meeting with Milner on 10 September, he presented evidence to the effect that 'The discipline of the German Army is quickly going, and the German officer is no longer what he was.' The character of the war had definitely changed. 'If we act with energy now, a decision can be obtained in *the very near future*.' Having learned his lessons, Haig was conspicuously reluctant to make any more specific predictions. 'Lord Milner fully agreed and said he would do his best to help.' Or so Haig thought. Wilson wrote at the time that Milner 'thinks Haig ridiculously optimistic and is afraid that he may embark on another Passchendaele'. Doubts, by Milner or others, would have been understandable. In the past, Haig had promised much but delivered very little. Though recent British advances were impressive, they were still less extensive than those made by the Germans earlier in the year. Furthermore, casualties on both sides remained nearly equal; by the end of September, losses would reach nearly 200,000. These may have been the acceptable price of victory but Haig could still not guarantee that victory was what they would buy.[68]

Ignoring the doubts of these 'cowards', Haig continued to attack. On 18 September, the 3rd and 4th Armies advanced on a forty-kilometre front to within 5,000 metres of the Siegfried Line. The success of the operation prompted a short note from Wilson:

> My General,
>   Well done, you must be a famous General!
>   Henry

Haig thanked Wilson for his kindness, but insisted, 'No, certainly not! I am not, nor am I likely to be a *"famous General"*. For that must we not have pandered to Repington and the Gutter Press? But we have a surprisingly large number of *very capable* Generals.' Haig used the success to bargain for more troops and equipment. Wilson was urged to send 'Yeomanry, cyclists, motor lorries . . . anything to add to our mobility'. Milner, visiting GHQ, was likewise told that 'it is possible to get a decision this year, but if we do not every blow that we deliver now will make the task next year much easier'. Therefore, *'every available man should be put into the battle at once'*. Milner in turn warned Haig that 'if the British Army is used up now, there will not be men for next year'.[69]

Meanwhile, preparations proceeded for what would turn out to be the final offensive on the Western Front. Haig and Foch had decided to strike with simultaneous and converging attacks on both flanks of the salient formed earlier in the year by the German offensive. The British would attack in Picardy; the French and the Americans in the Argonne. At the same time, the Belgians (aided by the British Second Army) would push forward in Flanders.

Early results were disappointing. On 26 September 1918, the Americans jerked forward on three cylinders; the French were hardly more successful. But, on the following day, the First and Third British Armies pushed through two lines of the Siegfried system around Cambrai. Then came the turn of Rawlinson, reinforced by two American and two Australian divisions. By the morning of the 29th, his force had captured two lines of the strongest sector of the Siegfried defences between St Quentin and Cambrai. Haig took obvious delight in proving his critics wrong. He noted that 'an Army Commander (I gather it was Byng) stated in August (last month) that we would never get beyond the Hindenburg Line! Now we *are* through that line.'[70] This was an exaggeration – the third defensive line had yet to be captured. But it was an exaggeration for which Haig could for once be excused.

On 6 October, the Paris newspapers carried the news that Germany, Austria and Turkey had requested an armistice based upon President Wilson's Fourteen Points. Haig, in a meeting with Foch when the news broke, remarked – correctly – that it was 'the immediate result of the British piercing the Hindenburg Line'.[71]

The possibility of an armistice brought with it an entirely new set of issues over which the principal actors could disagree. Foch at once insisted that 'the enemy should be told to retire to the Rhine as a guarantee of good faith, before any negotiations are begun'. Four days later, he told Haig that 'the enemy is so desirous of peace that he will agree to any terms of this nature which we impose'. He had therefore advised Clemenceau to demand the evacuation of Belgium, France and Alsace-Lorraine; the administration by the allies of all territory up to the Rhine; and the surrender of three bridgeheads on the river. The Germans would be required to evacuate within fifteen days, leaving all their heavy equipment behind them. Haig, distressed by Foch's attitude, noted that 'the only difference between his . . . conditions and a "general unconditional surrender" is that the Germany Army is allowed to march back with its rifles, and officers with their swords'. Whilst Haig planned 'to go on hitting [the enemy] as hard as we possibly can, till he begs for mercy'; he was, unlike Foch, prepared to grant mercy when it was requested. There was, Haig thought, no need to prolong the punishment and the humiliation (not to mention the dying) any longer than required.[72]

On 13 October, Haig met Clemenceau, who 'thanked me "in the name of France" for what I had done'. The French leader was 'evidently fully aware how the recent results obtained are entirely due to the boldness and tenacity of the British Army'. Taking the opportunity to voice his concern over proposed armistice terms, Haig argued that Foch's demands were 'too complicated . . . We ought to say "hand over Metz and Strasburg as a preliminary sign of your good faith".' He also thought that 'America ought not to be allowed to play so prominent a part in making peace since she has, as yet, done little to bring it about.' It seemed that Clemenceau agreed.[73]

Haig was worried about the effect which decisions taken far away from the fighting front would have upon his Army. 'Kindly let me know', he asked Wilson, 'how far Foch, as Generalissimo, has power to involve the British Army? If I do not concur in such terms as he may wish to impose, what am I to do?' Anticipating this inquiry with a simultaneous telegram, Wilson told Haig that 'until the terms of an armistice have been laid down by the allies and agreed to by the enemy, the operations now going on should be continued with all the vigour you consider safe and possible'. In other words, Haig was to mind his own business, and, in the meantime, should warn his men 'not to throw their caps up prematurely'.[74]

Considerably anxious about the recent course of events, Haig met Wilson in London on the 19th, and was dismayed to learn that he agreed with Foch. In a desperate attempt to inject some sanity into the debate, Haig argued that the Germans were still capable of determined resistance and not yet ripe for unconditional surrender. A similar message was conveyed to Lloyd George, Milner and Bonar Law later in the day: 'The German Army is capable of retiring to its own frontier, and holding that line if there should be any attempt to touch the *honour* of the German people, and make them fight with the courage of despair.' The French desired retribution but would not be doing the bulk of the dying. 'The British alone might bring the enemy to his knees. But why expend more British lives – and for what?' It therefore made sense to offer reasonable terms now, rather than prolong the war into 1919 and allow the Germans to recuperate over the winter. Haig proposed that these terms should be the evacuation of France, Belgium and Alsace Lorraine, the occupation by the Allies of Metz and Strasburg and the return of Belgian and French rolling stock.[75]

Lloyd George seemed to agree but Milner and Wilson demanded stiffer terms, particularly the evacuation to the Rhine. When asked about the attitude of his Army, Haig replied that though he remained confident of the determination of his men:

> everyone wants to have done with the war, *provided* we get what we want. I therefore advise . . . that we set our faces against the French entering Germany to pay off old scores. In my opinion, under the supposed conditions, the British army would not fight keenly for what is not its own affair.

Haig later suggested that the roles of civilians and soldiers should be kept distinct, 'i.e., the soldiers will arrange the Armistice. As soon as that is concluded, the diplomatists should take their place and arrange PEACE.' This was a naive wish. In the days that followed, Haig found common sense in short supply. Those furthest from the fighting seemed most strident in their demands for revenge. The naval terms, for instance, were 'most exacting and incapable of enforcement except by a land force'. After a discussion on 21 October, Haig concluded that Wilson wanted to continue the war so that conscription could be enforced in Ireland, and that country pacified in the process.[76]

On the 24th, Foch reiterated his terms for an armistice, which Haig dismissed as being 'political, not military'. He was also angry with Foch's insistence that the British Second Army should remain under the command of King Albert, as it had been in the recent offensive. According to Haig:

> Foch declines to return the Second Army to me because of the political value of having the King of the Belgians in command of an allied Army, when he re-enters his capital, Brussels! His real object is to use the British Second Army to open the way for the 'dud' Divisions . . . and ensure that they get to Brussels. France would then get the credit for clearing Belgium and putting the King back in his capital.

Haig gave Foch some 'home truths' about how '*the British Army has defeated the Germans this year*', but the Frenchman refused to budge. Foch, he concluded, 'is suffering from a swollen head and thinks himself another Napoleon!'[77]

Though Haig criticised Foch for allowing political considerations to take precedence over military ones, he did not himself ignore the former. The difference was that because he had no desire for immediate revenge, he was capable of a long-term political view. For instance, he feared that if harsh terms were imposed upon the Germans 'Bolshevism may get the upper hand in the country, and all law and order be at an end'. It also seemed possible that eventually a 'Militarist would return to Power and begin a life and death struggle'. At a meeting with Foch, Pétain and Pershing on 25 October, Haig stressed that harsh terms were a gamble hardly worthy of the risk since 'We don't know very much about the internal state of Germany.' Leaving aside the irony of this admission, he was absolutely right. Unfortunately, he was talking to a brick wall; Foch, Pétain and even Pershing, were bent on retribution. Haig was astonished at Pétain's proposal for 'a huge indemnity, so large that she will never be able to pay it. Meantime French troops will hold the left bank of the Rhine as a pledge!'[78]

Prior to a meeting of the Supreme War Council on 1 November, Haig conveyed his worries to his wife:

> The Peace of the World, for the next 50 years at least, may depend upon the decisions taken! So it is important that our Statesmen should think over the situation carefully and not attempt to so humiliate Germany as to produce the desire for revenge in years to come.

He soon learned that his was a lonely voice of reason. The surrender of Turkey and Austria-Hungary had convinced the allied representatives that it was safe to squeeze Germany. Astonished and disappointed, Haig recorded that 'the terms are very stiff, and include retirement beyond the Rhine with a strip of 40 kilos. on the eastern bank . . . Personally, I feel that there are many good officers in Germany like myself who would in a similar situation rather die than accept such conditions.' He predicted that the terms would be rejected and the war would continue. Intelligence reports (which had ironically so often indicated a demoralised Germany) revealed that *the enemy has not yet been sufficiently beaten as to cause him to accept an ignominious peace*.[79]

Haig was wrong. On the 9th, the Kaiser abdicated. Two days later, hostilities ceased. Accepting his error gracefully, Haig shifted his attention to the enforcement of the armistice terms, however iniquitous he felt them to be. His first priority, however, was to give thanks. To Doris he wrote: 'my first thought is to thank that Power that has guided and guarded me all these anxious years', adding that he wanted to 'thank *you* too for being such a good true little wife to me through these long black days since I left you at Aldershot'. When he learned, on the 11th, that the Kaiser had fled to Holland and that German soldiers had fired on their officers, he reflected:

> If the war had gone against us, no doubt our King would have had to go, and probably our Army would have become insubordinate like the German Army. cf, John Bunyan's remark on seeing a man on his way to be hanged. 'But for the Grace of God, John Bunyan would have been in that man's place.'

In the only way that mattered to Haig, his efforts had been a success.[80]

15

Consistent to the End

For Haig, the lessons of the past had always been sacrosanct. The war had been won not by ingenious tactics and new weaponry but 'by applying old principles to present conditions'. In the very same way, he thought, the fruits of victory would be reaped.[1]

But, as Haig soon found, this formula was as unpopular after the armistice as it had been during the war. Lloyd George, among others, seemed too eager to opt for short-term political gains at the expense of long-term social stability. Upon hearing that a snap election had been called, Haig wrote that he was

> disappointed to see that our rulers are entirely given up to electioneering now, apparently forgetful of all our War truths. In my opinion they should be on their knees, thanking God for having preserved the Old Country and our liberties in spite of the Government.

The Army, according to Haig, felt 'a general apathy' about the election; there was 'a feeling that "we have been got at" [by] . . . the Prime Minister'. He felt 'much the same' – commenting (once again) that 'I do not think that Lloyd George is really to be trusted.' Unfortunately, Labour and the Liberals were even more untrustworthy; therefore, on 14 December a disenchanted Haig 'voted for four Coalitionists, viz., one for Kingston, and three for the Scottish Universities'. He did not derive a great deal of comfort from the coalition landslide, announced two weeks later.[2]

Difficult as it may be to imagine, Haig's regard for Lloyd George had actually diminished since the armistice. He felt particularly hurt by the Prime Minister's plans for a ceremony in honour of Foch scheduled for 1 December in London. 'I heard that I was to be in the fifth carriage along with General Henry Wilson. I felt that this was more of an insult than I could put up with, even from the Prime Minister.' Though he was expected to take part in the procession, he was not invited to the subsequent reception. In a letter to Doris, Haig surmised that Lloyd George was 'trying to belittle the British Army' because 'it might interfere with him and his schemes of revolution and bolshevism'. Venting his anger in his diary, he wrote that he had 'no intention of taking part in any triumphal ride with Foch, or with any pack of foreigners, through the streets of London, mainly in order to add to L.G.'s importance and help him in his election campaign'. He was thus conspicuously absent.[3]

A proper homecoming took place on 19 December, when Haig returned to England to spend his first Christmas with his family for four years. The welcome accorded by the cheering crowds who lined the streets of London was indeed impressive. Haig was especially delighted that

> The reception was essentially a *welcome by the people*, without any official interference, and I could not help feeling how the cheering from the great masses of all classes came from their hearts. As A.D.C. to King Edward, I have taken part in many functions, but never before have I seen such crowds, or such whole hearted enthusiasm. It was indeed most touching to take part in such a ceremony.

After a reception with the King and Queen, Haig returned to his home. At 8.30 that evening a crowd of some 10,000 people descended upon Kingston Hill, there to pay further homage to the Commander-in-Chief. Genuinely touched, Haig reflected:

> To-day, indeed, has been a red letter one in my life. To receive such a spontaneous welcome . . . shows how the people of England realise what has been accomplished by the Army and myself. This more than compensates for the . . . coldness displayed towards me by the Prime Minister since the Armistice.[4]

Another sore point between Haig and Lloyd George pertained to the matter of rewards. On 19 November 1918, Haig received a telegram from Downing Street, offering him a viscountcy. He immediately rejected the offer, noting in his diary 'that when F.M. French was *recalled* from the command of the Armies in France for *incompetence*, he was made a Viscount!' But Haig did not reject the offer solely out of pique; it was, he explained, impossible for him to accept a peerage 'until the P.M. has fixed allowances for Disabled Officers and men as well as "batta" for all ranks of the Armies under my orders'.[5]

Haig's concern for disabled soldiers was no mere post-war whim inspired by a guilty conscience. Over the previous few years, appalling cases of poverty and neglect had come to his attention. With state aid virtually non-existent, the disabled were forced to rely on overstretched charities. On 30 July 1918, Haig told his wife that 'it is a mistake to ask the public to subscribe to help Disabled Officers when it is the *duty* of the State to do so. The voluntary funds should be *in addition* to state aid. The latter must be fixed at a minimum of what is necessary to keep the poor fellows from want.' Apparently confused by her husband's message, Lady Haig subsequently proposed donating £5,000 to a disabled officers charity. A somewhat stunned Haig replied that he wanted to know a lot more about the 'organisation, rules, and who is on the committee, etc.' before making any donation. He nevertheless promised that he would 'give not only money, but all the energy which I may have left after the war is over, to help Disabled Officers and men who have suffered in this war'.[6]

He was as good as his word. The refusal of a peerage was a calculated and ingenious ploy to embarrass the government and galvanise it into action on the pensions problem. And embarrassed the government was. Wilson, replying to Haig's rejection of the Prime Minister's offer, wrote that Admiral Sir David Beatty (the First Sea Lord) had accepted a similar award, and added: 'It would be a wholly false situation, generally misunderstood by the public and distressing to the King, if only Beatty was honoured at this moment, indeed, unless you assent, I do not see how his name can be put forward alone.' Wilson gave his assurance that the disabled would be dealt with 'in no niggardly spirit, though it may take a little time to get everything settled'. Haig, merciless in his righteousness, had decided to be neither patient nor understanding. This benevolent blackmail continued over the next two months, with Wilson repeatedly arguing that the disabled were well looked after by the charities, and Haig persistently countering that 'Officers and their wives . . . will not, and ought not to be asked to, accept *Charity*.' The King, who intervened on two separate occasions, was no more successful than Wilson in denting Haig's resolve.[7]

On 23 February 1919, Sassoon went to Downing Street to discuss the pensions and peerage issues with Lloyd George. Haig told Sassoon beforehand to make it clear that no personal rewards would be accepted until the government demonstrated its commitment to the disabled. The private secretary was further advised to tell the Prime Minister that Haig was 'well satisfied with the rank and honours conferred on me. I only want a sufficient pension to live in a simple way without monetary anxieties for the rest of my life.' If the government insisted on a peerage, Sassoon was to stress that 'unless an adequate grant is made to me to enable a suitable position to be maintained, I must decline such an honour'. Haig had no desire to become a poverty stricken peer.[8]

The Downing Street meeting brought some progress towards an agreement. Lloyd George blamed the pensions fiasco on the minister responsible (who had recently been sacked) and assured Sassoon that the problems would be resolved within two months. As to the question of a peerage and grant, the Prime Minister sympathised with the argument that Haig could not accept the former without the latter. But, 'with so much unrest about – miners demanding an extra shilling, etc. – this was a bad time to go to the House for a large sum of money'. There was also the problem of Beatty, whose services could not be compared to those of Haig, but who nevertheless had to be given an equal sum, so as not to offend the Navy. As to the size of the grant, Lloyd George thought £100,000 appropriate. Sassoon had in mind £250,000.[9]

Though details remained to be settled, it appears that by the beginning of March Haig was satisfied with the government's promises to help the disabled, and was therefore ready to accept his reward. Though Lady Haig disapproved of a large grant, her objections were easily brushed aside. So too were the reservations of Lord Elibank who advised Haig that the working class resented rewards made to officers. 'You have saved the nation in war; it may devolve upon you to save her in Peace' (in other words by refusing a grant). Haig politely reminded Elibank that he had 'until quite recently taken up the attitude you advise solely in order to help the ex-soldiers'. Nevertheless,

I was induced to abandon my previous attitude because I had no wish to appear to be setting myself up as superior to all the rest, and too superior to accept reward! Nor did I wish to join the Bolshevists by refusing the title which the King proposed to give me! Moreover any further refusal to accept the reward on my part won't benefit the ex-soldier. The Govt. has promised to do its duty in the matter – indeed the whole country is now behind me in its determination to see that these gallant fellows and their dependants are *properly* treated.

On 6 August, Haig was granted £100,000, and eight weeks later was made an earl. The package of rewards was completed in 1921, when a grateful nation presented him with the ancestral home of Bemersyde.[10]

During his homecoming in December 1918, Haig came for the first time into contact with Woodrow Wilson, who had crossed the Atlantic to take part in the peace negotiations. First impressions were not very positive. 'He talks well and seems pleasant and agreeable', Haig thought, 'but is he a practical man?' Wilson's main fault was apparently his idealism, an attribute which Haig thought out of place in the modern world. Some comfort was derived from a speech the President made at the Mansion House, on 28 December, in which 'There was less rubbish talked about the League of Nations, "self-determination" and democracy.'[11]

This sort of rubbish must not, Haig thought, pollute the peace process. Since, in his view, the need to preserve the security of the British Empire was paramount, it was imperative that the Continent be stabilised – by whatever means necessary. His advice was something of a mixed bag. On the one hand, he suggested 'dividing up the German people into independent States . . . A great block of 70 to 80 million Germans in the centre of Europe must produce trouble in the future.' At the same time, it was 'to our interest . . . to have Germany a prosperous, not an impoverished country'; nor was it wise 'to make Germany our enemy for many years to come'. If the country were too severely weakened, the result would be anarchy. Fearing such a situation, Haig urged Henry Wilson and Milner to send emergency food supplies to the German people. 'If we don't feed her, Bolshevism will spread. This will result in the destruction of Germany and probably in our having to intervene. And, further, Bolshevism is likely to spread to France and England.' For similar reasons, Haig scorned the attitude of the French, whose object it was to 'grind Germany to powder'. 'The French don't want peace! They want "revenge" and the destruction of the German people . . . so that there will be no competitor against French trade.' Haig warned Hankey that 'If the French were allowed to have their own way, the British would lose much of their fruits of victory and the war would go on without end.' Many of these suggestions made sense. Unfortunately, after the armistice (unlike during the war) Haig's advice could easily be ignored.[12]

Upon Haig's return to France in the New Year, he was confronted with a problem which had been virtually non-existent during the war years – that being the spread of serious discontent within his Army. On 8 January, he sent 'a strongly worded wire to the W.O. pointing out that the Army is being disturbed by the Demobilisation Orders'. He was especially concerned about the policy of 'pivotalism' under which men with promised places in industry were demobilised first, regardless of when they had actually entered the Army. When this scheme was first proposed in November 1917, Haig warned that it was unfair and potentially dangerous. Men who had delayed joining the Army (in other words those who had resisted the call to volunteer) were those most likely to have jobs waiting for them at home and would consequently be the first to be released. Unpatriotic behaviour would therefore be rewarded. In addition, Haig worried that the scheme would give rise to serious social dislocation. The discipline and cohesion of the military would be too quickly relaxed and a 'mass of individuals' set loose upon society, with predictable consequences. Far better, Haig thought, to demobilise 'by complete formations' – and thus use the military structure as a tool by which to ease the reintegration of the soldier into society.[13]

This advice was ignored and, at the end of January, a very serious riot occurred at Calais when soldiers returning from leave refused to rejoin their units. Faced with what he perceived to be a potential revolution, Haig reacted with characteristic severity:

> I directed the CGS and AG to tell the Commander on the spot that they *must keep order*. We are all 'on active service'. If men start disturbances in the town of Calais or elsewhere, *the disturbances are to be quelled at all costs, and as soon as possible. Discipline must be maintained*, and rioters if they cannot be arrested must

be shot. Those men who have returned from leave have no ground for complaint and appear to be led astray by Bolshevist agitators.

Order was quickly restored, whereupon the question of punishment arose. In a letter to Churchill, the new War Minister, Haig emphasised 'How important . . . it is that the ringleaders of the mutiny should suffer the supreme penalty. If any leniency is shown to them the discipline of the whole Army will suffer, both immediately and for many years to come.' Churchill, fearing that executions would only exacerbate the tension, counselled leniency. In response, a disgusted Haig recorded: 'I have power, by warrant, to try by Court Martial and shoot in accordance with Army Act; and no telegram from S. of S. can affect my right to do what I think is necessary for the Army.' The steam released, Haig then did as Churchill wished.[14]

It is significant, in the light of their disagreement, that Churchill not long afterwards asked Haig to become Commander-in-Chief, Home Forces. The War Minister announced that the position had become profoundly important because 'Very serious strikes for which colliers, railwaymen and dockers are organised to combine together, seem imminent.' In other words, the severity advocated by Haig after the Calais incident did not disqualify him for a position in which the requisite characteristics would seem to have been moderation and tact. As it turned out, Haig was surprisingly well suited to his new assignment. Upon taking up his post in April, he assumed an uncharacteristically low profile. He recognised that in Britain the Home Office was the official law enforcement authority and he its servant. No attempt was made to exploit or expand upon the very limited power he possessed. Thus, when a general strike threatened in the autumn of 1919, he directed

> that troops should be kept concealed as long as possible, and should only appear when the civil authorities required their help. As soon as the necessity for action was over the troops must at once be withdrawn out of sight. Troops must be armed and act as soldiers. It is not their duty to act as policemen.

To Haig's profound relief, the strike did not materialise. Never very comfortable in his new post – in which the 'enemy' was often former soldiers – he was quite pleased when it was abolished in January 1920, despite the fact that his active military career had thus been brought to an end.[15]

With the completion of his duties as Commander-in-Chief, Home Forces, Haig was able to devote undivided attention to the needs of the men he had commanded. For the last nine years of his life, this was his consuming passion. In the immediate aftermath of the Great War, a number of associations were founded to advance the interests of ex-soldiers. All had the same basic end, but very different means. Aware that veterans were not likely to get fair treatment from society unless they presented a united front, Haig immediately pushed for an amalgamation of these organisations. In a letter to a former colleague who was keen on an association in which membership would be restricted to officers, Haig explained that

> any attempt now to start a special 'Ex-Officer Assn.' would be harmful, first because it would withdraw the real leaders from the ex-service men, and secondly because such action at once divides officers and men into two camps. Whatever we do must be towards, not against unity.

Haig wanted '*one association* to include all who have served in H.M.'s service, regardless of their rank and present position'. Though such an amalgamation was not at first popular, through the sheer force of his personality and reputation, Haig was able to bring it into being. The British Legion, formally established in June 1921, owed its existence and its success above all to Haig.[16]

It is impossible here to do justice to the complex history of the Legion, or to Haig's tireless efforts on its behalf. But it should be mentioned that the organisation had for him a dual purpose. Aside from the obvious one of safeguarding the welfare of the ex-soldier, he saw an equally important need to curb the discontent of those who, returning from war, did not find the 'land fit for heroes' which they had been promised. It was necessary to wean these men away from the radicalism to which their disillusionment made them susceptible. Haig, as has been seen, recognised this 'danger' very early in the war, and, immediately after the armistice, warned that his men

> are still soldiers though without arms, and no doubt will go in for fresh groupings for new objectives, hitherto unthought of by

the present race of politicians! Above all, they will take vigorous action to right any real or supposed wrong! All this seems to me to make for trouble unless our Government is alert and tactful.

The Legion, in Haig's view, would be uniquely qualified to offer understanding, guidance and support to discontented ex-servicemen. Equally important, social stability would be promoted by perpetuating the cohesiveness and camaraderie of the wartime Army. This would be accomplished by directing the attentions of members outward: the Legion would 'foster the spirit of self sacrifice which inspired ex-servicemen to subordinate their individual welfare to the interests of the Commonwealth'; it would 'perpetuate [the] spirit of comradeship and patriotism through the Empire'. To this end, it was especially important that the Legion steer clear of politics. 'I think our politics should be imperial and in no sense partisan,' Haig advised. Thus the organisation took on the character of its founder. Politics and radical change were abhorrent; the Empire took precedence over the individual; the aim was essentially conservative.[17]

Haig was able to bring about the same amalgamation of ex-servicemen's associations in South Africa in 1921 and Canada in 1925. Similar trips to Australia and New Zealand were planned but could not be arranged before he died. In Capetown, in 1921, the British Empire Ex-Service's League was formally founded with Haig as Grand President (the body has since become the British Commonwealth Ex-Service's League). Though he died before his goals were fully realised, the spirit of his work survived. It was work which consumed most of his waking hours; it has been said, with some accuracy, that he toiled even harder than he did during the war. All correspondence was answered in his own hand, without the aid of a secretary. Despite doctor's advice, he refused to lighten his load.

One particularly loathsome facet of Haig's British Legion work was the vast number of speeches which he had to deliver to or on behalf of local branches. He was, in addition, during the post-war period in great demand at remembrance ceremonies, speech days, and the like. Inarticulate and rather shy, he had always dreaded speaking in public. Unfortunately, neither his proficiency nor his confidence improved through constant practice. But, though the delivery was invariably muddled, the message always managed to shine through. That message seldom varied: listeners – be they schoolboys or old

404

soldiers – were reminded of their duty to the Empire. For example, at Clifton in June 1922, Haig emphasised that

> Only by work and worth can a man attain true eminence or a nation remain great. We have received from the hands of our forefathers an Empire that is yet greater in ideals and qualities for which it stands than in the wide territories of which it is composed. It is for us to preserve these qualities and seek after these ideals, no less than to keep these territories free from the foot of the invader. Courage, manliness, truth, clean-living and honest dealing are the qualities that have made our nation great and must be preserved if that greatness is to last.

Haig went on to elucidate his personal principle of war: 'Tanks, guns, and aeroplanes would not have sufficed to bring us victory in the Great War if the character of our people had been other than what it was.' He ended with a clarion call more suited to a bygone age: 'Let your actions and your thoughts be worthy of the burden you will one day have to bear as a citizen of the greatest Empire that has ever taken manliness, liberty and justice for its purpose and ideals.'[18]

The passage of the years provided evidence that the message was not being heeded. Haig deeply regretted the way post-war Britain recklessly discarded pre-war standards. Authority crumbled; morals slipped. Workers seemed constantly on strike. Abroad, the Irish and Indians trampled on the Union Jack. Perhaps most disenchanting was the way the workers rejected the guidance of their benevolent superiors and turned in ever greater numbers to the Labour Party. Though glad of the departure of Lloyd George in 1922, Haig feared that Bonar Law and Stanley Baldwin did not have the manliness and courage necessary to put the nation back on the right track. During a trip to Italy in 1926, he discovered what he thought was the solution to Britain's problems:

> Yesterday evening I had an interview with Mussolini. I found him most pleasant. There is no doubt that he has already done much good in this country. His view is, that everyone is a servant of the State and must honestly do his best to serve the State. If anyone fails he is punished. We want someone like that at home at the present time.[19]

Though concerned by the course of events, Haig remained, as ever, confident and optimistic. The fact that his message appeared not to be heeded did not discourage him from repeatedly delivering it. Eventually, the pace became too much, the strains too great. On 29 January 1928, his heart surrendered

At memorial services, the British people paid their respects with genuine grief and affection. The bitterness and animosity which would eventually surface were not in evidence. Huge crowds lined London's streets as the funeral procession made its way to Westminster Abbey. Later, the High Street in Edinburgh was packed with silent mourners who watched the cortège wind its way slowly to St Giles. In accordance with Haig's wishes, he was laid to rest in the grounds of Dryburgh Abbey, a short distance from Bemersyde.

It is commonly held that Haig, to his credit, avoided the urge to defend his war record, engaging – unlike Lloyd George, Wilson, French, and Robertson (to name but a few) – in neither accusation nor self-justification. Like most popular opinions of Haig, this one is not entirely accurate. He did for instance, encourage the publication of his despatches, a volume released, by no coincidence, just before the 1922 election. The passages embarrassing to Lloyd George were not, however, responsible for bringing about his defeat – Haig could do little further damage to a reputation which was by then severely tarnished. He also reacted angrily (as has been seen) to French's allegations in his book *1914*, and to other criticisms – real, perceived or anticipated. It is nevertheless true that, generally speaking, Haig decided to rest upon his reputation, making little effort to defend it. Thus, he directed Kiggell and Lawrence to prepare the 'Memorandum on Operations on the Western Front, 1916–18' – a glowing tribute to his leadership – but insisted that the document be sealed until 1940. He considered for a time releasing his diaries, but eventually decided against it. He found it quite easy to steer clear of the sordid cesspool of public debate. As in the past, his quiescent image enhanced his reputation.[20]

The explanation for Haig's attitude is quite simple. He saw no reason for self-justification because he perceived of no faults in his command. As far as he was concerned, he had fulfilled his duty to the British Empire – there was no more devoted servant than he. The pursuance of duty had taken him to South Africa and the Sudan to fight two imperial wars. In 1914, he went to France to fight a third. The Great War was for him not a crusade to rescue poor little Belgium, it was a defence of Empire – God's Empire. Victory (he thought) would purify and strengthen Britain; it would expand the Empire; it would spread even wider the righteous and benevolent influence of English culture and of the English people. No price was too high for so sublime a prize. Victory was therefore its own justification; there was no need to question its cost. A formula for victory less costly than Haig's probably existed, but it was not part of his make-up to search for it. Death and suffering caused him grief, but never distracted him from his single-minded purpose of defeating the German Army.

In the end, Haig won. He accomplished what he had been trained to do; what his country required of him. In the Victorian age that would have been enough for him to qualify as a hero. But, unbeknownst to him, during his lifetime standards changed. When Britain became a people at war instead of simply an Army at war, there was a corresponding alteration in the definition of victory. It was no longer enough just to win. Costs and consequences became important. It was Haig's ironic fate that he, an eminent Edwardian, eventually came to be judged according to the very different standards of another age.

Notes

Numbers in the text are positioned at the end of a paragraph when the quotations in that paragraph are taken from more than one source. When there is only one quotation to be cited, the number is positioned at the end of that quotation. Citations from the Haig Papers are listed in the notes as 'Acc. 3155', followed by the specific file number. Citations from the Haig Diaries are simply referred to as 'Diary', followed by the date. 'HTLH' signifies 'Haig to Lady Haig'; and 'HTH' – 'Haig to Henrietta Jameson'. Other letters to or from Haig, unless otherwise cited, are contained in the Haig Diary. References to published sources, listed in the Bibliography, are by the author's name, unless more than one work by that author was consulted, in which case the title is included.

Introduction

1. Duff Cooper was not Lady Haig's first choice as official biographer. She first approached Sir Frederick Maurice, Sir James Edmonds and J.H. Boraston, but all refused, for different reasons. Duff Cooper's work, for reasons which remain unclear, upset her intensely. She tried to stop its publication, and when this proved impossible attempted to publish her own biography before Duff Cooper's. Faber and Faber, the publishers of *Haig*, in response initiated legal proceedings blocking her from doing so. The original biography by Lady Haig, much longer and more detailed than *The Man I Knew*, was never published. The manuscript is contained in the Haig Papers at the National Library of Scotland. Correspondence pertaining to the publication of the official biography and Lady Haig's work can be found in volumes 321 and 325 of the Haig collection.
2. Lloyd George, *War Memoirs*, forward to Volume I.

1 'And the Training Makes a Gentleman'

1. John Haig was six generations removed from Robert Haig of St Ninian's – the second son of the 17th Laird of Bemersyde.
2. John Haig to Lady Haig: 16 Feb. 1930, Acc. 3155/322(a). Rachel Haig to Douglas: 20 July 1877, Acc. 3154 (a).
3. Thomas Houston to Lady Haig: 6 April 1929, Acc. 3155/324(a). John Haig to Lady Haig: op. cit.
4. Ibid.
5. Janet Haig to Douglas: 10 Aug. 1920, Acc. 3155/346(d). An envelope containing the curls can still be found in the Haig collection in the National Library of Scotland.

6. Emily Haig to Lady Haig: 7 April 1928, Acc. 3155/322(a). Janet to Haig, op. cit.
7. Rachel to Douglas: 15 May 1874. John Haig to Lady Haig, op. cit.
8. The date of the document is not known. It was enclosed in the 10 August 1920 letter from Janet to Douglas.
9. Rachel Haig to unknown: 4 April 1859, Acc. 3155/3(a).
10. Rachel to John: 9 June 1885, Acc. 3155/3(a).
11. Dr Robertson to Lady Haig: n.d., Acc. 3155/324(a).
12. Norman Dixon argues – without secure foundation – that Haig's failures in school and his mother's strict upbringing resulted in 'pathological achievement motivation'. See Dixon, p. 250 ff.
13. The Countess Haig, *The Man I Knew*, p. 14. Rachel to Douglas: 21 May, 8 Oct. 1875.
14. Rachel to Douglas: 15 July, 29 Sept., 16 Oct. 1875. Rachel to John: 24 Sept. 1875.
15. John Haig to Lady Haig, op. cit. Rachel to Douglas: 7 Dec. 1878; 29 May, 18 June 1875. Rachel to John: 18 June 1875. C.C. Hoyer-Millar to Lady Haig: n.d., Acc. 3155/324(a). Charteris, *Field Marshal Earl Haig*, p. 5.
16. Rachel to Douglas: 25, 28 Feb., 4 March 1879.
17. Askwith, 'Haig at Oxford' p. 347. Diary: 21 Jan. 1883.
18. Duff Cooper, p. 20. Diary: frontispiece; 17, 18 June 1882.
19. Askwith, p. 347.
20. Diary: 18 April 1883.
21. Diary: 16 Jan., 22, 29 April 1883. Askwith, p. 348.
22. Askwith, p. 347.
23. Ibid. Diary: 18 April 1883.
24. Diary: 23, 28 April 1883. Askwith, p. 348.
25. Diary: 6, 14 March 1883. Askwith (p. 348) wrote that Haig had no time for the bawdy conversations common to groups of men. 'I have seen his face set in silent but obstinate protest, against any loose jokes about women. My impression was and is that he disliked any remarks derogatory to women, and showed it, without speaking, so clearly that any would be raconteur "dried up".'
26. The Sandhurst admission system may also have been a factor in his decision to go to university in the first place, since 'Regular Candidates' – those direct from school – had to be under 19 years old. Haig was already 19 when he returned from America. He therefore may have decided to go to Oxford in order to keep alive the possibility of an Army career.

2 A Martinet

1. L. Marshall to Lady Haig: 9 Oct. 1929; Acc. 3155/324(a). G. Drummond to Lady Haig: 10 Jan. 1929; Acc. 3155/324(a).
2. Diary: 19, 23 July 1883.
3. Congreve's observations are taken from the unpublished autobiography of Brig.-Gen. Sir James Edmonds, Edmonds MSS, III/2/10.
4. 'Report of the Royal Commission on Military Education' (1870), quoted in Harries-Jenkins, p. 148.
5. Bond, 'Doctrine and Training in the British Cavalry', in M. Howard (ed.) *The Theory and Practice of War*, p. 120.
6. The letter is no longer in existence but is mentioned in the Diary, 17 Aug. 1892.
7. All the quotations from H. J. Harrison are from his letter to Lady Haig: 17 April 1937, Acc. 3155/324(a).

8. Diary: 12, 13 Feb. 1889.
9. Diary: 29 Nov. 1889.
10. Diary: 8 June 1891. Bengough to Haig: 20 June 1891, Acc. 3155/6(e).
11. The quotation is from the Diary, 14 Aug. 1892. Haig was quoting a tribute given to him by Hunt at a farewell dinner.
12. Haig to Henrietta Jameson (hereafter HTH): 1 Sept. 1892. Acc. 3155/6. (All the letters to Henrietta are from this file.) Diary: 9 Sept. 1892.
13. HTH: 10 Oct., 3 Nov. 1892.
14. HTH: 17, 19 March, 4 April 1893.
15. HTH: 6 May 1893.
16. Draft copy of Haig's petition to the War Office, n.d., Acc. 3155/6(e).
17. K. Fraser to H. Jameson: 19 Aug. 1893, Acc. 3155/6(g).
18. All quotations pertaining to the French cavalry are from Haig, *Report on the French Cavalry Manoeuvres in Touraine – September 1893*. Acc. 3155/68.
19. H. Reid to Haig: 5 April 1894, Acc. 3155/6(e).
20. HTH: 23 April 1895.
21. HTH: 4, 31 May, 9 June 1895.
22. All the comments on German cavalry are from Haig, *Notes on German Cavalry*, 1896, Acc. 3155/74.
23. E. Wood to Haig: 1 July 1895, Acc. 3155/6(g). (All letters from Wood are contained in this file.) HTH: 4 July 1875.
24. Diary: 22 Aug. 1895.
25. Harries-Jenkins, p. 121. Godwin-Austin, p. 214.
26. The farcical situations which periodically resulted from these quotas are described in Adye, pp. 137–9.
27. The various definitions of a 'general staff' are described in Bond, *The Victorian Army and the Staff College*, pp. 30–2.
28. Edmonds Memoirs, op. cit., chapter XIV. Edmonds to Lord Wavell: 27 Aug. 1936, and Barrow to Wavell: n.d., Allenby MSS, 6/III.
29. Edmonds Memoirs, op. cit., chapter XIV.
30. Edmonds Memoirs, op. cit., chapter XIV. Bond, op. cit., p. 154.
31. B. H. Liddell Hart, *The Remaking of Modern Armies*, pp. 170–1.
32. Travers, *The Killing Ground*, pp. 87–8.
33. See Travers (p. 87) for an excellent (and more detailed) discussion of this subject.
34. Haig Staff College Notes, 'Tactics', Acc. 3155/17 and 'Strategy II', Acc. 3155/20.
35. Haig, 'Strategy II', op. cit.
36. See Charteris, *Field Marshal Earl Haig*, pp. 36, 39. Barrow, p. 105. Edmonds' comment was recalled by Liddell Hart, who heard it from J. F. C. Fuller. Liddell Hart MSS., 11/1929/16.
37. Edmonds, op. cit., chapter XIV. Haig, 'Military History Exam Papers – 1896', Acc. 3155/10. 'Military History Exam Paper on Wellington's 1815 Campaign', n.d., Acc. 3155/29.
38. Barrow, p. 43.

3 A Taste of War

1. Wood to Haig: 13 April 1898. See also 25 April 1898.
2. The 'arme blanche' technically means the steel weapons (lance and sword) used by the cavalry. In a wider sense, it also means the spirit and ethos associated

with the use of those weapons and with the cavalry. The latter meaning is used in this book.

3. HTH: 6, 11 Feb. 1898. Haig to Wood: 14 Feb. 1898.
4. Diary: 15 Feb. 1898. HTH: 17, 20 Feb. 1898.
5. HTH: 17 Feb., 2 March 1898.
6. HTH: 2, 25 March 1898.
7. Haig to Wood: 15 March 1898.
8. Diary: 13, 17 March 1898.
9. Haig to Henrietta: 1 April 1898. Wood to Haig: 25 April 1898.
10. Haig to Wood: 15 March, 25 June 1898.
11. Haig to Wood: 26 March 1898. See also Diary: 19 Jan. 1898, for discussion of machine-guns.
12. HTH: 11 April 1898.
13. Ibid.
14. Ibid.
15. Haig to Wood: 12 April 1898. HTH: 11 April 1898.
16. HTH: 11 April 1898.
17. Haig's comments on the Battle of the Atbara are from his letter to Wood, 29 April 1898.
18. HTH: 11 April 1898. Diary: 13 April 1898. See also Magnus, *Kitchener*, p. 121.
19. Haig to Wood: 29 April 1898. HTH: 5 June 1898.
20. HTH: 29 April, 7 July 1898.
21. HTH: 21 April, 1 May, 5 June 1898.
22. Haig to Wood: 29 April, 7 Sept. 1898.
23. Diary: 2 Sept. 1898. HTH: 6 Sept. 1898.
24. Haig to Wood: 7 Sept. 1898.
25. Diary: 2 Sept. 1898.
26. Churchill, *The River War*, pp. 135–6.
27. Haig to Wood: 7 Sept. 1898.
28. Haig to Wood: 7, 21 Sept. 1898.

4 Chasing Boers

1. HTH: 16 May 1899. The loan was repaid ten years later, despite French's problems in meeting the payments. See HTH: 9 December 1903: 'I am astonished at what you say re the loan to General F. . . . I am afraid the trustees have been hustling for payment and in fact I felt that I would prefer to lose the money myself than that General F. should be pressed for it.'
2. HTH: 26 Sept. 1899.
3. Diary: 10, 18 Oct. 1899.
4. Haig, Memorandum to General Forestier-Walker, contained in 1899 Diary, following entry for 13 October.
5. Haig's thoughts on the Boer problem are from 'Notes on the Transvaal', n.d., Acc. 3155/38(i).
6. HTH: 26 Oct. 1899.
7. HTH: 3 Nov. 1899. Diary: 2 Nov. 1899.
8. The preceding observations on the Boer problem are from Haig's 'Notes on Operations: 20 October to 2 November', Acc. 3155/38(c).

9. HTH: 26 Nov. 1899. Haig, 'Notes on Operations', op. cit.
10. Diary: 23 Oct. 1899. HTH: 12 Dec. 1899.
11. HTH: 23 Dec. 1899.
12. French to Roberts: 18 Jan. 1900; Kitchener to French: 19 Jan. 1900; Acc. 3155/6(c).
13. J. F. Laycock to Lady Haig: 13 Feb. 1930. Acc. 3155/334(e). HTH: 4 Feb.1900.
14. Cavalry Division Diary, 10 Feb. 1900, Acc. 3155/34. Roberts' speech is quoted in Selby, p. 168.
15. *The Times*, 6 April 1900. HTH: 22 Feb. 1900.
16. Haig to Lonsdale Hale: 2 March 1900, Acc. 3155/334(e).
17. Ibid.
18. The letter is no longer available but is quoted in Duff Cooper, pp. 88–9.
19. HTH: 22 Feb. 1900. Laycock to Lady Haig, op. cit.
20. Pakenham, p. 374. HTH: 16 March 1900.
21. HTH: 16 March 1900. See also Badsey.
22. Haig to Hugo Haig: 5 May 1900. HTH: 7, 14 April 1900.
23. HTH: 7 April, 14 May 1900.
24. HTH: 14 May 1900.
25. HTH: 17 June, 15 Aug. 1900.
26. HTH: 13, 19 Oct., 14, 30 Nov. 1900.
27. HTH: 18, 26 Dec. 1900.
28. HTH: 20 Jan. 1900.
29. HTH: 9 Sept., 18 Dec. 1900.
30. HTH: 7 Dec. 1900; 11 April, 7 Sept. 1901.
31. HTH: 8 July, 25 Aug., 7, 14 Sept. 1901.
32. HTH: 14 Sept., 26 Oct. 1901.
33. HTH: 9 July 1900.
34. HTH: 9 July, 7 Aug. 1900.
35. HTH: 14 Dec. 1900; 26 Nov. 1901. The 'lady-killer' was Wolseley, who had left the Horse Guards shortly before.
36. French to Hugo Haig: 20 April 1900. French to Haig: 20 May 1901, Acc. 3155/334(e). Kitchener to Roberts: 19 April 1901, Roberts MSS, NAM 7101-23-33-24.
37. Roberts to Kitchener: 4 May 1901, Roberts MSS, NAM 7101-23-33-24. HTH: 1 July, 22 Sept. 1901.
38. HTH: 20 April 1902.
39. HTH: 20 April, 5 June 1902.
40. HTH: 12 June, 13 July 1902.
41. HTH: 4 Feb. 1900; 13 July, 5 Aug., 17 Sept. 1902.

5 A Cavalry Counter-Reformation

1. Quoted in Duff Cooper, pp. 90–2.
2. HTH: 5, 25 Aug., 17 Sept. 1902.
3. HTH: 17 Sept. 1902.
4. Lady Haig, *The Man I Knew*, pp. 31–2.
5. Diary: 4 Oct. 1903. HTH: 4 Oct. 1903.
6. Roberts to Kitchener: 2 March 1904, Roberts MSS, NAM 7101-23-122-13. Roberts, preface to *Cavalry Training* (Provisional) 1904.

7. E. Childers to Roberts: 4 Nov. 1908. Roberts MSS, NAM 7101-23-222.
8. Roberts to Kitchener: 24 Sept. 1903, 28 Jan. 1904, Roberts MSS, NAM 7101-23-122-6, 7.
9. Quoted in Bond, 'Doctrine and Training in British Cavalry', in M. Howard (ed.) *The Theory and Practice of War*, p. 109.
10. Haig to 'Jessel': 14 Feb. 1903, Acc. 3155/334(e). Roberts to Kitchener: 30 June 1903; French to Roberts: 6 Nov. 1904, Roberts MSS, NAM 7101-23-122-5, 8.
11. Quoted in Dundonald, pp. 252–3.
12. Charteris, *Field Marshal Earl Haig*, pp. 27–8. The schedule of inspection is included in the 12 Nov. 1903 letter to Henrietta.
13. Roberts to Kitchener: 30 June, 24 Sept. 1903, op. cit.; and 8 Oct. 1903, Roberts MSS, NAM 7101-23-122-6.
14. Kitchener to Roberts: 5 Nov. 1903, Kitchener MSS, PRO 30/57/29/Q17. Roberts to Kitchener: 28 Jan. 1904, op. cit.
15. Kitchener to Roberts: 5 May 1904, Kitchener MSS, PRO 30/57/29/Q3. Diary: 4 May 1904. Kitchener to Roberts: 12 May 1904, Roberts MSS, NAM 7101-23-122-7.
16. HTH: 23 March 1905.
17. Ibid.
18. Haig, 'Notes on Inspections' (contained in 1903 Diary). HTH: 26 Nov. 1903.
19. HTH: 7 Aug. 1900, 26 Nov. 1903.
20. HTH: 1 Sept. 1904. See memo in 1910 Diary: 'The General Staff must be . . . a band of brothers.'
21. See collection of newspaper clippings pertaining to social scene in Acc. 3155/41.
22. Quotation from unknown newspaper in ibid.
23. Charteris, op. cit. p. 32.
24. French to Haig: 6 Aug. 1905, Acc. 3155/334(e).
25. HTH: 11 Jan. 1906. See also Esher to Kitchener: 26 Nov. 1905, Kitchener MSS, PRO 30/57/33/AA3.
26. See Haig, *Cavalry Studies*, pp. 1–19.

6 Politicians and Paperwork

1. Esher to Haig: 12 Jan. 1904, Acc. 3155/334(e).
2. HTH: 1 Sept., 25 Oct. 1905.
3. HTH: 13 Dec. 1905; 8 Feb., 29 March, 3 April 1906.
4. Diary: 20 Sept. 1906; 24 Nov. 1908; 9 Nov. 1907. The inquiries regarding the existence in the spirit world of the pet dogs is found in Henrietta Jameson, *Selections from letters of George Ogilvy Haig Written through the Hand of His Sister Henrietta Jameson*.
5. Diary: 3 Nov. 1907.
6. Haldane, *Autobiography*, p. 199.
7. Diary: 9, 10 June 1906. See entries for 12 Jan. and 4 Nov. 1907 for examples of Haig's praise of Haldane's political talents.
8. Haldane, *Before the War*, pp. 30–1. Marshall-Cornwall, p. 76.
9. The Militia was not technically one of the Auxiliary forces, but a separate and distinct body. For simplicity, however, 'auxiliary' will be taken to include the Militia.
10. Haig to Esher: 9 Sept. 1906, Acc. 3155/334(e).

11. Diary, 12 Nov. 1906, 3 Jan. 1907.
12. See Spiers, *Haldane, An Army Reformer*, pp. 151–3.
13. Ibid., p. 150.
14. *Parliamentary Debates*, 12 March 1908.
15. Diary: 10, 25, 27 June, 4 July 1907.
16. Diary: 8 Nov. 1907.
17. Barnett, *Britain and Her Army*, p. 43.
18. See Terraine, *Douglas Haig: The Educated Soldier*, p. 43 and Marshall-Cornwall, p. 75.
19. *Field Service Regulations*, vol. I, p. 12.
20. Diary: 11 Sept. 1907.
21. Haldane, *Autobiography*, pp. 199–200.
22. Haig claimed that he weighed 12 stone 11 pounds, a gain of over a stone since his Boer War days. See the Diary, 18 Jan. 1908. Visits to the 'magnetic health giver' occurred in February and March 1907.
23. Diary: 18 Feb. 1909.
24. Quoted in Marshall-Cornwall, p. 77.

7 Many Important Questions

1. Charteris, *Field Marshal Earl Haig*, p. 50.
2. Diary: 15 March 1909. Haig to Kiggell: 24 April 1909, Kiggell MSS, I/1.
3. Haig to Kiggell: 24, 27 April 1909 (I/2).
4. Haig to Kiggell: 18, 21 May, 3 July 1909 (I/3–5).
5. Haig to Kiggell: 27 April 1911 (I/11), 14 July 1910 (I/7).
6. Haig to Kiggell: 15 June 1911 (I/15).
7. Haig, 'Report on the 1911 Indian Staff Tour', Acc. 3155/85. Haig to Kiggell: 13 July 1911 (I/18). Terraine (*Douglas Haig: The Educated Soldier*, p. 49) makes some rather wild generalisations on the basis of a few enlightened sentences in the staff tour report.
8. Another misguided assumption by Terraine, pp. 46–50.
9. See the previously cited 27 April 1909 letter to Kiggell for an outline of Haig's goals for his Indian tour.
10. Diary: 2, 20 Aug., 1910; 31 March 1911.
11. Haig to Kiggell: 29 June, 29 Sept. 1911 (I/16,24).
12. Diary: 17 Aug. 1911. Haig to Kiggell: 3 Aug. 1911 (I/22).
13. Haig to Kiggell: 5 May, 18 April 1911 (I/8,13).
14. During the Great War, for instance, Haig sent Charteris home to negotiate the sale of his car and to help Lady Haig move out of Government House. In 1912, Haig sent Charteris to the Balkans to investigate the war there, but the order was quickly rescinded by a perturbed War Office.
15. Esher was one of many to refer to Charteris as the 'principal boy' – see his letter to Haig, 21 Oct. 1916, Acc. 3155/214(f). Charteris was often the brunt of some rather cruel and childish jokes; see Haig to Lady Haig: 7 April 1915 and Lady Haig (op. cit.), p. 108.
16. Charteris, op. cit., p. 64.
17. Haig to Kiggell: 29 June 1911 (I/16).
18. Charteris, op. cit., pp. 55–6. Diary: 19 Sept. 1912.

19. J. Gough to Haig: 20 March 1914; Haig to J. Gough: 21 March 1914; Acc. 3155/91(a).
20. See Beckett, *The Army and the Curragh Incident*, p. 218 and passim. I am extremely grateful to Dr Ian Beckett for guiding me through the Curragh labyrinth.
21. Diary: 25 March 1914.
22. French to Haig: 26 March 1914, Acc. 3155/91(a).
23. Haig to L. Rothschild: 13 Oct. 1916, Acc. 3155/214(e).
24. Haig to Haldane: 4 Aug. 1914, Haldane MSS, 5910, ff. 251.
25. Ibid.
26. Diary: 5 Aug. 1914.
27. French, *1914*, p. 6. Hankey to Haig: 25 July 1919 (includes notes of War Cabinet meeting, 4 Aug. 1914). It is clear that the diary entries for 4–12 August 1914 were written after the fact because they are not contained in Haig's handwritten original, but only in the typewritten copy compiled by Lady Haig.
28. Hankey to Haig, op. cit.
29. Diary: 5 Aug. 1914. Hankey to Haig, op. cit.
30. Diary: 9, 10 Aug. 1914.
31. Diary: 11 Aug. 1914.
32. Diary: 13 Aug. 1914. Haig to Kiggell: 18 May 1911 (I/13).
33. Diary: 13 Aug. 1914.
34. Diary: 14 Aug. 1914.

8 An Abnormal War

1. G. Haig (Henrietta) to Haig: 4 Aug. 1914, Acc. 3155/347(25).
2. Diary: 14, 15 Aug. 1914.
3. Diary: 13 Aug. 1914.
4. Diary: 18, 20, 21, 22 Aug. 1914.
5. Diary: 23 Aug. 1914.
6. Diary: 24 Aug. 1914.
7. Ibid.
8. Diary: 28, 31 Aug. 1914. Haig to Lady Haig (hereafter 'HTLH'): 8 Oct. 1914.
9. Diary: 27 Aug. 1914. HTLH: 31 Aug., 3 Sept. 1914.
10. HTLH: 3 Sept. 1914.
11. Diary: 4, 5 Sept. 1914.
12. Diary: 6, 7, 9, 11 Sept. 1914.
13. French to Haig: 15 Sept. 1914. Diary: 14 Sept. 1914.
14. Diary: 18, 20, 23 Sept. 1914.
15. Diary: 13 Oct. 1914.
16. Diary: 16, 19 Oct. 1914. HTLH: 8 Oct. 1914.
17. Diary: 22 Oct. 1914.
18. Diary: 20, 25, 26 Oct. 1914.
19. Diary: 25 Oct. 1914.
20. Diary: 30 Oct. 1914.
21. *Official History*, II, p. 303. Diary: 31 Oct. 1914.
22. Diary: 31 Oct. 1914.
23. Diary: 5, 7 Nov. 1914.

24. Diary: 7, 11, 13 Nov. 1914.
25. French to Haig: 14 Nov. 1914.
26. Diary: 18 Nov. 1914.
27. Marshall-Cornwall, p. 134. HTLH: 9 Nov. 1914. Diary: 21 Nov. 1914.
28. Diary: 23, 24, 26 Nov. 1914.
29. Diary: 4 Dec. 1914.
30. Diary: 27, 28 Nov., 1 Dec. 1914. HTLH: 13 Dec. 1914.
31. Diary: 12, 17, 18 Dec. 1914.
32. Diary: 18 Dec. 1914. HTLH: 19 Dec. 1914.
33. Diary: 15 Dec. 1914.
34. Diary: 24, 25 Dec. 1914. Haig to Rothschild: 26 Dec. 1914, Acc. 3155/214(e).

9 The Search for a Way Forward

1. Diary: 30 Dec. 1914.
2. Diary: 29 Dec. 1914.
3. Diary: 4, 22 Jan. 1915.
4. Diary: 8, 28 Jan. 1915.
5. Haig to Rothschild: 6 Feb. 1915, Acc. 3155/214(a). Diary: 9 Feb. 1915.
6. Diary: 11 Feb. 1915.
7. Diary: 4 Jan. 1914. HTLH: 12 Jan. 1915.
8. Diary: 9 Jan., 5, 13 Feb. 1915.
9. Diary: 12, 13 Feb. 1915.
10. Diary: 23 Feb. 1915.
11. Diary: 10, 22, 25 Feb., 2 March 1915.
12. Rawlinson Diary: 22 March 1915, Rawlinson MSS, 1/1. HTLH: 13 March 1915.
13. Diary: 14, 16 March 1915.
14. Rawlinson Diary: 16, 17 March 1915. Bidwell and Graham, *Firepower*, p. 75.
15. Diary: 27, 28, 31 March 1915.
16. Haig to Rothschild: 13 March 1915, Acc. 3155/214(a).
17. Diary: 20, 30 March 1915.
18. HTLH: 10 April 1915. Haig to Rothschild: 17 April 1915.
19. Haig to Rothschild: 17 April 1915. Diary: 12 April 1915. HTLH: 1 April 1915.
20. Diary: 4, 19, 24 April 1915.
21. Diary: 11, 30 April, 8 June 1915.
22. Diary: 30 April 1915.
23. Diary: 10 May 1915. Haig to Rothschild: 20 May 1915.
24. Diary: 10, 11 May 1915. Bidwell and Graham, op. cit., pp. 70–1.
25. Diary: 15 May 1915. HTLH: 16, 17 May 1915. Haig to Rothschild: 20, 30 May 1915.
26. *The Times*, 14 May 1915.
27. HTLH: 24 May 1915. Haig to Fitzgerald: 24 May 1915, Kitchener MSS, PRO 30/57/53/WD3.
28. Diary: 26 May 1915. Haig to Rothschild: 30 May 1915.
29. HTLH: 27 May, 1 June 1915.
30. Haig to Rothschild: 30 June 1915.
31. Haig to Rothschild: 17 April 1915. Diary: 21 May 1915. Haig to Fitzgerald: 24 May 1915, op. cit.
32. Haig to Rothschild: 20 May 1915.
33. Diary: 7, 13 June 1915.

34. Diary: 8, 14 July 1915.
35. Diary: 8 July 1915.
36. Diary: 9, 28 July 1915.
37. HTLH: 28 June 1915. Wigram to Lady Haig: 12 July 1915, Acc. 3155/213(d).
38. Diary: 14 July 1915.
39. HTLH: 1, 21 June, 1 July, 15 Nov. 1915.
40. Diary: 7 June 1915. Hunter-Weston to Haig: 15 July 1915, Acc. 3155/213(d).
41. Diary, 14, 23 June 1915.
42. Diary: 23 June 1915. Haig to Wigram: 27 June 1915.
43. Haig to Wigram: 27 June 1915. Diary: 26 June 1915.
44. Diary: 23, 26 June 1915.
45. Diary: 29 June 1915.
46. Diary: 22 June 1915.
47. Diary: 25, 29 June, 30 July 1915.
48. HTLH: 10, 15 Aug. 1915. Diary: 26 July, 12 Aug. 1915.
49. Diary: 16, 17, 19 Aug. 1915.
50. HTLH: 24 Aug. 1915. Diary: 6, 12 Sept. 1915.
51. Rawlinson Diary: 19 Sept. 1915. Diary: 26, 30 Aug. 1915.
52. Diary: 18 Sept. 1915. See Travers, *The Killing Ground*, pp. 16–19 for a discussion of the controversy of reserves at Loos.
53. Diary: 22 Sept. 1915. See also Bidwell and Graham, op. cit. pp. 77–9.
54. Diary: 17 Aug., 20, 24 Sept. 1915.
55. Diary: 25 Sept. 1915.
56. Rawlinson Diary: 28 Sept. 1915.
57. Diary: 28, 29 Sept. 1915. Haig to John Haig: 5 Oct., 2 Nov. 1915, Acc. 3155/214(b).
58. Haig to Kitchener: 29 Sept. 1915. See also Travers, op cit.
59. Diary: 2 Oct. 1915.
60. Diary: 11 Oct. 1915. HTLH: 18 Oct. 1915. Haig to Rothschild: 20 Oct. 1915.
61. Diary: 15 Oct. 1915. HTLH: 15 Oct. 1915. Haig to Rothschild: 25 Oct. 1915.
62. Diary: 17 Oct. 1915.
63. Diary: 24 Oct. 1915.
64. *The Times*, 2 Nov. 1915. HTLH: 3, 4 Nov. 1915. Diary: 8 Nov. 1915.
65. HTLH: 10 Nov. 1915.
66. Diary: 13, 14 Nov. 1915. Lees-Milne, p. 292.
67. Diary: 14 Nov. 1915.
68. Diary: 23, 24 Nov. 1915.
69. Diary: 25 Nov. 1915.
70. King George V to Haig: 17 Dec. 1915. Hankey Diary: 14 Dec. 1915, Hankey MSS, I/1.
71. Diary: 13 Feb. 1916.
72. Diary: 14 Dec. 1915. Haldane, *Autobiography*, vol. II, p. 385, Quoted from Travers, *The Killing Ground*, chap. 1 and 'The Hidden Army'.
73. Diary: 12, 14 Dec. 1915.
74. HTLH: 18 Dec. 1915. Diary: 18 Dec. 1915.
75. HTLH: 16 Dec. 1915. Haig to Rothschild: 9 Dec. 1915.

10 'Patience, Self-Sacrifice and Confidence'

1. George Haig (Henrietta) to Haig: 6 Jan. 1916, Acc. 3155/347(24). HTLH: 27 Dec. 1915.

2. Diary: 2 Jan. 1916. Duncan, pp. 22, 43.
3. Duncan, p. 22. Diary: 12, 15 Jan. 1916.
4. Duncan, pp. 119, 121, 123. Diary: 19 March 1916.
5. Diary: 12, 21 Dec. 1915. Kitchener to Haig: 22 Dec. 1915.
6. Duncan, p. 69.
7. Kitchener to Haig: 28 Dec. 1916.
8. Strachey to Haig: 31 Dec. 1915, Acc. 3155/213(d).
9. Diary: 3, 17 Dec. 1915. Robertson to Haig: 5 Jan. 1916.
10. Robertson to Haig: 13 Jan. 1916. Kitchener to Haig: 14 Jan. 1916, Kitchener MSS, PRO 30/57/53/WD16. HTLH: 13 Jan. 1916.
11. Diary: 16, 27 Jan. 1916.
12. Robertson to Haig: 5, 13 Jan. 1916.
13. Kitchener to Haig: 14 Jan. 1916 (op. cit.). Robertson to Haig: 13 Jan. 1916.
14. Haig to Kitchener: 19 Jan. 1916, Kitchener MSS, PRO 30/57/53/WD18.
15. Diary: 14 Jan. 1916.
16. Haig to Kitchener: 19 Jan. 1916. See also Diary: 14, 18 Jan. 1916.
17. Diary: 14 Jan. 1916. Haig to Robertson: 9 Jan. 1916.
18. Diary: 26 Dec. 1915; 10 Jan. 1916.
19. Diary: 6 Nov. 1915; 16 Feb. 1916.
20. See, for example, D. Winter, Liddle, Fussell, etc.
21. Diary: 31 Jan. 1916.
22. Lloyd George to Haig: 8 Feb. 1916. Diary: 30 Jan. 1916. HTLH: 6 Feb. 1916.
23. Diary: 9, 12 Feb. 1916.
24. Diary: 29 Dec. 1915; 14 Feb. 1916.
25. Diary: 14 Feb. 1916.
26. Haig to Robertson: 19 Feb. 1916. Diary: 10, 19 Feb. 1916.
27. Diary: 20 Feb. 1916. HTLH: 23 Feb. 1916.
28. Diary: 25 Feb. 1916.
29. Diary: 27, 28, 29 Feb. 1916.
30. Robertson to Haig: 6 March 1916. Diary: 8 March 1916.
31. 'Report to Armies on Recent German Attacks', 3 March 1916.
32. Ibid.
33. Ibid.
34. E. Swinton, 'Notes on the Employment of Tanks', March 1916.
35. 'Notes on conference of Army Commanders', 18 March 1916. Diary: 24 March, 9 April 1916.
36. Sassoon to Rothschild: 20 March, 2 April, 3 July 1916. Haig to Rothschild: 10 April 1916.
37. Haig to Rothschild: 14 May 1916. Diary: 11 June, 27 Dec. 1915. *Daily Graphic*: 11 Feb. 1916.
38. D. Winter, pp. 53–4. Diary: 31 March 1916. Lytton, p. 67.
39. Charteris, 'Notes on the Present Situation', 21 March 1916, Acc. 3155/215(l). Diary: 29 March 1916.
40. Rawlinson Diary: 1 April 1916, Rawlinson MSS, 1/5. Diary: 7 April 1916. Haig to Joffre: 10 April 1916.
41. War Committee, 7 April 1916, CAB 42/12/5. Diary: 29 March 1916.
42. Diary: 14, 15 April, 28 March 1916.
43. Diary: 4, 20 May 1916.
44. Charteris, 'Probable Movement and Operations of the Germans', 8 May 1916, Acc. 3155/215(l). Diary: 8 May 1916. Haig to Rothschild: 14 May 1916.

45. Diary: 7, 21 May, 23 April, 4 June 1916.
46. 'Memorandum on Policy for the Press', 26 May 1916.
47. Diary: 2, 26 May 1916. Charteris, 'Forecast of the State of German Resources', 24 May 1916, Acc. 3155/215(1).
48. Diary: 31 May, 16, 17, 24 June 1916. HTLH: 2 June 1916.
49. Diary: 3, 6 June 1916.
50. Diary: 7 June 1916. Haig to Robertson: 29 May 1916. Haig to Robertson: 20 May 1916; and War Committee, 24 May 1916, CAB 42/14/10.
51. Diary: 7 June 1916.

11 'Drive on, Illustrious General'

1. Maurice, *Life of Lord Rawlinson*, p. 155. Rawlinson, 'Plan for Offensive by 4th Army', 3 April 1916, PRO: WO 158/233. Diary: 5 April 1916.
2. Rawlinson Diary: 31 March, 30 June 1916. Occleshaw, p. 417. Diary: 27 June 1916.
3. Diary: 7 April, 28 June 1916.
4. On 14 April 1916, Haig saw Swinton, who informed him that the tanks would not be available in sufficient numbers by 1 July.
5. HTLH: 20 March 1916.
6. HTLH: 20, 22 June 1916. Diary: 25 June 1916.
7. HTLH: 30 June 1916. Diary: 30 June 1916.
8. HTLH: 1 July 1916. Diary: 29 June, 1 July 1916.
9. Diary: 2 July 1916. Haig to Rothschild: 3 July 1916. HTLH: 6, 7, 8 July 1916.
10. HTLH: 8, 13, 17 July 1916.
11. Diary: 9 July 1916.
12. Diary: 11 July 1916. See Travers, *The Killing Ground*, p. 171.
13. Diary: 16 July 1916.
14. Diary: 25 July 1916. Anon. to Haig: 30 July 1916, Acc. 3155/213(d).
15. Robertson to Haig: 7 July 1916, Robertson MSS, 1/22/51. Robertson to Haig: 29 July 1916.
16. War Committee, 30 May 1916, CAB 42/14/12. Robertson to Kiggell: 5 July 1916, Kiggell MSS, IV/3. Robertson to Rawlinson: 26 July 1916, Robertson MSS, I/35/100. See Wilson Diary, July–August 1916, Wilson MSS, DS/MISC/80.
17. Charteris, 'Note on German Casualties on the Somme', 31 July 1916. Haig to Robertson: 1 Aug. 1916, (O.A.D. 90).
18. Haig to Robertson: 1 Aug. 1916.
19. Diary: 6, 8, 9 Aug. 1916.
20. Diary: 6 July 1916.
21. Diary: 21, 23 July 1917.
22. HTLH: 23 July 1916. Fletcher to Lady Haig: 25 July 1916; Lady Haig to Fletcher: 29 July 1916; Acc. 3155/144.
23. Quoted in Marshall-Cornwall, pp. 201–2.
24. Diary: 15 Aug., 1 Sept. 1916. HTLH: 17 Aug. 1916.
25. Diary: 12 Aug. 1916.
26. Haig to Robertson, 23 Aug. 1916, (O.A.D. 119).
27. Diary: 27, 28 Aug. 1916.
28. Robertson to Haig: 29 Aug., 7 Sept. 1916.

29. HTLH: 13 Sept. 1916. See also Woodward, *Lloyd George and the Generals*, p. 105.
30. Diary: 15 Sept. 1916. Haig to Robertson: 28 Sept. 1916.
31. Diary: 4 Sept. 1916.
32. Diary: 14 Sept. 1916.
33. Swinton, 'Notes on the Employment of Tanks', 19 March 1916. Diary: 5 April 1916.
34. Diary: 14 April, 26 Aug. 1916. Haig to Robertson: 22 Aug. 1916.
35. Diary: 29 Aug., 10 Sept. 1916. Kiggell, Orders, 31 Aug. 1916.
36. *O.H.*, 191, II, p. 300.
37. Diary: 28 Sept., 1, 15 Nov. 1916.
38. Rawlinson Diary: 19 Sept. 1916. Haig to Robertson: 7 Oct. 1916, (O.A.D. 173).
39. Haig to Robertson: 7 Oct. 1916. Diary: 2 Oct. 1916.
40. Diary: 20 Oct., 18 Nov. 1916.
41. Diary: 25 Sept. 1916. HTLH: 1 Oct. 1916. Haig to Rothschild: 13 Oct. 1916.
42. Diary: 6 Oct. 1916. Haig to Rothschild: 4 Oct. 1916.
43. Strachey to Haig: 27 Oct. 1916. Diary: 11, 30 Sept., 9 Oct. 1916.
44. Diary: 25 Aug., 16 Oct. 1916.
45. HTLH: 16 Oct. 1916.
46. Diary: 7, 10 Oct. 1916.
47. HTLH: 21 Oct. 1916.
48. War Committee, 3 Nov. 1916. CAB 42/23/4.
49. Quoted from Travers, op. cit., p. 188.
50. Diary: 13 Nov. 1916.
51. Ludendorff, *My War Memories*, pp. 244–5.
52. Haig to Robertson: 21 Nov. 1916.
53. Diary: 31 March 1917; 24 Sept., 5 Oct. 1916.
54. HTLH: 22, 24 Oct. 1916. Diary: 15 Oct. 1916.

12 Two Wars

1. Diary: 29 Nov., 3, 16 Dec. 1916.
2. Diary: 25, 26 Nov. 1916. HTLH: 4 Dec. 1916.
3. HTLH: 6 Dec. 1916. Diary: 2 Dec. 1916.
4. See Woodward, *Lloyd George and the Generals*, p. 129. Diary: 15 Dec. 1916.
5. Diary: 15 Dec. 1916.
6. Ibid.
7. Diary: 13, 14, 20 Dec. 1916. HTLH: 20 Dec. 1916.
8. Diary: 20, 27, 28 Dec. 1916. HTLH: 20 Dec. 1916.
9. HTLH: 22 Dec. 1916. King George V to Haig: 27 Dec. 1916.
10. Diary: 31 Dec. 1916.
11. Diary: 4 Jan. 1917. Haig to Nivelle: 6 Jan. 1914.
12. Haig to Nivelle: 6 Dec. 1917.
13. Ibid.
14. Diary: 1, 4 Jan. 1917.
15. Diary: 4, 5, 6 Jan. 1917.
16. Kiggell to Haig: 10 Jan. 1917. Diary: 15 Jan. 1917.
17. Diary: 15, 16 Jan. 1917.

18. Robertson to Haig: 19 Jan. 1917. Stevenson Diary (ed. Taylor): 15 Jan. 1917. Hankey, *Supreme Command*, p. 629.
19. Diary: 18 Jan., 7 Feb. 1917.
20. Diary: 31 Dec. 1916; 1 Feb. 1917.
21. Robertson to Haig: 7 Feb. 1917. Diary: 27 Nov. 1916.
22. Robertson to Haig: 13 Feb. 1917.
23. Derby to Haig: 11 Feb. 1917. Diary: 15 Dec. 1916.
24. Diary: 4, 11 Feb. 1917.
25. Charteris, *At GHQ*, p. 126. Marshall-Cornwall, p. 214. Occleshaw, p. 392.
26. Charteris, *At GHQ*, pp. 12, 74; and *Haig*, p. 180. Fox, p. 37. Esher, p. 30.
27. Terraine, *Douglas Haig: The Educated Soldier*, p. 176.
28. HTLH: 7 April 1915.
29. Charteris, *At GHQ*, pp. 67, 76. Esher, pp. 58–9.
30. Charteris, *Haig*, pp. 109–10.
31. Quoted in Liddell Hart, *Through the Fog of War*, pp. 54–5. Morton to Liddell Hart: 17 June 1961, Liddell Hart MSS (File of 'Evidence on Haig'). See also Occleshaw, chapters 7, 8.
32. Diary: 18 Feb. 1917. *The Times*, 15 Feb. 1917.
33. Diary: 18, 22 Feb. 1917. HTLH: 22 Feb. 1917.
34. Derby to Haig: 20 Feb. 1917.
35. Haig to Derby: 22 Feb. 1917. Derby to Haig: 24 Feb. 1917. HTLH: 24, 25 Feb. 1917. Hankey Diary: 24 Feb. 1917, Hankey MSS, I/1.
36. HTLH: 25 Feb. 1917. *The Times*, 19 Feb. 1917.
37. Hankey Diary: 1 Nov. 1916.
38. Robertson to Haig: 14 Feb. 1917, Robertson MSS, 1/23/7. Diary: 16 Feb. 1917.
39. Diary: 18, 22 Feb. 1917. War Cabinet, 20 Feb. 1917, CAB 23/1.
40. Quoted in Marshall-Cornwall, p. 217.
41. See Woodward, op. cit., p. 146.
42. Diary: 26 Feb. 1917.
43. Ibid.
44. Ibid.
45. Spears, p. 43. Diary: 26 Feb. 1917. Hankey Diary: 26 Feb. 1917.
46. Diary: 27 Feb. 1917.
47. Ibid.
48. HTLH: 28 Feb. 1917.
49. Haig to King George V: 28 Feb. 1917. Stamfordham to Haig: 5 March 1917. HTLH: 2 March 1917.
50. Diary: 28 Feb. 1917.
51. HTLH: 3 March 1917. Diary: 25 Feb. 1917.
52. Diary: 2 March 1917. HTLH: 2 March 1917.
53. See Woodward, op. cit., p. 151. Diary: 7 March 1917.
54. Hankey, memo to Lloyd George, 7 March 1917, CAB 63/19.
55. Diary: 9, 11 March 1917. See Woodward, op. cit., p. 150.
56. Diary: 12, 13, 14 March 1917.
57. HTLH: 5, 6, 16 March 1917. Diary: 6 March 1917.
58. Diary: 28 Feb. 1917.
59. Diary: 12, 16, 23, 24 March, 8 April 1917.
60. Diary: 11 April 1917.
61. HTLH: 10, 13, 20 April 1917. Diary: 12 April 1917.
62. Diary: 12 April 1917. Haig to Robertson: 15 April 1917.

63. Diary: 16 April 1917.
64. Maurice to Haig: 18 April 1917. Robertson to Haig: 19 April 1917.
65. Charteris, 'Effect of British Action on German Moral', 13 April 1917. Diary: 18, 20 April 1917. HTLH: 30 April 1917.
66. Diary: 24 April 1917.
67. Diary: 24, 26, 27 April 1917. HTLH: 26 April 1917.
68. Diary: 28, 29 April 1917. Haig to Robertson: 29 April 1917.

13 High Hopes, Deep Mud

1. Robertson to Haig: 26 April 1917.
2. Haig to Robertson: 29 April 1917. Diary: 30 April, 1 May 1917. Haig, 'Present Situation and Future Plans', 30 April 1917.
3. Diary: 1 May 1917.
4. Diary: 3 May 1917.
5. Diary: 3 May 1917. Robertson to Haig: 20 April 1917. Haig, 'Present Situation and Future Plans', op. cit.
6. Quoted in Woodward, *Lloyd George and the Generals*, pp. 163–4.
7. Woodward, pp. 163–4. HTLH: 5 May 1917. Diary: 4 May 1917.
8. HTLH: 6, 7, 8 May 1917.
9. Diary: 14 May 1917. Lloyd George, *War Memoirs*, II, p. 1258. Haig to Robertson: 16 May 1917.
10. Haig to Robertson: 16 May 1917. HTLH: 15 May 1917. Diary: 10 May 1917.
11. Diary: 18 May 1917. Wilson to Haig: 20 May 1917.
12. Diary: 22, 26 May 1917. Derby to Haig: 27 May 1915.
13. Haig to Robertson: 28 May 1917.
14. Diary: 2, 7 June 1917.
15. Diary: 2 June 1917.
16. 'O.A. 79 – Memo to Army Commanders', 5 June 1917.
17. Diary: 9, 10 June 1917.
18. 'Present Situation and Future Plans', 12 June 1917. Robertson to Haig: 13 June 1917.
19. Robertson to Haig: 13 June 1917.
20. Diary: 17, 19, 20 June 1917. Lloyd George, op. cit., p. 1 277. Charteris, *At GHQ*, p. 233.
21. Diary: 21, 22 June 1917. Robertson, memo to War Cabinet, 23 June 1917, CAB 27/7.
22. Diary: 25 June 1917.
23. Diary: 5, 7 July 1917.
24. HTLH: 24 Oct., 24 July, 30 Jan. 1917.
25. Lady Haig to Fletcher: 29 July 1916, Acc. 3155/145. HTLH: 10 Dec. 1916.
26. Diary: 28 June, 2 July 1917.
27. Diary: 28 June, 10 July 1917. HTLH: 16 July 1917.
28. Robertson to Haig: 18, 21, 25 July 1917.
29. HTLH: 22, 26 July 1917. Haig to Derby: 29 July 1917.
30. Diary: 3, 5 July 1917. Lytton, p. 100. Haig, O.A.D. 538, 5 July 1917. HTLH: 23 July 1917.
31. Davidson, pp. 26–9. Rawlinson and Plumer, memo to GHQ, 14 Feb. 1917. Gough, *The Fifth Army*, p. 195.

32. Davidson, pp. 26–32.
33. Ibid. Morton to Liddell Hart, 17 June 1961, op. cit. Travers, *The Killing Ground*, p. 211.
34. Davidson, p. 35. HTLH: 1 Aug. 1917.
35. Marshall-Cornwall, p. 239. Diary: 4 Aug. 1917. Charteris, *At GHQ*, p. 241.
36. Haig to Robertson: 4 Aug. 1917. Diary: 19 Aug. 1917. HTLH: 24 Aug. 1917.
37. HTLH: 3, 13 Aug. 1918.
38. HTLH: 15 Aug. 1917. Whigham to Haig: 9 Aug. 1917. Hankey to Esher: 30 Aug. 1917. Esher to Haig: 3 Sept. 1917, Acc. 3155/214(f), (encloses letter from Hankey).
39. Whigham to Haig: 9 Aug. 1917. Robertson to Haig: 9 Aug. 1917. Haig to Robertson: 13 Aug. 1917.
40. Haig to Robertson: 13 Aug. 1917. Diary: 27 April, 22 July, 7 Dec. 1917; 2 Jan. 1918.
41. Diary: 4, 7 Sept. 1917.
42. Diary: 13, 14 Sept. 1917. HTLH: 13 Sept. 1917.
43. HTLH: 1 June 1917. Robertson to Haig: 15 Sept. 1917.
44. Diary: 23 Sept. 1917.
45. Diary: 28 Sept., 4 Oct. 1917. Charteris, *At GHQ*, pp. 258–9.
46. Diary: 26 Sept. 1917. HTLH: 26 Sept. 1917.
47. Robertson to Haig: 27 Sept. 1917. Haig to Robertson: 6 Oct. 1917. Diary: 30 Sept. 1917.
48. Diary: 29 Sept., 3 Oct. 1917.
49. Memo: Haig to CIGS, 8 Oct. 1917. Haig to Charteris: 5 March 1927, Acc. 3155/334(a). The conflict between the letter to Robertson and that to Charteris will probably always plague historians. In one letter he was definitely not being entirely truthful, but in which one is not clear. It is possible that the lack of evidence for the pleas which Pétain allegedly made to Haig can be explained by a solemn pledge by the latter to remain silent. Unfortunately, in order to accept this possibility requires an act of faith beyond the capacity of this historian.
50. Charteris to Liddell Hart: 11 Oct. 1935, Acc. 3155/337. Memo to CIGS, op. cit.
51. Robertson to Haig: 9, 11, 12 Oct. 1917. War Cabinet: 10 Oct. 1917, CAB 23/13. Diary: 11 Oct. 1917.
52. See Woodward, op. cit., pp. 211–12.
53. Charteris, *At GHQ*, p. 239. Diary: 11, 13 Oct. 1917.
54. Macdonough, 'The Manpower and Internal Conditions of the Central Powers', (W.P. 49), 1 Oct. 1917. Diary: 15 Oct. 1917. Haig to Robertson: 16 Oct. 1917.
55. Diary: 27, 28, Oct. 1917.
56. Diary: 6 Nov. 1917.
57. Diary: 19 Sept., 1, 4 Nov. 1917.
58. Haig to Robertson: 12 Nov. 1917.
59. Diary: 4 Nov. 1917. HTLH: 9 Nov. 1917.
60. *The Times*, 13 Nov. 1917.
61. Diary: 14 Nov. 1917. HTLH: 14, 18 Nov. 1917.
62. HTLH: 11 Nov. 1917.
63. Haig to Robertson: 15 Nov. 1917.
64. Ibid.
65. Diary: 19 Nov. 1917.
66. Bidwell and Graham, *Firepower*, p. 91. Diary: 13 Nov. 1917.
67. Marshall-Cornwall, p. 252. (Marshall-Cornwall was one of the junior intelligence officers involved.) Diary: 28 Nov. 1917.
68. GHQ orders to Byng, 3 Dec. 1917.

69. HTLH: 30 Nov., 1, 3, 12 Dec. 1917.
70. Robertson to Haig: 6 Dec. 1917. Haig to Robertson: 9 Dec. 1917.
71. Derby to Haig: 7 Dec. 1917. Haig to Derby: 10 Dec. 1917. HTLH: 23 Nov. 1917. Diary: 9 Dec. 1917.
72. Derby to Haig: 11 Dec. 1917. *The Times*, 12 Dec. 1917.
73. HTLH: 13, 14 Dec. 1917. Diary: 9 Dec. 1917.
74. Diary: 20 Dec. 1917.

14 But for the Grace of God . . .

1. Diary: 9, 13 Jan. 1918.
2. Diary: 7, 9 Jan. 1918. War Cabinet: 7 Jan. 1918, CAB 23/13.
3. HTLH: 16 Dec. 1917. Diary: 17 Dec. 1917; 7 Jan. 1918.
4. Diary: 14 Jan. 1917.
5. Diary: 20 July, 8, 28 Dec. 1917.
6. Robertson to Haig: 15 Sept. 1917. Diary: 23, 26 Dec. 1917; 2 Jan. 1918.
7. Kiggell's breakdown is described in the Edmonds MSS, VI/9/205. Diary: 20 Dec. 1917; 1, 5, 12 Jan. 1917.
8. Diary: 1 Jan. 1917. HTLH: 14 Jan. 1917.
9. Robertson to Haig: 19 Jan. 1917. Lloyd George *War Memoirs*, IV pp. 2266–7. Woodward, *Lloyd George and the Generals*, pp. 244–6. HTLH: 22 Jan. 1917.
10. HTLH: 25, 28 January 1918.
11. Diary: 27, 29, 30 Jan. 1918. Hankey Diary: 30 Jan. 1918.
12. Diary: 31 Jan., 1 Feb. 1918. HTLH: 31 Jan. 1918.
13. Diary: 2 Feb. 1918. HTLH: 2, 5 Feb. 1918.
14. Derby to Haig: 30 Jan., 7 Feb. 1918. Haig to Derby: 8 Feb. 1918.
15. Diary: 9 Feb. 1918.
16. Diary: 9, 11, 18 Feb. 1918.
17. Robertson to Haig: 15 Feb. 1918.
18. Lloyd George, op. cit., II. p. 1689. Diary: 17 Feb. 1918.
19. Diary: 20 Feb. 1918. HTLH: 5 Feb. 1918.
20. Woodward, op. cit., p. 275. HTLH: 4 March 1918. Diary: 17, 19 Feb. 1918.
21. Diary: 13, 15, 16 Feb. 1918.
22. HTLH: 13 Feb. 1918. Derby to Haig: 5 March 1918.
23. Diary: 2, 3 March 1918. HTLH: 28 Feb. 1918.
24. Diary: 25 Feb., 10, 13 March 1918.
25. Diary: 25 Feb. 1918. Wilson Diary: 13 March 1918. HTLH: 25 Feb. 1918.
26. Diary: 14 March 1918.
27. Diary: 19 March 1918.
28. Diary: 5 March 1918; 24 June 1917. HTLH: 20 March 1918; 4 Aug. 1917. Esher to Haig: 18 March 1918.
29. Diary: 17, 19 March 1918.
30. HTLH: 21 March 1918. Diary: HTLH: 21 March 1918.
31. Diary: 22, 23 March 1918. HTLH: 23 March 1918.
32. Diary: 23, 24 March 1918.
33. Diary: 25, 26, 29 March 1918.
34. Diary: 29 March, 3 April 1918. See Woodward, *Lloyd George and the Generals*, (esp. chap. 12 and p. 238) and 'Did Lloyd George Starve the British Army of Men Prior to the German Offensive of March 1918?'

35. Woodward, *Lloyd George and the Generals*, pp. 288, 290.
36. HTLH: 21 March 1918.
37. Gough to Edmonds: 3 May 1923. Farrar-Hockley, *Goughie*, pp. 270–1.
38. Diary: 26 March, 3 April 1918.
39. Diary: 4, 5 April 1918. Derby to Haig: 4 April 1918. HTLH: 6 April 1918. Wilson Diary: 4 April 1918. Haig to Derby: 6 April 1918. Farrar-Hockley, op. cit., p. 324.
40. Diary: 3 April 1918.
41. Diary: 8, 9 April 1918.
42. Haig, Despatch, 11 April 1918.
43. Haig, Despatch, 11 April 1918. HTLH: 11 April 1918.
44. Diary: 14 April 1918.
45. Diary: 19, 26, 29 April 1918.
46. Diary: 28 April 1918.
47. HTLH: 7, 11 May 1918. *Parliamentary Debates*: 9 May 1918.
48. HTLH: 11, 14 May 1918.
49. Diary: 27 May 1918.
50. Diary: 1, 3 June, 21 May 1918.
51. HTLH: 1 June 1918.
52. Diary: 4, 13 June 1918.
53. Diary: 7 June 1918.
54. Diary: 17 June, 2 July 1918.
55. HTLH: 12 May, 16 June 1918. Gough to Haig: 1 June 1918. Haig to Gough: 6 July 1918.
56. Diary: 28 June, 12 July 1918.
57. Diary: 15 July 1918.
58. Diary: 24 July, 3, 5 Aug. 1918.
59. Diary: 7 Aug. 1918. Woodward, op. cit., pp. 322–3.
60. Diary: 8 Aug. 1918. HTLH: 8 Aug. 1918.
61. Diary: 10, 15 Aug. 1918.
62. Diary: 13, 19 Aug., 1 Sept. 1918. Liddell Hart, *The Tanks*, II, pp. 181–4. Haig to Wilson: 1 Sept. 1918, Wilson MSS, 2/7B/11.
63. Diary: 21 Aug. 1918.
64. Diary: 22 Aug. 1918. Haig, Memo to Army Commanders, 22 Aug. 1918. HTLH: 27 Aug. 1918.
65. Diary: 12, 25, 27 Aug. 1918. Haig to Pershing: 27 Aug. 1918.
66. Diary: 29, 30 Aug. 1918.
67. Wilson to Haig: 1 Sept. 1918. Diary: 1, 3 Sept. 1918. Haig to Wilson: 1 Sept 1918; Wilson to Haig: 2 Sept 1918, Wilson MSS, 2/7B/11,12.
68. Diary: 10 Sept. 1918. Wilson Diary, 23 Sept. 1918.
69. Wilson to Haig: 19 Sept. 1918; Haig to Wilson: 20, 24 Sept. 1918, Wilson MSS, 2/7B/15,16,18. Diary: 21 Sept. 1919.
70. Diary: 29 Sept. 1919.
71. Diary: 6 Oct. 1918.
72. Diary: 6, 10 Oct. 1918.
73. Diary: 13 Oct. 1918. HTLH: 13 Oct. 1910.
74. Haig to Wilson: 13 Oct. 1918. Wilson to Haig: 13 Oct. 1918.
75. Diary: 19 Oct. 1918.
76. Diary: 19, 21, 29 Oct. 1918.
77. Diary: 24, 27 Oct. 1918.
78. Diary: 25 Oct. 1918.

79. HTLH: 26, 31 Oct. 1918. Diary: 31 Oct., 1 Nov. 1918.
80. HTLH: 11 Nov. 1918. Diary: 11 Nov. 1918.

15 Consistent to the End

1. Diary: 30 July 1915.
2. HTLH: 30 Nov. 1918. Diary: 14 Dec. 1918.
3. Diary: 30 Nov. 1918. HTLH: 1 Dec. 1918.
4. Diary: 19 Dec. 1918.
5. Diary: 19 Nov. 1918.
6. HTLH: 30 July, 4 Oct. 1918.
7. Wilson to Haig: 20 Nov. 1918; Haig to Wilson: 21, 27 Nov. 1918; Wilson MSS, 2/7B/23a, 25. Diary: 27 Nov., 19 Dec. 1918.
8. Diary: 23 Feb. 1919.
9. Sassoon, notes of meeting with Lloyd George, 25 Feb. 1919, quoted in Blake, *Private Papers*, pp. 357–8.
10. HTLH: 26 Feb. 1919. Elibank to Haig: 25 July 1919; Haig to Elibank: 27 July 1919; Acc. 3155/347(3).
11. Diary: 28 Dec. 1918.
12. Diary: 27 Nov. 1918; 26 Jan., 11, 12, 19 Feb. 1919.
13. Diary: 8 Jan. 1919; 3 Nov. 1917.
14. Diary: 28 Jan., 1 Feb. 1919. Haig to Churchill: 31 Jan. 1919.
15. Diary: 18 March 1919. Duff Cooper, pp. 418–19.
16. Haig to H. Baird: 29 Aug. 1919, private collection.
17. Diary: 26 Jan. 1919. D. French, 'Sir Douglas Haig's Reputation', pp. 956–7.
18. Haig, speech at Clifton, 30 June 1922, Acc. 3155/337(k).
19. Haig to J. P. Allison: 27 Feb. 1926, Acc. 3155/324(a).
20. HTLH: 26 July 1917. Haig to Edmonds: 5 Aug. 1926; 26 April 1927, Edmonds MSS, II/4/43,47. See also D. French, op. cit.

Bibliography

I. Manuscript Collections

British Library
  Haig Memorandum
Churchill College, Cambridge
  Hankey MSS
  Rawlinson MSS
House of Lords Record Office
  Lloyd George MSS
Imperial War Museum
  Fitzgerald MSS
  French MSS
  Miscellaneous Great War MSS
  Wilson MSS
Intelligence Corps Museum
  Charteris MSS
Liddell Hart Military Archives, King's College London
  Allenby MSS
  Edmonds MSS
  Kiggell MSS
  Liddell Hart MSS
  Maurice MSS
  Robertson MSS
National Army Museum
  Roberts MSS
National Library of Scotland
  Davidson MSS
  Haig MSS
  Haldane MSS
  Lawrence MSS
Public Record Office
  Hankey MSS
  Kitchener MSS
  Various Cabinet and War Committee files

II. Books, Articles and Theses

Adams, R. J. Q. 'Asquith's Choice', *Journal of British Studies*, 1986.
Adams, R. J. Q. *The Conscription Controversy*, 1987.
Adye, J. *Soldiers and Others I Have Known*, 1925.

427

Andreski, S. *Military Organisation and Society*, 1968.
Anthony-Morris, A. J. 'Haldane's Army Reforms', *History*, 1971.
Arthur, G. *Haig*, 1928.
Askwith, G. R. 'Haig at Oxford', *Oxford Magazine*, 1928.
Asquith, H. *Memories and Reflections*, 1928.
Badsey, S. D. 'Fire and Sword: The British Army and the *Arme Blanche* Controversy, 1871 1921', Cambridge University Ph.D., 1982.
Barnett, C. *Britain and Her Army*, 1970.
Barnett, C. 'The Education of Military Elites', *Journal of Contemporary History*, 1967.
Barnett, C. *The Swordbearers*, 1963.
Barrow, G. *The Fire of Life*, 1942.
Beaverbrook, *Men and Power*, 1956.
Beaverbrook, *Politicians and the War*, 1960.
Beckett, I. *A Nation in Arms*, 1985.
Beckett, I. *The Army and the Curragh Incident*, 1986.
Bethune, E. C. 'The Uses of Cavalry and Mounted Infantry in Modern War', *Journal of the Royal United Services Institute*, 1906.
Bidwell, S. *Modern Warfare*, 1973.
Bidwell, S. and D. Graham. *Firepower*, 1985.
Blake, R. (ed.) *The Private Papers of Douglas Haig, 1914–1919*, 1952.
Blake, R. *The Unknown Prime Minister*, 1955.
Bond, B. 'The Late Victorian Army', *History Today*, 1961.
Bond, B. 'Richard Burdon Haldane at the War Office', *Army Quarterly*, 1963.
Bond, B. *The Victorian Army and the Staff College*, 1972.
Bond, B. *Victorian Military Campaigns*, 1967.
Bonham-Carter, Victor. *Soldier True: The Life and Times of Field Marshal Sir William Robertson*, 1963.
Boraston, J. H. (ed.) *Sir Douglas Haig's Despatches*, 1919.
Brodrick, G. C. 'A Nation of Amateurs', *Nineteenth Century*, 1900.
Callwell, C. E. *Field Marshal Sir Henry Wilson*, 1927.
Carrington, C. E. *Soldier From the Wars Returning*, 1965.
Charteris, J. *At GHQ*, 1931.
Charteris, J. *Field Marshal Earl Haig*, 1929.
Charteris, J. *Haig*, 1933.
Childers, E. *The War and the Arme Blanche*, 1910.
Churchill, R. *Lord Derby*, 1959.
Churchill, W. *Great Contemporaries*, 1937.
Churchill, W. *The River War*, 1899.
Churchill, W. *The World Crisis*, 1927.
Clark, A. *The Donkeys*, 1961.
Collier, B. *Brasshat*, 1961.
Coppard, G. *With a Machine Gun to Cambrai*, 1969.
Cruttwell, C. R. M. F. *A History of the Great War*, 1982.
Davidson, J. *Haig: Master of the Field*, 1953.
De Groot, G. 'Educated Soldier or Cavalry Officer?' *War and Society*, 1986.
De Groot, G. 'The Pre-War Life and Military Career of Douglas Haig', University of Edinburgh Ph.D., 1983.
Demeter, K. *The German Officer Corps in Society and State*, 1965.
De Wet, C. *Three Years War*, 1902.
Dixon, N. *On the Psychology of Military Incompetence*, 1976.

Duff Cooper, A. *Haig*, 1936.
Duncan, G. *Douglas Haig As I Knew Him*, 1968.
Dundonald. *My Army Life*, 1926.
Dunlop, J. K. *The Development of the British Army*, 1938.
Ellis, J. *Eye-Deep in Hell*, 1976.
Ellison, G. *Home Defence*, 1898.
Englander, D. 'Jack, Tommy and Harry Dubb', *Historical Journal*, 1978.
Esher, R. *Journals and Letters*, 1934–8.
Falls, C. *The Art of War*, 1961.
Falls, C. *The Great War*, 1959.
Falls, C. *The Nature of Modern Warfare*, 1964.
Farrar-Hockley, A. *Goughie*, 1975.
Farrar-Hockley, A. *The Somme*, 1964.
Farwell, B. *Queen Victoria's Little Wars*, 1973.
Ferguson, J. *The Curragh Incident*, 1964.
Foch, F. *Memoirs*, 1931.
Forrester, C. S. *The General*, 1975.
Fox, F. *Battle of the Ridges*, 1918.
Fox, F. *G.H.Q.*, 1920.
Fraser, P. 'British War Policy and the Crisis of Liberalism in May 1915', *Journal of Modern History*, 1982.
Fraser, P. *Lord Esher*, 1973.
French, D. *British Strategy and War Aims*, 1986.
French, D. 'Sir Douglas Haig's Reputation', *Historical Journal*, 1985.
French, J. *1914*, 1919.
Fuller, J. F. C. *The Army in My Time*, 1935.
Fuller, J. F. C. *Generalship: Its Diseases and Their Cure*, 1932.
Fuller, J. F. C. *Memoirs of an Unconventional Soldier*, 1936.
Fussell, P. *The Great War and Modern Memory*, 1977.
Gill, D. and G. Dallas. 'Mutiny at Etaples Base in 1917', *Past and Present*, 1975.
Godwin-Austin, A. *The Staff and the Staff College*, 1927.
Goldman, C. S. *With General French and the Cavalry in South Africa*, 1902.
Gooch, J. 'The Maurice Debate, 1918', *Journal of Contemporary History*, 1968.
Gooch, J. 'The Origins and Development of the British and Imperial General Staff to 1914', University of London Ph.D., 1969.
Gooch, J. *The Plans of War*, 1974.
Gooch, J. *The Prospect of War*, 1981.
Goodspeed, D. *Ludendorff*, 1966.
Gorce, P. *The French Army*, 1963.
Gorlitz, W. *History of the German General Staff*, 1953.
Gough, H. *The Fifth Army*, 1931.
Gough, H. *Soldiering On*, 1954.
Guinn, P. *British Strategy and Politics, 1914–1918*, 1965.
Haig, D. *Cavalry Studies*, 1907.
Haig, D. M. *The Man I Knew*, 1936.
Haldane, R. B. *Army Reform and Other Addresses*, 1907.
Haldane, R. B. *Autobiography*, 1929.
Haldane, R. B. *Before the War*, 1927.
Hale, L. 'The Staff Work in the War', *Nineteenth Century*, 1900.
Hamer, W. S. *The British Army: Civil Military Relations 1885–1905*, 1970.

Hamley, E. B. *The Operation of War*, 1907.

Hankey, M. *The Supreme Command, 1914–1918*, 1961.

Harington, C. *Plumer of Messines*, 1935.

Harington, C. *Tim Harington Looks Back*, 1940.

Harries-Jenkins, G. *The Army in Victorian Society*, 1977.

Harrison, J. *Alpha and Omega*, 1915.

Hazlehurst, C. 'Asquith as Prime Minister', *English Historical Review*, 1970.

Hazlehurst, C. *Politicians at War*, 1971.

Holt, E. *The Boer War*, 1958.

Howard, M. *The Continental Commitment*, 1972.

Howard, M. *The Franco-Prussian War*, 1961.

Howard, M. (ed.) *Lord Haldane and the Territorial Army* (Haldane Memorial Lecture, Birkbeck College), Oxford, 1966.

Howard, M. (ed.) *Soldiers and Governments*, 1957.

Howard, M. (ed.) *Studies in War and Peace*, 1970.

Howard, M. (ed.) *The Theory and Practice of War*, 1965.

Huntingdon, S. P. *The Soldier and the State*, 1957.

Hynes, S. *The Edwardian Turn of Mind*, 1968.

Jameson, H. *Selections from Letters of George Ogilvy Haig Written Through the Hand of His Sister Henrietta Jameson*, n.d.

Janowitz, M. *The Professional Soldier*, 1960.

Janowitz, M. *Sociology and the Military Establishment*, 1965.

Jenkins, R. *Asquith*, 1964.

Judd, D. *Someone Has Blundered: Calamities of the British Army in the Victorian Age*, 1973.

Keegan, J. *The Face of Battle*, 1978.

Kennedy, P. *The War Plans of the Great Powers*, 1979.

Kitchen, M. *The German Officer Corps, 1890–1914*, 1968.

Koss, S. *Lord Haldane: Scapegoat for Liberalism*, 1969.

Koss, S. *Asquith*, New York, 1976.

Koss, S. *The Rise and Fall of the Political Press*, 1981.

Lees-Milne, J. *The Enigmatic Edwardian*, 1986.

Lehman, J. *All Sir Garnet*, 1964.

Liddell Hart, B. H. *The British Way in Warfare*, 1932.

Liddell Hart, B. H. *History of the First World War*, 1972.

Liddell Hart, B. H. *The Remaking of Modern Armies*, 1927.

Liddell Hart, B. H. *Reputations Ten Years After*, 1928.

Liddell Hart, B. H. 'The Tale of the Tank', *Nineteenth Century and After*, 1932.

Liddell Hart, B. H. *The Tanks*, 1959.

Liddell Hart, B. H. *Through the Fog of War*, 1938.

Liddle, P. *Home Fires and Foreign Fields*, 1985.

Liddle, P. *Testimony of War, 1914–18*, 1979.

Lloyd George, D. *War Memoirs*, 1938.

Lloyd George, F. *The Years That Are Past*, 1967.

Ludendorff, E. *My War Memories*, 1919.

Ludendorff, E. *The General Staff and Its Problems*, 1920.

Luvaas, J. *The Education of an Army*, 1964.

Luvaas, J. *The Military Legacy of the Civil War*, 1959.

Lytton, N. *The Press and the General Staff*, 1920.

MacCurdy, J. J. *The Structure of Morale*, 1943.

Macdonald, L. *Somme*, 1983.
Macdonald, L. *They Called it Passchendaele*, 1978.
McEwen, J. M. 'Northcliffe and Lloyd George at War', *Historical Journal*, 1981.
McGill, B. 'Asquith's Predicament', *Journal of Modern History*, 1967.
Magnus, P. *Kitchener: Portrait of an Imperialist*, 1958.
Magnus, P. *King Edward the Seventh*, 1964.
Mangan, J. A. *Athleticism in the Victorian and Edwardian Public School*, 1981.
Marshall-Cornwall, J. *Haig as a Military Commander*, 1973.
Marwick, A. *The Deluge*, 1965.
Maud, P. D. 'Lord Haldane's Reorganisation of the British Army', *Army Quarterly*, 1947–8.
Maude, F. N. *Cavalry: Its Past and Future*, 1903.
Maurice, F. *British Strategy*, 1929.
Maurice, F. *Life of Lord Rawlinson of Trent*, 1928.
Maxwell, H. 'Are We Really a Nation of Amateurs?' *Nineteenth Century*, 1900.
Maze, P. *A Frenchman in Khaki*, 1932.
Morgan, K. *Lloyd George*, 1974.
Morgan, K. *Lloyd George Family Letters*, 1973.
Morgan, K. 'Lloyd George's Premiership', *Historical Journal*, 1970.
Newsome, D. *Godliness and Good Learning*, 1961.
Occleshaw, M. E. 'British Military Intelligence in the First World War', Keele University Ph.D., 1984.
Ottley, C. B. 'The Social Origins of British Army Officers', *Sociological Review*, 1970.
Pakenham, T. *The Boer War*, 1982.
Panichas, G. A. (ed.) *Promise of Greatness*, 1968.
Parker, P. *The Old Lie: The Great War and the Public School Ethos*, 1987.
Pitt, B. *1918: The Last Act*, 1963.
Playne, C. *The Pre-War Mind in Britain*, 1928.
Pound, R. and G. Harmsworth, *Northcliffe*, 1959.
Protheroe, E. *Earl Haig*, 1928.
Richards, F. *Old Soldiers Never Die*, 1964.
Richmond, H. 'The Service Mind', *Nineteenth Century and After*, 1933.
Robertson, W. *From Private to Field Marshal*, 1921.
Robertson, W. *Soldiers and Statesmen*, 1926.
Rosinski, H. *The German Army*, 1966.
Roskill, S. *Hankey, Man of Secrets*, 1970.
Royle, T. *The Kitchener Enigma*, 1985.
Ryan, A. P. *Mutiny at the Curragh*, 1956.
Secrett, T. *Twenty-Five Years with Earl Haig*, 1929.
Selby, J. *The Boer War: A Study in Cowardice and Courage*, 1969.
Sixsmith, E. K. G. *Douglas Haig*, 1976.
Skelley, A. R. *The Victorian Army at Home*, 1977.
Smyth, J. *Sandhurst, 1741–1961*, 1961.
Spears, E. *Prelude to Victory*, 1939.
Spiers, E. M. *The Army and Society, 1815–1914*, 1980.
Spiers, E. M. 'The British Cavalry, 1902–1914', *Journal of the Society for Army Historical Research*, 1979.
Spiers, E. M. *Haldane: An Army Reformer*, 1980.
Spiers, E. M. 'The Reform of the Front Line Forces of the Regular Army in the United Kingdom', University of Edinburgh Ph.D., 1974.

431

Springhall, J. O. *Youth, Empire and Society*, 1977.
Steiner, Z. *Britain and the Origins of the First World War*, 1986.
Stone, N. *The Eastern Front, 1914–1917*, 1975.
Strong, K. *Men of Intelligence*, 1970.
Summers, A. 'Militarism in Britain Before the First World War', *History Workshop Journal*, 1975.
Swinton, E. *The Green Curve Omnibus*, 1942.
Taylor, A. J. P. (ed.) *My Darling Pussy: The Letters of Lloyd George and Frances Stevenson*, 1975.
Taylor, A. J. P. (ed.) *Lloyd George: A Diary by Frances Stevenson*, 1971.
Taylor, W. T. 'The Debate Over Changing Cavalry Tactics and Weapons', *Military Affairs*, 1965.
Terraine, J. *Douglas Haig: The Educated Soldier*, 1963.
Terraine, J. *The Road to Passchendaele*, 1977.
Terraine, J. *The Smoke and the Fire*, 1980.
Terraine, J. *The Western Front*, 1965.
Terraine, J. *To Win a War*, 1978.
Thomas, H. *The Story of Sandhurst*, 1961.
Travers, T. *The Killing Ground*, 1987.
Travers, T. 'The Hidden Army', *Journal of Contemporary History*, 1982.
Travers, T. 'The Offensive and the Problems of Innovation in British Military Thought, 1870–1915', *Journal of Contemporary History*, 1978.
Travers, T. 'Technology, Tactics and Morale', *Journal of Modern History*, 1979.
Trotter, W. *Instincts of the Herd in Peace and War*, 1953.
Vagts, A. *The History of Militarism*, 1959.
Waites, B. *A Class Society at War*, 1987.
Watt, R. *Dare Call It Treason*, 1964.
Waugh, A. *The Loom of Youth*, 1929.
Wavell, A. *Soldiers and Soldiering*, 1953.
Wilkinson, R. *The Prefects*, 1964.
Wilkinson, S. *The Brain of an Army*, 1890.
Wilson, T. *The Myriad Faces of War*, 1985.
Wilson, T. *The Downfall of the Liberal Party*, 1966.
Winter, D. *Death's Men*, 1979.
Winter, J. *The Great War and the British People*, 1985.
Wolff, L. *In Flanders Fields*, 1958.
Wood, E. 'British Cavalry, 1853–1903', *Cavalry Journal*, 1906.
Woodward, D. *Lloyd George and the Generals*, 1983.
Woodward, D. 'Did Lloyd George Starve the British Army of Men Prior to the German Offensive of March 1918?' *Historical Journal*, 1984.
Woodward, E. L. *Great Britain and the War of 1914–1918*, 1967.
Worsley, T. C. *Barbarians and Philistines: Democracy and the Public Schools*, 1940.
Young, F. W. *The Story of the Staff College*, 1958.

III. Government Publications

Official History of the War.
Cavalry Training (Provisional, 1904).
Cavalry Training (1907).
Field Service Regulations (1909).
Parliamentary Debates.

Index

Index